COLLECTED WORKS OF GEORGE GRANT
VOLUME 1
1933–1950

George Grant in London, 1941

# COLLECTED WORKS OF GEORGE GRANT

## Volume 1
## 1933–1950

*Edited by*
*Arthur Davis and Peter Emberley*

UNIVERSITY OF TORONTO PRESS
Toronto Buffalo London

© University of Toronto Press 2000
Toronto Buffalo London
Printed in Canada

ISBN 0-8020-0762-7

∞

Printed on acid-free paper

---

**Canadian Cataloguing in Publication Data**

Grant, George, 1918–1988
  Collected works of George Grant

  v. 1. 1933–1950.
  Includes bibliographical references and index.
  ISBN 0-8020-0762-7

  1. Philosophy.   2. Political science.   3. Religion.   4. Canada – Politics and
  government.   I. Davis, Arthur, 1939–   .   II. Emberley, Peter C. (Peter
  Christopher), 1956–   .   III. Title.

  B995.G74 2000      191      C99-931317-7

---

This volume has been published with the generous financial assistance of
W.H. Loewen.

University of Toronto Press acknowledges the financial assistance to its
publishing program of the Canada Council for the Arts and the Ontario
Arts Council.

University of Toronto Press acknowledges the financial support for its
publishing activities of the Government of Canada through the Book
Publishing Industry Development Program (BPIDP).

Canadä

# Contents

# Acknowledgments

A large project entails the collaboration and goodwill of innumerable friends, colleagues, critics, and interested parties. These individuals cannot all be mentioned, but we single out particularly Sheila Grant, who extended her wonderful hospitality during our many visits to work on the papers at her Halifax home, giving her wise counsel, sharing her special knowledge of Grant's writing, and contributing countless hours of hard work to the preparation of the papers; and Ron Schoeffel, editor-in-chief of the University of Toronto Press and our editor, who deserves our heartfelt gratitude for years of advice, support, and assurance. We also want to give special thanks to Edward Andrew, for his early faith in the project and his ongoing support; Gerald Owen, for his extensive and invaluable editorial assistance; Dennis Lee, for indispensable and timely editing; Michael Burns, for support and advice in the early stages; Jon Alexander, for assisting us early in the project by scanning much of Grant's published writing; Mark Haslett, for working so diligently in compiling an exhaustive bibliography and tracking down obscure journals; Louis Greenspan, for unflinching support and assistance; Harris Athanasiadis, for assistance with the background of Grant's thesis on John Oman; and William Christian, for sharing the knowledge of Grant he had garnered and for finding Grant's early writings at Upper Canada College and Queen's together with the 1942 journal. Some of the many others who have helped us along the way include David Cayley, Bob Davis, H.D. Forbes, Nita Graham, Douglas Hall, David Jones, Henry Roper, Lawrence Schmidt, and Kassie Temple.

The editors are grateful for financial assistance from the Canadian Studies Directorate, Secretary of State, the Jackman Foundation, the Henry White Kinnear Foundation, the McLean Foundation, and Atkinson College, York University, during the period in which we performed the editorial work of the project.

*Special Acknowledgment*

We are particularly indebted to W.H. Loewen for his commitment to support financially the publication of these volumes.

# Permissions

We thank the following for permission to reprint material in this volume: Upper Canada College for Grant's three writings in the *College Times*; *Queen's University Journal* for three reviews and one article; Sheila Grant for the unpublished journal of 1942, the poem 'Peace,' 'Have We a Canadian Nation?' (*Public Affairs* ceased publication in the 1950s), and Grant's DPhil thesis (Oxford University's Bodleian Library stated that copyright rests with the author's heir); the Canadian Association for Adult Education for various articles, columns, and letters published in the journal *Food for Thought* and for the Citizens' Forum bulletins; McGraw-Hill Ryerson for *The Empire, Yes or No?*; the Canadian Institute of International Affairs for *Canada: An Introduction to a Nation*; and *Dalhousie Review* for two 1948 reviews.

# Chronology:
# George Grant's Life

1918  Born in Toronto on 13 November to William Grant and Maude Parkin.

1927  Enters Upper Canada College in Toronto. Graduates in 1936.

1935  Father dies.

1936  Enters Queen's University to study history. Completes Honours BA in 1939.

1939  Awarded Ontario Rhodes Scholarship. Enters Balliol College, Oxford, to study jurisprudence.

1940  Works as Air Raid Precaution Officer on the London docks in Bermondsey during the Battle of Britain.

1941  Tries to join the Merchant Marine but contracts tuberculosis. Works on a farm in Buckinghamshire. Converted after period of despair to a belief in 'order beyond space and time.'

1942  Convalesces in Canada.

1943  Works under Dr E.A. Corbett as national secretary of the Canadian Association for Adult Education. Writes for the journal *Food for Thought* and, with Jean Hunter Morrison, for the radio program *Citizens' Forum*.

1945  Returns to Balliol to study theology. Influenced by A.D. Lindsay, Austin Farrer, and C.S. Lewis. Meets Sheila Allen.

1947  Marries Sheila Allen. Begins work at Dalhousie University as Professor of Philosophy. Begins association with Professor James Doull, 'who taught me to read Plato.'

1948  Daughter Rachel born.

1950  Son William born. Awarded DPhil degree for dissertation entitled 'The Concept of Nature and Supernature in the Theology of John Oman.'

1952  Son Robert born.

1954    Daughter Catherine born.

1957    Daughter Isabel born.

1959    Son David born. Delivers a series of nine talks on CBC Radio's
        *University of the Air.*

1960    Publishes *Philosophy in the Mass Age,* a revised version of the
        nine radio talks. Accepts and then resigns a position at the
        newly founded York University in Toronto. While in Toronto
        writes for Mortimer Adler of the Institute for Philosophical
        Research in Chicago.

1961    Contributes 'An Ethic of Community' to *Social Purpose for Can-
        ada,* a book published to coincide with the founding of the New
        Democratic Party. Accepts a position as Associate Professor of
        Religion at McMaster University.

1963    Writes first essay on Simone Weil (unpublished). Mother dies.
        Appointed Fellow of the Royal Society of Canada.

1965    Publishes *Lament for a Nation.* Addresses the International
        Teach-In at the University of Toronto.

1966    Publishes a new introduction to *Philosophy in the Mass Age,*
        indicating an important change of mind.

1969    Publishes *Technology and Empire.* Delivers Massey Lectures on
        the CBC, which are published as *Time as History.*

1970    Reassesses *Lament for a Nation* in a new introduction to the book.

1971    Begins work on 'Technique(s) and Good,' a proposed book.

1974    Delivers Josiah Wood Lectures at Mount Allison University,
        which are published as *English-Speaking Justice.*

1976    Begins work on 'Good and Technique,' a proposed book.

1980    Resigns teaching position at McMaster University. Accepts
        Killam professorship in the Department of Political Science at
        Dalhousie University, with a cross-appointment to the Depart-
        ments of Classics and Religion.

1982    Begins work on the idea of history in the thought of Rousseau
        and Darwin.

1983    Publishes essay on Céline, intended as part of a proposed book
        on Céline and the nature of art.

1984    Retires from teaching.

1985    Publishes Notre Dame University Press edition of *English-
        Speaking Justice.*

1986    Publishes *Technology and Justice* (House of Anansi and Notre

Dame University Press). Publishes *Est-ce la fin du Canada? Lamentation sur l'echec du nationalisme Canadien*, the French edition of *Lament for a Nation* (reprinted 1992). Begins work on a book responding to Heidegger's *Nietzsche* with a defence of Christianity and Plato.

1988    Dies in Halifax on 27 September.

# Editorial Introduction:
# Collected Works of George Grant

Dalhousie students in the 1950s regularly saw George Grant leaving the library with an armload of books piled literally to his nose, heading for his home on the edge of the campus. The volumes not only were from philosophy and theology, but covered a bewildering sweep of subjects, including history, politics, economics, science, and biography, as well as poetry, novels in English and French, and mystery stories. The same intensity that drove him to read so widely made classes with him come alive. Students sensed a fire within him. He obviously did not treat the academic life as detached from the concerns and suffering of everyday existence, or as 'the passionless pursuit of passionless intelligence' – a characterization he once quoted from Jack London.[1]

Grant's search for the truth about existence was always under way, whether he was talking about local businessmen; new scientific developments; Dostoevsky's Grand Inquisitor; or the ideas of Plato, Kant, and Augustine. Students were drawn to a teacher embarked on a quest for answers to questions that mattered to them – questions about morality, religion, politics, economics, all intertwined. When he asked them to look at what was happening to their traditional beliefs and whether they knew what they should do with their lives, he nurtured their questioning minds and spirits in a way that was not common at other universities in the 1950s. Later he also jolted the readers of *Lament for a Nation* and *Technology and Empire* when he pointed to the danger that technology could engulf their political and religious traditions and institutions, transform their communities, and put the future of their country in jeopardy.

As editors of this project, our aim is to enable readers to get as close as possible to Grant's intellectual and spiritual quest through the medium of his written works. George Grant is among the few Canadian thinkers of the later twentieth century who continue to command the attention of Canadians. They are still examining his arguments about what has happened and is happening to their country, and they are still learning from his scepticism regarding the age of technology. Whether or not readers agree with Grant, they need to read his texts in order to make their assessment. We have provided those texts and we believe that critical work will follow. We have not considered it part of our task as editors to evaluate either Grant's style or his substance in our editorial interventions. Our editorial task is limited to drawing attention to comparable ideas in Grant's works and to clarifying obscure points and references.

Grant's six books (*Philosophy in the Mass Age, Lament for a Nation, Technology and Empire, English-Speaking Justice, Time as History,* and *Technology and Justice*) ranged from commentaries on other thinkers to meditations on politics, education, technology, and war. Yet these books contain only a fraction of what he wrote. Grant also produced a large corpus of unpublished essays, chapters for books in development, manuscript proposals, and lectures, all of which help to illuminate the relationships linking the many dimensions of his thought. Grant's *Collected Works* will thus provide scholars complete access to the thought-provoking ideas of one of Canada's most important philosophers.

This eight-volume edition provides scholars and general readers with a complete collection of Grant's published work, and a selection of his unpublished work from his years at Upper Canada College in the 1930s until his death in 1988. The aim of the project is to gather Grant's work together in a readable, accurate, scholarly edition, together with whatever editorial intervention is needed to give confidence in the accuracy of the text, and to explain references and allusions in Grant's work that may puzzle or confuse some readers.

We began work on this edition in 1989. Sheila Grant enthusiastically supported the project and undertook to organize and make available the materials in her possession. These include unpublished manuscripts of essays and books, along with lectures, addresses, broadcasts, research notes, and letters. We have used these unpublished documents to supplement Grant's published books as well as the reviews and articles he produced for various magazines and journals from the 1930s to the 1980s. Mrs Grant sorted the papers so that, where paginated, they ran successively; dated them where possible; and labelled his forty notebooks in alphabetic and numeric sequence. She also sought to bring some coherence to an additional clutter of papers that lacked clear indication as to their purpose and date. At the time of the printing of this volume, the papers remain in the care of Mrs Grant in her Halifax home. They will eventually be catalogued and housed in the National Archives of Canada.

We were assisted by John Robson's account of the principles and methods used in the *Collected Works of John Stuart Mill*, and were guided by his suggestion that 'an ideal audience has to be postulated, but the needs of the actual audience cannot be ignored in that postulation.' We are assuming that our audience consists of scholars with a knowledge of the history of Grant's period, and also general readers (and younger readers) less familiar with the context of his work and therefore in greater need of editorial annotations. At the end of each volume, in an appendix entitled 'Editorial and Textual Principles and Methods,' as well as in the second section of each volume's introduction, on texts, we describe the use of annotations and the headnotes that identify the sources and dates for each text reproduced in the volume. We have compiled a chronology of Grant's life, which appears in the front matter of each volume.

The guiding motive of the project has been the conviction on the part of the editors that Grant's work needs to be understood as a unified and coherent whole. From the beginning we deliberated whether to adopt a chronological or a thematic approach, and decided to take the former route. In some exceptional cases we adopted a thematic approach when it seemed more important to gather together certain writings (on Simone Weil, for example), rather than have them scattered, in several volumes. We decided against separating the published and unpublished materials, and also against presenting the broadcasts, the notebooks, and lectures, each in a distinct volume. We hope that by integrating the materials chronologically we have offered the reader a better sense of the unity in the diversity of Grant's concerns. We have divided the material into six volumes, covering the following periods: 1933–50, 1951–9, 1960–8, 1969–73, 1974–9, and 1980–8.

We have included a small number of letters with the corpus when they seemed necessary to provide a bridge, but the whole, extensive collection of correspondence will appear by itself in two final volumes, the seventh and eighth. At all stages of our work, to ensure consistency in the system of reference, we have coordinated our efforts with those of William Christian, who is gathering and editing Grant's correspondence.

We inform readers about variants of essays that Grant revised; where variants have survived, we have chosen in most cases, unless so noted, the last version as the copy-text. By 'copy-text' we mean the version that appears to be the closest to the author's final intentions and preferences. In the textual notes we have indicated changes in successive versions, most of which are manuscript variants.

To ensure that the texts presented to readers are accurate representations of the originals, we have corrected all the materials that were keyed and scanned into computer files, until we were confident that we had eliminated as many human and mechanical errors as possible. We have flagged mistakes in Grant's original texts, sometimes with square-bracket indicators and sometimes with textual notes. Other changes made to the original texts for purposes of standardization and the house style of the University of Toronto Press are described in 'Editorial and Textual Principles and Methods.' In addition we have included in each volume an introduction to the period it covers. These introductions describe the biographical circumstances and the recurring themes of Grant's writing, with second sections giving an account of the sources, location, and preparation of the texts in the volume.

We have selected pieces from the unpublished work with the general aim of bringing out the surviving writings of interest, while avoiding, whenever possible, repetition of what Grant expressed well in his published work. We consider the most important of the larger unpublished works to be the DPhil thesis on the theologian John Oman (1950); a three-chapter manuscript written prior to *Philosophy in the Mass Age* entitled 'Acceptance and Rebellion' (1958); draft manuscripts for book-length studies of 'technology and the good' (1972, 1976); and the notebooks (most from the 1970s) containing lectures and notes on Plato, Aristotle, Kant, Nietzsche, Céline, Weil, and Heidegger.

Where we selected lecture notes, we adopted the principle that we would reproduce the material if the lectures contained Grant's own thought. But we also realized that we could not present only the original parts of a lecture extracted from their context. Consequently, in order not to lose the flow of the thought, we left intact those lectures

which brought together both Grant's views and other familiar interpretations such as those of Strauss, Kojève, or Weil. From the notebooks we extracted some short aphoristic sections (we ordinarily
found these between summaries of books Grant had read), and we
have supplied an informational heading indicating the context in
which these sections appeared.

After long deliberation we decided that it was not financially feasi-
ble, or logistically convenient, to reproduce all the radio and television
broadcasts. We decided, instead, to bring forward a small number of
exemplary broadcasts, and to provide readers with a list of the identified broadcasts available in the CBC archives. Our sustained efforts to
investigate whether local radio stations still had copies of broadcasts
were unsuccessful, and even the CBC mapping we provide may be
incomplete.

Hand-written unpublished writings such as the 1942 journal and
the later notebooks (often very difficult to decipher) have been carefully transcribed by at least three different readers. Where doubt still
exists about a word or phrase we have flagged the particular word
with [?] and provided a textual note for the phrase. Rationales for the
selection of unpublished work are provided in each volume in the second section of the volume's introduction. When particular items could
not be dated exactly, we have assigned them to a period by assessing
their style and content.

Arthur Davis and Peter Emberley


**Note**

1 Grant, in a 1944 Citizens' Forum column in the Adult Education magazine
   *Food for Thought*, referred to a speech Jack London (1876–1916) gave at Yale
   on 26 January 1906 titled 'The Coming Crisis.' London said he 'found that
   the American university had this ideal, as phrased by a professor [Paul
   Shorey] in Chicago University [*sic*], namely: "The passionless pursuit of
   passionless intelligence" – clean and noble, I grant you, but not alive
   enough ... And the reflection of this university ideal I find – the conservatism and unconcern of the American people toward those who are suffering, who are in want.' See Philip S. Foner, ed., *Jack London: American Rebel*
   (New York: Citadel Press 1947), 74–5.

# Introduction to Volume 1: 1933–1950

## The Formative Years

George Parkin Grant was born in Toronto on 13 November 1918 to William Grant and Maude Parkin.[1] His father and grandfathers had all been leading figures in Canadian education. His father, William Lawson Grant (1872–1935), had held professorships in history at both Oxford and Queen's Universities before becoming principal of Upper Canada College (UCC; a private boys' school) in 1917, a position he held until his death. George Monro Grant (1835–1902), his paternal grandfather, had been principal of Queen's from 1877 until his death, and his mother's father, Sir George Parkin (1846–1922), had been a predecessor as principal of Upper Canada College from 1895 until 1902, when he became secretary of the Rhodes Scholarship Trust. George Grant attended UCC and then studied history at Queen's, taking a BA in 1939, the year in which he won a Rhodes Scholarship. He enrolled in law at Balliol College, Oxford, in October 1939, just after the outbreak of the Second World War and just before he turned twenty-one.

This volume, covering the years from 1933 to 1950, contains the writings of Grant's formative years as a thinker. They include his precocious first reviews and literary efforts at UCC[2] and Queen's University, a brief journal written as he recovered from tuberculosis in 1942, the social and political writings about Canada and international affairs produced between 1943 and 1945 while he was working for the Canadian Association for Adult Education (CAAE), and finally the Oxford DPhil thesis he completed in 1950 on the Scottish philosopher of religion John Oman, in which we can see the main themes of Grant's thought worked out for the first time.

*England in 1941: Two Formative Experiences*

It is possible to enter into the central concerns of Grant's thought by examining two momentous experiences that occurred in England during 1941, when he was in his twenty-third year. He later called these events 'primals' in his life and thought. Both took place at a time when he said he was 'living poetically': responding to events immediately and passionately rather than deliberately and thoughtfully.

As a child, Grant had been bought up in the Presbyterian Church and the United Church of Canada. In spite of his Christian upbringing, he spoke of his wartime experience as a true conversion because his family had taught him to think of religion as something necessary for public order, rather than something intellectually and spiritually true.

Grant experienced his first 'primal' during the intense bombing of the London Blitz. The declaration of war in 1939 had presented him with a difficult dilemma. Because of the horrors of the First War, he had become a pacifist in his teenage years, and after his undergraduate studies his pacifism was reinforced by new friends at Oxford. He therefore held back from enlisting, even though he felt at the same time a deep loyalty and responsibility to Britain, and many friends and family members urged him to join the armed forces. He solved this dilemma in September 1940 by joining the Air Raid Precaution Service, a decision which placed him in the heart of the Blitz, as he was stationed at Bermondsey, near the London docks. During a bombing raid on 17 February 1941, Grant's post at Stayner's Arch (a railway arch in Bermondsey) suffered a direct hit. More than 300 of the people under his guardianship, many of whom had become well-loved friends, were killed or seriously wounded. The horror of this event shook his confidence that the world was a good place where joy was possible and where he could feel he belonged.

Shortly after the Blitz ended in the fall of 1941, Grant experienced his second 'primal' while working on a farm in the English countryside. He had reluctantly renounced his pacifism – sufficiently, at least, to attempt to join the merchant marine – but was rejected for service when a medical examination revealed that he had tuberculosis. Shattered, he fled to the country and found work on a farm. One morning, on his way to work, he experienced a revelation:

The great experience for me was the war of 1939 ... [I] went into the English countryside to work on a farm. I went to work at five o'clock in the morning on a bicycle. I got off the bicycle to open a gate and when I got back on I accepted God ... I have never finally doubted the truth of that experience since that moment ... If I try to put it into words, I would say it was the recognition that I am not my own. In more academic terms, if modern liberalism is the affirmation that our essence is our freedom, then this experience was the denial of that definition, before the fact that we are not our own.[3]

John Calvin used the phrase 'not being our own,' meaning that we are 'God's instruments.' The original source may be Paul, 1 Corinthians 6: 19: 'Do you not know that your body is a temple of the Holy Spirit within you, which you have from God? You are not your own; ...' Grant used this language on many occasions throughout his life and in many of his works. At one point he credited the Scottish cleric and storyteller George MacDonald as his source. Grant was struck by MacDonald's statement 'The first principle of hell is "I am my own",' when he first read it in C.S. Lewis's *Surprised by Joy*.[4] As had been the case with C.S. Lewis's, Grant's conversion was not fully to Christianity. It took as long as ten years for all the elements of his experiences and thought to come together in an 'agnostic' Christian Platonism. His later recollection of the 1941 conversion was that it had revealed to him the existence of an order beyond the world of space and time, an order which would endure no matter what happens here.

Grant wrote little about the nature of his Christian faith. A notable exception was his Oxford DPhil thesis, where we see his attachment to the theology of the cross.[5] That work, however, was not published, and most of what was known to his general readers about his reliugious beliefs comes from remarks he made during interviews in the last fifteen years of his life. In any case, the *fact* of Grant's conversion is not in doubt. In Volumes 5 and 6 of the *Collected Works*, which cover the period from 1972 to 1988, it will be possible to look more deeply at the question of his faith and its relation to his philosophy.

The conversion seems to have helped him come through the shattering experience of the Blitz, although he does not mention it in the 1942 journal, written in Toronto as he emerged from a year of convalescence from tuberculosis and stress. When he recovered from his illness, his convictions about what was worth doing in the world had not, on the surface, changed. He spent the later war years working in the Canadian Association for Adult Education (CAAE) with progressive colleagues, most of whom were either Catholics or communists. Beneath the surface, however, his social action was less sustained by the faith in progress he had inherited from his family than by the newly found but still undigested faith in God.

*Canadian Public Thinker, Educator, and Broadcaster, 1943–1945*

Shortly after Grant's conversion, his aunt's husband (Vincent Massey, then Canadian high commissioner in London), arranged for him to return to Toronto. There Grant convalesced for about a year in the care of his mother, his sisters, and Sarah Barclay, who had cared for the Grant children in their early years.

After his recovery, in February 1943 he accepted a position as national secretary with the CAAE. (Before his death in 1935, Grant's father had been one of the founders of the association.) He was hired by Dr Edward A. Corbett, who was a close friend of his mother's. Corbett (1887–1964), the first director of the CAAE from 1936 to 1951, was instrumental in setting up the weekly radio programs *Farm Forum* and *Citizens' Forum* for the Canadian Broadcasting Corporation (CBC). During his two years as national secretary, Grant wrote extensively for the association's magazine *Food for Thought*, and for the *Citizens' Forum* program.

When he took the CAAE position, Grant was stepping into one of a number of interlocking organizations seeking to influence public policy that had grown up in response to the harsh conditions of the 1930s and 1940s. Grant's father had been a leading figure in a number of them. 'He was a founder and first president of the Workers' Educational Association of Ontario; he played a leading role in the establishment of the Canadian Association for Adult Education; and he was a founding member of the World Association for Adult Education, an Executive member of the National Council of the Young Men's Christian Association, and President of the League of Nations Society of Canada.'[6]

In a volatile, reform-oriented atmosphere, the CAAE attempted to organize and educate a broad group of Canadians for thoughtful participation in the shaping of Canada's domestic and foreign policies. Although Grant was considered left-of-centre, he opposed the CAAE or *Citizens' Forum* being used for the purposes of any particular political party.[7]

Grant's approach to reform at this time was based on the assumption that there were members of the dominant classes, 'the big boys' as he once called them, who could be pressured into making significant changes in the economy and the politics of Canada. In a June 1944 letter to a colleague, Harry Avison, about appointments to the board of *Citizens' Forum*, he wrote that 'it should be comprised of [sic] two sorts of people. First the majority – people like yourself who know what the project is about both spiritually and physically and who always emphasize that ... Secondly people like Malcolm Wallace who can approach the big boys in the community with some hope of success. However it would be disastrous ... if there were only this latter type and not the former.'[8] Grant and another colleague, Jean Hunter Morrison, wrote bulletins to accompany the *Citizens' Forum* programs. These contain a remarkable compendium of progressive Canadian thinking in the 1940s; they deal with unemployment; social security; health care; education; the constitution; agriculture; and external relations involving the United Nations, the Commonwealth, the Soviet Union, Asia, and the United States.

The speedy growth of membership in the CAAE and *Citizens' Forum* chapters, followed by a speedy decline, shows that there was a short-lived period of public awareness heightened by the Depression and the war. During the wartime period, Grant and others believed it was possible to strengthen public participation in policy making. These hopes were dampened in the late 1940s and 1950s, when most Canadians turned their attention to what Grant called 'the expanding economy.'

Grant's early experience in public broadcasting in the 1940s with *Citizens' Forum* was the beginning of a second career as a radio and television personality. The work he did with the CBC Talks Department in the 1950s and after had been forged in this earlier period. Grant had a flair for preparing and delivering radio talks. He often took part in *Fighting Words*, a popular CBC television and radio panel show (1952–62), and he contributed talks on Sartre, Dostoevsky, and Jung to the series *Architects of Modern Thought* (1955, 1958, 1961). Grant also interviewed prominent Canadians, including Robertson Davies and Wilder Penfield, about 'belief' for CBC Television's *Explorations* series in 1959. His skill as an interviewer lay in his ability to draw out the thoughts of others, to listen carefully to them, and then to respond appropriately. His first book, *Philosophy in the Mass Age*, was originally a series of talks given on the *University of the Air*. Praising Grant's 'marvellous radio personality,' Robert Fulford later wrote: 'Two years ago, Grant was assigned to give a series of half-hour radio lectures on moral philosophy. The result was stunningly effective. Grant's talks, obviously the products of a supple and curious mind, were models of their type – learned but clear, original but persuasive, highly personal but intensely communicative. It would be hard to imagine a more successful use of educational radio.'[9] Grant continued to work with radio and TV throughout his life.

Grant's early work with the Adult Education movement had pressed him to think about the special demands of educating a broad range of Canadian citizens. This public engagement made his writing more vital and immediately accessible than most academic work. By the same token, the demands of talking on the air to a broad audience influenced the character of his writing.

The George Grant who later became familiar to readers of *Lament for a Nation* and *Technology and Empire* can be heard in these writings of the early 1940s. He was becoming the Canadian nationalist, loyal to British traditions and deeply concerned about social injustice and economic inequality – sympathetic to socialism though not a socialist. His religious, economic, and political concerns joined together to form the special voice of the widely respected thinker, educator, and broadcaster he would later become.

*Imperial Power and Canadian Nationalism in 1945*

In two writings of 1945 – *The Empire: Yes or No?* and *Have We a Canadian Nation?* – Grant began to construct the complex web of thought about war and empire that eventually emerged in 1969 in *Technology and Empire*. In the circumstances of the 1940s, he began to take up the difficult question about Canada and its relation to empires, a question his grandfathers and his father had pondered before him. His grandfathers had been leading voices in the Imperial Federation League in the 1880s. George Monro Grant and Sir George Parkin had argued that

Canada needed to maintain the British connection in order to become a nation strong enough to resist U.S. 'manifest destiny,' and to maintain a tradition of peace and order that differed from the U.S. revolutionary approach.

Even in his early twenties, George Grant's special strength was his mixture of deep moral concern with an awareness of real political power. His opposition to war had grown out of his understanding of the conflict that began in 1914. He believed the greed and imperial aspirations of the great nation-states of Europe had taken them into that terrible catastrophe. In a letter to his mother from England in 1941, he expressed his moral opposition to empire: 'The whole thing centres around the tremendous paradox of this country, the giant defender of freedom maintaining the greatest and most barbaric of empires ...'[10] But he also belonged to that empire, and that left him deeply ambivalent. Eventually, the real circumstances of the 1939 war had forced him to accept the necessity of fighting the Nazis.

By 1945, he had decided that his pacifist position had been mistaken. His belief that imperial domination was wrong did not mean it was not a given; in the real world, one power could be blocked or balanced only by another. As Grant pointed out, '[t]he three great dominating powers of the world after the war will be three great empires. The two immense continental empires of the U.S.A. and the U.S.S.R., and the maritime empire of Great Britain ... However much people may inveigh against such imperialism, in this spring of 1945, it is clearly the emergent pattern.'[11] This prediction for the postwar period turned out to be wrong in the case of Great Britain, but this did not alter the fact that Britain had been the empire that rose up against the Axis powers. Grant believed that there were British traditions which could be used to 'control the more ruthless forms of expansionism.' Canada's right choice was to support the British Empire so that it could withstand and balance the new U.S. and Soviet empires. He believed that '.those empires with past experience and traditions of liberty will be the ones most liable to be empires of law and not of power alone.'[12]

The writings of 1945, then, seem to show that Grant had abandoned his pacifism by the end of the war. But, at a deeper level, he had not changed his overall stance towards war and empire. He had conceded that the war had to be fought; but, at the same time, he believed that the world wars showed the failure of progressive civilization to live up to its own aspirations. Looking back ten years later, Grant asked himself in a notebook: 'Was my conservatism at 25 a return to domination?' In later years he sometimes considered the possibility that his pacifism and Chamberlain's policies had perhaps been appropriate after all.[13] The darker implications of his vision of the failure of progressive civilization, which he had yet to think through coherently, were still held in check in 1945 by his faith that somehow the West would find a way to transcend its failure, and to progress to a more just and peaceful future.

At this time, Grant thought Canada's task in external relations should be to strengthen the balance of the 'Atlantic Triangle' in the new conditions of 1945. He believed with John Bartlet Brebner that the events of 1939–44 had reminded a whole generation of North Americans of the continuing importance of Great Britain in the affairs of Canada and the United States.[14] U.S. and Soviet power was a fact, but their imperial domination could perhaps still be tempered by the influence of a united British Commonwealth of Nations, and by a strengthened and broadened United Nations.

In addition to this support of the United Nations, Grant thought that Canada should maintain its ties with the British Commonwealth as a counterweight to the emergent U.S. superpower. Canadians, he said, have to struggle to sustain and build a national identity, since they live in a young country lacking a deep-rooted national tradition. 'For unless we know why we exist, unless we know what we are trying to build here in Canada, unless we make a conscious effort to build it – we will inevitably be shaped by the REPUBLIC. There always has been and always will be an alternative to building a Canadian nation. And that is the submerging of our nation in the USA.'[15]

Grant did not address the French-/English-speaking cleavage that had been evident in the conscription crisis of the Second World War; he argued that both French and English Canadians were conservative in character. Both had avoided revolution, and the forward-looking orientation that rejected the heritage from France and England. Canadians, he said, have 'realized that true progress can only be made step by step – layer on layer – if it is going to stick.' French Catholics, Scots Presbyterians, and English Anglicans placed social order and responsibility ahead of individual rights and freedoms. This Canadian conservative tradition marked us off from our more liberal neighbour to the south.

## Philosophy, Theology, and Philosophy of Religion, 1946–1950

Grant took up philosophy with unusually high expectations because he came to it after studying history and law – and motivated by his experiences in 1941. Those events had transformed a twenty-two-year-old George Grant who was being groomed for public life, 'programmed for the practical' as he later put it.[16] At Upper Canada College in his teens, however, he had wanted to be a poet, perhaps partly in rebellion against the family's wishes. He studied history at Queen's, and jurisprudence at Oxford in 1939. And then, when the war had influenced the course of his life for ever, he turned to the study of theology and philosophy. He thus was able to bring to his studies both the poetic and religious passion that had been such an important part of his earlier experience, and the practical orientation of the progressive public servant he was raised to be but never became.

In 1945 Grant stepped down at the CAAE and went back to Oxford. There he studied the great Western tradition of philosophy and theology that was dominated, as he saw it, by Plato and St Augustine. He found at Oxford thinkers who were still in touch with this older tradition; he stumbled upon the tradition 'by accident,' as he said, but also because his experience had produced in him the hunger for the comprehensive and 'religious' truth that tradition offered.

> At Oxford, I found the teaching of philosophy dominated by the narrowest tradition of linguistic analysis – people such as [Gilbert] Ryle and A.J. Ayer. They simply saw philosophy as the errand boy of natural science and modern secularism. They were uninterested in the important things I wanted to think about. By accident I went to some lectures by [Austin] Farrer on Descartes, and I recognized immediately this was what I had come to Europe for. [Farrer] spoke with marvellous clarity and relevance about what had made the European tradition of philosophy and theology – not the minor logical twitterings which dominated Oxford philosophy when I was there. Farrer wrote books not only on philosophy – but about the Gospels ... What Farrer introduced me to was theological rationalism – the heart of Christian intellectual life ...[17]

Grant wanted to learn how to argue the case for Christianity in the context of contemporary ethical, political, and economic struggles. How could modern human beings come to know God's love in their actions and their contemplation, even though they operated within a way of thinking and acting which excluded God? He attended C.S. Lewis's Socratic Club at Oxford. There he heard arguments for and against Christianity advanced and debated 'directly, clearly and lucidly.' Lewis, himself a convert, as has been said, first from secular thought to religion, and then to Christianity, was for Grant an example of a religious thinker who took the experience and language of modern people seriously.

## Doctoral Thesis on John Oman, 1950

Grant's religious and philosophic thought took shape during his years studying theology and philosophy at Oxford (1945–7). His doctoral (DPhil) thesis, written mostly in England, completed in 1949, and examined in 1950, already contains many of the essential elements of his later political philosophy. Grant wrote on the Scottish liberal theologian John Oman (1860–1939), following the suggestion of his mentor, Lord Lindsay, Master of Balliol. We have provided an introduction to this important work in the headnote to the work itself.

For Grant, as for Oman, philosophy could not be confined to the natural world. Grant was looking for a kind of philosophy that could comprehend 'the whole,' including the mystery of God, the affliction of human beings, and the ongoing search for the wisdom that tells us how we should live our lives. He was beginning to shape his unusual approach to thinking, combining traditional religious faith and Greek philosophy with a strong involvement in the contemporary secular world. One of Grant's early Dalhousie students later described this recollection:

> What struck me about him, and what strikes me to this day, is very strange when you think of George's general reputation as a man who lives in the past. What struck me about his mind then, as today, was how modern he is. George was able to see the world through the eyes of Freud, Marx – at that time, Jean-Paul Sartre – and others, with a total clarity, and I don't think he's ever lost that. I just cite as one well-known

example his reading of Nietzsche in *Time as History*. Now what attracted me at that time [the 1950s at Dalhousie] was that he combined this with a strong religious faith. This was absolutely spectacular. Here was a man who was totally modern and totally traditional.[18]

Grant's teaching and writing were strong because of a tension in his thought between the answers he gave to questions based on Christian faith and classical reason, and the questions he continued to ask in the wake of his experiences in the mid- and late-twentieth-century world. He embraced Plato's teaching that we can apprehend the good and the beautiful and he asserted that we can know that some actions are categorically wrong. But he also emphasized the ongoing need to ask questions because we do not have final answers. He asserted that Plato was agnostic, that the seeker of the good and the beautiful knew them to be a mystery that must be revealed to us.

## The Perfection of God and the Misery of Man

The way Grant lived, and the questions he addressed in his teaching and writing, remained constant throughout his life. Shifts in emphasis at turning points along the path of his thought reflect the complexity of a consistent search for truth. His Christian faith and his philosophic convictions led him to accept the world as good, and yet the fact of human suffering and injustice horrified him and led him to rebel against the way things are. These two conflicting facets of reality seemed to him irreconcilable even though he was convinced they must somehow be linked and held together. The need to fathom that mystery drew him to philosophy. 'The great statement for me of all modern statements,' he said, 'is Simone Weil's statement that "I am ceaselessly torn between the perfection of God and the misery of man".' Grant had discovered Weil as early as 1951, when he reviewed *Waiting on God* for the CBC, beginning a lifelong encounter which was to influence his thought decisively.[19]

But we do not get to the heart of the Grant that Canadians knew if we concentrate only on his religious faith. He had a passion to communicate about what was going on in the world. He wrote also for non-religious people in the terms of their own experience. His voice reached a broad cross-section of Canadians, pressing them to think more deeply and carefully about matters of justice and responsibility to others – in a way that was no longer typical in technological North America; Christians, at the same time, were hearing a voice that was urging them to stay true to the Gospel and warning them not to underestimate the secular world as it co-opted them.

In summary, the most important of Grant's formative years as a thinker were those he spent at Oxford after the war, culminating in the writing of his DPhil thesis during the 1949–50 period after one year of teaching at Dalhousie. It was in that time that his early education, his wartime experiences, and his involvement in adult education were brought together in the thought that would stay with him in later years. His discovery in England of a tradition of European philosophy that predated the age of progressive enlightenment set the stage for the work he was going to do at Dalhousie in the 1950s. His teachers in England brought to his attention the idea that reason, unassisted by revelation, can teach us what we are as human beings, and that we are subject to natural laws and limits to our actions, just as, in the same way, reason teaches us that nature as a whole is structured and limited. Reason can guide and limit our actions because it expresses both the nature that surrounds us and the nature that makes us what we are. Grant realized that this older understanding of reason contrasted sharply with the modern view that reason is an instrument with which we transform the world to obtain what we want. During the 1950s he pursued the question whether the modern spirit that had raised him and to which he was still deeply committed, the spirit that presses human beings to change the world, could restore some natural limit to its own dynamism.

**The Texts of Volume 1: Sources and Presentation**

Most of the works in this volume are published poems, articles, reviews, pamphlets, and letters, all of which appeared over Grant's name. They have been gathered together from relatively scattered sources such as the CAAE magazine *Food for Thought* and *Dalhousie Review* and they presented no editorial problems. The three works that did raise some editorial questions are the journal, the *Citizens' Forum* bulletins, and the DPhil thesis.

There are no existing manuscripts or early drafts of these published and unpublished materials from the 1930s and 1940s. Nor did we have reason to doubt that Grant is the author of any of the writings, or to think they might have been altered in any way against his will. Our task was to transcribe the handwritten journal and to reproduce the printed and typed texts accurately, providing notes where necessary. (The exception, where a question of authorship is raised, is the collaboratively written *Citizens' Forum* bulletins: see below.) Our annotations consist of notes identifying Grant's allusions to places, events, and persons, and identifying corrections made to copy-texts. The notes, the chronology in the front matter of this volume, and the individual headnotes are designed to help readers with questions they may have about the writings.

### Upper Canada College and Queen's University Publications

Apart from childhood letters, the earliest of Grant's writings that have survived consist of a handful of short works he published during his high-school and undergraduate years. William Christian found them while preparing to write his biography of Grant – an article and three poems written at Upper Canada College and an article and three reviews published in the Queen's University literary journal. We decided to begin the collection with the Queen's material and to place the earlier works in an appendix.

### The Journal of 1942

Grant wrote this journal at his mother's home on Prince Arthur Avenue in Toronto during the closing months of 1942, when he was recovering at the end of a one-year convalescence. The journal, though short, gives us a substantial look at Grant's thoughts about religion at the time, along with some fragmentary glimpses of his developing artistic, political, and social sensibilities. Located in the forty-volume Grant–Parkin papers in the National Archives of Canada (MG 31 D, vol. 75), the original journal is written in Grant's hand in a large scrapbook. We worked with a photocopy obtained by William Christian. Several editors helped with the transcription of some of the more difficult passages.

We have retained the casual punctuation Grant used in the journal, to avoid giving the writing a misleadingly finished or polished appearance. Grant used dashes frequently, for example, where a period or a comma might be expected. We kept the dashes rather than 'correct' the text with periods and commas. We have indicated a word or phrase we could not decipher with the designation [?]. We have tried to provide useful annotations for as many of Grant's references as possible.

## Writings during the CAAE Period, 1943–1945

While he worked for the Canadian Association for Adult Education (CAAE), Grant wrote several monthly *Citizens' Forum* columns, some reviews, and a letter to the editor, all in the association's journal, *Food for Thought*. During the same period he published one small history text for the Canadian Institute of International Affairs, and two substantial pamphlets about Canada for the Ryerson Press and the journal of Dalhousie's Institute of Public Affairs. We decided to deviate slightly from our chronological format in order to gather all the *Citizens' Forum* columns together in a section of their own, though they came out regularly from 1943 to 1945. The rest of the works from the period are presented in chronological order, with the further exception of the bulletins written collaboratively and distributed across Canada for *Citizens' Forum* radio programs.

In the CAAE archive (at the Archives of Ontario) we found eighteen of the twenty bulletins that Grant wrote with Jean Hunter Morrison, a colleague at the association. Because they are collaborative works and because we were unable to find out exactly what part Grant played in the writing, we decided not to publish them all. We have presented, instead, a selection of excerpts – apart from the main body of Grant's writings, in Appendix 2. Our rationale for the selection of the excerpts is given in the introductory note there.

## Reviews Written at Dalhousie in 1948

Grant published three book reviews during his early years at Dalhousie and before he had finished his DPhil thesis. These reviews, published in *Dalhousie Review* and *Food for Thought*, posed relatively few challenges to the editors and we are not aware of any early drafts having survived.

## DPhil Thesis: Oxford 1950

We worked with Grant's own copy of the thesis, the copy Sheila Grant found with Grant's other papers and made available to Mark Haslett for duplicating when he was working on Grant's bibliography at McMaster University. A carbon copy of that original copy (except for the abstract, which is an original typescript) is lodged at Oxford. We compared Grant's copy with the Bodleian carbon and found that most of the minor corrections in Grant's copy were made by him to both copies at the time he submitted the thesis. We have noted the few corrections in Grant's copy that were not made to the Oxford copy.

We had Grant's copy scanned into computer files. Then we corrected the text until we were convinced it was an accurate representation of the original. In separate sessions, one editor read the entire text aloud while another corrected the computerized version. We continued this process until we were sure our text was completely reliable.

Because the thesis is so important in the formation of Grant's thought, we have provided a substantial headnote to help readers to understand its relation to Grant's thought as a whole. For the thesis, once again, we have provided annotations to help readers with Grant's references, attempting to give the information readers need to understand Grant's specific allusions in the text. All Grant's quotations from Oman's works have been checked and amended against the original sources. Further details about standardization, spelling, upper- and lower-case usage, and house style can be found in Appendix 4, entitled 'Editorial and Textual Principles and Methods Applied in Volume 1.'

*CBC Radio and Television Broadcasts*

We have compiled a list of Grant's radio and television broadcasts for the CBC, as complete (or incomplete) as it can be, given the limitations of the CBC's records and our resources. We consider the list valuable because it indicates a surprisingly large amount of broadcasting work by Grant. We decided to print the list in this volume as well as in later ones (even though all but one of the broadcasts were aired after 1950), because Grant's 'second career,' as we have called it, really began with his behind-the-scenes work with the CAAE and the *Citizens' Forum* programs.

Arthur Davis

## Notes

1 See the chronology in the front matter this volume. For a complete account of Grant's life see William Christian's *George Grant: A Biography* (Toronto: University of Toronto Press 1993).
2 See Appendix 1 for the writings from the Upper Canada College period.
3 See 'Conversation: Intellectual Background,' in *George Grant in Process: Essays and Conversations*, ed. Larry Schmidt (Toronto: Anansi 1978), 62–3.
4 C.S. Lewis, *Surprised by Joy* (London: Collins 1959), 201. MacDonald's statement, slightly different from the version given by Grant, is in 'Kingship' in the Second Series of the Unspoken Sermons in *George MacDonald: Creation in Christ*, ed. Rolland Hein (Wheaton IL: Harold Shaw 1976), 140.
5 For a discussion of 'the theology of the cross' see the editors' introduction to the DPhil thesis (162–6, 401n). I am grateful to Sheila Grant, Douglas Hall, and Harris Athanasiadis for their assistance with the interpretation of the DPhil thesis. See Sheila Grant, 'George Grant and the Theology of the Cross,' in *George Grant and the Subversion of Modernity: Art, Philosophy, Politics, Religion, and Education*, ed. Arthur Davis (Toronto: University of Toronto Press 1996), 243–62; Douglas John Hall, 'Toward an Indigenous Theology of the Cross,' in *Theology and Technology*, ed. Carl Mitcham and Jim Grote (Lanham, MD: University Press of America 1984), 247–69; and Harris Athanasiadis, 'George Grant and the Theology of the Cross: Religious Foundations of His Thought,' doctoral dissertation (1998) prepared for Dr Douglas Hall at McGill Department of Religious Studies. See also Christian, *George Grant: A Biography*, 147–50.
6 See D.P. Armstrong, *William Lawson Grant* (Toronto: Dept. of Adult Education, Ontario Institute for Studies in Education, 1969).
7 Ron Faris, *The Passionate Educators: Voluntary Associations and the Struggle for Control of Adult Educational Broadcasting in Canada, 1919–1952* (Toronto: Peter Martin Associates 1975), 109.
8 The original source is CAAE, *Citizens' Forum*, Letter, G. Grant to H. Avison, 22 June 1944. See Faris, *The Passionate Educators*, ch. 6, note 81, which cites 'Citizens' Forum: Its Origins and Development, 1943–1963' by Richard Mackie (MA thesis, University of Toronto, 1968), 67–8.
9 'The Enemy of Uplift' in his column in *The Toronto Daily Star*, 'Robert Fulford on Books,' 11 November 1959.
10 George Grant to his mother, 15 June 1951. Grant's letters have been gathered by Professor William Christian of the University of Guelph, and he has published *George Grant: Selected Letters* (Toronto: University of Toronto Press 1996). This letter is not in that selection.
11 George Grant, *The Empire: Yes or No?* (Toronto: Ryerson Press 1945), 3.

12  Ibid., 11.
13  George Grant, Unpublished Notebook 1, 5.
14  See John Bartlet Brebner, *North Atlantic Triangle: The Interplay of Canada, the United States and Great Britain* (Tornto: McClelland & Stewart, 1966). It was originally published in 1945.
15  George Grant, 'Have We a Canadian Nation?', *Public Affairs* (Institute of Public Affairs, Dalhousie University) 8/3 (Spring 1945): 162.
16  In *The Owl and the Dynamo*, a film profile of George Grant produced by Vincent Tovell and narrated by William Whitehead for CBC Television's *Spectrum* series, 13 October 1980.
17  Schmidt, ed., *George Grant in Process*, 62.
18  Professor Louis Greenspan of McMaster University, interviewed by David Cayley in 'The Moving Image of Eternity,' CBC *Ideas* series transcript, Part III, 10 February 1986, 11.
19  'The Moving Image of Eternity,' CBC *Ideas* series, Part III, 10 February 1986, produced by David Cayley. Transcript, 19. The exact statement by Weil, which Grant had paraphrased, is in a letter to Maurice Schumann in *Gateway to God*, ed. David Raper (London: Collins–Fontana 1974), 64.

*Queen's University, 1937–1939*

# Review of *Grey of Fallodon*[1]
# by George Macaulay Trevelyan, OM[2]

A review written at the age of seventeen at Queen's University. It appeared in *Queen's University Journal*, 16 November 1937, in the column 'The Bookshelf.' *Grey of Fallodon: The Life and Letters of Sir Edward Grey, afterwards Viscount Grey of Fallodon* was published in London by Longmans, Green and Co. (1937).

After the indiscriminate propaganda of the war had subsided with the declaration of peace in 1918, the historians of the world tried to discover what really were the causes of the cataclysm which had just ended. This search for the basic facts which underlay the seemingly simple outbreak of war was quickened by the insertion of a clause in the Treaty of Versailles stating Germany's guilt. Immediately, in a definite reaction, the historians of the world and particularly Germany tried to vindicate the honour of the defeated country. In the process of this vindication, much criticism was levelled at the head of the British Foreign Secretary of 1914. Viscount Grey of Fallodon was accused on the one hand of uniting the powers of Europe against Germany, and on the other of maintaining a front of ambiguity up to the very day of the British entry into the war. In answer to this criticism this book has been written, by one of England's greatest historians, to prove that Grey was really a great humanist and a great pacifist who realized after many searchings of his soul that the aggressive nationalism of Germany could not be allowed free rein in Europe.

It is doubly fitting that Professor Trevelyan should write this life of Grey, firstly because he has written previously a life of Grey's famous ancestor, the father of the Reform Bill of 1832,[3] and secondly because he has been brought up in the same liberal tradition as was Grey himself. He can interpret for us, as few others could, Grey with all his inconsistencies and sensitivities. He gives us the picture of a great statesman who had four main principles of foreign policy. Primarily he believed that everything should be done to prevent the war, but that if war came England should not stand alone and unprotected. Secondly, England could not allow the aggressive domination of Europe by an irresponsible nation. Thirdly, the friendship of the United States was to be maintained at all costs. And fourthly, when war did come Grey realized more and more that at the end of the war a League of Nations would have to be established which would help to guarantee the future security of the world.

But it is in the less controversial sphere of Grey's study of birds, his passionate love of fishing (on which he wrote several books) that Professor Trevelyan becomes most interesting. His lucid and naturally simple style is no longer being forced into propounding a very complicated argument, but in telling the tale of a man who in private life was a very great human being. The extracts from the letters of Grey prove without doubt that he would have been a most charming individual to know. Although all British statesmen are traditionally supposed to wish to retire from public office, Grey is one of the very few who one feels would have been happier living his quiet life in the country. But even when he was overcome with practically total blindness he thought that it was his duty to continue his trying to work at the Foreign Office. In a style almost Latin in its simple brilliance, Trevelyan intersperses scenes of idyllic English country life with the devastating scene of a blind Europe approaching the inevitable catastrophe of 1914.

## Notes

1 Sir Edward Grey (1862–1933), first Viscount Grey of Fallodon (1916), Liberal MP and statesman, was Foreign Secretary from 1905 to 1916 and thus archi- tect of British foreign policy at the time of the outbreak of the First World War and in the Balkan peace negotiations (1913). He was ambassador at Washington (1919–20) and chancellor of Oxford (from 1928). He published *Memoirs* (1925) and, as Grant says, wrote well on fly-fishing and birds.

2 George Macaulay Trevelyan (1876–1962), Regius Professor of Modern History (1927–40) and Master of Trinity College at Cambridge (1940–51). In

recognition of his position as Britain's premier historian, Trevelyan was awarded the Order of Merit in 1930. In addition to *Grey of Fallodon: The Life and Letters of Sir Edward Grey, afterwards Viscount Grey of Fallodon* (1937) and *Lord Grey of the Reform Bill: Being the Life of Charles, Second Earl Grey* (1920), his works included *Garibaldi* (1907; 1909; 1911), *History of England* (1926), and *English Social History* (1944)

3  Charles Grey, second Earl Grey (1764–1845), Whig MP (1786–1807) and English statesman, formed the government in 1830 that passed the Great Reform Bill of 1832, giving the franchise to the middle classes. Grant is referring to Trevelyan's *Lord Grey of the Reform Bill: Being the Life of Charles, Second Earl Grey* (1920).

# Review of *The Higher Learning in America* by Robert Maynard Hutchins[1]

A review written at the age of nineteen at Queen's University. It appeared in *Queen's University Journal*, 18 January 1938, in the column 'The Bookshelf.' *The Higher Learning in America* was published at New Haven by the Yale University Press in 1936.

Robert Maynard Hutchins the American educational revolutionist was appointed President of the University of Chicago at the age of twenty-nine. Writing copiously on the educational problems of all ages, he has now produced his 'credo' on university education in America.

*The Higher Learning in America* is a concise catechism in less than one hundred and fifty pages. Hutchins believes primarily that young men and women are not trained to think but rather to get a job. Their minds (I should say our minds) are filled with myriads of detail of a purely temporary nature and no equipment is given them to face constantly recurring problems in a changing world. They have no rationally stable mental process when they leave college. Secondly, he disagrees with the fundamental factor of a university system which believes that by exposing any individual to university life an education may be gained. A mixture of custom with a lack of initiative has crowded uninterested and lazy youngsters, totally unfit for the higher learning, into universities where a make-shift for education is shoved down their unwilling throats. The serious student of higher intelligence is choked by these herds, for the standard of teaching has to be kept down to a low level to accommodate the lowest intelligence in the class. Thirdly, by catering to the individual's varying taste, the unity of curriculum is lost in a group of trivialities. Here Hutchins is criticizing the state-controlled universities which place education at the changing whim of the legislature.

These ills are due to two main reasons, President Hutchins believes. The American worship of money and business has led to the position where nearly every student wants to train himself to become a large money-maker (which is unfortunately not uniformly possible) rather than to train himself to live 'the good life.' Also the omnipotence of the dollar has given the teaching profession no tradition of respect either economically or socially. The second of President Hutchins' reasons for educational incompetence is the current belief that the general public is completely trained to choose its own educational programmes. In other forms of life, the expert is respected, but in education the educationalist is merely meant to carry out the ideas of an easily influenced general public.

After his brilliantly destructive attack on the modern bases of American education, President Hutchins turns to constructive suggestions in the second half. He bases his assumptions on the premise that every student at a university is seriously seeking knowledge and the ability to think. Therefore there must be no compulsion or spoon-feeding for this ability to think will be used in no too easy world. With no compulsory attendance a student may write his examinations when he feels that he is ready. This time will of course vary with the amount of work he is willing to do and his ability to do it. The courses of study must be those that will give the student a sense of tradition of the great thought of the world. His ability to think must be based on a knowledge of what his forefathers have thought.

Written in a vividly strong and virile style *The Higher Learning in America* is a challenge to the people of North America. Many of the unconscious bases which underlie our educational system are exposed as ludicrous. Supremely confident in the undoubted truth of his argument, President Hutchins carries both his illustrations and situations to the extreme. But, despite his unconscious colouring of the subject, this book gives a picture which is alarming in an age when democracy must produce an intelligent electorate for its increased efficiency, if it is to exist. As Dorothy Thompson has said, the choice lies with us.[2] Are we to grovel in an unsatisfactory *status quo* or are we going to follow intelligent educational leaders such as President Hutchins?

**Notes**

1 Robert Maynard Hutchins (1899–1977), president and later chancellor of the University of Chicago from 1929 until 1951. As Grant reports, he criticized overspecialization in the college curriculum and argued for a balance that would maintain the Western intellectual tradition. In 1954 Hutchins founded the Center for the Study of Democratic Institutions and became editor in chief of the *Encylopaedia Britannica*'s series, the Great Books of the Western World. Grant wrote in a 1960 letter, discussing his prospects for a new position, that 'the other possibility is through Robert Hutchins of the Fund for the Republic. He is chairman of the editorial board of the *Encyclopaedia Britannica* and has been trying to persuade the board to make me editor and to make an entirely new encyclopedia which synthesizes all knowledge ... I would work for him because he is a great man, and his purposes and mine in the educational world are closely similar.'

2 Dorothy Thompson (1893–1961), American newspaper columnist, lecturer, and radio commentator whose second husband was Sinclair Lewis and who was editorial writer at *The Ladies' Home Journal*. Her column at *The New York Herald Tribune* was syndicated with 151 papers. We were unable to find any specific reference to Hutchins's book in Thompson's writings. Grant may have been simply calling attention to a similar position held by someone he respected.

# Art and Propaganda

A short essay written at the age of nineteen at Queen's University. It appeared in the Literary Supplement to *Queen's University Journal*, 1 March 1938, pp. 6–7.

No art is more completely convincing than that in which the artist sets out with a unity of subject that will not allow complexity to shadow the central theme of his work. It is this unflinching directness that makes the portrait of a fanatical cardinal by El Greco more powerful than the fleshy and innocuous females of Rubens. Beethoven, by the emphatic use of a strong motif, achieves the grandeur that Wagner misses in his passionate incoherence. In alternating this purposeful simplicity, the artist becomes so inculcated with his own form of expression that he tends to become intolerant of other aspects of life which he unconsciously considers of minor importance beside his own work. The artist may be a sophisticate within his own field, but he cannot be versatile, for in diffusing his ability he loses his intensity. He is not the confident optimist who has no intellectual basis for his ideals, but he must remain limited, if he is to direct his thoughts and emotions into positive channels that can be coherently interpreted. Samuel Butler, the outstanding satirist of the Victorian age, highly conscious of the foibles of the society in which he lived, was at the same time oblivious to some important issues at stake in the world at large.[1]

In modern society where the individual is losing the control of his own conscience before the growing encroachments of mass movements, the artistic forms of expression are being perverted into propaganda for the cause of divergent economic and political creeds. Art is no longer the expression of the individual; it is now an effective weapon in the hands of large groups who exploit it for their own ends. These insidiously corrupted forms of expression have submitted hypothetical proof for analysis. In Shakespeare a problem is honestly presented and left to the audience to solve. Odets presents a distorted problem that is solved by the ideals of a political party.[2] Rembrandt painted humanity with the eyes of an unbiased personality; de Rivera [sic] paints with the ideas of a class movement.[3] But unfortunately an integral characteristic of effective propaganda is that intensity of purpose also essential to great art. This common characteristic has led critics and laymen alike to confuse the two so that in many minds they have merged into one. The uncertain author sincerely probing the bases of his conscience is despised as a decadent pessimist, while the confident propagandist, so immaturely sure of his convictions that he can charge blindly ahead, has been lauded as a constructive artist. The bigoted certainty of cor-rupted art is mistaken for purposeful uncertainty by an eye that is seeking some new ideology to replace its defeatist cynicism.

Although one characteristic is common to both art and propaganda, there are many that differentiate between them. Above all, propaganda is ephemeral; art is permanent. The former, dependent for success on its ability to sway the emotions of the untrained mind, must base its efficiency on superficiality so that it can be understood easily. The lat-ter, dependent on the studied analysis of the trained sections of the community, must remain basic so that it does not prove shallow when examined closely. The pamphlets of the seventeenth century parlia-mentarians are forgotten by all except the historian, while the poetry of Milton based on constructive principles rather than personal invective remains immortal. Propaganda, in its superficiality, must indulge in the worst orgies of sensationalism and insincerity if it is to drug the uneducated mind so that it loses its ability to balance issues. Art, per-manent and basic, cannot indulge in these abuses, if it is to gain funda-mental importance rather than brief notoriety.

The effects of this surge of propaganda over the world in civilized and uncivilized countries has devastated the human mind. Satiated with this cheapening drug, the appetite of the public becomes so dead-ened that it is unable to distinguish between truth and lies concocted for political purposes. The process whereby the individual submerges himself into mass movements becomes accelerated. For if men and women are to negate their individuality so that their aims remain iden-tical for long periods of time to those of their fellows, their finer senses must be drugged to the point where they accept easily the political ideals of their leaders. Propaganda, far more effective and far more insidious than physical force, becomes the means whereby civilization may lose its finer instinct and political freedom may become the despised product of a past age.

## Notes

1 Samuel Butler (1835–1902), English author, painter, and musician, wrote the Utopian satire *Erewhon* (1872; the work to which Grant refers), in which conventional practices and customs are reversed, and *The Way of All Flesh*, an autobiographical novel that was published posthumously in 1903.
2 Clifford Odets (1903–1963), American playwright of the 1930s, wrote works that were marked by a strong social conscience growing out of the conditions of the Great Depression. His plays include *Waiting for Lefty, Awake and Sing, Till the Day I Die* (all in 1935), and *Golden Boy* (1937).
3 Diego Rivera (1886–1957), Mexican artist, painted murals in public buildings depicting the popular uprisings of the Mexican people. From 1930 to 1934 he executed a number of frescoes in the United States, mainly of industrial life. His art is a blend of the rhetorical realism of folk art with a message of revolution.

# Review of *Searchlight on Spain*
# by the Duchess of Atholl, MP[1]

A review written at the age of nineteen at Queen's University. It appeared in *Queen's University Journal*, 11 November 1938, in the column 'The Bookshelf.'

The Duchess of Atholl follows directly in line from Gladstone in that she believes that moral right is the fundamental aim in human relations.[2] With a strong tradition of landed aristocracy behind her, she had still the basic judgment of the true British Conservative so that she realized where the ethical right lay in the Spanish conflict, even if that realization entailed the throwing over of her own selfish class-interest. After her journey through Spain as an English Conservative Member of Parliament, she returned to England to write *Searchlight on Spain* to counteract the mercenary or fanatical propagandists of fascism who had polluted the mind of the world with falsities. With no personal axe to grind save her unflinching desire for truth she has set down a story that must horrify most of her readers. In telling the story of the fascist invasion of Spain, Her Grace has three main aims. The first of these is to refute such propagandists as Douglas Jerrold[3] and to correct the biased leaning of misguided intellectuals like Professor Peers.[4] Her condemnation of these conscious perverters of truth based upon concrete evidence embodied in footnotes is convincing in its completeness.

Her Grace's second aim is to paint a true picture of what is happening in Spain founded upon authentic documents into which she has delved deeply. She tells the story of a reactionary army and a selfish class of landowners combining with a decadent Roman Catholic hierarchy to regain control of the Spanish state which they had lost in a recent election to the predominant liberal elements in the population.

Realizing that they can gain vast support from the expansionist fascist powers of Italy and Germany, they were willing to raise a revolt based on Moorish troops and foreign intervention, knowing full well the terrors of civil war. She tells the tragic story of a government composed neither of socialists or communists but of liberal republicans who had to face the issue of rebellion when it had no trained army and when a deluded world refused it arms while its rebellious fascist opponents received aid of the fullest kind. Her greatest tribute and our greatest debt is to the strength and courage of the Spanish people who resisted fascist invasion for the cause of international democracy and freedom. Her most damning comparison is between [the] orgia[s]tic cruelty of Franco's rule and the liberalism, even in conditions of siege, which the government of Spain has shown. Millions of refugees have left their homes rather than live where Franco rules because they believe that the establishment of his rule based upon foreign support and repressive land laws would be the final catastrophe for Spain.

The third aim of Her Grace is by far the most significant for us, for it is in this third part she shows us the terrible results for liberalism if Franco wins in Spain. A satellite of Germany and Italy, Franco would be adding a terrible burden to French defences. German airports in the Pyrenees, German and Italian guns trained at Gibraltar, Italian control of the Balearic island have already placed the democracies at an almost overwhelming disadvantage in Europe. Both England's natural interest and her democratic interests are being washed down the drain by a futile policy of unfair non-intervention.

This book is written in the vigorous style of a crusader but at the same time it has none of the faults of a fanatic. *Searchlight on Spain* is a book that makes one afraid and makes one think, but it is well worth reading.

**Notes**

1  Katharine Marjory Stewart Murray (1874–1960), Duchess of Atholl, fourth daughter of Sir James Henry Ramsey, tenth Bart, in 1899 had married Lord Tullibardine, who succeeded as the eighth Duke of Atholl in 1917. She served as Conservative MP for Kinross and Perthshire from 1923 to 1939. In addition to publishing *Searchlight on Spain* (1938) opposing on principle

Britain's policy of 'non-intervention' while not supporting the Spanish Republic, she campaigned against ill-treatment of women and children in the British Empire (1929–39) and worked to aid refugees from totalitarianism (1939–60). Her other publications include *Women and Politics* (1931).

2 William Ewart Gladstone (1809–1898), Liberal statesman and founder of the Liberal party, 1859, was four times prime minister and a supreme master of parliamentary debate. He was returned by Newark in 1832 as a Conservative to the reformed Parliament but broke with traditional Toryism over the corn-law agitation in the 1840s and later led Liberal governments as prime minister in 1868 and 1880.

3 Douglas Francis Jerrold (1893–1964), English author, publisher, and historian, was a staunch Catholic and considered a man of the Right in British politics. In the early years of the Spanish Civil War, he was a strong supporter of General Franco, and for a time he was unquestionably drawn to Hitler. His works in the 1930s include *Storm over Europe* (1930) and *Georgian Adventure; Autobiography* (1938).

4 Edgar Allison Peers (1891–1952), English Hispanic scholar and professor, taught Spanish at Liverpool after 1920. He edited *Casell's Spanish–English, English–Spanish Dictionary* (1959) and published the works of St John of the Cross and other Spanish mystics. He wrote 'Spain Week by Week,' a regular feature of *The Bulletin of Spanish Studies*. In *Spain, the Church and Orders* (1939), he gave a warm defence of the Catholic Church in Spain, though he himself was an Anglican. His other works on Spain in the 1920s and 1930s include *Spain* (1929), *the Pyrenees, French and Spanish* (1932), *The Spanish Tragedy 1930–36: Dictatorship, Republic, Chaos, Rebellion, War* (1936), and *Our Debt to Spain* (1938).

*Journal: Autumn 1942/Untitled Poem*

Oct 21st 1942 Last night in the interval of mental wandering before sleep I decided to keep a journal – partly for the sake of recording events but mostly for the practice in perseverance it would give me – the discipline. So here it is – I don't know what caused the mood last night but it was as if suddenly the sickness that had enveloped me since 1940 was over. I knew that all the moral weaknesses of character – procrastination – etc would in time God how can one experience them but that the utter sense of defeat masque. Was the mood temporary? what caused it? has it sexual – ? have it the people who had been in for the evening? Further there are asked myself the next morning all the doubting negative questions about it – but at the time it was peace beyond peace – calm beyond calm. I looked out of the east window at the Park Plaza a moment above us with its pattern of lights on the back & side – at the trees – blowing their leaves in the moonlight lit the amber yellow Chestnut leaves almost in their reach out the window – all mostly so close – it was as if I hadn't looked out the window since early spring or then now, it was autumn – all the oldness of the change, having not been seen – I did not think it saw it therefore as something plum organic – inevitable – but the terrible change to life to the beginning of death. well anyway it does fill one with a glow sense of rest – of having thrown off the sickness – the first sure & peaceful moment since that June 1940 – or I suppose May 1940 the first moment of life's opening with wholeness since the February 7th episode 1941 – a year & a half to feel like that. Is it real – or is it romantic steering in the juice of ones sorrow so it real – or is it romantic steering in the juice of ones sorrow to take solace to renew – why does one learn to depend one a person like that? has it that one gave me sexual peace & a sense also of real manhood for the first time & then to find it broken into by the offerings suddenness or worse

# Journal, Autumn 1942

Grant wrote this journal in longhand in a large scrapbook during two months at the end of 1942. He was beginning to recover his spirits after a year convalescing at his mother's home at 7 Prince Arthur Avenue in the shadow of Toronto's Park Plaza Hotel. William Christian found the journal in the forty-volume Grant–Parkin papers in the National Archives (MG 31 D, vol. 75, George Grant, 1922–54). On the cover page Grant had written in large letters, 'Take what you want said God – take it and pay for it.' He writes what this Spanish proverb meant to him in his December 13 entry:

> What a tremendous truth for men and societies – with the individual he or she can choose to be cruel – to want power – to be over-sensual – to be decadent – to be (like myself) slothful – he can take any or all of these things – He can take them – but will pay for them. Also with nations – they can take empire – or power or wealth – or on the other side isolation and irresponsibility – they can take them but will pay for them.

He probably first saw the proverb in a novel by Winnifred Holtby that he later recommended to his daughter Rachel, called *South Riding: An English Landscape* (London: Collins 1936). It is the epigraph at the head of the novel and plays a part in the story's development. Forty-four years later Grant returned to this proverb in his preface to *Technology and Justice*, using it to make the point that not only individuals and nations, but also civilizations, constrain later generations with their fateful choices.

*October 21, 1942*
Last night in the interval of mental wandering before sleep I decided to keep a journal – partly for the sake of recording events but mostly

for the practice in permanence it would give me – the discipline. So here it is – I don't know what caused the mood last night but it was as if suddenly the sickness that had enveloped me since 1940 was over. I knew that all the usual weaknesses of character – frustrations – etc. would continue – God how can one conquer them – but that the utter sense of defeat was gone. Was the mood temporary? What caused it? Was it sexual? Was it the people who had been in for the evening? [?] And one can ask oneself the next morning all the doubting negative questions about it – but at the time it was peace beyond peace – calm beyond calm. I looked out of the window at the Park Plaza rising above us with its pattern of lights on the back and side – at the trees – blowing their leaves in the moon light – the amber yellow chestnut leaves almost within reach out the window – all rustling so close – it was as if I hadn't looked out the window since early spring and then now it was autumn – all the slowness of the change having not been seen – I did not see it therefore as something slow organic – inevitable – but the terrible change from life to the beginning of death. Well anyway it does fill one with a glorious sense of rest – of having thrown off the sickness – the first sane and peaceful moment since that June 1940 – or I suppose May 1940, the first moment of life's overpowering worthwhileness since the February [1]7th episode 1941[1] – a year and a half to feel like that. Is it real – or is it romantic stewing in the juice of one's sorrow to take so long to recover – Why does one learn to depend on a person like that? Was it that she gave me sexual peace and a sense also of real manhood for the first time and then to find it broken into by the shocking suddenness and worse completeness of death? Anyway it was wonderful to think it is over as a destroying force – the part of one it has corroded into is still there but it can corrode no farther. But what a bastard I have been in the last year – emptiness – sleeplessness – the grossest animalism – then even worse emptiness and finally a long illness. Really if there was some way of recording one's thanks to older people. Mrs Lovett.[2] Aunt Lal.[3] – Mother – Br...[?] Pooh.[4] Sarah.[5] Joan A[rnoldi].[6] – but of course 3/4 Mrs Lovett. On the other hand it is better not to record one's bitterness at the people who have not fathomed one, who have just plainly let one down[7] – Alison,[8] Peter,[9] Morin,[10] Margaret.[11] Anyway one is reborn and I hope it comes to something.

*October 22nd*
Tony Chapman in[12] – talked of Wilfred Owen. Chapman does not like him, does not realize what a part war has played in Europe. He sees it intellectually but does not comprehend it emotionally – How typical of this continent at the moment. I quoted him these two or three lines of Owen –

My friend, you would not tell with such high zest
To children ardent for some desperate glory,
The old Lie: Dulce et decorum est
Pro patria mori.[13]

Of course I shut up – it just acts like alum on one's heart – anyone who does not even attempt to fathom the terribleness of what war is – does not see that it corrodes everything[;] to write of anything else seems futile. So I switched to trying to convince him of Owen's greatness as a discoverer of new keys in poetry, especially his newer rhymes. But how 19th century; it is these people who cannot see that art taken away from the war at the moment must be non-existent – He says Owen is ephemeral – my answer is the lily-minded boys like Stephen Spender and Auden who have only seen these problems in the light of eternity, not in the light of their own lives, are the ephemeral ones – Owen in the intensity of his temporariness is the lasting one. Poetry is not criticism, it is not analytical interpretations of theories of history, it is not erudition – it is – and of course there it sticks – I cannot say what it is – what I can say however is Owen is poetry –

*October 23*
Shalom in today[14] – Story of how Racine compared himself as a writer to a prostitute – Like a prostitute he started his writing because he liked it – he then did it for his friends and finally for money.[15]

*October 24*
The sense of recovery does not seem to have lasted. I am just as bad-tempered, just as despairing – just as lustful as before. Read an article by Joad on the English 1922 Tory report on education – Joad (and quite rightly) calls it fascist – The idea of service of the state as the most vital

training for youth and a state that is to be leader among nations i.e. the Herrenvolk – also a state that has supported and strengthened, has been founded on the basis of capitalism – leaders from public schools – the leaders and the led.[16] What I can never understand – why it isn't patently obvious to the people (British German Japanese or American) who preach the Herrenvolk idea, that other nations will soon learn the idea – then when Herrenvolk meets Herrenvolk the result is chaos – what we have now. That is what makes me so angry at the people here like Sandwell, Wallace, etc. who stress the superiorities of those Canadians who are British[17] – see the danger of the immigration platform of the Port Hope Tories.[18] Who can deny the power of Wagner (e.g. *Tristan and Isolde*) when he really gets there?

*October 25*
Everybody from soup to nuts in yesterday. I suppose the soup was Charles MacI. the Tory[19] – and the nuts McD. the R.C.[20] – Also Dorothy Dew – a nice person – God she looks tired – away from her husband for a year and a half.[21] The actual physical celibacy must be one of the most difficult things for her, yet – I think she maintains it. Though she is beautiful her face is getting through this long period of unhappiness – [to be] the face with the signs of a virgin tortured by her virginity after too long. Yet of course she isn't – one can see that at one time she was not – but now that pinched look is there – the lined face.

*October 26*
Have felt lousy all day – bad-tempered tired and headachy – interspersed with periods of glory when all I could do was to chant the romantic theme from the second movement of Tchaikovsky's 5th. But a totally unproductive three days – this has been just blank – One pays and pays and pays. But one learns – I looked out into the garden this morning – a typical late autumn garden – leaves everywhere and the beds full of foliage that was tired. But tomorrow I will and must wake to work – no thought of anything else. Mrs Agnes Macd. in – *still* in widow's weeds after years and with the white – dead-looking skin of one who has fed on her grief[22] – Mother is so different – her grief is immense – she is always talking not only of father – but what a bitch life has been for her – but her grief has not acted like a fester within her – Amusing and beautiful letter from Mrs Lovett –

*October 28*
Two Toronto people in (if one can use the word typical at all one can use it here). Prosperous, secure, bewildered, good-willed but goodwill overlain with too great a desire for personal comfort and safety to make it worth while. They quoted a wonderful phrase by the fat G. Stanley Russell that there must be a Christianity after the war as we have never known[23] – They then proceeded to be unChristian about India and our relation to it – they went on to be unChristian about the unemployed who bought chocolate biscuits and bought radios with relief (I nearly told the coals in the bathtub story)[24] – they were unChristian about these radicals – these people who think everything's wrong – In fact they may have wanted Christianity – but they don't know what sacrifices it entails – it will not come with words – it won't come even from the institutional changes they would be willing to have. For that matter how much does Stanley Russell know about Christianity – his comparison of the cross to the commando dagger I thought carrying things just a little too far – even for our fat hearts

*October 29*
Finished an article on India [?] – never so expressive as one would hope – but tried to stress the point that we have to think of the East in terms of equality – not only because it is the right thing to do but because we will pay in terms of their hostility in the future – Of course the old chickens coming home to roost story. Dr George came [?] today.[25] he evidently thought he better see me before Jim came back – which will be next week.[26] Mrs George has been disgracefully rude to mother about me – but that is in character. Terry MacDermot[27] in with Elizabeth – a frequenter of intellectual brothels married to a nice piece of fluff. Yet I like the hamster and the fluff. But there is a terribly negative quality about him – as if he not only did not feel like affirmation but also feared it 'per se' – We were talking about the TVA and Wilkie's fight against it[28] – Norris's support of it and Roosevelt[29] – His remark was that you can't talk about right and wrong in politics – He did not mean merely that politicians do not think in terms of right and wrong – but that he did not think it cogent either. Of course one is bound to come into that cynical state of mind – but surely one should be ready to come out of it by 45 – most people come out of it at 21 – Was it the last war with Terry. Of course carried to the logical conclusion – like Céline has – this nega-

tion will make one a fascist[30] – For the argument is obvious if one doesn't believe in right and wrong – then take what you can – how you can – when you can. His is a thin pointed Puckish face – with sharp chin and pointed cheek bones and a dome-like surface of baldness rising from his forehead – When one carries Puckish irresponsibility over to the fields where it is not appropriate – one becomes half unreal, and half merely asinine. Why he has this disappointing quality – I wish I knew – Of course I suddenly realize his intellect is without wisdom – his Puckish quality is without warmth. Elizabeth plays the beautiful calm woman who in her Mona Lisa silence conceals the wisdom of the ages – yet from my own observation (and people more qualified) she is a very stupid woman. Altogether I can't remember a more thoroughly sad evening – for after all there is nothing sadder than being disappointed in people – I guess one grows out of the shock and sadness from this disappointment – it is essentially a youthful characteristic.

## October 31

I read something about *War and Peace* by Eddie McCourt[31] – hopeless, inadequate – hopeless misunderstanding of its depth – talking of it simply as an allegory of the present conflict. Even in English *War and Peace* is the greatest symphony in the world – the opening themes of society and the family at home – weaving up to the early battles. The intricate personal themes woven into each other and woven into the whole. The crashing and the thunder of the battles – the terribleness of the fall of Moscow – To me the greatest theme is Kutuzov – the old – dirty – novel-reading old Russian – like the earth itself – like the force that drives the Volga. Berated first by the talkers because he retreats – berated finally because he will only beat the enemy and drive them out of Russia, no farther – He is past pleasure and past pain – The noblest portrait in literature. Of course after the tumult and the shouting – comes the wonderful peace of the family life – like a great placid theme from Bach and then the end – the discourse on history, on God in history – on man in God – on Life itself and more than life – the most profound yet simple – beautiful yet overwhelmed by the consciousness of sin – optimist yet founded on the rock of little hope. As he says somewhere in it – the point about life is to live it despite its misery and unhappiness – misery and unhappiness even if it is not one's own fault. Of course it would be the Master's favourite book.[32]

*November 1*

One thing that is consistently forgotten among leftists of a certain class – The Anglophobe leftists – is that English imperialism is not the only side to the life of England – and that English capitalists have performed almost as great an exploitation within their own country as without – that the average Englishman has had little benefit from the Empire other than fighting to maintain it – that the average Englishman (and by that I mean the average income group – 3£10 – etc.) has had little of the economic benefit of the Empire – Take Joe Penney.[33]

*November 2*

The bairns were here today[34] – Alison so excited with a pink dress – Before she had always worn blue – so today she was thrilled in pink. As soon as she came in she unbuttoned her coat except for the button at her throat, pulled the coat sideways and said, 'Look at Kitten's new dress.' It is one of those small children's frocks that come up cottonish and is hard to keep straight – She was very proud of the whole business and was just like an older woman in her showing it off – except (one) she was much more excited externally and made no effort to hide her excitement (two) unlike an older woman she was just excited about her dress, however it was, and insisted on her underwear showing down her arms instead of being hidden by the puff on her sleeves. I said, 'Turn round and show me the back' and so every time anybody else, Mother or Sarah, wanted to see the dress she would turn round – graceful and extremely feminine and her face smiling and expectant, looking over her shoulder to see how the admirer is admiring – They are such dear children because Eddie is so masculine and Alison so feminine – so intrinsically feminine – Ed careering around the room – pushing over everything, stumbling, wanting – with an intense physical want – to eat or to play – He will be an extraordinary child with this intense physical motivation and intensity of feeling – when he smiles – his fat pudgy Russian face breaks into a smile completely irresistible – when he cries he really cries. He was playing behind the mirror with Margaret (who adores him) and there was a great deal of laughter from Margaret and him. 'Where's guffinkus – where's guffinkus' and then roars of laughter – Then suddenly he banged his head – his fat face went blank for a moment – then began to pucker up, his underlip went forward in sadness and he went and laid his head against Margaret's knee for maternal healing. Kitten's smile is sweet and heart-touching – its gentle feminineness – Ed's is like the sun – he just grins – Yet though Ed is the more powerful of the two – Kitten will be the harder one to bring up – she is the moody one – she is the turbulent one emotionally –'I won't, I won't, I don't want to go home, I won't say goodbye.' Eddie's grief is less intense.

[There may be a page missing at this point.] [...] listened to Toscanini conducting the *Rhapsody in Blue* with Benny Goodman playing the solo clarinet[35] – evidently asked by Toscanini to do it – an amazing performance – glittering – blatant – colourful – all the qualities that Gershwin wanted in it. It is strange that the best performance of such a wildly American piece of music should be given by a European – but I guess technique counts – he can just get what he wants from the orchestra – Beside it the Brahms 4th by the NY Philharmonic under Bruno Walter was mediocre.[36] Goodman was amazing on the clarinet – it was like a wild shriek of New York's triumphant life. What genius of Toscanini to ask him.

Last night England and particularly Bermondsey was deeply in my thoughts – Mrs Lovett and Ellen[37] – it was as if I could have touched them. Also the playing of Amapola[38] brought back the memory of that girl, that squadron leader's wife – the luxuriant, healthy English country one – so meant for complete physical life, and with her husband away. I thought of her leaning against me in the night saying 'Stay' – a thick hot voice – war is brutal – I suppose I would not think of these things if I had started life again – It is the fact that one felt so intensely in those last months – everything was so tremendously heightened so that one's senses were magnified – I dreamt the night before that I got a letter from Peter Clarke from Guadalcanal and knew when I wakened that he was very near.[39]

*November 2, at night –*
Well it is the anniversary of father's birthday – How little I remember or ever knew of him – A passing remark, a little change of intonation have given me some picture of him, but so little.

Today Sarah came upstairs and ate her lunch with me as mother was out. When she stands up she is a portly and dignified woman – but when she sits down she is just the 'old bairn.' The weight of her body settles like a bag full of sand onto the chair – spreading out from where her buttocks are on the chair and her legs spread out over the edge of the chair hardly touching the ground. Her neck disappears as her head settles down right onto her shoulders so that it looks like a stone on top of the bag of sand. We were talking. As usual when she talks she is tremendous – vivacious especially about her early life in Scotland, a fund of miraculous stories told with every expression of her face and her eyes about to pop out of her head as she describes some incident that becomes so real not only to her but to the listener. Also when she starts talking about 'durrty greed and selfishness' that has caused the war her face very soon gets all ferocious – yet with all her wonderful gift of conveying a story – with all her amazing vivacity and humour, when you start explaining your point or when she is reading the newspapers she just doesn't get very far. The point is, would anybody who started work at eight and has worked like the devil at drudgery ever since ever get the point. They've worked so we can get the point – yet ever so many of us fail worse than they, failing from our selfishness – fail because we are natively stupid or fail because we cannot use our heart – or fail like myself because of native laziness. But Sarah had been eating, bending right over her food – dribbling at it as her head reached forward for the spoon above her plate. She turned to me suddenly smiling with a dribble of milk down her short stubbly little chin that sticks out from rolls of fat on her chin – and suddenly I was filled with how indescribably more beautiful and wonderful life is, than it can be described – We can never touch in our writings these moments of miraculous power and glory – reasonless and triumphant – They just come – it is as if one had seen a wonderful plumed bird – Katherine Mansfield gets the idea best in that story 'Bliss'[40] – but how could one ever describe the deep and real warmth of feeling one feels for Barc.[41] It is not just sentimental but based on the thousand incidents of growing up.

'O love that interests itself in thoughtless Heaven.'[42]

Miss Joy in. Looks exactly like a sheep – with the small head – negligible cranium and long ears.[43]

'Indeed A.J. Balfour pointed out to her [Lady Ribblesdale, Charles Lister's mother] that Charles would get all sorts of experience and some

sort of special knowledge which might be of more use to him in after life
than if he kept Selling Platers or ruining an actress.'

(This is Lord Ribblesdale writing of his son Charles Lister joining the
I.L.P.) And it is that attitude to the problem – that facetious attitude
that has in it a seed of a divine right of ruling – that was the failure of
the English ruling class – and the failure was in Charles Lister too – at
least 'au fond' for when the crisis came he left the I.L.P. – and reverted
to type.[44] Though the aristocrat can be a help in the social change – he
generally reverts to type. Roosevelt, a supremely great man, has also
tendency toward reverting to type. Also John Strachey[45] – Reading
Daniele Varè – the *Laughing Diplomat*[46] – a cynical selfish opportunist –
politically, economically, and sexually – an out and out bastard – yet
with the quality that that kind of opportunist and clear-sighted man
has – he sees the actual state of affairs – He does not cloak it in honeyed
phrases – He sees the picture of the world as it is and says I'm just
going to use that as best I can. For instance he laughs at the 'old pirate'
England taking a stand on sanctions over Abyssinia when after all Italy
was just doing what England had done in the palmier days – and on
the whole I prefer the person like that who goes after power, empire,
sensual gratification – than the old fools (particularly the Anglo-Saxon
and Germanic fools) who sugarcoat their power-seeking schemes
under the guise of morality. Varè, for instance, says that the 1914 War
should have been treated as a civil war in Europe – It was a great mistake to start fighting among ourselves (ourselves being the white man)
in the East as it lowered our prestige in China – especially when we let
China take part on our side – Oh glorious Europe.

*November 4*
What a sad thing the Americans' elections are on first glance. Of course
after Farley's perfidy[47] one could expect Dewey to have won N.Y.[48] but
the beating of so many U.S. New Deal Senators and worst of all the
beating of George Norris was a blow – also Josh Lee in Oklahoma[49] –
and Prentiss Brown in Michigan[50] – oh brave new democracy. Of
course as usual it makes one despair. Certainly if Wilkie means a quarter of what he says he is infinitely preferable to a pipsqueak like Tom
Dewey.
    Read Elliot Paul's *The Last Time I Saw Paris*[51] – a good pornographic

commentary on the fall of France – yet with the dreadful lack of any sense of history, or of what has caused things to be what they are. I suppose only very few artists – Tolstoy, and on a much lower plane Faulkner, have a sense of what history is – the importance of not only our past but the past of everybody living at the moment and those that have lived in all history – I would love some day to write a great chapter on free will and determinism – determinism as we are caught in our own environment, the state of the world and us, our parents – history – everything that ever was and everything that everybody has been. I am just not equal to it at the moment. Something like those great last pages of *War and Peace* – God, of course never that good – Have started *Madame Bovary* – too early to make any sort of judgment on it – but already one sees how exquisitely Flaubert chooses his words, how he balances his phrases – moulds his paragraphs, interweaving incident, simile, description – French is such an expressive language. The thing about Flaubert is the intense accuracy and analysis of his descriptive passages – what a range of vocabulary and accurate vocabulary he has – there are few like it – though of course for accurate classic prose, French is better than English.

*November 5*
'God sees the truth but waits'[52] – what a phrase that is – The whole tragic, futile, benighted, sublime, ridiculous grandeur of our lives is there. We sow and sow and sow without heed and not caring – and God in his infinite wisdom and perfect power just damn well waits – and then with that irony of all ironies we reap what we have sown – So many people will say 'but, but what nonsense.' A poor person does not reap what he or she has sown – yes they do – reap of all that they have been and everybody has been – So many have taken 'as you sow, so shall you reap' as a moral warning – it is not moral in the sense of right and wrong – it is the pitiable and wonderful truth – and that is the point – God sees the truth but waits. Personally it is a great emotional discovery – the discovery of God – the first glimpse of that reality – not amateurish or kind – not sentimental or moral – but so beyond our comprehension that the mere glimpse is more than we can bear – God not as the optimist – nor as the non-mover but God *who sees the truth but waits* – God waited through the selfish nationalism and ignorant self-seeking of the nineteenth century – God waited through the strug-

gle of the first war – and through the continuance of our sloth – our greed and our ignorance from 1918 to 1939 – he saw the truth – he saw what the policies that we were following would mean. He saw that each individual sin multiplied in countries and continents would bring us down to this – Yet he did not intervene, he waited –

Of course the approach to God is, I know not how. For me it must always be *Credo ut intellegam* – the opposite of that is incomprehensible.[53]

Who wrote another great title for a short story – 'Nothing Breaks But the Heart'?[54]

*November 6th*
Reading in Uncle Burgon's letter from England[55] one realises the old guard is still in power in the most important places.

Jim George married today.

Art is wonderful – it is part of all – it is the beauty that gets us nearer to the final and ultimate reality but the reality of living is greater, nobler than the art itself. The depth of one's own feeling is deeper than any art one could produce – and I think this raised to the highest degree, that the tremendous understanding of Tolstoy was greater than anything he did in Art from *War and Peace* to *Where God Is Love Is*. It is because the medium however well it is used – used to the full – yet not even [ping]? as in the case of Bach or Beethoven still it is a medium – and not the person – How much more wonderful to have been Emily Brontë's lover than to have read *Last Lines* – or whatever that last poem – for then one would have touched the very source of the fountain – felt the depth of that driven personality – Or is this all muck I write – made from too great a dinner and too emotional a day – After all depth of emotion is greater when one has fed well – that is why it is so limited.

*November 10*
Nehru's *Glimpses in World History* – what a great intellectual feat and what a good thing to read after the sloppy narrow approach to history – I have read many good things recently but none of them has meant anything to me like this book.[56]

[At this point in the journal, Grant drew a rough sketch of Asia, Africa, and Europe. The map he was probably copying, entitled 'Asia and

Europe about 1000 AD,' is in the Nehru book, which has fifty maps by J.F. Horrabin.]

The vital importance of the central Asian plain as a place from which people after people have come to dominate different parts of the world especially the Mongols – people for whom I can feel absolutely no sympathy – especially for their destruction of the great Arabian civilization – Ashoka a wonderful character[57] – It makes one humble but very proud – Just because Europe [...]

*November 18*
The attacks on Wilkie here seem to me to be very misguided. The point they seem to forget is that Wilkie has made no attempt to castigate the British Commonwealth but *imperialism* of the old school in whatever form it is. Of course what Americans do not understand in my opinion is that Churchill does not represent England's views as to a world of peace – merely the war years. They seem to equate imperialism with England – as Canadians do – The result is – the picture here is we like the Empire – we like Britain – they do not like imperialism in leftist circles in the States therefore they draw from that a conclusion as to England

*November 27*
I often think that the regime of W.L.M. King is like that of Walpole's – a regime – mightily attacked at the time of its being – by the more lively members of society – yet one that we will look back to as a ministry of great prudence – Not that it is the best ideally – but that it is so much better than any practical alternative – in fact the best possible.[58]

*December 4*
Time passes into time – but I am progressing fast – perhaps there is a chance that if I get over my mixture of sloth and sensualism I might turn myself into something.

Mrs Crooks with her hands curling over the arm of the chair like talons – her ugly black dress hanging on her gaunt body – her awful black hat – her voice slow and methodical not because she was dull but because she had trained herself not to say anything – her face quiet but neither from true calm or bovine placidity – but again based on this terrible restraint.[59] Also nothing on her in the way of ornament except thick gold and diamonds – as remembrance of her wedding – think of the story. Mrs Crooks remembering – her son – her beloved son sent away from home because of the scandal that broke around old Crooks' head – for swindling – going to England to the R.A.F. – crashes and now she hates her husband – proud and controlled – somehow unable to see any but the kindest of neighbours – but hating her husband.[60] Is it true? – does she hate him? – I doubt it.

*December 13*
'Take what you want said God – take it and pay for it' – What a tremendous truth for men and societies – with the individual he or she can choose to be cruel – to want power – to be over-sensual – to be decadent – to be (like myself) slothful – he can take any or all of these things – He can take them – but will pay for them. Also with nations – they can take empire – or power or wealth – or on the other side isolation and irresponsibility – they can take them but will pay for them. These people who believe that 'as you sow, so shall you reap' is merely a moral little lesson to be learned for the good of all and that if one doesn't learn it one is a bad boy – but nothing much else – are fools. As you sow – so shall you reap is the terrible and furious pronouncement of the law of human life. It is not an improving aphorism – it is the truth – Sow violence – you get violence – sow greed – you get greed. One pays and pays and pays for everything – Right now we are paying for the greed, selfishness, slothfulness and irresponsibility of the past years – and we are paying for it in an easy way – however strange that may seem. We never faced up to the issue – but gave over to the arbitrament of force without thinking. Therefore after the war we will pay for this –

In 'All This and Heaven Too' – war is described as the same kind of action as a man who burned down his house because there were rats in it.[61]

**Notes**

1 Grant is referring to the bombing of the railway arch in the East London docks at Bermondsey when he was an Air Raid Precaution Warden. See introduction to this volume, p. xxii.

2 Mrs Lovett was a dear friend who cared for Grant (as a kind of surrogate mother, according to William Christian) during his months as Air Raid Precaution Warden in Bermondsey. She cooked at the Oxford and Bermondsey Club, a Settlement House in the East End. See William Christian, *George Grant: A Biography* (Toronto: University of Toronto Press 1993), 69.
3 Alice Massey, sister of Grant's mother, Maude, was married to Vincent Massey.
4 'Pooh' was an affectionate nickname for his mother. It seems probable that the previous, indecipherable word, 'Br ...,' is another.
5 Sarah Barclay, the Scottish maid who had worked for the Grant family when the children were young. When she heard that Mrs Grant was going to have to take care of her son, she voluntarily gave up another job to come back and help out. See entry for November 2.
6 Joan Arnoldi was a close friend of the Grant family. She became national president of the Imperial Order Daughters of the Empire in 1920.
7 We don't know what Grant meant with this list of persons who 'did not fathom him' and 'let him down.' Perhaps he was referring to a failure on their part to understand and support him in his pacifist stance during the early years of the war, though we do not have any direct evidence that these persons took that position.
8 Grant's sister who later married the diplomat George Ignatieff.
9 Possibly his cousin Peter Macdonnell. In a letter dated December 13, 1941 Grant had written: 'Before the merchant navy episode I saw Peter Macdonnell. I admired him immensely although we have little in common. He lectured me on what the English people are really like. It is the kind of audacity of laying down the law left and right that only the extrovert has.'
10 Victor Morin was a wealthy Québécois with whose family he stayed as a young man.
11 Grant's eldest sister, who married Geoff Andrew. See entry for November 2 for Grant's account of a visit with Margaret's first two children, Alison and Edward.
12 Tony Chapman had been a friend of Grant's since his Upper Canada College days.
13 Wilfred Edward Salter Owen (1893–1918) was killed one week before the armistice at the end of the First World War at the age of twenty-five. His single volume of poems is thought by many to contain the most poignant English poetry of the war. It was written out of anger at the cruelty and waste of war and out of pity for its victims. Grant is quoting from the poem 'Dulce et decorum est.'
14 Michael Shalom Gelber was Grant's closest friend at Upper Canada College. The Gelbers were the first Jewish family to be admitted to UCC

after Grant's father changed the policy. Gelber and Grant were fellow paci-
fists during their school years. See Shalom's account of his years at UCC in
James FitzGerald, *Old Boys: The Powerful Legacy of Upper Canada College*
(Toronto: Macfarlane Walter & Ross 1994), 38–43.

15  We were unable to find the source of this Racine story.

16  See 'Tory Education' in *New Statesman and Nation* 24: 215–16, 3 October
1942, where Joad argues against two interim reports of the Conservative
Sub-Committee on Education. Cyril Edwin Mitchinson Joad (1891–1953),
pacifist and philosopher, taught at Birkbeck College, London, and was
known to the public at large for his appearances on the BBC 'Brains Trust'
radio programs.

17  Bernard Keble Sandwell (1876–1954), editor of *Saturday Night* (1932–51),
championed civil liberties, and believed in Canadian nationalism within an
imperial framework.
William Stewart Wallace (1884–1970), editor and historian, was university
librarian at the University of Toronto from 1923 to 1954 and as the first
editor of the *Canadian Historical Review* (1920–30) edited important reference works for Canadian Studies.

18  'At both the Port Hope conference and the Winnipeg convention of 1942 ...
Conservatives advocated a long-range immigration policy of encouraging
selected immigrants – preferably British – to make their homes in Canada.'
See John R. Williams, *The Conservative Party of Canada: 1920–1949* (Durham,
NC: Duke University Press 1956), 228.

19  Charles Stephen MacInnes (1872–1952), prominent Conservative lawyer
and the son of Donald MacInnes and grandson on his mother's side of
Chief Justice Sir John Beverley Robinson. MacInnes's wife, Rose (*née* Patte-
son), was a friend of Grant's mother's.

20  D.J. McDougall (1869–1969) was a University of Toronto historian blinded
during the 1914 war. Grant had read for him during the summer of 1938 at
his cottage near Lake Rosseau. Grant remarked in a letter at the time that
'[i]t is very hard to argue with such a strong Catholic, as I find him to be.'
See Christian, *George Grant: A Biography*, 41.

21  Dorothy Dew had been a friend of Alison's in England who later moved to
Canada, where she worked for Eaton's and maintained a connection with
the Grants. She was separated from her husband, Peter.

22  Agnes Macdonnell (*neé* Primrose) was mourning the death of her husband,
Norman Macdonnell.

23  G. Stanley Russell, minister at the Grant family's parish church, Deer Park
United Church, on St Clair Avenue West. The Grants had been Presbyterians and incurred the wrath of some friends and extended family members
by joining the United Church when it was formed in 1925.

24 Grant is probably referring to the typical story told in England by opponents of housing for the poor, that the ignorant and dirty poor would use
the bathtubs to store their coal.

25 Dr George was a medical doctor, possibly seeing Grant for a check-up.
Alternatively he may have been seeing him as the father of his close friend
Jim.

26 Jim George had been a good friend of Grant's since UCC days. They were
both Rhodes Scholars. He had been a pacifist, like Grant and Gelber, until
he changed his mind and enlisted in the navy. He entered External Affairs
after the war, and in 1967, at the age of forty-eight, was appointed to the
post of Canadian high commissioner in India. See Michael Shalom Gelber's
account of a religious pacifist discussion group at UCC attended by Jim
George along with Grant, himself, Ken McNaught, and a few others, in
FitzGerald, *Old Boys*, 38.)

27 Terence W.L. MacDermot (1899–1966) was selected to be principal of Upper
Canada College (1935–42) after Grant's father died. He was said to be
Maude Grant's appointment because she was able to influence Vincent
Massey who headed the selection committee. MacDermot had been teaching history at McGill and was associated with Frank Scott; his sympathies
lay with the left wing: socialists, pacifists, and Canadian nationalists. He
also had a deep interest in art, which he tried to share with the boys.
According to Richard Howard, 'MacDermot was a brilliant man with
quixotic attitudes, obviously torn between his educational ideals and the
fact that he was trying to work them out in an environment dominated by
big business, imperialism, and conservatism – against each of which he
instinctively rebelled.' See Richard B. Howard, *Upper Canada College, 1829–
1979: Colborne's Legacy* (Toronto: Macmillan 1979), especially ch. 14,
'Unsettled Years,' 222–30. After UCC, MacDermot entered the Canadian
Diplomatic Corps, serving in India, Greece, Israel, and Australia (1944–61).
He taught political science at Bishop's University from 1961 to 1969.

28 Wendell Wilkie (1892–1944), Democratic businessman who opposed
Roosevelt's New Deal and ran unsuccessfully for president as a Republican
in 1940. He tried to convince the Supreme Court that the Tennessee Valley
Authority (TVA), a major federal power project created in 1933, was uncon-
stitutional.

29 Senator George William Norris (1861–1944) of Nebraska (1912 –42), a
progressive Republican and a New Deal supporter, believed in public
ownership of water power under the New Deal, and the TVA's first dam
was named in his honour. His memoirs were posthumously published as
*Fighting Liberal*.

30 Louis-Ferdinand Céline (1894–1961) (Louis-Ferdinand Destouches), a

physician and novelist who practised medicine in a Paris suburb for much
of his life. Grant is obviously referring to two novels written in the 1930s,
*Journey to the End of Night* (1932) and *Death on the Instalment Plan* (1936),
though they are about nihilism and resentment rather than fascism. Céline
did write anti-Semitic works in the late 1930s and 1940s, but there is no
evidence that Grant had read these at the time. Céline later wrote the trilogy *Castle to Castle* (1957), *North* (1960), and *Rigadoon* (1961). Thirty-eight
years after writing his journal, Grant argued in 'Céline's Trilogy' that
the three books about his flight through Germany to Belgium during the
last months of the Second World War are the greatest work of art of the
twentieth century.

31  See 'Tolstoy's *War and Peace*,' *Queen's Quarterly* 49/2: 147–56. Edward
Alexander McCourt (1907–1972), Irish-born novelist and professor of
English at the University of Saskatchewan (1944–72), had taught at Upper
Canada College (1936–8) as well as at Ridley College, the University of
New Brunswick, and Queen's University. He wrote novels, literary criti-
cism, works on the 1885 North-West Rebellion, and travel books.

32  Alexander Dunlop Lindsay (1879–1952), first Baron Lindsay of Birker, 1946,
philosopher, Labour politician, and the Master of Balliol College during
both Grant's periods at Oxford (1939–40, 1945–7), was a Plato scholar as
well as a socialist, possibly influencing Grant to his own mixture of conservatism and socialism. In a 1939 letter Grant wrote: 'The master is really
a fine man. Exalted about the war, refusing (in a speech he made in the
Sheldonian) to answer any socialist argument, but still a fine character from
the short sermons he makes in Balliol Chapel on Sundays. Really fine, there
is no doubt. Whatever unreasoning principles he has he is like a prophet.'

33  Joe Penney was a friend of Grant's in Bermondsey during the Blitz.

34  Alison and Edward Andrew, the first two children of Margaret, Grant's
sister, and her husband, Geoff Andrew. At the time of this visit, Alison was
three and Edward was two months short of two.

35  The Benny Goodman performance of Gershwin's *Rhapsody in Blue* (1924) by
Arturo Toscanini and the NBC Symphony Orchestra with Earl Wild on
piano was broadcast and recorded live on 1 November 1942. It was issued
together with two other Gershwin works, *An American in Paris* and *Concerto
in F*. The Toscanini Discography Website lists the recording as 'Studio 8H,
Hunt 534.' The LP has been remastered for two CD issues, the Grammo-
fono 2000 series and the vintage Jazz Classics series (VJC 1034).

36  Bruno Walter (properly Bruno Schlesinger) (1876–1962) conducted the
Berlin Philharmonic from 1919, and became chief conductor of the New
York Philharmonic in 1951. He recorded Brahms symphonies with the New
York Philharmonic in a three- LP set for Odyssey 32360007 (mono). He

recorded it earlier with the BBC Orchestra in 1934 (KOCH 7120) and later with the New York Philharmonic in 1951 for Columbia (ML 5127, ML 4472). His 1959 version with the Columbia Symphony Orchestra is on Sony 44776 and Sony 64472.

37  Possibly a friend from Bermondsey, perhaps the woman he refers to in his opening entry of October 21 'who gave him sexual peace and a real sense of manhood,' and who may then have been killed on 17 February 1941.

38  'Amapola,' a popular love-song in 1941 written in French in 1924 by Joseph M. Lacalle and later given English words by Albert Gamse. The song was recorded by many artists, including Deanna Durbin.

39  Peter Clarke was Grant's friend from Oxford who, as a conscientious objector, was imprisoned in England during the war. He thus could not have been at Guadalcanal, the largest of the Solomon Islands in the southwest Pacific and the scene of the first Allied Pacific invasion northward in 1942.

40  The story by Katherine Mansfield (1888–1923) can be found in *Bliss and Other Stories* (1919) or in *The Collected Stories of Katherine Mansfield* (1945). Bertha Young tells the story: 'What can you do if you are thirty and, turning the corner of your own street, you are overcome, suddenly, by a feeling of bliss – absolute bliss! – as though you'd suddenly swallowed a bright piece of that late afternoon sun and it burned in your bosom, sending out a little shower of sparks into every particle, into every finger and toe? ...' 'Oh, is there no way you can express it without being "drunk and disorderly"? How idiotic civilization is! Why be given a body if you have to keep it shut up in a case like a rare, rare fiddle?' See *Bliss and Other Stories* (London: Constable and Co. 1920), 116.

41  Sarah Barclay. See note 5.

42  Grant lightly altered the first line of W.H. Auden's 'Prologue' in *Look Stranger* (1936). The first two stanzas read:

O Love, the interest itself in thoughtless Heaven,
Make simpler daily the beating of man's heart; within
There in the ring where name and image meet,

Inspire them with such a longing as will make his thought
Alive like patterns a murmuration of starlings
Rising in joy over wolds unwittingly weave;

The poem, dated May 1932, can be found in Auden's *Selected Poems*, selected and edited by Edward Mendelson (New York: Vintage 1979), 25.

43  Miss M. Joy was nurse at Upper Canada College from 1910 to 1935. She took care of William Grant after his first heart attack.

44  Thomas Lister, fourth Baron Ribblesdale (1854–1925), one of the last of the

old school Lords known at Oxford as 'the bloods.' His *Impressions and Memories* (London: Cassell & Company) with a preface by his daughter, Lady Wilson, was published in 1927. She mentions that her father wrote a life of her brother Charles Lister (1887–1915), the memoir from which Grant was quoting. It was probably given to him by Lord Lindsay, who had been Lister's tutor at Balliol in 1906. In the light of Grant's own struggle during the second war, he is understandably drawn to and troubled by the story of Charles Lister, who backed away from his early socialist rebellion against the ruling class to which he was born and was fatally wounded in 1915 fighting for Great Britain in the Gallipoli campaign. Grant takes note of the patronizing attitude of Ribblesdale, who says he 'enjoyed [Charles's] Socialist or Fabian period, and was sorry in a way when its blood-heat passed off.' Grant's quotation is taken from the following passage: 'But let me return to his relations with the I.L.P. The day came when he elected to be received into its bosom; we were neither pleased nor displeased. His mother thought it a mistake to contract himself out of being helped by the machinery and caucus support of either of the two great recognized parties – at that time a condition of adoption and grace - but she was reassured by Mr A.J. Balfour, who was mildly interested and approving. Indeed he pointed out to her that Charles would get all sorts of experience and some sort of special knowledge which might be of more use to him in after-life than if he kept Selling Platers or ran [not 'ruining,' as Grant wrote] an actress. I was present and I heartily concurred.' See *Charles Lister: Letters and Recollections. With a Memoir by His Father, Lord Ribblesdale* (London: T. Fisher Unwin 1917), 13. Arthur James Balfour, first Earl of Balfour (1848–1905), Conservative statesman and philosopher. The Independent Labour Party (ILP), socialist party formed in 1893 with the objective of sending working men to Parliament. Many of its leaders played a part in the founding of the Labour Party in 1906. The ILP was affiliated with the Labour Party but had its own MPs until 1946.

45 Evelyn John St Loe Strachey (1901–1963) resigned from the Labour Party in 1931 and gave his support to further left organizations, but then served in the Royal Air Force (RAF) during the Second World War and in 1945 became Labour under-secretary for air.

46 Daniele Varè (1880–1956), Italian diplomat and author, held diplomatic positions in Italian governments from 1907 to the mid-1930s, including Italian Minister to China (1927–32). *Laughing Diplomat* (1938) is a book of memoirs, but most of his works are novels such as *The Last Empress* (1936), *The Gate of Happy Sparrows* (1937), and *The Temple of Costly Experience* (1939).

47 James A. Farley (1888–1976) served under F.D. Roosevelt until breaking with him to make his own bid for the presidency in 1940.

48 Thomas Dewey (1902–1971), the racket-busting prosecuting attorney who was governor of New York for three terms from 1943 to 1955, was Republican presidential nominee in 1944 and 1948, losing both elections.

49 Joshua Lee (1892–1967), a teacher of public speaking who became the Democratic senator from Oklahoma (1937–42). After Lee lost the 1942 election, Roosevelt appointed him to the Civil Aeronautics Board (1943–56).

50 Prentiss Marsh Brown (1889–1973) was the Democratic senator from Michigan under Roosevelt (1936–43) and then he became chairman of the board of Detroit Edison Company. The Library of Congress has several reports on trade, finance, and industry that he produced during his years as senator.

51 Elliot Paul (1891–1958), an American who belonged to the expatriate community of writers and artists in Paris in the 1920s and 1930s. *The Last Time I Saw Paris* (New York: Random House 1942) is a novel telling how the coming of the Second World War destroyed the life of rue de la Huchette, a small side street on the Left Bank. A British version was published in the same year by Cresset with the title *A Narrow Street*.

52 'God Sees the Truth But Waits to Tell' is the title of a Tolstoy short story.

53 'I believe so that I may understand.'

54 'Nothing Ever Breaks Except the Heart' was a short story by Kay Boyle (1902–1992), also a member of the American literary set that flourished in Paris early in the twentieth century. She and her husband, Joseph von Franckenstein, were blacklisted in the 1950s by Senator Joseph McCarthy and his communist-hunting investigators.

55 John Burgon Bickersteth, MC, MA (1888–1979), warden of Hart House (1921–47) and a close family friend of the Grants. He had come from England first to Western Canada in 1911 and then to Ontario in 1921. He visited Grant in Bermondsey in February 1941 (see Christian, *George Grant: A Biography*, 74–9).

56 Jawaharlal Nehru (1889–1964), Indian statesman deeply influenced by Mahatma Gandhi, was prime minister of India from 1947 to 1964. *Glimpses in World History* was subtitled 'Being Further Letters to His Daughter, Written in Prison and Containing a Rambling Account of History for Young People,' [2d Indian Edition 1962; Oxford University Press edition 1985]).

57 Ashoka (or Asoka) the Great (c 268–226 BC), an exemplary ruler of India, the King of Magadha (c 259 BC). Nehru writes about Ashoka's reign (also quoting H.G. Wells on the subject), paying special attention to the king's turn away from war and his attempt to teach his kingdom the Buddhist dharma. Ashoka had been disgusted by the bloody slaughter that had ensued when he extended his empire at the beginning of his reign. See Jahwaharlal Nehru, *Glimpses of World History* (New Delhi: Oxford University Press 1985), 61–7.

58  William Lyon Mackenzie King (1874–1950), leader of the Liberal party
    (1919–48) and prime minister of Canada (1921–6, 1926–30, and 1935–48). Sir
    Robert Walpole, first Earl of Orford (1676–1745), British Whig statesman
    generally regarded as the first British prime minister, was in power from
    1721 to 1742 under George I and George II.
59  Mrs Crooks (*née* Ellis) was a friend of Mrs Grant's. She had been married to
    a prominent lawyer and former mayor of Toronto who had taken his own
    life after being disbarred.
60  David Crooks, a friend of Alison's and Charity's, was killed in the war.
61  *All This and Heaven Too* was one of Grant's favourite movies, according to
    Sheila Grant. It was made in the United States in 1940, starring Bette Davis,
    Charles Boyer, and Barbara O'Neil, based on the best-selling 1938 romantic
    novel of the same title by Rachel Field (1894–1942). It tells the story of a
    French nobleman who falls in love with his governess (due to their mutual
    love of his children), and who then, in tragic circumstances, ends up mur-
    dering his wife and dying himself.

# Untitled Poem

This poem was found in a file folder with some other poetry of the 1950s, but its sensibility suggests that it does not belong to that period. Though it cannot be dated with any certainty, it probably was written in England in 1941, or in Toronto in 1942, at the time of the journal.

They told me that your arms held only lust –
A birthright lost to win a mess of pottage
Emptiness was their word – that I would lose
My soul within the compass of your breasts.

God – I believed them and lost forever
The sweet forgetfulness of your enchanted lips
The fading wander into bliss and dreams
The heliotrope of your soft-scented things.

Gain from that loss was but the gain of myrrh
The smell of bitter almonds in the gloam
The right to walk in loneliness again
The dreadful terror of the night alone.

*Canadian Association for Adult Education:*
*1943–1945*

# Food for Thought Columns: 1943–1945

During his two years at the Canadian Association for Adult Education (CAAE), Grant wrote extensively for the association's magazine, *Food for Thought*, including a monthly column that enabled him to report to the members of Citizens' Forum. When he took the CAAE position, he had stepped into an organization that was part of an interlocking group of agencies seeking to influence public policy making. In a volatile, reform-oriented period following the Depression and during the war, the CAAE (and Grant) were attempting to organize and educate a broad group of Canadians for thoughtful participation in the shaping of Canada's domestic and foreign policies. Grant was considered to be left of centre, but he opposed the CAAE or Citizens' Forum being used for the purposes of a particular political party such as the Co-operative Commonwealth Federation (CCF).

Work with the Adult Education Movement, and especially writing for *Food for Thought*, had a long-term effect on Grant's thinking and his style of writing. He learned in that job to write in response to the special demands of educating a broad range of Canadian citizens. Public engagement made his later writing more vivid and immediately accessible than most academic work.

## CITIZENS' FORUM – SO FAR

Appeared in *Food for Thought*, volume 4, issue 3, November 1943.

Have you ever started a snowball down a slope, and seen it become the size of a cannon ball? This is rather like the momentum and size that the *Citizens' Forum on Canada in the Post-War World* is gaining as it rolls along. All across Canada, the response has been more enthusiastic than we had dared to hope. This response has shown, if anyone needed proof, that the people of Canada are deeply concerned with thoughts of tomorrow. They want to learn more of the facts, and to express their opinion on the problems. It has demonstrated, too, that literally hundreds of organizations were waiting for some such opportunity to come along.

A month before the starting date, before the promotion of the Citizens' Forums had even got well under way, scores of groups have written in to the national office, at 198 College Street, Toronto, saying that they are ready to go. Each day the mail brings a dozen requests for more information about the project, from all over the country.

The greatest achievement to date is the fact that offices have now been set up in all the provinces, to organize and service the forums on a provincial basis. All local Citizens' Forums will register with these regional headquarters, and receive from them study-bulletins, guides on conducting forums, lists of films, and so on.

In British Columbia the provincial organization is in the hands of Dr Shrum of the Department of Extension at the University of British Columbia, and Mrs Kern of the Parent–Teachers' Association is working with him.

In Alberta, the scheme has been handled by the Provincial Adult Education Council through the cooperation of the Department of Extension at the University of Alberta, under Donald Cameron. Wide plans have been instituted throughout the province.

Professor K.W. Gordon of the Department of Extension at the University of Saskatchewan is in charge of the work in this province. A large meeting has been held with representatives of many provincial organizations, and an extensive scheme of publicity and promotion has been set in motion.

In Manitoba, the project is being handled through the Department of Extension at the University of Manitoba, with Watson Thomson in charge. In Winnipeg the Central Volunteer Bureau have offered their full cooperation, and Mrs Tannis Murray has been appointed urban listening organizer.

A meeting for the province of Ontario was held on October 2nd. A provincial committee was formed under the chairmanship of Harvey

Mitchell, President of the Ontario Secondary School Teachers' Federation. A provincial office has been set up in Simcoe Hall, at the University of Toronto. In cities such as Ottawa, Hamilton, Toronto, London, and Peterborough, local committees will work in cooperation with the provincial office.

Several meetings have been held in Montreal, out of which a Quebec Council of Citizens' Forums has been formed. Alex Sim of Macdonald College has been appointed executive secretary. An office will be opened in Montreal. Close cooperation has been received from Mrs Ware of the Local Council of Women, A.C.Lawson of the Young Men's Board of Trade, Dr Morley, and Mr Harry Avison.

In the Maritimes Dr Blakeny and Dr Peacock of the Department of Education, New Brunswick, are contacting organizations throughout this province. In Nova Scotia the project is being carried under the leadership of Dr Richter of the Institute of Public Affairs, Dalhousie University. Dr Croteau is directing the work in Prince Edward Island.

Members of our armed services will be participating in Citizens' Forum through the cooperation of the educational branches and the Canadian Legion Educational Services.

**1944**

*CITIZENS' FORUM*

Appeared in *Food for Thought*, volume 4, issue 7, April 1944.

Among the experts there is a widespread feeling that while domestic matters allow for democratic participation in framing policy, external relations can have little to do with the people. Canadian foreign policy must be made by politicians and administered by well-dressed young men in the Department of External Affairs. It can be written about by erudite professors and discussed by societies on international affairs, open only to the socially acceptable. Canada's foreign policy has nothing to do with the individual citizen. After all, it is too difficult for him to understand.

The weekly reports coming in from Citizens' Forums prove this wrong. Groups of ordinary citizens all across the country have met and discussed Canada's place in the world, and have come to conclusions that have all the colour and progress and sanity that many of our experts lack. From Saskatchewan to Nova Scotia, from young civil servants in Ottawa to church groups in small towns, the reports on such subjects as Canada in the British Commonwealth, the new relationship with Soviet Russia, and many other topics, have proved in considerable measure that Canadians know what it is all about.

It is unfair to quote one of these reports alone – they are all so good. One thing does emerge. *Citizens' Forum* members recognize that we are living in a world of challenge. They feel that a new world order must be born and Canada must play her full part in building it. Are the experts – professors and diplomats alike – ahead of or behind these ordinary Canadians?

Another gratifying thing about *Citizens' Forum* is the number of action projects that are being undertaken by groups. Some have sent in plans to their municipal government; others have tried to do something to eliminate racial prejudice in their areas; others again have written to the government for information about what kind of foreign policy we are pursuing. This development of action from study is amazingly encouraging. Out of this discussion and action a fuller group consciousness is being born.

George Grant

## CITIZENS' FORUM

Appeared in *Food for Thought*, volume 4, issue 8, May 1944.

More than a year ago, when Dr E.A. Corbett, the Director of the Canadian Association for Adult Education, first thought of a large-scale educational venture which would aim to set up discussion groups on post-war problems in the cities and towns of this land, many people told him that it couldn't be done. They said: city people just won't meet together; there are too many distractions; people don't know their neighbours, even if they have lived in a place twenty years. Well, this year *Citizens' Forum* has disproved this.

Local Citizens' Forums, to the number of some 1500, have sprung up all across the country to work out for themselves the problems that confront them in the world that is coming. Some are in small prairie towns like Ituna and Humboldt in Saskatchewan; some in wartime Halifax, or industrial Montreal. There are church groups in Ontario towns like Bloomfield, or St George and Plaster Rock in New Brunswick. There are forums in schools, libraries, and in plain ordinary neighbourhoods. Hundreds of men and women in the navy, army, and air force swell the numbers.

Many of the forums have emphasized the need for action to implement the conclusions they have reached in discussion. 'We must not be accused of idle chatter,' said one forum. In Manitoba, conferences have been held at Carmen, Gilbert Plains, and Souris, and out of such meetings a fuller understanding of community needs and responsibilities is arising. In Fredericton, the teachers are hoping to use *Citizens' Forum* as part of their annual conference.

During April, provincial *Citizens' Forum* meetings are being held in all the Western Provinces, to evaluate the progress made this year, and to lay plans for the future. Quebec is arranging a meeting for May 6th, and other provinces will undoubtedly follow suit. The mail coming in to the national office continually bears witness to the value of this project, and the need for its continuance.

CALLING ALL CITIZENS

Appeared in *Food for Thought*, volume 5, issue 1, October 1944.

Dear *Citizens' Forum* Members:
Citizens' Forums will again get under way on Tuesday, November 7th, at the usual hour. Again groups of people right across the country will meet once a week to thrash out the problems that confront them as democratic citizens of Canada. And in the winter of 1944–5 what could be more important than intelligent and constructive thought by Canadians?

For in this year significant new things are happening in the world. After five years of struggle, victory seems at last in sight, and the fall of the Nazi barbarians appears imminent. No longer can we think in terms of things to come – but of things already here. As the objective of victory becomes more certain, the objective of a peaceful and ordered world becomes more pressing.

In the world picture the United Nations, having worked together for war, turn their attention to the solution of world problems so that the war will be a fruitful basis for enduring peace. Already conferences are being held; decisions are being made. At Dumbarton Oaks the problems of international security are being thought through.[1] At Montreal plans for the effective relief and rehabilitation of devastated countries are being discussed.[2] It is the duty of every citizen in Canada to understand these plans and to help to make them lasting and effective. Only by widespread understanding among all Canadians of our international responsibilities will we play a role worthy of this country.

At home, too, the same knowledge, the same responsibility, is demanded of all Canadians. Soon thousands of men and women, who have been away for years, will be returning after the accomplishment of victory. What must be ready for them? How can we prepare the way to bring them back into a fruitful civilian life? At home the Canadian nation, built around two major racial groups, faces new difficulties in living together. How are we to meet this problem? Can we preserve the nation we have built?

With these and other questions to face, it is clearly important that Canadians resolve them, not blindly and with prejudice, but constructively and with thought. And this does not mean thought by the few, but by the many. For we have built a democracy and that obviously means a vote for all of us, a part for all of us, responsibility for all of us.

In such a Canada then, *Citizens' Forum* is clearly a vital instrument in our democratic process. For through it, groups of all kinds across the country can sift through the facts and sort out the problems, whether they be local, national, or international. Through it all of us can play our part and take our responsibility for a better Canada and a better world.

Sincerely yours,
George Grant

## CITIZENS' FORUM 1944–5 PRESENTS

Appeared in *Food for Thought*, volume 5, issue 1, October 1944.

### REGULAR DISCUSSIONS ON THE AIR EVERY TUESDAY EVENING BEGINNING NOVEMBER 7

*Main areas of discussion:*
A New Generation of Citizens, Canada as a Nation, Jobs for Soldiers and Civilians, Can We Build a Lasting Peace?, The Citizen and His Government

Maritimes 9:30 ADT, Ontario and Quebec 8:30 EDT, Manitoba 7:30 CDT, Saskatchewan and Alberta 9:00 MDT, British Columbia 8:00 PDT

Two introductory broadcasts on Thursday, October 26th, and Thursday, November 2nd, will open up the winter series, and will provide an opportunity for local Citizens' Forums groups to become organized before the main series begins.

For further information, write to George Grant, *Citizens' Forum* , 198 College Street, Toronto, Ont.

## CITIZENS' FORUM LAST YEAR

Appeared in *Food for Thought*, volume 5, issue 1, October 1944.

When something new like *Citizens' Forum* is starting, it is particularly necessary that everybody who is part of it should help to shape its development so that out of this common and cumulative experience and thought a more effective instrument may be forged. This is, after all, the basis of the democratic method. As part of this process for *Citizens' Forum*, a questionnaire was sent out to all groups at the end of last year's programme, and out of the answers that came back the *Citizens' Forum* is being shaped for this coming year. This is the only way that the failures of one year can be changed into the successes of the next.

The first important piece of information is the list of occupations of people who took part in the forums last year. For in it one can see the wide variety of human beings who thought about and discussed our national problems. It is impossible to list it completely here for it takes up a page and a half of type and covers the wide range of varying occupations that make up our modern community. The occupation mentioned most often is the housewife. This obviously is because the wives of men of many differing occupations met with their husbands in the forums. It is interesting, however, that women should take such a large part and is indicative of the fact that the petticoat will no longer reside in the kitchen but is going to take its place on the public rostrum.

The next largest group were teachers. Some led forums in their schools; some led them among their friends; others were part of their neighbourhood group. Next came clerks and white-collar workers; next, business and professional; then engineers, ministers, and so on. The rest of the occupations range from hotel manager, harbour master, railway employees, artificers, veterinary surgeons, librarians, judges, loggers – every category in the complicated working of modern Canadian life. On the whole, the list is weighted on the side of the more economically prosperous, and one thing that the forums must do is to try to make its influence more powerfully felt among such groups as the union movement. It would be wise if any neighbourhood groups brought in local members of a trade union who live in the district. Unfortunately, these questionnaires could not be sent out to the groups in the armed forces. This summary of the different occupations does not, therefore, include these men and women.

The next important category was the various nationalities in the Forum. Here, almost without exception, all forums mentioned members of British origin (i.e., English, Scottish, Irish). But as well as this, 28 other national origins were mentioned. The highest [incidence] of these were French, American, German, Polish, and Jewish, but others include every corner of the world, from Hindu to Swedish, West Indian to Icelandic. Some of the best work of the forums was bringing people of varying national origin into the same group so that they could discuss together common problems and feel a greater unity of purpose as Canadians. In the future one of the most important parts of the forum's work may be in bringing Canadians, newly arrived in this country, into connection with the problems that confront them.

The next few answers give a picture of how the forums got started and what was the moving force in keeping them together. In the case of well over half the forums they were called together by some individual and were composed of groups of friends and neighbours. This fact is significant. For it shows that the greatest potential of the forums is in getting people together in the same neighbourhood or street. In most towns people are grouped together, not according to geography but according to occupation, through a Board of Trade or union. The result has been that often one doesn't know one's neighbours on the same street, and there is little neighbourhood feeling.

The forum may be a way of reintroducing that neighbourhood feeling into our cities. Another thing that will affect this is that people often have to go so far away for their entertainment, and neighbourhood forums being near at home will be an attraction on a cold winter night. Next to neighbourhood groups, the next largest number were forums started within certain organizations. Ten per cent of all forums were from church organizations; others centred around Home and School clubs, Y.M.C.A.s, unions and other types of organizations. Among church groups it was found particularly that Citizens' Forums gave a great opportunity for members to discuss what their responsibility was in the social world as members of the Christian Church.

It is difficult to analyse the answers to the question on which topics were considered of most importance by the forums, for one cannot tell whether people happened to like the individuals on the broadcast or whether they liked the subject intrinsically itself. Anyway, it is interesting to note which subjects are considered most stimulating last year. By a long shot the evening of discussion on 'The Rise of Asia' was considered most interesting. Next came the broadcast on education; then on our relations with French Canada, and fourthly our relations with the U.S.S.R. It was often said before the *Citizens' Forum* started that the ordinary people in Canada weren't interested in international affairs. The fact that two of the most popular broadcasts were on Canada's relations with other parts of the world is evidence that Canadian people are deeply concerned with their relations with other people. This fact and the reports that come back from the forums show little trace of isolationism or self-centred concentration on our own problems. There is a realization that Canada's problems are part of larger world questions.

The broadcast considered the least stimulating was the one on the Constitutional question in Canada. The reason given was because it was given by three lawyers who all talked in the highest of technical jargon, which was un-understandable. The next most unpopular broadcast was the one on the French-Canadian relations. This had at the same time been one of the most popular among other people, so it may be considered to be one that roused either praise or blame from those who heard it (and not surprising in the light of present Canadian politics).

The question of what topics should be discussed next year brings out clearly the varied interests of the forum members. It certainly brought out a multiplicity of answers. The most popular demand was for a series of discussions on the economic problems of Canada, and how they fit into the world economic problems. There was a general demand for a further discussion of monopolies and cartels, the effects of tariffs on world trade, and the whole complicated structure of the world economy. Next most popular demand was for a general discussion of citizenship and government – how the citizen fitted into government, and what part he should play in political parties and other institutions. Interestingly enough, though last year the most unpopular broadcast had been on our Constitutional problem, there was a widespread demand for further and more detailed study of this subject. Many people wanted education discussed in more extensive form than it had been last year. A large percentage wanted a discussion of the organization for world peace. A large section wanted race and minority problems discussed, especially in relation to French Canada. Many other topics of use were mentioned. These ranged from women's place to the place of press and radio in a democracy, from housing to immigration. It is interesting that a majority of the forums wanted the same subject discussed for several evenings in a row so that they could get down to more detailed discussion than was possible in one evening, and therefore reach saner and sounder conclusions.

Many other questions were raised. Many forums wanted better and more pertinent report questions; others wanted better and more comprehensive library lists; others again talked of forming new forums in their town or city next year. From this questionnaire a vast amount of useful information was amassed. And above all, out of it one gets a picture of the living society, with all its varying shapes and changing colours, that is Canada. One can picture forums as they worked last year all across the country. A group of church people in western Ontario, a group of teachers in New Brunswick, the Knights of Columbus in Regina – these and many others discussing together the emerging and changing facts of our Canadian democracy. Yes, from these questionnaires and the reports that came in, throughout the year, one gets a picture of the vitality and determination of that democracy. One sees, in fact, the effort that was *Citizens' Forum* last year.

## CALLING ALL CITIZENS

Appeared in *Food for Thought*, volume 5, issue 2, November 1944.

Dear *Citizens' Forum* Members:
The difference between a forum that is successful and one that is having difficulties seems to me to be definitely based on whether a group knows clearly what it is doing and why it is doing it. This struck me forcibly about a group that met in Halifax the other night. In size this group is a good deal larger than most other forums, having an average attendance of about 30 people – approximately two-thirds of these being service personnel and one-third civilians from Halifax. This group had an extremely successful season last year and was starting on its second season. They had themselves helped to get other groups going on shore and certain of their members had taken the discussion guides to sea and had started informal groups on their ships. And apart from their able chairman and secretary, the clearest reason for this success was that they knew why they were meeting together, what they were trying to accomplish at these meetings and what that accomplishment would lead forward to in their lives. *Citizens' Forum* was not something that was carried out in a fit of absent-mindedness, but something that had a reason.

The first thing that this group realized was that if they were to be capable citizens of Canada – playing the productive role that democracy demands – they had to know more about the country. In the year 1944, knowledge is power and only those who know what is happening in Canada will be able to play a real part in shaping that country.

Secondly, it was obvious that by discussing these facts together and by the interplay of opinion against opinion, each individual member of the Forum sharpened and clarified his own mind on the anvil of controversy. Clearly, if the ideas you voiced had to stand up before 29 other minds, flaws in them were quickly thrown out. As one of the members said, 'A lot of my ideas that were sort of misty in my head, I've brought out and heard people criticize them and praise them and this has helped me to adjust them and revise them in the light of what the others said.' A lot of half-formed ideas have been put into shape. A lot of prejudices have been unable to stand up in front of other people's criticisms. Of course, just expressing our own ideas before other people often clears them up in our own minds.

The third fact that many of this group realized, and this was one of the things that made them most effective, was that the whole idea wasn't just 'pie in the sky,' but that answers to these Canadian problems are tough. Finding the answers means real thought – not just a last-minute airing of prejudices on a Tuesday night. They realized that sifting the facts by their own experience, reading other facts in other places, were necessary if they were to get anywhere – and that after the discussion was over it was up to them to learn more.

The last reason why this forum seemed so effective was that its members realized that this discussion was something to equip them for future life. Many of the service personnel could not apply the things they had learned right away in the places they were stationed, for their time was fully occupied with the prosecution of the war. But it was clear that what was learned was not going to be just sterile thought, but in the future would be applied to the vital problems of Canadian life. This was not just discussion in a vacuum, but discussion as an instrument to help produce more effective citizens.

Of course the essential quality of this forum was that it had a sense of purpose and a feeling of growth. And this is the most necessary quality; with it, each Citizens' Forum can do a useful job for Canadian democracy – without it they will die.

This sense of movement and growth perhaps will be intensified this year by the fact that the subjects will not be dealt with in a single evening, but will be discussed from different angles on three or four consecutive broadcasts.

However, quite apart from the subjects and their treatment on the radio or in the study bulletins, the responsibility for giving each forum growth and movement – so that each member of the group and the group as a whole knows that it is learning and expanding through this activity – is up to the chairman and to each member. This feeling that *Citizens' Forum* is something worth doing, that it is part of democratic living, is up to each group itself.

Sincerely yours,
George Grant

## CALLING ALL CITIZENS

Appeared in *Food for Thought*, volume 5, issue 3, December 1944.

Dear *Citizens' Forum* Members:
People often ask what is the relation of a discussion programme like *Citizens' Forum* to getting things done in the local community and in the country at large. They say: in this year 1944–5, why get together and discuss things? We should be doing things. These people are of course right in one way. At such a time in history we should all be doing things – that is, if we want to keep our democracy alive and to extend it to new fields. That is of course perfectly clear, and few would disagree. But this natural desire for action does not in any way preclude discussion. They both go together.

Discussion is, in fact, intelligent deliberation as to what is necessary to be done. Action is the putting of decisions into effect. Discussion, like most thought, is sterile if it doesn't lead forward to practical conclusions. Action, to be constructive, must be well thought out.

Take voting, for instance – the most primary action in a democracy. There is not much use in voting – federally, provincially, or municipally [–] unless we first know the issues and work out which is the best candidate to vote for. On the other hand, after long thought on the question, it would be pretty sterile thought if we didn't go ahead then and vote. Discussion in Citizens' Forum means clear thinking on the part of the group, to equip themselves to be better citizens, to take the right kind of action. Even the most active people must decide what kind of a community they want before they act. They have to work out in their minds what they want and then go ahead and see that they get what they want.

Discussion programmes like *Citizens' Forum* have another real value as far as action is concerned. We will never have democratic action until people see the need for it. *Citizens' Forum*, by getting people to discuss, by helping them to see the problems that confront them as Canadians, can help them to start acting. Discussion can, if it is well and creatively led, be the best way to break down the apathy and sloth that often prevent human beings from moving forward to better things. People who have not been active citizens before can become so through *Citizens' Forum*. This certainly happened last year.

What are the ways that a group can act, if through its discussion it has seen the need for action? It seems to me there are two main ways.

1. The individuals in the group can take action in their community in any of the various spheres that present themselves, through some organization already existing in the community. If they are interested in education, they can get into their Home and School Association and make it work. If they are interested in rehabilitation, they can get into their rehabilitation organizations. If they feel the most important thing is our relations with the world, they can get into their League of Nations Society or an organization like it. If they are church people, let them get behind their church activities. If they are in a union, they can become a really active union member. If they want to get better housing, they can get into their local housing association and push it. Let them join the political party of their choice or get behind their local community centre. There are a myriad ways of doing this. The main thing is to see that in such action they are really being constructive.

2. Some groups, however, will want to act as a group, having been together as a group. They may not want to do it through other organizations but by themselves. Last year in *Citizens' Forum* for instance, many groups did different things. One forum in Fredericton, N.B., got interested in education and pushed for higher salaries for teachers and better school facilities. One forum in Winnipeg became interested in rehabilitation and started to welcome returned men back into the community. They did these things, acting together as a group, and went forward together through the various stages that were necessary to get things done as a group.

The first thing, it seems to me, that needs to be done by a group if they are to be effective, is to pick their objective and make it a very definite one. That is, before they decide on action they must decide what they want to accomplish by it, and secondly they should undertake something that is within their powers. For example, if a group undertook to change the structure of the United Nations, they wouldn't by themselves have much chance of success. If, on the other hand, they attempted to get a community centre for their own area they might well succeed.

The next thing, it seems to me, that is necessary if a group is undertaking action, is to know at what point they will need the support and cooperation of other groups in the community. For instance, if a group wants to get a good rehabilitation committee going in its area, it will soon need to get other people in on it. If it is to be successful, business men, clergy, trade unionists, and other appropriate people will need to get behind it. A discussion group is part of a community. It must recognize that it must work with others.

The key person in the relation between discussion and action in a Citizens' Forum is, of course, the leader or chairman of the group. It will be he or she, after all, who will fundamentally be responsible for the success or failure of both discussion and action. It is he who must see clearly exactly that the relationship between the two is going to be and what he can do to make it fruitful.

One fact is certain, what Jack London once called 'the passionless pursuit of passionless intelligence' won't interest many Canadians.[3] Most Canadians are practical and want their knowledge to be useful and constructive. If a group becomes merely sterile discussion, it won't have a very long life. On the other hand, it is impossible to push a group farther forward than they want to go. Free people always act as they want, when they want. The job of the leader is to maintain the balance between these two extremes. He must prevent the group from becoming sterile through inaction. On the other hand he must see that the group goes forward in its own way and at its own time. To achieve such a balance is a tough problem.

Sincerely yours,
George Grant

**1945**

CALLING ALL CITIZENS

Appeared in *Food for Thought*, volume 5, issue 4, January 1945.

Dear *Citizens' Forum* Members:
Wherever I go among *Citizens' Forum* groups, they ask me about the value of answering the report questions –'Why should we send in our reports? What's the use?' When *Citizens' Forum* first started, some people thought that the reports were being used for some sort of prying. Others thought that the reports were useless and that nobody ever looked at them. So why send them in?

Because of these misunderstandings about the purpose of reporting, it seems important to try and show exactly the role that it plays as a central part of the whole *Citizens' Forum* project. There are four main reasons for the importance of these reports.

1. *Sense of National Unity*: The reports serve the purpose of letting groups all over the country know not only what they themselves in their particular area are thinking, but also what others are thinking. They give people a sense that these matters are important not only in, say, Halifax, Winnipeg, or Vancouver; they are important problems for the whole Dominion. The provincial report summaries given over the air each week do that for the province. The national report summaries will do that for the nation as a whole.

This year, starting in January, each forum that reports regularly will receive from the National Office a mimeographed summary of the reports from all across Canada, so that they will know what the other provinces are thinking.

2. *Two-way Communication*: By the system of weekly reports, each forum can express its opinion about the study bulletins, the questions, and the broadcasts. In this way the people who are responsible for the programmes find out what the forums really want and can then, wherever possible, change the broadcasts and bulletins accordingly. A good example of this is the reaction this year to the report questions. Different forums have called them every name in the book.

3. *Clarifying Opinion*: Reporting helps a forum to make its conclusions real and down to earth, to keep them from being vague and woolly. Once an idea is written down on paper, it is much more real than when it is bounding about in somebody's mind. By reporting, the group is forced to express its conclusions and opinions in clear, con crete terms.

4. *Use of Reports*: This year a summary of the reports of the forums is to be sent to all the major political parties, to all the government departments concerned, both federal and provincial, and to all organizations that may be interested in the subject under discussion. For instance, reports on labour relations will go to the Chamber of Commerce and to the labour congresses. Reports on international policy will go to the Department of External Affairs. In this way, the people who are making and administering policy will come to know what a large, representative section of the thinking public wants in national policy. *Citizens' Forum*, in this way, will serve as a crucial part of the democratic process.

It is important to understand the difference between the 'discussion questions' and the 'report questions' on your study bulletins. A discussion question should open up the subject and provide a stimulant to discussion. Report questions, on the other hand, should be phrased so that groups can give a concise answer as to their opinion on certain subjects.

Often, in the past, we have tried to make report questions serve both purposes. Starting in January, however, the study bulletins will include – in two separate sections – questions to be used to stimulate discussion, and other questions for the group to report on. This division of questions should be a helpful technique for the group leaders. If they need a question that will take them into the core of the subject and promote good discussion, they can use the discussion questions. For their reporting, they can use the report questions, which will be clear, concise, and answerable in a short space. This type of question should not prevent the qroups from sending in other and fuller comments, but it will, we hope, promote better discussion and better reporting.

Reporting is indeed the measure of a forum. By doing so, a Forum enters into the project, sending in its findings to be used over the air the next week. In this way it unites with other forums all across the

country in expressing the opinion of its members on the major problems that confront Canadians. By doing this the forums can help shape
the democratic thinking of the Canadian people.

Sincerely yours,<br>
George Grant

## CALLING ALL CITIZENS

Appeared in *Food for Thought*, volume 5, issue 5, February 1945.

Dear *Citizens' Forum* Members:
There are always people who say it is a waste of time to study international affairs. 'There's nothing anybody can do about it. External policy
is something for the government, not for the ordinary citizen. What
*Citizens' Forum* should study are subjects like the local school, community councils, local job opportunities, and so on. Subjects which the
Forum members can do something about. Leave international relations
to the civil servants and professors.'

In this month of February, for three evenings, *Citizens' Forum* is
going to discuss international affairs. It is important therefore to know
exactly what we are doing and why, and what we expect to get out of
discussing these world topics.

The first reason, it seems to me, why we should tackle international
questions is that they affect us so greatly. In these days, that seems to
be something of a truism. The Canadians who faced the Nazis at Fal-
aise, Ortona, or on Walcheran Island would think it ridiculous even to
mention this. They don't have to be told the value of a peaceful world,
nor of world cooperation. We can build a perfect society at home here
in Canada, where everybody acts like an angel, and still it wouldn't do
us much good if every twenty-five years world security was so threatened that the best of the society had to go off to defend it. Denmark,
after all, was admitted by many to have a full and fine community life
and an active democratic society. Yet none of this saved it from barbaric conquest and exploitation.

But this does not answer the question – is there any point in discussing international questions, or is this a question only for the government? The only possible democratic answer is, of course, that it can't

be left to the government and that there *is* something for people to do. In Great Britain, for instance, after 1938, it was the gradual awakening of a determined public opinion that made the government change its mind about the aggressor nations. Between 1939 and 1941, Franklin Roosevelt could not have expanded American help to the allied nations if his electorate had not increasingly realised the need for such action. Here in our country, it was awareness on the part of public opinion that took us to war in 1939. An effective public opinion in Canada in the 1930s would have forced us to shoulder our responsibilities then. The same goes, of course, for all democratic countries. After the war, will a lethargic public opinion be only too willing to let our government back away from our international responsibilities? Or will there be a sufficient number of Canadians ready to insist that our government act wisely?

Many people say that our Members of Parliament aren't interested in foreign affairs in an election campaign. But if there were enough citizens in every constituency sufficiently well informed, they could insist on candidates stating their policy. Eternal vigilance is, as always, the price of freedom and of international security. That is why *Citizens' Forum* must study international affairs.

This is an easy answer which doesn't face the problem of the leader, who has to make the Dumbarton Oaks Proposals[4] or UNRRA[5] as real as the local school or jobs for all. And that is what the group leader has to do, if these discussions are to be concrete and realistic. The first essentials for the leader to know, in every corner of his being, how vital the subjects are. If a leader thinks that these discussions on world security and lasting peace are not very useful and only vague theorizing, then the discussion will be exactly that. If, however, the discussion leader is conscious of its real and living importance, he can constantly infuse that element into the discussion.

The second job of the discussion leader is to constantly bring the discussion on international affairs down to earth. Remind the participants of Canadians fighting and dying. Ask them exactly what the alternative to international collaboration is. Ask them how Canadians can have jobs without ordered international trade. If this is well done, the discussion won't get vague and distant.

Discussion on international relations can be made real and effective. And every time anybody says the field is too big for individuals, let us remind them of this war and the last. Let us realize that the prevention of a third war is our business.

Sincerely yours,
George Grant


## CALLING ALL CITIZENS

Appeared in *Food for Thought*, volume 5, issue 6, March 1945.

Dear *Citizens' Forum* Members:
When we see the flamethrower and the rocket bomb as the symbol of 1945, it is easy to lose courage. It is easy to ask ourselves what is the use of building small things. What is the use of better city government, what is the use of planning better cities, of building better houses, of seeing that our schools become the most alive institutions of their kind, if every twenty-five years we are going to be swept into the holocaust of war and the fruits of labour destroyed? We think of the peace-loving people of Denmark and Norway, of Great Britain and the Soviet Union, who worked hard for a better and freer society within their own borders, only to have it dashed down by invasion and bombing.

There is, of course, some truth in this thinking. Churchill, Roosevelt, and Stalin have a tremendous job of establishing a world order in which international harmony, law, and security will prevail. Every Canadian must work for that, strive for that. Citizens' Forums have recognized this in their discussions on 'Can We Build a Lasting Peace?'

But although this is true, we must not let it blind us to the immediate tasks and objectives we have here at home. While we recognize that the main job of outlawing the flamethrower and the concentration camp must fall on the leaders of the United Nations and our support of them, we know too that the eventual elimination of these horrors from the world will depend upon their elimination from the minds and hearts of human beings all over the world. The only way we can achieve that is by better education, better houses, more democratic city government, in every country of the world, in every town of the world. And to get these things we must start at home.

There are some people who seem to expect Utopia to appear suddenly in our midst as Minerva sprang fully armed from the forehead of

Jove. What nonsense this is. The brave new world we want will come only from hard thought and hard work, on the part of thousands and millions of people. We approach Utopia only as, bit by bit, selfishness and sloth are eliminated. And that means getting down to such subjects as local government, the planning of our towns, the establishment of community councils, the improvement of our schools. For after all, when we talk of Canada or the world in general, we mean thousands of small communities, towns, cities and villages. And when we talk of a better and more democratic Canada, we mean that Souris, Manitoba, is a better place to live in, that Halifax has fewer slums, that Toronto has a better city council, that Plaster Rock, Lethbridge, and Smiths Falls present more opportunities for a fuller life for their citizens.

If our communities are indeed to become better places to live in, that means hard work and hard thinking. There is, in fact, no part of the *Citizens' Forum* this year so important as the section on 'The Citizen and his Government,' particularly the last two discussions in March on THE CITIZEN AND LOCAL GOVERNMENT and TOWN PLANNING AND COMMUNITY CENTRES. For here are problems in which each citizen can directly play his part. Here are subjects about which it is impossible for the groups to say 'Oh, it is the government's responsibility' or 'This is the business of the Big Powers.' Here are subjects where the objectives can only be realized if thousands of citizens across the country play their part and make their influence felt. With these subjects *Citizens' Forum* moves out of the realm of vague discussion into the field of direct action. These problems demand an answer, and our treatment of them will prove whether Citizens' Forums are meeting their responsibility for Canada.

George Grant

## CALLING ALL CITIZENS

Appeared in *Food for Thought*, volume 5, issue 7, April 1945.

Dear Citizens' Forum Members:
About this time in the year it is good to try and assess what Citizens' Forums have accomplished. In numbers, the forums have not grown this year. In some provinces they have indeed decreased; in others they have increased. But there has been little net gain. Certainly there is a

need for more forums, and next year we must guarantee that, particularly in areas where there have been no forums, a vigorous effort to organize them is launched. The lack of increase this year has been a disappointment and, to a degree, a failure.

But we must not make the mistake of judging Citizens' Forum solely by numbers. If one had the choice between 10 good forums in a province and 500 ineffective ones, the only sensible choice would be 10 good ones. Mass education is a myth. Its exponents are deluded optimists. Worthwhile education is a slow process. It is not something which can be applied like a plaster. What matters, ultimately, is the degree to which each individual develops, and the way each group is strengthened. A very few effective citizens can change the face of the community. They can provide the spur to community effort and action. They can prod the inertia and smugness of our democracy. In trying to assess the actual value of *Citizens' Forum* this year, the quality of the groups must clearly be our criterion.

The question is, then, are the forums better developed this year? Are the members more thoroughly informed? Are they more conscious of local, national, and international problems? Have they become more responsible citizens? These, of course, are impossible questions for anyone sitting in the central office to answer. They are questions which only the individual forums can answer properly.

It is true to say, however, that, all in all, the calibre of reports this year has been better than last – they show more straight thinking and more investigation of the problems at hand. That means better-informed citizens. Also, many groups have decided after the broadcasts are over to go on with the study of a particular subject. Several forums in Toronto, for instance, are going on with the study of Dominion–Provincial relations. Others are going to undertake further study of international affairs, the Dumbarton Oaks Proposals, and the San Francisco Conference.[6] By concentrating on a single subject over a longer period, these groups will have more time for extensive reading, and thus make possible more satisfactory discussion. Our National Office would be only too delighted to hear from any groups across the country that are doing this, and to send them any further material that we might have available on their special request.

As for responsibility, that is even more difficult to gauge. But news does come in here to our office of groups giving proofs of their sense of responsibility. A group in B.C. writes about getting behind rehabilitation plans. Groups in Smiths Falls, Ontario, are pushing for proper town planning in their city. From Nova Scotia comes news of more community interest. From Barrie, Ontario, and from Winnipeg, we hear of groups getting interested in their schools and in the education of children in their community. Groups in Montreal are getting together for a housing meeting. And in all parts of the country groups are interviewing their municipal, provincial, and federal representatives and putting these representatives on the mat. This is responsible citizenship. It is the way a better Canada will be built.

It is no use fooling ourselves, however. *Citizens' Forum* has still a long, long way to go before it can become the force that it should be in this country. There are large areas where no groups at all exist, and there are many groups which still have a long way to go in the development and use of the discussion method. They are still not aware of the force the group can be in the community, not really convinced of its possibly as a leavening agency. Now, that must be for next year; but during the summer we must all be working to see that there will be more forums next year and, what is more important, better and more responsible forums. We can tell our neighbours, and the people we meet in our organizations and community activities, about Citizens' Forum. We can arouse their interest in this tool for making our democracy work. The more forums we have, the more representative they will be of opinion across Canada. And the more power they will have for action.

Yours sincerely,
George Grant

CALLING ALL CITIZENS

Appeared in volume 5, issue 9, of *Food for Thought*, June–July 1945. The column is headed: 'This is a summary of the report presented by GEORGE GRANT, National Secretary of Citizens' Forum, at the opening session of the Winnipeg Conference.'

REPORT ON *CITIZENS' FORUM*

*Citizens' Forum* has just completed a second year. Now is a good time, therefore, to assess how much has been accomplished. What have been our successes and what our failures? Indeed, only by such analysis of what has been done in these first two years can we see how to do better in the future.

The ultimate test of *Citizens' Forum* must be of course how many and how good are the forums that are organized. The number of groups this year indicates that *Citizens' Forum* has not expanded as it should. The quality of the groups this year and their location show that we have made strides ahead and also that the *Citizens' Forum* technique is one that will work and can be of growing significance, if we can perfect our techniques and our organization. At the end of this second year of *Citizens' Forum*, in fact, two main conclusions can be reached: (a) *Citizens' Forum*, where there has been good leadership, has been an outstanding success and can be of real significance in shaping the life of our country; (b) both in the provision of facilities and of imagination we have failed, as yet, to tap the potentialities for the expansion of this programme. There is still a large job to be done.

*Number of Registered Groups*

| | |
|---|---|
| British Columbia | 100 |
| Alberta | 70 |
| Saskatchewan | 155 |
| Manitoba | 125 |
| Ontario | 170 |
| Quebec | 80 |
| New Brunswick | 80 |
| Nova Scotia | 50 |
| TOTAL | 830 |

(This total does not include a large number of people who have used *Citizens' Forum* study material or broadcasts at different times for their differing purposes. Nor does it include 10,535 copies of the study material that went weekly to the armed forces through the courtesy of the Canadian Legion Educational Services and were used for discussion purposes there. It is impossible to estimate the number of groups organized in the services around this study material.)

These groups have one common factor. Nearly all of them are formed within neighbourhoods. This has been one of the great contributions of *Citizens' Forum*. In urban Canada it has often helped to change a geographic locality into a community – with all that that implies. Many a good forum on a street has brought people together. This creation of neighbourliness may not have any immediate effect in any specific way – but in the long run healthy, friendly communities will mean more productive people.

Though the forums are composed mainly of community groups, these have been mainly of two different kinds. First, those composed of friends and neighbours who come together informally and have a group which is their only common basis of meeting. Second, members of some organization, perhaps a church or a Home and School Association, who use the *Citizens' Forum* as part of their programme. Particularly this latter type present large opportunities for expansion in numbers, for organizations are discovering that the forum is useful to them. They are seeing that discussion (an active art in which all must take part) is producing more responsible members than would be the case with programmes of a more passive sort. Particularly at this point it is worth noting the wide potentialities for discussion in the schools through the use of *Citizens' Forum*.

*Action*
One of the best results of this second year is that Citizens' Forums are realizing, in an ever growing way, that discussion must lead forward to greater responsibility to our communities, our nation, and our world. Naturally, this responsibility takes differing forms in different places. There is no set pattern. In one place, a group is interested in education and starts a Home and School Association or gets a member elected to the school board; in another it organizes an election forum for the airing of issues; in another it pushes for adequate housing; in another for adequate town planning; in another it forms and supports a local rehabilitation committee. It is not possible here to give in any greater detail the variety or extent of the community projects that have been undertaken, but all these activities show clearly that *Citizens' Forum* is an important means of producing effective community spirit and responsibility.

*Leadership*
As in most programmes, the telling factor is leadership. In communi-

ties which have vital, intelligent leaders, interested in what discussion can do, then the *Citizens' Forum* can, and does, succeed. It is a question of finding such leaders, training them in the discussion method, and making as clear as possible the enormous gains that can be made for democratic Canada, through the creative discussion group. Only as we prove, with results, what the discussion group can mean, will our movement grow and flourish.

*Organization*
Without doubt our greatest failure this year has been in the field of organization. At the end of this second year it is abundantly clear that discussion groups will not be created merely by putting on broadcasts, sending out study bulletins, and casting publicity upon the waters. Personal contact is what creates a discussion group. Also, the media (broadcasts and bulletins) must be adapted to each local forum with its own local needs. This means that to run *Citizens' Forum* there must be sufficient paid staff to (a) go into new territory, pick out the potential group leaders, and explain how the *Citizens' Forum* technique may be developed; (b) to interest heads of organizations to use *Citizens' Forum* in their organization; (c) to hold leadership conferences; (d) to give personal advice and help to any forum that may need it. These functions must be carried out as well as the weekly mechanical work of sending out material, writing the radio reports from the material that comes in from the groups, and answering the regular correspondence. This need for paid organization staff is particularly felt in *Citizens' Forum*; for whereas *Farm Forum*, because it appeals directly to creating better farmers, will get the support and help of farm representatives, *Citizens' Forum*, because of its wider approach, is everybody's and nobody's responsibility. This means the latter is true.

Looking at the provincial organization, then, we can see how totally inadequate in numbers – however excellent in quality – our provincial organizations have been. In the Western provinces it has been carried on by the staffs of the Extension Departments, all of whom have had to do the job in the midst of other manifold and pressing responsibilities. None of these secretaries, despite great willingness, has had the time to get on the road to organize forums. In Ontario the situation is as bad – one full-time secretary (without adequate funds) to organize the enormous urban areas of Ontario. This has meant that the vast percentage of Ontario has never been touched by *Citizens' Forum*. Quebec, though smaller in English-speaking population, has had a difficult time raising funds. In Nova Scotia and New Brunswick, despite the support of the provincial governments and the valiant efforts of the secretaries, not enough organization has yet been done. Both the secretaries have other full-time jobs. Only their generosity has enabled them to accomplish so much in their spare time.

Clearly then, the first and foremost need of *Citizens' Forum* is an adequate number of full-time regional organizers who can really make the work effective and widespread. Otherwise we will, by necessity, only continue to skim the surface. As large an educational undertaking as *Citizens' Forum* cannot be carried only by a corporal's guard.

*Subject Matter*

Another area where more thought and experimentation must be carried out is in subject matter for *Citizens' Forum*. What kind of topic should be discussed? Clearly the most essential criterion is, what are the citizens of the country interested in? We must raise issues that people feel touch their daily lives and which people feel a need to discuss. But what are the 'felt needs' of people as far as discussion is concerned? For instance, where *Farm Forum* appeals to one functional group, *Citizens' Forum* appeals to all the varying folk of Canadian urban communities.

What are the common problems in which to interest people in urban communities? Certainly not function, for there are many, many varying functions. In one group there may be a teacher, a garage mechanic, a lawyer, two housewives, a baker. Obviously the common meeting ground is not a discussion of work, but in other common problems. We must see that subject matter is chosen that does interest the greatest number possible. Also, as one of our prime needs in *Citizens' Forum* is in the creation of community solidarity, we must have topics, the solution to which centres in the community. If all our topics are about subjects over which people have little or no control, the resultant sense of impotence will do much to wreck *Citizens' Forum*.

*Techniques*

Equally, as there is a need for experimentation in subject matter, so is there need for improvement in our techniques – whether in producing better broadcasts, sending out more useful written material, or in personal aid to the individual group. We must recognize the necessity for continually improving our techniques and seeing that they help to produce the kind of result we want.

This brings up the most important point of all about *Citizens' Forum*. There must be a continual recognition by those planning the programme in all its aspects, that its purpose is to get Canadians to think for themselves. All aspects of the programme must be seen in this light. This must be the criterion to judge its success, not, have we put on broadcasts that convince people that one point of view is right? But rather, have we put on broadcasts that have stimulated people to reach their own conclusions? Have we written study material that will help people to think for themselves and strengthen their own minds? Only in this way will we be doing our job. *Citizens' Forum* must be no media for any particular set of ideas; it must rather be a place where, through the help of the spoken and written word, Canadian citizens may find their own way and learn to think for themselves.

Citizens' Forum is a growing movement. But it can grow much faster and to far greater size if all concerned with it show intelligence, imagination, and hard work.

## CALLING ALL CITIZENS

Appeared in *Food for Thought*, volume 6, issue 1, September 1945.

Dear *Citizens' Forum* Members:
No sooner is *Citizens' Forum* finished one year than it is necessary to start building a programme for the next year. For building up a list of subjects for *Citizens' Forum* is no short or easy job. It is a question of first finding out what seem to the members of the forum the important areas of interest, then taking all the myriad suggestions that come in and putting them in some order. Then finding out what leaders in government, business, labour, agriculture, and education think of these areas, trying to guess whether these topics will be the ones in the public eye the next year. Finally taking these topics and giving them interesting titles that promote discussion. One of the main parts of this process is to remember the mistakes and failures of our first two sea-

sons. Learning for instance that a topic that is too broad is not good for discussion, remembering that all topics should be as close to the people's everyday lives as possible.

Well, this year, after careful analysis of what subjects the forum members wished to discuss and after a conference at Winnipeg at which men and women from every province in the Dominion were represented, we finally decided that there were five main areas of discussion for the coming season. These would, of course, be broken up into twenty or so titles later on.

### (1) Re-establishment

What could be more important than this? In the coming year, thousands of Canadian men and women will have to fit themselves back into civilian life, to take their part as nobly in peace time as they have in war. This is a subject matter for which all Canadians have a responsibility. It will not only require adequate planning by the Federal and Provincial Governments if it is to be carried out successfully. It will need the co-operation of every citizen of the country. Therefore if we are to do it well, we must discuss it. Therefore, re-establishment ranks as No. 1 priority on *Citizens' Forum*.

### (2) Jobs

Employment is also a subject in which Canadians have the most vital interest. More than anything else, what is on the minds of service men and war-workers is, 'Will there be a chance for remunerative and useful work for me after the war?' Without that, other things in our national life will be impossible of achievement. Nobody will debate the reasons for *Citizens' Forum* discussing employment.

### (3) National Unity

Clearly the subject of national unity is of crucial importance to Canadians. If this Dominion is to give fruition to the promise laid down in 1867 by the British North America Act, then we must attempt to lessen any differences between parts of this country, whether they be religious, racial, or regional. Can English- and French-speaking citizens work together better than in the past? Can we eliminate racial prejudice? In our Federal system, can we smooth out the differences between the Dominion and Provincial Governments so that we can go forward to more efficient government? These are questions we must settle if we in Canada are to maintain our nation.

## (4) *International*

V-Day and the San Francisco Conference increase Canada's responsibility to the world. What will be our relations with the U.S.S.R.? What is our responsibility as part of the British Commonwealth? What must we do to help feed the starving people of Europe and Asia? What will be our responsibility to the new United Nations body that has been formed at San Francisco? These questions are just as important to Canadians as any domestic or national problem. For without a solution to them, the threat of war and international anarchy appears before us.

## (5) *Community Problems*

Last, we have those problems of community interest, without which nothing is possible, for if we talk of having a good educational system and then not try to improve the schools in our own community, we fail. If we think of the moral fibre of Canada and do not put our weight behind our local church, then our thoughts are merely empty words.

If we want healthy adolescents in this country, then it is our responsibility to provide recreation in our towns and cities. Yes, questions such as these, education, community planning, and housing, are ones we must face in our own backyard.

These, then, are the main areas of interest for *Citizens' Forum* 1945–46. We hope you think they are well chosen. They are not completely frozen yet, so if anybody has any more suggestions, please send them along.

Yours,
George Grant

## Notes

1 The Dumbarton Oaks Conference on International Peace and Security was held at Washington, D.C., in 1944. The great powers drafted a blueprint for a new world organization to guarantee peace and security, with themselves at the helm.

2 The Council of United Nations Relief and Rehabilitation Administration (UNRRA) held their second session in Montreal in September 1944. Lester B. Pearson was elected chair.

3 Jack London (1876–1916), American left-wing novelist and writer, was known for his stories of adventure set in the Yukon such as *Call of the Wild* (1903). Grant is referring to a speech given at Yale on 26 January 1906 titled 'The Coming Crisis' when London said that he 'found that the American university had this ideal, as phrased by a professor [Paul Shorey] in Chicago University [*sic*], namely: "The passionless pursuit of passionless intelligence" – clean and noble, I grant you, but not alive enough ... And the reflection of this university ideal I find – the conservatism and unconcern of the American people toward those who are suffering, who are in want.' See Philip S. Foner, ed., *Jack London: American Rebel* (New York: Citadel Press 1947), 74–5.

4 See note 2.

5 See note 3.

6 At the San Francisco conference preparing for the United Nations in the summer of 1945, Canada sought to modify the Dumbarton Oaks proposals and thereby safeguard the rights of the middle powers in decision making.

# Canada – An Introduction to a Nation

Published by the Canadian Institute of International Affairs. Toronto 1943; 2nd edition, 1943; 3rd edition, 1944; 4th edition, 1945; 5th edition, 1946. French edition in 1944: *Le Canada est devenu une nation*. Quebec: Éditions des Bois-Francs.

## Canada

A person coming to Canada for the first time may well ask what kind of country he has arrived in. If he has passed through the United States on the way here, he may feel that the Canadians he meets are much the same as Americans and may wonder why they don't all belong to the same country. On the other hand, when he hears 'God Save the King' so generally played and sees the Union Jack so proudly flown, he may wonder whether this is not merely a British colony controlled from England. Let him, however, mention either of these possibilities to most Canadians and he will be met by either anger or amusement. He will be told that Canada is neither dominated from the south by the United States nor from the east by England, but is a united and independent country managing its own affairs.

But if, then, he moves from place to place across the country, he will not find a particularly unified population nor the kind of roots from which one would expect a nation to have grown. At one place he will hear people speaking French, at another English. He will see people crowding into Mass in one province, while the majority in another go to the Protestant churches. At one place he will see the factory workers and storekeepers of a large industrial town, at another the cowboys and farmers of the prairies. In the extreme east, in the Atlantic seaports, he will see ships from Europe lying at anchor; and from the coast of British Columbia in the far west, he will look out across the waters that wash the islands of the Far East. And through the length and breadth of the country he will meet people with names of diverse origin – not only British and French, but also Ukrainian, Scandinavian, German, Russian, Jewish, and many others.

If he thinks then about what he has seen, he may well wonder how and why this nation was created. What keeps so many different peoples and areas together under one flag? What has kept a country as small in population as Canada from being swallowed up by the 130 vigorous millions to the south? Why is it that a country that boasts of its independence still calls itself British and gives allegiance to a king thousands of miles away?

These and many other questions may well be asked by a visitor new to Canada. But in his search for answers he must not be too readily satisfied. Just as it is always necessary to take many factors into account in working towards an understanding of any nation, the stranger seeking an answer to his questions about Canada must consider the people and their history, their geography and their climate, their natural resources and their skills, their hopes and their fears, their loyalties and their aspirations.

## Geography

Canada covers the northern half of the North American continent. It stretches from the Atlantic and Labrador in the east, to the Pacific and Alaska in the west; from the extreme Arctic in the north, to the far flung borders of the United States in the south, which stretch three thousand miles from coast to coast.

With all her vast area Canada touches no other foreign territory besides that of her powerful neighbour to the south. But where in the past this meant a degree of isolation from the rest of the world, today this is no longer so. With the continual development of world transportation, Canada has close ties with nearly all the great centres of the world's activity. She is part of both the Atlantic and Pacific orbits that centre around the two great oceans. Even the Arctic draws her into world relations today for with the advance of aviation, the U.S.S.R. is straight across the Pole. The shortest air routes from the United States to

Europe and Asia cross Canadian territory. This nearness to the outside world does not apply to the coastal areas alone, for the St Lawrence and Great Lakes system penetrates Canada far inland from the east, while in the north Hudson Bay opens the world's oceans to the prairies. Of all the nine Canadian provinces only two have no sea-coast.

The vast area of Canada (3,694,863 square miles) makes it the third largest country in the world, smaller only than Russia and China. It is one-fifth greater than [the] continental United States and it constitutes twenty-seven per cent. of the total area of the British Commonwealth. Canada is truly a geographical giant. But what must be remembered by people who talk of its immense potentialities is that over sixty-five per cent. of this whole area is covered by the Laurentian Shield, a waste of barren rock, swamp, and bush, frozen solid for a good part of the year.

This Shield stretches over Canada in an immense arc, sweeping from the St Lawrence in the east, across northern Quebec and Ontario, along the top of the prairies, and on up into the Arctic. It is broken at one point by Hudson Bay, jutting down from the north, but otherwise it covers the northern and greater half of Canada. To see the Laurentian Shield is to understand its chilling significance. The soil is thin and found only in occasional pockets. Otherwise the surface of the area is bare rock. There are large tracts of unbroken forest, mainly pines and firs with a few scrub birches that can stand the climate. It is studded with beautiful lakes that were scooped out by glaciers centuries ago. Fish and game are abundant. In winter, sleigh and snowshoe, tractor train and 'snowmobile' are the only means of transportation. In summer, the swamps make it almost impenetrable. People who have seen both areas compare the Laurentian Shield to northern Siberia. Recent discoveries of mineral wealth in the area and development of pulp and timber industries are making it more productive than was ever deemed possible in the past. But even so its progress will be slow and Canada cannot look to the Shield for quick and easy wealth. Many speculate as to the golden possibilities of its future, but there is no question that, in the past, it has been a frontier wilderness where only the toughest dared penetrate. Certainly as an agricultural area its future is not bright for one cannot grow food on its bare rock. Because of the Laurentian Shield, the fertile areas of Canada, vast as they are, are by no means as expansive as a casual glance at a map might seem to indicate.

The most generally desirable areas of Canada in point of climate and soil fertility extend in a relatively narrow strip along the southern border. But even this fertile strip is divided into regions by barriers of barren country. The Atlantic seaboard area is cut off from the St Lawrence and Great Lakes section by four hundred miles of rock and wilderness. Central Canada is separated from the western plains by nine hundred miles of Laurentian Shield. The prairies are shut off from the Pacific coast by the most difficult barrier of all, the Rocky Mountains. And while these areas are isolated from each other, they are each of them intimately related to some American area to the south. The Maritime provinces are in effect an extension of American seaboard states. The rolling farmland of central Canada is a continuation of the same type of country in New York and Ohio. The western plains most of all are one continuous area, in spite of the existence of a political border. The Canadian Pacific coast with its backbone on the Rockies is the same as the coastline farther south in Washington and Oregon. It is this north-and-south division into regions that has made people say that Canada has been created despite its geography. For if geography had been the only active force, by far the strongest pull would have been towards a north-and-south union rather than the east-and-west one which makes up present-day Canada.

On the other hand, the Canadian rivers have done much to counteract this regionalism and give good geographic reason for Canada's independence of the United States. In the east, the St Lawrence and Great Lakes, with their tributaries running northwest towards the prairies, have provided from the earliest times a connecting like between east and west, a link that the railways were to follow and strengthen. On the western plains the rivers form a natural division between American and Canadian territory. For where the Canadian lands drain northward to Hudson's Bay and the Arctic, by such rivers as the Mackenzie and the Saskatchewan, the American area drains southward to the Gulf of Mexico by the Mississippi–Missouri system.

## The People

The population of Canada is today about 11½ millions – a figure that shows constant though gradual growth from the 3½ millions of seventy years ago. While there are some who argue that Canada should develop a vast population in the coming decades – from 50 to 100 millions – experts are by no means agreed on this point. Some say that with a normal rate of expansion Canada will probably have between 18 and 20 million people by the turn of the century.

Canada's population today (apart from the native Indians and certain Asiatic peoples on the Pacific coast) is divided into three main groups, all of European origin.

(1) *The French-Canadians*, who constitute about one-third of the population, are concentrated mostly around the St Lawrence in the province of Quebec. They are also a growing factor in northern and eastern Ontario and in certain parts of the Prairie provinces, particularly around Winnipeg. Sprung from the original 60,000 French colonists left in Canada when it was conquered by the British, these people now number approximately 3½ million. They have their own language, their own Church, their own laws, their own educational system, in fact their own way of life. It is, indeed, a story of amazing courage and determination that in the midst of an alien continent and with change all around them, they have kept to their own separate existence and not allowed themselves to be swallowed up by the rest of Anglo-Saxon America. In fact the shoe has often been on the other foot. It is not rare to find in a French-Canadian village people with Scottish names, descendants of the soldiers who captured Quebec, who now speak not a word of English and who have been completely assimilated into the French-Canadian world. In recent years the forces of the modern age have without doubt been penetrating more and more into this ancient life. But even industry and town life, the radio and the movies, have done little to break the Frenchman's fundamental belief in his farm, his family, and his Church. He remains to this day a unit cut off from the rest of Canada – a nation within a nation.

(2) *The people of British origin* constitute more than half the total population. Unlike the French, they are not concentrated in one area, but are spread out from sea to sea. Nor are they so tightly knit as a racial group. The reason for this is of course that they are not trying to preserve an ancient way of life against the pressure of change. They accept the changing world and are caught up in the same current as modern Britain and modern America. While the percentage of those of British

origin has been declining slowly in the Canadian population since 1870, the importance of this decline can be greatly exaggerated. People of British origin still hold the key positions in the political, business, and educational worlds and are able to wield great influence in shaping the loyalties of their fellow-Canadians.

(3) The third group are *the new Canadians* who poured into the country in the years following 1900, when Canada was expanding so rapidly. Today they represent between one-third and one-quarter of the total population and are concentrated particularly in the Prairie provinces. Ukrainians, Scandinavians, Germans, Russians, Jews, and many others have all enriched Canadian life in their own ways. The process of assimilation into the community has varied greatly with the diverse conditions encountered in different areas. But it can safely be said that as the second and third generations have grown up these new Canadians are no longer foreigners but true Canadians.

**History**

When one looks at the cleavages in her geography and in her population, there seems little reason why Canada has been built into a nation. Indeed both these factors seem to point in the opposite direction. Yet this nation, once created, has proven its ability to persist through all the stresses of both wars and depressions. Therefore, if we are to understand how this has been accomplished, we must look beyond geography and the origins of her population for an answer. It is in the history of the country that the answer is found.

**Origins.** The first people to come to what is now Canada were the French. They came in that great wave of expansion that swept Europeans in the sixteenth and seventeenth centuries to every quarter of the globe. What brought them was their search for the Orient; but they stayed to tap the wealth of the fisheries and the fur-trade. A permanent base was established at Quebec on the St Lawrence in 1603, from which they set out down the Great Lakes highway to bring back the riches of the interior. From Hudson Bay to the Gulf of Mexico, the French 'voyageurs,' 'coureurs de bois,' and missionaries explored the continent by canoe. Their story of heroism and daring, imagination and determination, is one of the finest in the world's history. Detroit, St Louis, Sault Ste Marie, remain to this day, as memorials of what they accomplished.

The English had also established colonies on the Atlantic seaboard, and though they were slower in making their way inland because of the Appalachian mountains they too wanted the wealth of the interior. A showdown was inevitable. After a fierce struggle, which ended in 1763, the British won the day and were left in control, not only of the interior, but of the colony on the St Lawrence – a colony of 60,000 people, completely alien to their conquerors. It is to the credit of the British that eleven years later they granted to these same people the right to their own laws, their own language, their own religion – in fact a guarantee of survival. To this day it is that guarantee more than anything else that keeps the French Canadians a partner within Canada and the Commonwealth. They look upon it as their Bill of Rights. This tolerant statesmanship served the British well in the next few years. When in 1776 the Americans appealed to the French to become the fourteenth state in the new republic they received little support. Through the turbulence of the American Revolution, French Canada remained loyal to Britain.

The American Revolution had another and greater effect on the future of Canada. Thousands of men and women in the rebellious colonies who had fought on the side of Great Britain turned to the northern lands when they saw that their cause was lost. As they poured northwards, into what are now the Maritime provinces and Ontario, they changed the future of those areas. Canada was now to be more than French – it was to be French and English. Both these elements had one thing in common, however. They were firm in their desire not to be swallowed up by the United States. The French did not want to become a hopelessly small minority in a unified Anglo-Saxon continent. The English did not want to be ruled by the people who had so recently harried them to final exile. Out of these two strong impulses to independence, so different in motive but so identical in result, dawned the future of Canada as a separate nation.

**Development.** In the hundred years that followed the American Revolution, British North America expanded in every way. The first major problem was to open up the wilderness and wrest from it the bare necessities of life. As in all pioneering countries, the early settlers' story is one of hard work and disappointment, of bad weather and hostile Indians, of calamity and courage. Yet through it all the great undertaking progressed. More and more land was broken to the plough; the country was crossed from Atlantic to Pacific; the western plains became known; shipping was developed; railways were built; the Pacific colony took shape despite difficulties and set-backs. The frontier of civilisation was rolled back.

The second great goal was the achievement of self-government. For whatever the loyalties of Canadians to Great Britain, they still wished to run their own affairs. It was a tough fight and a bitter one. But Britain had learnt the lesson of the American Revolution and by the middle of the century the various sections that were to make up Canada had won the right to govern themselves.

The third problem was the relationship of the various parts of Canada to the expanding United States. From the war of 1812 and the various disputes over boundaries that followed Canadians learned one thing. The only way to have any bargaining power, the only chance of not being swamped by the superior power to the south, was to stick close to the coat-tails of Great Britain. The loyalty of Canada to the Commonwealth is today more than a little the fruit of that early lesson.

**Formation of a nation.** But as the modern world arrived with its railways and steamships, its industries and world markets, it became increasingly clear that a lot of separated British units, spread out across northern North America, would have little chance of independent survival. The United States, at the end of its Civil War, was launched on a period of expansion the like of which the world has never seen. Canadians were fearful that that expansion might surge northwards across the border. Certainly unless some authority took charge of the western lands they would be swallowed up in the full tide of American settlement. Several disunited colonies were not strong enough to develop the required strength and resistance; a united country was needed. Wise statesmen saw the vision and acted upon it, and in 1867 four provinces, Quebec, Ontario, Nova Scotia, and New Brunswick, joined together to form the Dominion of Canada. In the following years Prince Edward Island, the western lands, and British Columbia were also brought in, with a transcontinental railway planned to give the union strength. The nation was extended from sea to sea.

**Expansion.** The history of the Dominion from the time of its formation up to the First Great War, is a story of tremendous development. The western plains were opened up to farming and became one of the leading granaries of the world. Immigrants poured into the country, not only from the British Isles but from central and eastern Europe as well. Railways and roads, schools and universities, factories and wheat elevators were built. Small towns became great cities. Between 1871 and 1911 the population more than doubled. Undoubtedly, as in all new countries, many excesses were committed and many stupid things were done. But still the object was accomplished, and by 1914 Canada had become a prosperous country. When the eighth Canadian Prime Minister, Sir Wilfrid Laurier, said that Canada was the country of the future, he expressed the optimism which most Canadians felt.

**Wars and maturity.** In the period of international breakdown and alternating booms and depressions that have been the world's lot since 1914, Canada has come to maturity. As for all countries, it has been a tough time and a time of chastening. Yet by its very toughness Canada has grown up. Out of the sacrifices and effort she made in the last war, there came the recognition by the rest of the world that she was a nation worthy of a nation's status. Out of the hardships of the great depression there came to Canada herself the realization that she must throw off her youthful complacency and get down to the business of tackling her own difficult problems. Finally in this Second Great War, Canada is showing what she is capable of as a nation. Through the year 1940–41 Canada was Britain's chief ally. Today she is the fourth largest producer among the United Nations. Whatever else may come of it, one thing is certain. Out of the turmoil of war, Canada will emerge a power to be reckoned with.

## The Economy

The people of Canada make their living in many different ways. At both extremes are the oceans with their fishermen and sailors. In between are the wheat farmers, dairy farmers, ranchers, lumbermen, miners, trappers, factory workers, store-keepers, business men, bankers, teachers, and doctors. The list is long and much the same as in other new countries like Australia or the Argentine. In recent years, however, the picture has changed. For where Canada was once primarily a producer of raw materials, today her economy is a more even balance between industrial and raw material production. The industries that began their life as subsidiaries helped into existence by the friendly aid of tariff walls are today sturdy elements in Canadian life. Indeed, under the stress of war, industrial production has more than doubled and this new potentiality will not disappear with the coming of peace. The war has made Canada an important industrial nation. Of course the change to increased industrialism will only be a modification, not a complete alteration, of our economic life. Raw material production, particularly for export, will continue to play its vital rôle. Wheat, minerals, newsprint, timber, and fish will still find customers in the markets of the world.

The centre of Canadian wealth is in Southern Ontario and Quebec. These provinces are not only rich in mixed farming land, they are also the home of most Canadian industry. Here are situated the commercial and financial capitals of the Dominion. In the two great cities of Montreal and Toronto are located the head offices of most of the banks, business houses, shipping organizations, and railways that keep the economic machinery of the country running. Recently these provinces have further benefited by the opening up of the Laurentian Shield. The extension of newsprint production, constant mineral discoveries, and the development of hydro-electric power, all from the north country, are bringing with them a wave of new prosperity.

The Prairie provinces were for years almost completely a one-crop area. The particularly fine grade of wheat they produced found a market all over the world in years of plenty. But when in the 1930s drought coincided with the collapse of the world wheat market, this dependence on one crop caught the prairies vulnerable to the full onslaught of the depression. Now, wheat is no longer the magic word it once was, and much marginal land is being put back to the raising of livestock. In the western part of the prairies there is also wealth in coal and oil. With the realization this year of the presence of further oil potentialities of great extent westerners are beginning to look to a brightening future.

British Columbia on the Pacific Coast has riches in fisheries, timber, minerals, and fruit. Also, as the possibility of an expanding trade with the Orient develops, the rôle this area is to play will become increasingly more influential. Vancouver, but half a century ago a small local settlement, is fast becoming one of the great ports of the Pacific.

On the Atlantic seaboard, the Maritime provinces (Nova Scotia, New Brunswick, and Prince Edward Island), though the oldest settled parts of the Dominion, are, generally speaking, the least prosperous. They have the only Canadian Atlantic ports open through the winter. But this advantage is overweighed by the remoteness of these ports from the interior. The war has, however, brought them increased prosperity and a renewed development of their resources. Halifax, at one end of the Atlantic lifeline to Great Britain, has become on of the busiest and most crowded ports of the world.

**Trade.** The two countries most important to Canada, as far as trade goes, are the United States and Great Britain. They are by far her biggest customers. From them she buys most of her imports. With the United States particularly, the Canadian economy is inextricably linked. Over sixty per cent. of her imports come from there. Over forty per cent. of her exports go there. This close connection in peacetime has been an important advantage during the war. It has enabled the two countries to establish a joint economic collaboration so that Canada does certain jobs, the United States others. Great Britain has always been a steady market for Canadian raw materials, particularly wheat and other foodstuffs. In exchange Canada buys back from Great Britain textiles, machinery, and other manufactured goods. As, however, newsprint and materials grow in importance and wheat ceases to be king in Canadian life, the economy of the country becomes orientated more to the United States and less to Great Britain.

### Social Life

The everyday life of the ordinary English-speaking Canadian is much the same as that of his neighbour across the border. If we went to two small towns, one in the United States and one in Canada, we would find little difference in the way people lived. Family life, the school, the Church, social activities, and the various forms of entertainment are all very similar, irrespective of the boundary line. In recent years indeed this similarity has grown by leaps and bounds, as the ways of the larger country have influenced the smaller one more and more. Movies, the radio, magazines, and swing music come up to Canada from the south and mould Canadian tastes into an American form.

Yet with all this undeniable influence, there is nevertheless a quality about Canadian life that is distinctive. Perhaps it is due to the surviving British tradition, perhaps to the particular Canadian conditions. Whichever of these it is, Canadian life has an independent character in many ways. The Canadian invented games like hockey and lacrosse, the distinctive quality of education, the tone of our churches are all indications of the national flavour. Also one finds that the nearness to the frontier, which all Canadians are aware of in varying degree, imparts a freshness unknown to most industrial countries. The Laurentian Shield with its tracts of wilderness brings to nearly all young Canadians opportunities for canoeing and swimming, hunting and fishing – a yearly escape from the artificial life of the city.

French life in Canada, as has been said before, is quite different again. Even when he has come in contact with the life of a modern industrial society, the French Canadian generally bases his personal life on the habits and customs he has inherited from his forefathers. And in the country, where the majority still live, the mode of life has remained almost unchanged for generations. Large families on small farms, living simply and producing most of their requirements at home, are still the general rule as they were in the past. One does not have to go far in Quebec to see oxen ploughing and women spinning wool for clothing. So also in the things of the spirit, the 'habitant' (as the French-Canadian farmer is called) turns still to his ancient church. Nowhere in the world does the Roman Catholic religion wield a greater influence than in Quebec.

**Education, the Press, and the Arts**

As in any new territory, in Canada the first job was to open up the country. Till the ordinary necessities of life were provided there was little time for education and all the various accoutrements of civilization. Only when the country was settled and beginning to prosper did these things appear. All the main stocks, Scottish, French, and English, brought with them a tradition that made education a key-stone of life. The schools and universities that cover the length and breadth of the country today are a product both in their number and excellence of that original spirit. They are potent instruments in shaping a true national feeling. The tradition of a free press as a basis of vigorous democracy was also brought here by the early settlers. Out of the early printing presses of the pioneer world, the influential newspapers of today have developed.

The radio, the influence of American programmes with their powerful facilities and highly paid talent, is enormous. By developing our own radio corporation, however, modelled on the lines of the British, we Canadians have been able to encourage native talent and foster Canadian ideas. More recently the National Film Board has attempted to do the same thing for the Canadian film. Its success was acknowledged last year, when it won one of Hollywood's coveted 'Oscars' against the competition of the world.

It is through painting that Canada has made her chief contribution to the arts. In the scenery of the Laurentian Shield Canadian artists have found a subject of unlimited possibilities through which they have been able to produce their own kind of painting with style and feeling of its own. As the country matures, other arts are maturing with it. Native Canadian music, writing, and the drama are advancing steadily, if slowly. More and more the formation of home-grown Canadian art is however beset with many obstacles. So much of the brightest talent is drained off to the greener fields of New York and London.

### Government

In matters of government Canada has borrowed from both Great Britain and the United States. From Great Britain she has taken the system of parliamentary government; from the United States, the federal system of government. She has blended these two together and produced her own particular brand.

Federalism is a divided system whereby the governing power is split into two parts: matters of general interest for the country as a whole are in the hands of a central authority, while matters of purely local interest remain under local control. Thus in Canada the Dominion Government looks after those matters affecting the whole country. The provinces look after the particular affairs of their respective areas. In their own domains both powers are sovereign. Neither can encroach upon the sphere of the other. This form of government, while it seems very complicated to an outsider, is really the only possible form for a country like Canada. We are not sufficiently united either by geography or racial make-up to have one central government with power over everything, like the British Government at Westminster. In its present form, our divided government gives ample room for minorities to protect their own special interests, and for certain areas to maintain their local customs, without constant fear of being trampled on by the majority. In this way the French Canadians through their control of Quebec province can keep their own education, their own laws, their own religion, without fear of interference from the English-speaking majority. On the other hand, the country is well unified in structure, for on matters of general policy like foreign affairs, tariffs, and defence, the central government has to power to act. Of course the maintenance of this balance between power at the centre and power in the provinces has not always been easy to maintain in practice. Friction has been caused by one side or the other wanting more than its fair share. Still, despite this friction, the federal system of government in Canada has succeeded in reconciling all the various elements and interest under one flag.

The system of parliamentary government works much the same in Canada as it does in all the British countries. The elected representatives of the people are returned to Parliament, and from them a government is chosen of a Prime Minister and Cabinet. That government remains in office only as long as it maintains a majority in Parliament. The rôle of permanent figurehead that the king plays in England is played in Canada by his representative, the Governor-General. As in most countries, there are two parts of the legislature. However, the upper one, a Senate, wields less and less power compared to the elected House of Commons.

To keep the democratic machinery moving, Canadians have much the same kind of party system as has England or the United States. These parties are active not only in the central sphere but in each individual province. Their well-knit organizations, indeed, often do much to bind the various sections of the country together. The two traditional parties that have alternated in power since the formation of the Dominion are the Liberals and the Conservatives. The difference in platform between the two is on the whole not great. The Liberals, who are in power at the moment under Prime Minister Mackenzie King, tend traditionally towards lower tariffs and more independence of action for Canada within the Commonwealth. The Conservatives (lately become the Progressive Conservatives) are theoretically the party favouring higher tariffs and a closer maintenance of the Imperial connection. In recent years the Liberals have almost completely monopolized the French-Canadian vote, while the strength of the Conservatives has been greater in Ontario. Out of the great depression of the 1930s several other parties emerged, standing mainly on platforms of social and economic reform. Of these only the Co-operative Commonwealth Federation (known as the C.C.F.) survives today as a party of national significance. One thing it is wise to remember about Canadian parties is that they draw their support from a wide variety of voters, with the result that their platforms must be broad if they are to satisfy everybody. In the past this broadness has often meant mere vagueness, and things have been left undone for fear of offending some particular group. This weakness, however, is likely to lessen as the period of post-war re-organization moves closer. The parties are beginning to realize that they must make their platforms concrete, if they want to gain support in time of crisis.

**Canada and the World**

In a country as large and as divided as Canada, decisions as to the part she is to play in the world are generally ones of compromise. The government will act only when it has weighed and balanced the various desires and loyalties of the different groups and reached a careful decision. To do otherwise and impose a policy that a large section of the population would not stomach, would be to end any hope of holding the country together. This has often meant that Canada's foreign policy seemed to be driving in several different directions at the same time, having nothing definite about it. This is not necessarily a criticism, since conditions in a sense create policy. Out of all the conflicting elements, however, there are certain fixed principles which may serve as guides to any understanding of future Canadian attitudes.

**Loyalty to the Commonwealth.** When Canada along with the other Dominions won official recognition of her complete independence by the Statute of Westminster, there were many prophets of doom who spoke of it as the beginning of the end, as far as Canada's loyalty to the Commonwealth was concerned. Events of recent years have proven this conclusion to be quite false. In September 1939, when Great Britain went to war, Canada made the grave decision to go to war beside her. So often has this decision been accepted as merely natural that what it actually meant in concrete terms has often been forgotten. Canada had the right to stay neutral. Eire, with the same status and much nearer the war-zone, did exactly that. But Canada refused neutrality and declared war. Loyalty to the Commonwealth was responsible for that decision, above all else. Other American countries were equally menaced strategically. Others like the Argentine had just as much interest in keeping the European markets free. Only Canada had an imperial connection with a European country. Only Canada went to war. Though there may be a few who deplore this loyalty, there can be none who doubt its existence. Whatever the motives behind it, it is a very real fact in Canadian life.

**Friendship with the United States.** Friendly relations with the United States are absolutely essential to Canada. When eleven million people are neighbours to one hundred and thirty million, they have the choice of friendship or extinction. Canada has chosen friendship. Of course, the roots of this friendship are much deeper, much firmer, than mere necessity. The ways of life, the tastes, the interests, of the two countries are so much the same, so much real friendship exists between individuals in the two countries, that anything but friendship is, in fact, unthinkable. Like all good things, those relations have not been built easily. The hundred and twenty-five years of peace since the War of 1812 were filled with crises and disputes. The triumph is that despite all this friction peace was maintained. Arbitration rather than war became the habit. It is a habit that, with all the different kinds of co-operation this war has brought, cannot but persist and grow in the coming years.

**General good-will and a desire for peace.** Few would deny that Canada had anything but peaceful intentions. Like most smaller nations she has everything to gain from a world of order, justice, and stability – a world where she can sell her goods and conduct her life, free from the ever-pressing fear of war. Yet like many other countries she has not always realized that peace cannot be gained without sacrifices. Thus though Canada was always a member of the League of

Nations, she was not always ready to bear her responsibility as a member of the organization. This war has, however, brought so many lessons home to the average citizen that, more than ever before, Canada is ready to play her part in building a fair international order.

So Canada moves into the future, a future full of hope and with infinite possibilities. She still has a lot to learn from the rest of the world. At the same time the world can learn something from her. In one sphere she stands as a meeting-ground that can draw the two great Anglo-Saxon peoples of the world together. She is British by tradition, she is American by nature. Her very existence affirms that these two loyalties are not contradictory. In another sphere she stands as an example to a divided world of how people of different origins and creeds can live together, not without friction, but without disruption and strife. For all these reasons and because of what she has done in this war, Canada hopes that her future will be worth watching.

# Integration through Education

Appeared in *Food for Thought*, volume 4, issue 2, September 1943.

A review of *The Universities Look for Unity [: An Essay on the Responsibilities of the Mind to Civilization in War and Peace* (1943)] by John Ulric Nef.[1] (Pantheon Books, Inc., N.Y.) Price, 25 cents (American).

This short pamphlet by the professor of economic history at the University of Chicago has particular significance for the adult educationalist. For however much we have come to think that our chief job is to compete with David Sarnoff[2] and Samuel Goldwyn,[3] we must still look to the universities to help us find some sane and moral content for our teaching. However much we busy ourselves with techniques for getting ideas across to the community we serve, what ideas we intend to get across will continue to be the more vital question to interest us. Healthy universities are the places for us to turn for those ideas. Our Canadian universities may seem to be becoming increasingly sterile, but that is only more reason to look for the causes of their failure. For without successful universities, the adult educationalist will be like a ship without a rudder, an explorer without a compass.

Professor Nef starts from the idea (as patently true for Canada as he makes it for the U.S.A.) that our physical response to the war, has not been accompanied by any equal moral or intellectual response. He sees that this lack will have very immediate and very tragic results. For it will mean that when the day of peace arrives, we will have nothing creative enough to replace the Hitlerian New Order and we will therefore fall back into an old world, out of the failure of which Hitlerism itself sprang. The reason for this moral dearth is not only in the transitory phenomenon of the moment – but in the deep-seated materialism and the misdirected individualism of our civilization. During the development of the natural sciences and their Gargantuan infant, industrialism, we lost as a community, any real belief in either art or philosophy. And as art and philosophy are the only means of achieving those transcendent values, out of which the climate of a civilization is born, without them we became as arid and as unstable as the shifting sands. This does not mean that Nef wishes to turn back from science and its amazing fruits. All he wants is that 'knowledge in the kingdom of the transcendental and knowledge in the realm of the physical ... should coexist to their great mutual advantage and to the advantage of the legitimate aspirations of men and women throughout the world.' Like the blind man and the deaf man, they must cross the stream together. For only in the combination of the two will the roaring torrent of today's crisis be crossed successfully.

In this vast problem, symptoms of which are found in every corner of our civilization, Professor Nef is primarily interested in how it has affected our universities and what role the universities can play in its solution. First, how have the universities failed in the past? They have been dogged by specialization and departmentalism so that each little segment of knowledge, cut off from the rest of knowledge, has been as colourless and unproductive as grass under a stone. Universities have served to produce techniques and technicians rather than sane ideas and thinking citizens (certain heads of Canadian Universities please note). Nef goes even deeper, he says that the objectives of the university, as much as of the society as a whole, are out of date. They are 'bankrupt.' The old idea that the function of the universities was a utilitarian one (utilitarian in its most materialistic connotation) has ceased to have any validity. It has ceased to serve as a dynamic. The university must become in the future a place where all knowledge is made over, and out of that integration, the meaning and destiny of our civilization are discovered.

There is not room here to describe the reforms that Professor Nef would institute to achieve the ends he desires. Like most good means, they are closely identified with the ends in question. Let readers buy the pamphlet and read it for themselves. They will be well rewarded. Quite apart from its content they will learn much in the sensitive and accurate use of the English language as an instrument for conveying ideas.

At the end Professor Nef quotes from an editorial printed on Armistice Day, 1924, in the *Manchester Guardian*. It is a plea that in the eleventh hour we start building a moral edifice to save us from the storm. It is a plea, so true and so terrible for us today, that everyone who remains in the security and optimism of the North American Continent should let it eat into his heart.

> The dead in war are terribly at the mercy of the living. Those whom we shall remember in the two minutes of silence today, gave their lives, which most of them treasured, in the hope that their gift would help to make a cleaner and less sour world. But, their lives once given, they lost all their own power to insist, when peace came, that this price should not have been paid for nothing. Once they were out of the way, it rested with us who have survived them to decide whether the dead should be remembered for ever as founders of a nobler new Europe.

George Grant

## Notes

1 John Ulric Nef (1899–1988), economic historian at Chicago (1939–64), published (in the 1930s and 1940s) in addition to *The Universities Look for Unity*, *The Rise of the British Coal Industry* (1932), *A Comparison of Industrial Growth in France and England from 1540–1640* (1936), and *The US and Civilization* (1942).
2 David Sarnoff (1891–1971), American industrialist and chairman of RCA, pioneered the bringing of radio and television into American homes.
3 Samuel Goldwyn (1882–1974), American motion picture producer, started the company that would later become Metro Goldwyn Mayer (MGM).

# The Failure of Nerve

Appeared in volume 4, issue 3, of *Food for Thought*, November 1943: 23.
*The Machiavellians: Defenders of Freedom* was published at New York
by The John Day Company in 1943. Grant takes his title from Sidney
Hook, who wrote two articles in *Partisan Review* (Jan.–Feb. and Mar.–
Apr. 1943) entitled 'The New Failure of Nerve' and 'The Failure of the
Left.' In the context of the war against Hitler, Hook defends scientific
rationality and America-led democracy against a wide selection of their
religious and political detractors, who, he claims, are symptomatic of a
growing flight from responsibility. Céline, Spengler, Pound, and Burnham
are not actually named by Hook in those articles, but he does emphasize
loss of faith in ordinary people and a turn to heroic leaders. Hook actually
begins with an attack on Rheinhold Niebuhr and particularly opposes an
idea which later became central for Grant – that egalitarianism must be
based on religion.

Review of The Machiavellians by James Burnham.[1]

This is the fitting and necessary successor to the author's earlier book
*The Managerial Revolution.* For where the first book described the next
stage in the development of human society (the revolution by the managers), this one is an exposition of his general theory of history, as it
has evolved through the ages. This theory of history, in barest outline,
is that mankind is divided always and irrevocably into two divisions:
first, a small minority of energetic rulers; second, a lazy mass of dull
ruled. The character of any given civilization is always found in the
character of its particular elite or ruling class, who produce typical

institutions, typical art, and typical myths. The rest of the population are merely passive instruments, who work for their masters, accept the institutions and are kept quiet by the myths. All they want is bread to fill their stomachs and circuses to drug their minds. This division of society into two parts, the ruled and rulers, has always been true and will be true in the future. Anybody who dares to think differently, is, according to Burnham, a woolly-headed idealist.

This theory of history is, of course, the complete opposite to any the adult educator could possibly accept. The very fact that one enters a profession like education (unless one is either dishonest or blind) is that one believes mankind is capable of development – is worth developing. If one did not, if one believed as Burnham does that the life of man is 'nasty, brutish and short,' then there would be no point in working with people. The best thing would be to go out and rook the suckers as best one could, to get a good place for oneself at the top of the scrambling heap. Our whole idea of democracy would be, of course, destroyed. Such work as that at St Francis Xavier University[2] or through the Farm Forums or in labour unions becomes pointless idealism. Life would become dog eat dog, or as Burnham describes it, by quoting from Shakespeare's *Pericles*: '3rd Fisherman – "Master I marvel how the fishes live in the sea." 1st Fisherman – "Why as men do a-land, the great ones eat up the little ones."'

Yes, if we accept the low opinion of mankind's nature that Burnham has, we might as well give up education. It would be a waste of time. That is his challenge to us.

The kind of thought Burnham represents is indeed one of the sights most symptomatic of our world of wars and depressions. Fine and sensitive brains such as his have been pushed back into the cork-lined room of their lonely isolation, there to sneer at the vulgarity and barbarity of their own species. Before the terrible events of 1914–1943, they didn't have the courage to keep their belief in human dignity and progress. They surrendered to the all too easy pessimism that said most men were selfish fools or ignorant knaves.

Democracy was too difficult for them. They became fascists. Sidney Hook has described this process[3] that has happened to Europeans like Céline and Spengler[4] and to Americans like Burnham and Pound[5] as 'the failure of nerve.' They haven't had the courage to keep on believing in the goodness of people. They have taken the quick way out, forgetting that it is easy to despair, but difficult to believe. They are products of a sick civilization. Let us pity them.

George Grant

## Notes

1 James Burnham (1905–1987), American philosopher and prominent cold-war theorist, was for years a well-known Trotskyite, but abandonned leftist politics in his best-known work, *The Managerial Revolution* (1941). He argued a new type of managerial society was emerging that was neither capitalist nor socialist. Two years later he followed with the *The Machiavellians,* here reviewed by Grant. He was a colleague of Professor Sidney Hook at New York University (see note 3).

2 St Francis Xavier University in Antigonish, Nova Scotia, established its Department of Extension in 1928. Father Moses Coady was the leader of the liberal Catholic 'Antigonish Movement,' which used adult education as a means towards social improvement and economic organization in the fishing, mining, and agriculture communities of eastern Nova Scotia.

3 Sidney Hook (1902–1989), American professor of Marxism who evolved into a social democrat, also taught at New York University (in the same department as Burnham) from 1927 to 1972. See headnote above for a discussion of Professor Hook on 'the failure of nerve.'

4 Louis-Ferdinand Céline (1894–1961). See note 30 in the Journal of 1942. Oswald Spengler (1880–1936), German historian and political philosopher, argued in *The Decline of the West: Outlines of a Morphology of World History* (1918–22) that our destiny in the twentieth century is the death of the soul of Western civilization.

5 Ezra Westin Loomis Pound (1885–1972), American poet and critic, expressed in *Hugh Selwyn Mauberly* (1920) his view that modern Western civilization was decayed and had given itself over to false values. His pro-Fascist anti-democracy broadcasts from Italy in the early years of the Second World War led to his indictment for treason in 1945.

# The Empire: Yes or No?

Printed by the Ryerson Press at Toronto in 1945, this pamphlet was one in the series called *Canada Must Choose: a Series dealing with our immediate problems*. Other titles included *Must Canada Split* and *The Revenge of the Cradles*, by C.E. Silcox; *Baby Bonuses: Dollars or Sense*, by Charlotte Whitton; *Civvy Street: Red Light or Green*, by O.T. Williamson; and *Family Allowances: Facts and Fiction*, by Margaret Gould.

## PART I

The origin of Canada as a nation is in the British North America Act. And in the name of that Act we see indeed the main forces that have shaped our country. British, yes, and North American too; and from the amalgam of these two influences has come the Canada of today. The particular Canadianism, that we feel from the grey streets of Halifax to the foothills near Banff, from the wide horizons of the prairies to the lakes and rivers of Algonquin Park, has been created from these two sources. Yes, Canada as a nation can truly be called British North America.

Today, however, there are in our midst certain English- and French-speaking citizens who decry the significance of our membership in the British Commonwealth. There are others, more numerous, who though paying lip service to the Commonwealth belie their attachment to it in their activities or their apathy. It is necessary, therefore, that those Canadians who believe deeply in the value of the Commonwealth, for Canada and for the world, should reiterate their faith in it – the faith that not only for the progress of the civilized world, but also for the existence of our nation as a free and democratic state, our membership in the Commonwealth is essential. Indeed, our reasons for remaining in the Commonwealth are not based on colonialism, or attachment to the past, but on the cold logic of the present. In this year 1945, every interest of Canada demands that we should remain intimately attached to the other British nations.

## The World Today

The first job in seeing our rôle in the British Commonwealth must be to look at what is happening in the world today. The first fact of the world today is that the United Nations have won complete victory over the forces of the fascist axis. This coalition of United Nations now comes out of the war as a possible nucleus for future world order. The gradual and organic development of the United Nations from a mere coalition of powers in 1942, towards greater and greater unity has spoken well for the sagacity of its leaders. In this the atomic age the failure of world order is too appalling to contemplate.

## Imperialism

But though the first and most hopeful fact of the modern world is this developing new world order, let us not blind ourselves to the fact that the development of this world order into perfection will not happen overnight, and that every step of the way will be fraught with dangers and difficulties. Only if we recognize how difficult the job will be, shall we be clear enough and tough enough to accomplish it. The creation of the United Nations will by no means take us over into an ideal world. Friction between great and small powers will still remain. Self-interest and self-complacency will continue to beset nations and groups of nations, as they have beset individual men and nations in the past. Merely by vaguely inveighing against such words as imperialism and power politics we will not destroy them. By the very nature of life itself, power exists. By the very existence of life, it will be necessary to balance the stresses and strains of that power within the United Nations. Only if we recognize this will we be able to move forward gradually to the more perfect world order we desire.

## Three Empires

The three great dominating powers of the world after the war will be three great empires. The two immense continental empires of the

U.S.A. and the U.S.S.R., and the maritime empire of Great Britain. There will be other powers. Perhaps in the near future France will return to its former noble stature, or China and India will become other great empires. But at the moment there is little doubt that these three are the mainspring of the United Nations. The U.S.A. will remain the dominant power in this hemisphere, and in most of the Pacific. The U.S.S.R clearly is going to hold and expand its imperial sway from Central Europe to the Far East. The British Empire and Commonwealth will continue to encircle the globe. However much people may inveigh against such imperialism, in this spring of 1945, it is clearly the emergent pattern.

## Continental Regionalism

The greatest menace to the creation of an international organization in this present situation is undoubtedly the division of the world into great competing continental regions. Already there are signs that nothing is more truly undermining the basis of world order than the fact that the great continental empires feel they do not need an international body, but can retire back into regional isolation. This would mean the division of the world into competing regions, rather than into the truly world order that we need. Continental regionalism cannot mean world unity. It inevitably means a division of the world.

These large continental blocs, established by the large nations and at first merely holding imperial sway over near-by countries, but at last spreading out till they come in contact with one another, presage wars beside which the past wars between nation states would be mere storms in teacups. In the future, the most immediate threat of this kind is that the U.S.A. will form a great hemispheric empire centred in capitalist Washington, while the U.S.S.R. forms another empire out of Asia and Europe with its power concentrated in state-socialist Moscow. At first living in fear and isolation of each other, then gradually expanding their respective spheres of influence, they may meet in head-on collision. In such a world, international organization would be impossible.

## The Commonwealth

At a time when the greatest menace to world organization is the existence of these great hemispheric blocs or regions, the British Commonwealth and Empire takes on a new and particular significance. It is not a continental region. Its interests are world-wide. It is an association of nations whose various members belong to every part of the globe. By the very fact that it cuts across the regionalisms of the world, it serves to break down the isolation of these regions and bring then into co-operation with each other. By its very existence it says to the world, don't just be American or European or Asiatic or African; be something more than that, be world-wide. It is an organization whose members have something more in common other than the mere sharing of a continent, and as such can bring the continents together. Australia is part of a southeastern Asiatic region, but also part of the Common-wealth. South Africa is part of the African continent, but also part of the Commonwealth. Canada is part of the North American region, but also part of the Commonwealth. The United Kingdom is part of the European continent but also a member of the Commonwealth. These nations, because they have interests not only in their particular region but in a world organization, will inevitably tend to prevent their par-ticular region from going isolationist. By preventing that region from being isolationist, they make it more world-minded and more a part of any world organization. That is why the British Commonwealth is so vital and real a force in making world co-operation effective. There would be much less chance of world order if it did not exist.

## Cannot Be Isolationist

The British Commonwealth cannot be isolationist. The huge continen-tal empires, each composed of one geographic region, can pursue a unified policy and retire into isolation, pursuing one-sided interests alone. The British Commonwealth, spread out all over the world, can-not pursue such an isolationist policy. Each part of it is sufficiently small (including the United Kingdom) that it cannot depend on itself alone for security. It depends on a world organization. In this way each part of it has realized the need of it depends on effective world secu-rity. Therefore, as a group of nations, nobody can fear that it will retire into isolationism. By its structure, it can't. All its interests tend to world order; therefore it will work for world order. The work of the British nations at San Francisco has abundantly proved this.[1]

## Cannot Be a Power Bloc

It is strange that the British Commonwealth, least likely to be a power bloc, should most consistently be accused of being one. Its development has always been towards decentralization and autonomy for its member parts. And today, though it is united together, it is unity achieved by consent, not by other means. The formation of a maritime empire (as the British Commonwealth is) spread around the world, broken up by vast expanses of sea, and with differing people and interests, means a decentralization of power and the working out of policy by consent. This is the very opposite to power bloc politics. No unwilling member, for instance, can be forced over a long period to stay in the Commonwealth unless it wants to. Eire is a good example of this. Even India, now that it has revitalized and modern leadership of its own, will never be kept within the limits of the British orbit unless it so desires. Canada, Australia, South Africa, all stay united only of their own free will. Indeed, far less than either the empire of the U.S.A. or that of the U.S.S.R., can the British Commonwealth become a unified and centralized power bloc.

## The Necessity for a Third Power

But whereas the British Commonwealth and Empire helps to mitigate continental regionalism by its world-wide nature, and at the same time cannot be just another power bloc, it is still in the realities of the present political situation the only group of nations with sufficient unity of purpose that can prevent a world organization from being totally dominated by the U.S.A. or the U.S.S.R. Without the British Commonwealth, the world organization will fall into two opposing camps.

For though the British Commonwealth is decentralized, it still has enough unity within itself to stand as a power between these two colossi. And power split three ways will surely be a much safer preserver of the peace than power divided between Washington and Moscow. The triumvirs of Rome in the dim past recognized that power was better divided three ways than two. For two always meant a division into two decided and hostile camps. Three means a more even balance.

So in the world we are coming into, it will be much safer to have, as well as Washington and Moscow, a third force like the British Commonwealth to stand with a firm heart in the councils of the world, and to keep it as strong as possible. For, it must be repeated, a world in which Washington and Moscow were supreme would be a world in which one empire controlled the Eurasian heartland and another the Americas, and no power on earth stood between them. It is as clear as crystal that we are moving in that direction today. Only the free maritime Commonwealth is sufficiently strong to prevent that division of power between them. Surely it is important that such a Commonwealth should exist as an effective body.

## What Does This Mean for Canada?

It must be clearly stated that if the world is divided between Washington and Moscow (and the situation is sufficiently imminent not to be a mere bogeyman), nobody would have more to lose than Canada.

For if such an immense tragedy as conflict between these powers should take place, it would not take place in some distant corner of the globe, but on our soil. Canada has indeed in the last years become the potential cockpit of the world, as Belgium was thirty years ago. As our north and south connections run to the U.S.A., so they run across the Pole to Moscow. As our east and west connections join us together, so they carry us towards Siberia and Asia in the east and to Great Britain and Europe in the west. We would be at the very centre of the conflict between the two great continental empires. It is clearly in our most direct and immediate interest to prevent that. If we do not, we will be caught like the nut in the nutcracker.

Our best means of preventing that tragedy is our continued membership in the Commonwealth. Cut off from the British nations, as an independent country, we would have little alternative but to join the South American nations in the hemispheric Empire of the U.S.A. And as part of that we would be strengthening the power of the U.S.A. to retire into isolation. We would be abetting its ability to establish an anti-Russian bloc. We would be increasing the chances for an American–Soviet conflict. On the other hand, as a member of the Commonwealth, we would be doing exactly the opposite. Friendly to the U,S.A. we would still not be her satellite. By our world-wide interests, we

would, as her chief neighbour, be pulling her out of continental isolation and towards effective commitments to a world order.

In fact, time and time again in the past we have played this constructive rôle. We are a country of 1914 and 1939 rather than 1917 and 1941.
Both times we were the first country of the American continent to take
responsibility for the rest of the world. Both times the fact that we were
taking such responsibility influenced the U.S.A. Canada historically,
rather than abetting the U.S.A. in continental isolation, has been an influence in bringing that nation into a community of nations. The reason we
have done that is because of our membership in the free association of
nations, the British Commonwealth, and our world-wide connections.
Surely it is important that we should continue to do so in the future. If
we look at it from the view of world peace, by our membership in the
British Commonwealth we are helping to make effective a real world
organization and practical international co-operation. If we look at it
from our own selfish interests, we are helping to prevent that division of
the world into continental power blocs that would probably come into
conflict over our soil and be the savage end to our era of safety.

Winston Churchill once wrote of Canada's place in the world:

> The long unguarded frontier, the habits and intercourse of daily life, the
> fruitful and profitable connections of business, the sympathies and even
> the antipathies of honest neighbourliness, make Canada a binder-
> together of the English-speaking peoples. She is a magnet exercising a
> double attraction, drawing both Great Britain and the United States
> towards herself and thus drawing them closer to each other. She is the
> only surviving bond which stretches from Europe across the Atlantic
> Ocean. In fact, no state, no country, no band of men can more truly be
> described as the linchpin of peace and world progress.[2]

It is our membership in the British Commonwealth that reserves for us
that job. Surely from such a wonderful destiny we should not shrink.

## What Is the British Commonwealth?

Of course those who decry our membership in the Commonwealth
often don't know what it is. The British Commonwealth is a number of

sovereign democratic states bound together by common allegiance to a common crown. These countries are joined together into a world-wide federation for the purposes of security and other common interests. What an amazing political experiment it is. Always in the past, nations if bound together were only united by force into a union with all power concentrated at the centre. The British Commonwealth, though an effective union, is bound together in freedom with power decentralized so that each member state has control over its own destiny.

This is surely an example of world order on a small scale. What we all want for the world is that peoples all over the world, large and small, should work and live together in harmony and co-operation. That is clearly the ideal the world must strive for. The Commonwealth shows how it can be achieved.

The rise of fascism and organized barbarism in the 1930s should never be forgotten. Previously we had been apt to scorn the Commonwealth. For, after all, in a few years the age of perfection was going to be ushered in. Such limited instruments as the British Commonwealth were unnecessary! In a few years we were going to have a perfect world of universal brotherhood. We didn't have to guard the institutions we had developed. Utopia was nearly here.

But then the rains descended and the floods came. We began to realize that our joyous optimism as to mankind's perfection was not as true as we had once believed it. We saw that, instead of universal brotherhood about to be ushered in, a wholesale return to the jungle and to despotism was not far distant. The tolerance and dignity of mankind were, indeed, a thin veneer laid over the desperate beast. In such an atmosphere, a freely co-operating body of liberty-loving nations like the Commonwealth was not something quickly to be thrown on the scrap heap. *And in 1940 we saw that it was not the pious talk of idealists that stopped fascism and the forces of evil, it was the practical co-operation of the free nations of the British Commonwealth.*

Some always knew this lesson; some learned it very late (like this writer). But let us all remember it after the war, and never forget it. Let us not sell down the river an organization like the British Commonwealth that did such a magnificent job. At least, before we do, let us be dead certain that we have something as sane and practical to take its place, and as useful and necessary for the development of civilization and world order.

## What of the British Empire?

More nonsense is talked about imperialism these days than almost any other subject. It is a bright and shining catch-word that people can use as a whipping boy without knowing what it is. Yet after all, it is nothing but the expansion of one vital people from its own native heath into other areas. It varies from the extreme barbaric invasion with fire and the sword, carried on by the *Herrenvolk*, to the peaceful infiltration of a country like Canada by the U.S.A. When speakers proclaim that this war will mean the end of imperialism, I presume that they mean the end of that ruthless form of rapine that is the extreme form of imperialism. If they mean that large nations are not going to influence other countries, they are denying the whole nature of human life. If they mean that powerful nations like the United States are not going to maintain security in the Pacific, they cannot be reading their newspapers. In this hemisphere, the U.S.A. is inevitably going to influence South America. In eastern Europe the U.S.S.R. will naturally dominate the satellites around it. As the strong member of a family inevitably influences that family, so also inevitably in human affairs there will be imperialism.

Of course this does not mean that by now we are not past the stage where the imperialism of exploitation and brutality cannot be left behind as one of the less glorious parts of man's inglorious past. More and more we will be able to control the more ruthless forms of expansionism. More and more empire will become a trust and less and less the imposition of the will of the powerful on the weak. More and more will it be the strong bearing responsibility and authority. Power, it is hoped, will find in the world its concomitant morality. Eventually blatant power can be reduced and voluntary law take its place. Human freedom is, in fact, our goal.

But how is this to be achieved? It is all very well to want perfect freedom for all the world. But merely wanting it will not make it come. It will not spring, like Minerva, fully formed from the head of Jove. It will come with our travail and our sacrifices. Nothing is more clearly the lesson of the last years. And at the present stage of human development, varying forms of empire must remain as steps toward that world of perfection. Liberty can only exist with law. And only the empires, be they American or Chinese, British or Russian, have the strength to make that law. And those empires with past experience and traditions of liberty will be the ones most liable to be empires of law and not of power alone.

It is all very well for people to attack imperialism, but that does not in itself meet the practical problems that make such imperialism necessary: (1) security, (2) the development of retarded people.

## Security

During the nineteenth century, Britain, because it was the first industrial country and because of its strong maritime commerce, had such a preponderance that it could impose world-wide security. Many of the qualities of the British hegemony were not perfect, but with it came a large degree of freedom and, most important of all, freedom of the seas. The British policed the seas, guaranteed their freedom, and made it possible for large areas of the world to develop in freedom. To achieve this, Britain had to control many strategic bases around the world. Now in 1945 another pattern is emerging. No one power is sufficiently preponderant to do the policing alone. Three great empires are clearly going to maintain world security. That is the basis of the present world organization. It emerges from the Teheran and Yalta declarations.

And the two new powers will find that they need bases for that security job, just as much as the British ever did. And as they find out, there may be less talk of the evils of such bases. For it is all very well to say that Malta, Panama, the Dardanelles, and Singapore should be handed over. But the question is, when and to whom? If, before the war, the British had handed Gibraltar over to Franco's Spain, would world security have been advanced? Should it give Malta to Italy? Should the Americans be asked to turn over their control of the Panama Canal? Should the Russians be asked to give up their strategic bases on the Baltic?

Certainly as the international organization develops and its ability to police the world becomes clear, more and more duties can be turned over from individual empires to the common whole. When these halcyon days arrive, the British can give up Suez, for there will be somebody safe to give it to. The Americans can give up Panama. And the

U.S.S.R. will need no guarantee of its western boundaries. But till that perfect world emerges, empire, however much it may be abused, is the only concrete and practical way yet guaranteed to insure world security.

### Development of Retarded People

Also, though it has made countless mistakes and like everybody else has indulged in exploitation and repression, the British Empire stands today as the best practical proponent of one of the world's most difficult jobs. It stands for the ordered helping of people in backward areas to move towards fuller political consciousness and the modern use of their resources. Stalin's fine accomplishments in this field are the only ones that can compare with the British. If anyone wants to read anything on this subject, let them look at Lord Hailey's report on the Colonies in Africa[3] or the new constitution of Jamaica, or the work of the British Council in the Caribbean. Lord Cranborne stated recently the basic policy of Great Britain towards these colonies:

> ... The ultimate objective of our policy is to promote self-government in the Colonies. We seek to retain all that is good in the existing social and political system. We aim, also, to graft it on to modern ideas and the lessons of our own experience, so that finally the peoples of even the most backward colonies may become fit for free institutions, self-government by the people as a whole; and the problem of making free institutions understood and worked in backward and primitive communities is not an easy one. It is not surprising if many of the people in the British Colonial Empire are not yet ready for full self-government, and will not be ready for some considerable time; nor is it by any means certain that to give them self-government prematurely, before they are educated up to it, would be for the happiness and prosperity of the peoples themselves. At the same time it must clearly be our aim to equip Colonial peoples to administer their own affairs, whether this goal is near or far. We have made, and are making considerable progress; the British Colonial Empire is a living organism and is constantly changing and developing.[4]

Over the whole British Empire there are areas in different stages of development. Yet there are people who constantly attack this work and say that it is based only on exploitation. What is their alternative? These backward areas are going to be brought into the stream of modern life. And if that is so, the job has to be done by somebody. That is unavoidable.

Surely it is better that this be accomplished under the aegis of a country like Great Britain, with long traditions of both parliamentary government and of colonial administration, than that they be left alone at the mercy of private investors and of private companies who are responsible to no one. For that is exactly what would happen, if there were no government supervision.

Would they be better controlled by other nations which have little or no experience? A Canadian told me recently of going down to a conference in Virginia on a train marked 'For Whites Only,' to hear the Americans at the conference lecture the British, the French, and the Dutch on their enslavement of colonial peoples. Would these people be so much better off under the U.S.A. or the U.S.S.R. administration? The British have much knowledge of colonial administration and fair administration at that. Surely their experience on this matter should not be lost to the world. Certainly the British have admitted that in the future all colonies must be opened to international inspection. But international inspection and international control are two different things. If one had international control, it would mean that each colony was run by a series of administrations from different traditions – Russian, American, Dutch, British. It would be a question of too many cooks spoiling the broth. It would result in confusion.

The question is one of responsibility. This is a job that has to be done. Who is, in fact, going to bear the responsibility? (And as a corollary it must be remembered that not only must those with power bear responsibility, but also those who want to bear responsibility must also have the power to fulfil that responsibility. Many of us are only too willing for the British to bear the high responsibility, but then we aren't willing to let them have the power without which that responsibility cannot be borne.) If we scrap the experience of the British in this matter, will we be much further on? The world will still have to find others to do the job. It will merely have lost the vast experience of the British. Canada should be proud of its connection with the British Empire in the development of backward people. It should see that it bears its share in the work of that Empire.

## Certain Arguments

There are certain arguments that are constantly being raised against Canadian membership in the Commonwealth. It is well that they should be answered.

1. The first and foremost one is that our connection with the British Commonwealth somehow detracts from our stature in the world. The hated word "colony" is generally thrown in, to appeal to our emotions. Let it be stated categorically that under the Statute of Westminster we are a sovereign state within the Commonwealth, and any limitations on our sovereignty or stature, such as appeals to the Privy Council, remain simply and solely because we in Canada desire it. The United Kingdom continues to amend our B.N.A. Act – not because they want to do so, but because we want them so to do.

Second, let it be said that in this writer's view it is long overdue that we have a flag and anthem of our own. We must establish our Canadian nationhood. But this in no way interferes with our glorious Commonwealth connection. And as for it interfering with our stature, surely just the opposite is true. Why is it that Canada has twice been the scene of meeting between Churchill and Roosevelt? Why is it that Canadians are so often chosen for leading positions in the United Nations bodies? Why are we, a country of approximately eleven and a half million souls, listened to in the councils of the world? Why are we a leader among the small nations? The answer is simple. We are a North American nation and also a member of the British Commonwealth. We have not only prestige as the U.S.A.'s northern neighbour; we are also the senior Dominion of the British Commonwealth. If we were a small little nation without outside connections, how much would we be listened to? We would be a small nation, no more important than many of the Latin American nations. The U.S.A. would certainly listen to us far less. For we would only be a Little Orphan Annie of small importance, where now we are part of a huge family. Certainly if we went out of the Commonwealth we could expect no special privileges from the British nations. Anybody who has travelled around the world doesn't have to be told the advantages of Canada's membership in a huge world-wide organization. When people intimate that Canada loses status by its membership in the Commonwealth, they are talking through their hats. By being Canadians and British at the same time, we have a double status. It is only necessary to speak to men of other small nations, such as Holland, Belgium, Poland, etc., to know how much our status is increased in their eyes by our membership in the British Commonwealth.

2. A second argument used against our membership in the Commonwealth is made by those who say that it prevents us from being internationally minded. This is pernicious and patently ridiculous. First, our membership in the British Commonwealth does not prevent us from being members of other federations, e.g., the Pan-American, any more than it will prevent Australia being part of a Southeast Asia federation. Secondly, it does not prevent us being part of a world order. (It did not prevent us from being part of the League of Nations.) In fact, our membership in the British Commonwealth was the factor that took us to Geneva, when the U.S.A. was not there.

Canada has already had a greater tradition of internationalism than the U.S.A. Without doubt, what has made us internationalist is our membership in the British Commonwealth. We have always been, in fact, part of an international organization. Would it not be the height of folly that on the road to complete internationalism we should drop our membership in the practical international organization that has worked so well in the past? Would it not mean that instead of taking a step forward, we would be taking a step backward – away from a world view? We would be retiring out of international responsibility rather than into it. For it can never be denied (however much some people may not like it) that what made Canada bear its responsibility to the world in 1939 was not some vague internationalism, but the concrete internationalism of our membership in the Commonwealth. Till we can arrive at an equally concrete membership in an equally concrete world organization, let us not give up the British connection. Our aim must be the upward climb of mankind to a perfect and effective world government, and on the ladder upwards the British Commonwealth is an important step.

In fact, those of us who before the war attacked Canada's membership in the British Commonwealth, generally did it in the name of high-minded and pious internationalism. We said, we can't stay in this imperfect international organization. We can only go into a perfect world organization. As this perfection wasn't forthcoming, it was perfectly simple to retire back into irresponsibility and let the rest of the world go hang. The same attitude is prevalent today. English-speaking or French-speaking Canadians who say Canada shouldn't be a member of the Commonwealth, still use the noble vocabulary full of phrases such as 'power blocs,' etc. But what they are really singing is the same old isolationist tune. André Laurendeau may talk about our independence from the Commonwealth, but what in effect he means is being relieved of any responsibility for the rest of the world.[5] Isolationists may say that we should get out of an empire power bloc, but what they really mean is that we should retire *into* the power bloc of American isolationism, free from world responsibility. The anti-Commonwealth forces in Canada, indeed, talk much the same language as the isolationists in the United States. They sound much like Senator Wheeler[6] or ex-Senator Nye.[7] Talking against the British Commonwealth may be done in the name of noble internationalism – it is really tedious isolationism.

For indeed is it not more unity among all the nations that we want, rather than less? As General Smuts has written, everything in the natural world is tending to form greater and larger 'wholes.'[8] Canada as a nation has been created out of separate provinces. The Commonwealth has been created out of separate nations. In God's good time the perfect world order will finally be created. Why should we split up and give way to the divisive forces in a world that so badly needs more unity, more cooperation? Surely the Commonwealth is a step towards greater unity. Why must it be weakened or broken up? Certainly to many of us the unity of the Commonwealth is of equal importance with the smaller unity of Canada or the greater unity of the United Nations. In a world sadly divided it stands for practical cooperation.

3. A third argument used against our membership in the Commonwealth is made by those who are all for the western hemisphere. They are all for Canadian participation in the Pan-American Union, and seem to imply that that militates against our membership in the Commonwealth. First of all, it does not seem to me correct that our membership in the Commonwealth means we cannot be a part of Pan-America. Second, we certainly should cooperate with the people of this hemisphere in every way we can. But, thirdly, if it ever comes to a

choice between the Commonwealth and the Pan-American Union, the former is of vastly greater importance to us as a nation than the latter. For what the believers in the western hemisphere forget is geography. Canada is even more intimately bound up with the northern hemisphere than with the western hemisphere. Most Canadians don't have to have the obvious fact explained to them that Canada is more vitally dependent on London, the Atlantic Ocean, and the North Sea, than on Buenos Aires and Cape Horn. And our connection with the British Commonwealth guarantees our interests in the Atlantic and the northern hemisphere, as 1940 so adequately proved. Finally, it must be reiterated again, Canada's membership in Pan-America must not let us become part of an American hemispheric power bloc, dominated from Washington and hostile to the other continents of the world, and as such inimicable to world order.

### Practical Decisions Must Be Made

Those people who wish Canada to retire from the British Commonwealth and Empire, and thereby greatly weaken that great organization, should think of a world in which it did not exist. What would such a world be like?

1. It would be a world in which the only free association of nations with membership in every part of the globe did not exist. A world where the only effective organization of free nations, cutting across regional and hemispheric boundaries, was destroyed.

2. It would be a world where the most effective experiments in the development of backward peoples towards political democracy and economic maturity did not exist.

3. It would be a world where the mainstay of Western Christian civilization did not exist. And Western Christian civilization, for all its faults, has developed in practice, more than any other, the practical concept of man's intrinsic and ultimate worth as an individual and the right of mankind to be free and to develop freely towards a higher and fuller destiny. And, as both André Siegfried, the Frenchman, and Cohen-Portheim, the Austrian, have pointed out, Western Christian

civilization has little chance of survival if the British Commonwealth and Empire goes down.[9]

It was all very well for us in the 1920s and 1930s to think of the British Empire and Commonwealth as being dismembered, and to talk glibly of some uncertain perfection taking its place. But surely the terribleness of the last years has taught us that there is a good chance that what would take its place is not something better, but something a lot worse; that though the Empire and Commonwealth must be improved and many of its anachronisms wiped away, in 1940 it at least stood for a certain modicum of liberty, dignity, and decency when these values were all but swept away. And it bore this responsibility before either of the other two empires, the U.S.A. or the U.S.S.R., had accepted their responsibility for the maintenance of freedom.

## PART II

### Should We Preserve Our Nationhood?

Quite apart from what the British Commonwealth has meant to the world and Canada's role in that world-wide organization, it must be clearly stated at this time that our membership in the British Commonwealth has been, is, and will be the only basis on which our nation can be built and its unity maintained. Often in the past certain Canadians have pleaded that our membership in the Commonwealth somehow took away from our nationhood, and it was therefore the policy of those people to deny that membership. Anybody who is willing to look at that argument clearly and without prejudice, however, will see how spurious it is – *particularly today*, in 1945. The meaning and significance of Canada as a nation is that on the northern half of this continent a sovereign state has been created, friendly to the U.S.A., but essentially different. And the basic reason why we are not part of the U.S.A. is because we have remained in the British orbit. The U.S.A. broke its ties with Western Europe. We never did. We kept our close connection, not alone with the United Kingdom, but with Europe in general. It is that difference that kept us separate from the U.S.A. It is that difference that made us a nation. It is that difference that preserved our individuality. Let us not fool ourselves. The same factors will continue to operate in our history in the future as did in the past. If we have no link with the British Commonwealth, we will soon cease to be a nation and become absorbed in the U.S.A. On the other hand, within the Commonwealth we will be able to develop the form of government and social order that we desire.

Those who want to destroy our membership in the British Commonwealth in the name of a greater Canadian nationhood are fooling themselves. They are really destroying our nation. Because without that membership no power on earth can keep us from being absorbed by the U.S.A. And with that we cease to be a nation.

Too long have we been silent when we were told that our membership in the British Commonwealth is a foolish sentiment from the past. Too long have we listened to those who told us that loyalty to the Commonwealth meant disloyalty to Canada. Too long have we accepted the old worn-out cliché that Anglo-Canadians, because they believe in the Commonwealth, are colonials and not good Canadians. These fatuous platitudes are not good enough. For they come from those who are too lazy to think. Let us examine them and see what they mean.

Canadians who believe in the British Commonwealth have a loyalty to the Commonwealth not because they are bad Canadians but just because they are good Canadians and want to keep Canada alive. The loyalty of English-speaking Canadians to the British Commonwealth is not because they feel subservient to the United Kingdom (God knows how many superior and complacent Englishmen we have all suffered from). Because their first loyalty is to Canada, they realize that the best chance for Canada's national survival is in that Commonwealth. In fact, those who don't believe in the Commonwealth are the bad Canadians. They are the colonials. They would destroy our nationhood and submerge us in the U.S.A.

The other day a noted Canadian author was raising his voice against Canada's membership in the Commonwealth, saying that it militated against our true nationhood. When I asked him how this could be reconciled with the fact that the basic factor in our national survival had been our Britishness, he replied, 'Of course, when you look at it straight, the whole existence of Canada is a lie.' What he meant was, of course, that Canada should never have been created, and that we should long ago have entered the U.S.A. And yet, these are the people who call themselves Canadian nationalists. What a perversion of the name!

If our connection with the British Commonwealth is broken, it will not be the beginning of a free and sovereign Canada. It will be the end of such a Canada. When certain French Canadians preach this so-called independence, they may do so in the name of nationalism, but they would achieve the opposite. For if we were not part of the Commonwealth, most English-speaking Canadians would see no reason for remaining separate. And how long would French-Canadian culture keep its integrity in such a union? The French Canadians may not have received perfect treatment from the Quebec Act of 1774, but it did guarantee them the right to their religion and their civil law. They cannot both have their cake and eat it. *They cannot both want the right to their independent culture that the British connection has given them, and then want to destroy that connection. By destroying one, they may destroy both.* The great Canadian dream of a nation with its origins in the two great civilizations of Western Europe, drawing sustenance from the logic and form of the French and the sagacity and compromise of the English, would be destroyed.

## Our History

Like a plant, a nation develops organically. Like a plant it is dependent on its root for survival. Only by an examination and understanding of our past can we renew ourselves, and make straight our course for a glorious future. In Canada we have an obligation to look at our history so that we can see clearly the basis for building our future and in our history the lesson can be read with crystal clearness. The basis of our sovereign nationhood on this continent is our connection with the British Commonwealth. Only by balancing our geographic North Americanism with our political Britishness have we created the nation we are today.

## Our Origins

The two decisive steps in the formation of our Canadian nation were taken at the time of the American Revolution. First when the French Canadians refused to accept the overtures of the American revolutionists (brought by Benjamin Franklin and John Carroll),[10] and made plain that they considered they had better hope of maintaining a free national way of life within the British Empire than within the newly-formed U.S.A. They had seen two things: in 1774 they had been guaranteed by the British Government's Quebec Act the right to their own civilization – that is, their own civil law and religion. They had also heard the objections that had been raised in the south to these guarantees, at the Continental Congress of 1774. Therefore when the Americans invaded French Canada, the French Canadians saw it not as a glorious liberation but as an invasion, and resented it as such. It is well for all Canadians to remember clearly these days, that had it not been for French-Canadian resistance, at a time when the number of Anglo-Saxons was negligible, the whole course of Canada's development would have been different.

The second great fact on which Canada as a nation was based was the treatment by the American revolutionists of those who opposed them within the colonies. This sent some of the best American stock into Nova Scotia and New Brunswick in the east and to Ontario in the west. These were people who remembered two things: (1) they had been hounded out of their homes to the south by the republic and had had to start life on this hemisphere all over again from scratch; (2) they did not want to become part of the U.S.A. again. They, too, preferred to remain British. In every civilization there are the same kind of conservatives. These [are] men and women who feel that a break with the past may endanger the future. These people brought this feeling to Canada.

From these two beginnings, then, Canada was built: (1) by French Canadians who wanted to maintain their own particular way of life; (2) by English-speaking Canadians who feared the U.S.A. Both realized that if they were to protect themselves they depended on support from Great Britain, and of course that support would only be forthcoming if Canada was part of the British Empire. It is often said, by people who wish to minimize Canada's attachment to the British connection, that Canada is and always has been held to Great Britain by ties of foolish sentiment alone. Our ancestors were smarter than that, however; they instinctively knew that their only chance for free survival was through that attachment.

## Responsible Government

Of course, as much as the settlements desired the support of the British protector, they did not want to be bossed from that country. Those who truly understand the British people know that they refuse to be bossed by anybody. Their political genius and tradition demands that each share in the determination of policy. So during the next years took place one of the brightest chapters in Canadian history – the way the scattered settlements, small and struggling, achieved self-government. Unless we should minimize this or take it for granted, let us remember that older countries in Asia and Europe, products of more ancient civilizations, have never yet achieved democratic government to this day. The Canadian settlements, still in the pioneer stages, achieved this in the 1840s.

In this development towards self-government, particularly as it relates to our membership in the British Commonwealth, it is necessary to remember two basic facts: (1) the popular leaders who made self-government effective at home always saw the importance of our British connection. They were not interested in breaking with Great Britain; they were interested in ending the power of political and religious oligarchs in our own country; in establishing in Canada responsible and democratic government. Lafontaine, Baldwin, and Howe, in their various regions, wanted democratic government at home, but they wanted this inside the Empire.[11] Responsible government made them more British, not less.

The second fact that must be remembered about our struggle for self-government is that the government in London gave full support to the democratic forces as soon as the settlements showed themselves ready to run their own affairs. In 1838 Lord Durham's Report laid down that responsible government was a necessity for the Canadian people. In 1846 [*sic*] Lord Elgin brought it in.[12] Unless we should think of the British Government as ruthless imperialists trying to keep us from our well-deserved freedom, it is well to remember that Lord Elgin was stoned on the streets of Montreal by local commercial elements, because he insisted that the government of Canada should be chosen from the democratically elected representatives of the people, whether French or English, and not from the local oligarchs.[13] His insistence, which was backed by the government in London, is hardly the mark of a power that wanted to keep Canada subservient. British policy to the settlement was, indeed, based on the common sense of a good parent. As soon as the child was ready to bear responsibility, responsibility was granted. The British realized that all true political theory should have as its origin not the doctrinaire concept of rights that pushed the child faster than it could go, but the known results of sound education and pedagogy. Namely, that a growing human being must be gradually developed to responsibility. And, after all, what is common sense in politics but the practical sanity of the family? What is good economics but the laws of the household?

## Relations with the U.S.A.

At the same time as this basic evolution to self-government was going on, another equally basic policy was being evolved by Canada in our relations with the U.S.A. In 1812 Canada was invaded by the U.S.A., and the capital of Upper Canada burned. From that time onwards it became increasingly clear to Canadians that if they were to maintain their independence of the U.S.A. their only hope was not to try and fight the colossus with their own flea-like strength alone, but to defend themselves as a loyal part of the British Empire. Otherwise they would have been swallowed up in short order. In the series of border disputes (Maine, Oregon, Alaska, etc.) they saw that they would always be thoroughly rooked unless they had some backing. Without that backing the young nation would not have had a hope of survival. This became particularly clear as in the U.S. congress voices were constantly being raised to talk of 'manifest destiny' and the invasion of Canada. Indeed, in the disputes between Canada and the U.S.A., Canadians were constantly complaining that the British sometimes did not support them sufficiently forcibly. But they realized that without the British support they would have done even worse. It would have been like going into a poker game without any reserves, when playing with a millionaire. Every time the big fellow would have cleaned us out.

## 1867

It was this fact above all else that brought about the union of the scattered settlements into the Dominion of Canada. The civil war in the U.S.A. was at an end, and it was openly feared in Canada that the victorious armies of the north would be looking for some other fields of conquest. Union seemed the best way of combatting such an eventuality. Numerous other factors did, of course, operate in Confederation, but that was the most crucial one. So in 1867 the Dominion of Canada was formed out of Nova Scotia, New Brunswick, Ontario, and Quebec. In 1869 the prairie area of the west was taken over by the new country, and in 1870 British Columbia came into the Dominion. So our country was formed across the northern half of this continent.

## Since 1867

The settlements of 1867 have, by 1945, developed into a nation. There are few Canadian today who do not feel pride in that nation. Difficulties between regions may beset us, difficulties between races and religions may stir our tempers, but at the same time a real consciousness of nationhood has developed. This is not the place to describe that development, but several points as to our relationship to the rest of the world should be described.

First, since 1867 all the essential characteristics of a sovereign nation have become ours. Through the years we have developed to complete self-government. After the last war we entered the League as a nation in our own right. The work of Sir Wilfrid Laurier[14] and Sir Robert Borden[15] can never be forgotten.

In 1931 the Statute of Westminster laid down in final and unequivocal form that the Commonwealth was an association of free nations co-operating freely. In 1939 we went into the war, by the act of our own Parliament, when we were quite at liberty to stay neutral.

The second point is that, though we have completed our sovereignty, since 1867 we have remained of our own free will in the Commonwealth, and twice went to war. Many of us had believed, in the vacuous thinking of the 'thirties, that the Statute of Westminster would mean a gradual dissolution of the Commonwealth. But the average Canadian was clearer-headed than that. The years since 1931 have shown that Canada's sovereignty, through the Statute of Westminster, has only made us a firmer member of the Commonwealth. Our nationalism has not loosened our connection to the Commonwealth. It has made it more real.

## Our Culture

Another and less tangible way that our membership in the Commonwealth has affected our history is in the general pattern of our national way of life. Many of us, who have suffered from remittance men and second-rate Scotsmen, are apt to forget that which has been more important. From the United Kingdom has come a continual stream of men and women bringing the best of Western civilization to enrich and mature the life of this nation. And it does not make a nation colonial to accept such enrichment; it makes it more adult. These men, however, would not for the most part have cast in their lot with Canada unless they had felt sympathy with us because of our connection with the Commonwealth. This British connection has kept the door wide open, and we have benefited.

The other side of the picture is that because of our connection with Great Britain that country has been wide open for thousands of young Canadian men and women, who have studied there and brought back the rich stream of Western European thought and maturity to this young country. Is that colonial?

This does not mean that we are merely second-rate Englishmen, nor that we are imitation Americans. We are Canadians. We are that distinctive product that is Canadian. It is the blending of the best of the ancient civilization of Western Europe with its maturity and integrity, with the best of North American life. That is what makes a Canadian. That is what gives us our particular colour and our particular quality. That is what gives to every branch of our life its distinctive and vital element. That is not being colonial. It is a blending of what is best in two worlds. We should be glad to have it.

**What Is Canada?**

Of course, in the final analysis this question boils down to what we consider Canada to be. There are now, and have always been in the past, two distinct versions of this. One is that it is only an unfortunate accident that we were ever created and that the sooner we join the United States, the better. The other (and what seems to the present writer a much nobler version), the vision of Macdonald, Laurier, and Borden that on the northern half of this continent has been created a nation, raised in a different tradition from the U.S.A. and dedicated to the extension of certain different political and social concepts.

But what are these concepts? It is always difficult to define such things in bald and general terms. We Canadians feel them in our daily lives, and we see them in intimate and immediate ways. We understand them in particular instances, as they affect us, rather than rationalizing them into generalizations. But now that they are challenged, they must be enunciated. The essential principle around which Canada has been established is embodied in the age-old struggle in human society as to how free each individual can be and yet live in an ordered society where that freedom is not so abused that it infringes on the freedom of others. Where does freedom for one person to do what he likes mean lack of freedom for other people? This conflict, so continuous in human life, can be expressed in many ways: the relation of the one to the many, of freedom to authority, of liberty to order. But it is the same old question, how do individuals live together in peace and harmony [?]

The main thought of Americans on this subject has emphasized the inalienable right of the individual to be free to do as he chooses, whatever effect it might have on society as a whole. We in Canada have put the balance far more on the side of order or the good of society. The individual has certain rights, but these rights must be strictly prevented from causing any disruption to the society as a whole. This stress on order in our society has been true of French as well as English Canada. In the opening of the West, also, we saw to it that the forces of law and order preceded settlement and did not follow it, as was often the case in the U.S.A. The R.C.M.P. was an instrument of the central government for maintaining order in the new territories, the like of which there never was in the U.S.A. or any other country of this hemisphere. Now, in modern times, on the question of wartime restrictions, for instance, there has been a widespread realization in Canada that, because these restrictions were for the good of society as a whole they must be accepted, and they have been. In the U.S.A. there has been widespread attack on them as limiting the freedom of the individual.

It is unwise and presumptuous to say which balance is better – that of the U.S.A. or that of Canada. But let us admit frankly that it is important that this continent should have this diversity of social philosophy. The great question of the modern world is going to be to what extent, within the complicated pattern of industrialized civilization, freedom and authority can be truly integrated. How far in this new and intricate world will it be possible for men to have individual freedom without disrupting too many other men by their actions? How far will men have to be curbed by authority, so that they do not interfere with others? In 1929 the U.S.A. saw the results of complete freedom. Yet that nation still, more than anywhere else, deifies the right of the individual to do as he likes. In the U.S.S.R. the other extreme has been tried, wherein the individual has been subordinated to the good of society as a whole, and his acts are ruthlessly curbed for the sake of general order.

The whole tradition of the British nations has been to effect a compromise between the two extremes of liberty and order. The new Labour government in the United Kingdom, the New Zealand social security laws, the growth of the C.C.F. and Social Credit in Canada, all show that the British nations are moving towards a greater social ordering than the freer, more individualistic society of the U.S.A. On the other hand, the true Britisher is the last person to submit to the overwhelming control of the centralized totalitarian state. We are true individualists to our very core. Ernest Bevin's recent speech on foreign policy is proof of that.[16] It is particularly important that there should exist on this continent a nation such as Canada with the tradition of the middle course between individual liberty and social order. For by extending and working out these differing forms of social structure we can strongly affect the tendencies that the U.S.A. will follow. In this way, because we share this contact with the U.S.A., we can influence that country to move in the direction of greater social order by the power of our example. But we can do this best be preserving our own individuality as a nation and by remaining part of the stream of social thought that flows through the British Commonwealth.

**Our Obvious Responsibility**

Of course too much of this pamphlet has been written on the defensive. As if to true Canadians it was necessary to defend our membership in the Commonwealth! Neither is there ever need for Canadians to put our membership in the Commonwealth on the basis of selfishness – though, of course, our membership in it is our interest. But it is too great an institution for that. Let it be stated that this war has proved as never before how important the British Commonwealth is to the world. Many of us were foolish enough to doubt it before. The events of the last years are overwhelming proof.

Two dates must emblazon themselves on our minds if we are to understand modern history: 1933 and 1940. In 1933 the dream of liberal mankind that we were on the edge of Utopia was rudely shattered by the rise of sadism and perverted tyranny in the very centre of our Western world. Signs of the evil in the heart of man had been appearing with alarming frequency, but here was the final outcrop of it in organized form to tear our footling optimism into shreds. For this was a state that not only acted with barbarism but preached that barbarism was the true way of life. That all our Christian virtues of love and co-operation were a mockery, and that, as Spengler said, man should be 'the hammer.'[17]

The second date that must be remembered is 1940. For in that year barbarism was first checked – not by the vague hopes of the idealists, but by the organized strength of the free nations of the British Commonwealth. The last five years have been cruel. Millions of people's hopes have been smashed by war. But let us learn from this waste. Whatever our illusions before the war may have been, we cannot hold on to them now.

People who attack or weaken the Commonwealth as late as this year 1945 are like people who grow tired of the very dykes which have protected them. The dykes have been there for years. The people have been brought up with the dykes. Eventually they begin to believe that the unflooded world is the natural world, and that the dykes are unnecessary. They feel that the dykes are outmoded institutions standing in the way of progress. Therefore they don't tend the dykes and the floods come. Before the war our pleasant tolerant world had depended more than on anything else on the order that depended on the British fleet. But gradually we began to accept freedom as the natural state of human affairs, and we neglected the order that had made that freedom possible. We, in fact, began to believe that that order was the only thing standing in the way of more perfect freedom. But in 1940 the floods came, and it was only the worn-out dykes of the British Commonwealth and of gallant and alert people in that Commonwealth that kept the floods back. Yet now, when the floods have subsided, once more in our innocence we start to ignore the dykes. But if we do scrap the dykes, let us be ready for the floods to come again, and this time perhaps to sweep down for a thousand years.

We cannot judge the British Commonwealth from our petty interests alone (however well these are satisfied), but on the highest criteria of political morality. For today in the modern world, with it more than with any other political institution, lies the hope of Christian man, of ethical man, of man the reasonable, moral being who stands before God and history. One can indeed say that ethical man, reasonable man, is a last remaining fragment of the dark ages, and that the new man is one ruled by Marxian economics or Freudian sex – mankind, in fact, who is brutal and unreasonable, unethical and material, and who is ruthlessly dominated by his appetites. Then we can disavow the British Commonwealth. But if we believe in Christian man, the finest flower of all that Western civilization has produced, then there can be no doubt that our chief hope in the survival of such values is in the survival of the British Commonwealth. Canada has a vital responsibility. Canada must choose.

## Notes

1  For the 1945 San Francisco conference that prepared for the founding of the United Nations, see note 6 in *Food for Thought* columns section, p. 73.

2  Sir Winston Leonard Spencer Churchill (1874–1965). We have not been able to trace this quotation.

3  William Malcolm Hailey (1872–1969), first Baron Hailey, 1936, was a British public servant who served from 1896 to 1934 in India, where he was committed to the gradual development of Indian responsible democratic government. Grant is referring to *An African Survey* (1938).

4  Sir Robert Arthur James Gascoyne-Cecil, Viscount Cranborne (1893–1972), elevated to the Lords as Baron Cecil of Essendon in 1941, succeeded his father as fifth Marquess of Salisbury in 1947. An English Conservative statesman from a family distinguished by public service, he became foreign under-secretary in 1935 and colonial secretary in 1942. He represented Britain at the founding conference of the United Nations Organization at San Francisco in 1945, and later became secretary of state for Commonwealth relations in 1952 under Churchill. He was leader of the House of Lords from 1942 to 1945 and from 1951 to 1957. We were unable to trace the source of Grant's quotation.

5  André Laurendeau (1912–1968), journalist, politician, playwright, French-Canadian nationalist, and leader of the anti-conscription party Le Bloc Populaire, was, at the time of Grant's reference, the editor of *Le Devoir*.

Later he was co-chairman (with Davidson Dunton) of the Royal Commission on Bilingualism and Biculturalism (1963–8).

6 Senator Burton Kendall Wheeler (1882–1975), American lawyer and Democratic senator from Montana, was one of the leaders of the isolationist movement preceding the entry of the United States into the Second World War.

7 Senator Gerald Prentice Nye (1892–1971), newspaperman and the Republican (Progressive) senator from North Dakota (1925–45), was a strong advocate of isolationism and a prominent member of the 'America First' Committee.

8 General Jan Christian Smuts (1870–1950), South African soldier and statesman, was prime minister of South Africa (1919–24; 1939–48) and Commander-in-Chief during both World Wars. Grant is referring to his *Holism and Evolution* (1926), a study of the creative forces in nature. One of the chief advocates of the concept of the Commonwealth of Nations, General Smuts was a major builder of both the League of Nations and the United Nations.

9 André Siegfried (1875-1959), French economist, historian, and sociologist, published several works on Canada, the United States, and the British Empire. Grant is referring to *What the British Empire Means to Western Civilization* (1940).
Paul Cohen-Portheim (d. 1932) wrote *Time Stood Still: My Internment in England 1914–18* (1931), *England: The Unknown Isle* (1932), and *The Spirit of London* (1935).

10 Benjamin Franklin (1706–1790), John Carroll (1735–1815), and Samuel Chase (1741–1811) were sent in 1776 by the Continental Congress on an unsuccessful foray to obtain French-Canadian support for the American Revolution.

11 Sir Louis-Hippolyte Lafontaine (1807–1864), Lower Canadian Liberal politician, became the first prime minister of the united Canadas in 1848 when Lord Elgin fully recognized responsible government.
Sir Robert Baldwin (1804–1858), the rallying figure in rebuilding the post-rebellion Reform opposition in Upper Canada, became prime minister of Upper Canada (1842–3) and later forged an alliance with Lafontaine's Lower Canadian Liberals in the successful fight for responsible government.
Joseph Howe (1804–1873), journalist and politician, was premier (1863–70) and lieutenant-governor (1873 for 3 weeks before his death) of Nova Scotia. He was a reformer and great orator who secured responsible government for Nova Scotia in 1848 and, after unsuccessfully opposing confederation, entered the cabinet of the first Canadian government at Ottawa in 1869.

12 James Bruce (1811–1863), eighth Earl of Elgin and twelfth Earl of Kincardine, was named governor general of Canada in 1846, took office early in

1847, and held it until 1854. Grant's date is incorrect since Elgin commissioned LaFontaine to form the first responsible government in Canada in 1848.

13 Elgin was attacked by Tory forces when he gave assent to the Rebellion Losses Bill of 1849.

14 Sir Wilfrid Laurier (1841–1919), seventh prime minister of Canada (1896–1911). Grant is referring to Laurier's work towards the future independence of Canada when he resisted efforts made by the British Empire to promote unification at the colonial conferences of 1897 and 1902.

15 Sir Robert Laird Borden (1854–1937), eighth prime minister of Canada (1911–20), was the leader of Canada during the First World War and a leading figure in the achievement of Dominion status and the transition from the British Empire to the British Commonwealth of Nations. In his later years he was recognized as a firm advocate of the League of Nations and was president of the League of Nations Society in Canada.

16 Ernest Bevin (1881–1951), self-educated English trade unionist and Labour statesman, Minister of Labour 1900–45, Foreign Secretary 1945–50, said in a speech to the House of Commons on 26 October 1945: 'If every country could get free parliaments and free expression without dictatorship or orders, and if people could express themselves freely on these problems, we might make a better world for the future than we have experienced in the last 25 years ... [The German people, having lived under a dictatorship,] have no sense of judgment because so long as there is a dictator at the top giving all decisions, the power of decision is lost lower down. I think that one of the greatest tributes to democracy is that it retains the power of responsibility and decision.' See Alan Bullock, *Ernest Bevin: Foreign Secretary, 1945–61* (New York: W.W. Norton 1983), 107.

17 Oswald Spengler (1880–1936). See note 3 in 'The Failure of Nerve,' a review of James Burnham.

# Have We a Canadian Nation?

In volume 8, no. 3, of *Public Affairs* (Institute of Public Affairs, Dalhousie University), Spring 1945: 161–6. According to Sheila Grant, *Public Affairs* was run by a very fine man, Lothar Richter, whom her husband had gotten to know when visiting Halifax for Adult Education events in the 1940s. Grant wrote several pieces for him, and the Grants became close friends of the Richters. Sadly, Richter was killed on the road soon after the Grants arrived, and Grant ceased to have much contact with the Institute of Public Affairs.

## I

What is it that makes a nation? How is it formed? From what elements does it get its peculiar character? In any attempt at analysis, one inevitably finds that a nation is compounded out of so many parts, woven together in so many strands, existent because of so many interdependent factors, that it is impossible to determine exactly what gives it its cohesive strength. Race (if there is such a thing), language certainly, geographical area, long remembrance of life under a distinctive form of government (this is not always there), love of common traditions and beliefs, a solid core of common religious ideals, and many other factors are blended together. Some of these factors are basic, some merely incidental. And all these elements have, like a complicated chemical compound, ceased to be merely a mixture of separate differing substances, but have fused into a distinctive entity.

It is impossible to analyse its substance intellectually, and so it becomes a mystery, and the nation a mystic symbol, deeply important in itself. We see this in French or Polish nationalism, in Russian (more powerful to-day than ever before) or Greek. We see it in that unpretentious variety that is so sure of itself that it need not be talked of – the English. And we see the nationalism of Germany – once in part fine, but now dominated by the half-farcical, half-tragic legend of the master race. Yes, nationalism is a great thing. When embodied in a glorification of the state it is capable of fantastic outrage and barbarity; when embodied in an individual culture it is capable of unique contributions to the world. The latter is what is meant by nationalism in this article.

Do we have this kind of nationalism in Canada? Have we something that is unique in itself and which will be our particular contribution to the world. The tentative answer must be that as a young nation we are only just beginning to develop it. But there is no doubt it is developing. One can see it in the open horizons of the prairies on Portage Avenue; in the stolid fertility of rural Ontario; in the grey mists of Halifax Harbour. One can feel it in the quiet villages of French Canada, in the comfortable towns of the Ottawa valley, in the clear lakes of Algonquin Park. We can hear it in the voice of Canadian war correspondents telling of Canadians overseas; one can hear it on Saturday might in a bright-lit Ontario town; one can hear it at the exciting political meetings in the province of Quebec.

But that is not sufficient answer. What is this particular Canadian spirit? We must define it and find what it is. For we are not in the position of the French, the English, or the Russians, whose nationalism is so deeply rooted in the past that it is almost impossible to uproot it. We are a new nation, established on this continent. Our foundation and development are recent. We have not time for the slow maturing of national feeling. It must be created around some principles. It must be consciously based on certain conscious ideas. Too often in the past certain Canadians have talked about the development of Canadian nationalism without knowing what it was they hoped would develop. They thought that nationalism would grow if we talked about it in [the] abstract. But of course it will only grow if we make it. And to do that we must know what it is we are trying to produce.

This is particularly true of this country, where we live so intimately and closely with the mighty U.S.A. For unless we know why we exist, unless we know what we are trying to build here in Canada, unless we make a conscious effort to build it – we will inevitably be shaped by the REPUBLIC. There always has been and always will be an alternative to building a Canadian nation. And that is the submerging of our nation in the U.S.A. This is a perpetual challenge to us who believe deeply in the importance of the Canadian nation. Have we within our nation enough depth, sufficient resources, to build something of our own?

## II

What then is Canadian nationalism and what created it? Is it a gigantic accident that across the northern half of this continent a nation has been built? I think not. For surely the basis of our nation is rooted in one historical fact. Where the U.S.A. broke away from its past and its connections with Western Europe, we never did so. The original people of both English- and French- speaking Canada were those men and women on this continent who did not wish to be part of the new American experiment but wished to build a different society. The French Canadians did not want to become part of the new republic. The English Canadians were mainly made up of those who left the U.S.A. rather than accept the new society. Both were able to accomplish their desired ends by maintaining their connection with the British Empire and eventually by uniting together into a nation. It is on this basis that our nation was founded and maintained.

Yes it was this refusal to break, the fact that the people who made Canada were those (English- and French-speaking alike) who did not accept the American Revolution, that laid down the character of our country and gave us our individuality. This meant first of all that we were a conservative nation. In these days, that adjective has come to mean solely reaction and the defence of property rights. But it is not meant in that way here. What is meant is that we were a nation who believed that the past could tell us something of the future. A nation that realized that true progress can only be made step by step – layer on layer – if it is going to stick. And that the progress that is made by dashes forward will probably involve equally violent backward lurches. We were a country, in fact, careful to its very foundations.

Second, this origin of our country has meant that we are a society where social order is of prime importance. The very origin of the U.S.A. is in the concept of revolution and the rights of the individual to be free. The origin of Canada (both English- and French-speaking) is in the concept of holding the social fabric together and of the duty of the individual to preserve a decent order in society. The U.S.A. has produced a society where freedom of the individual is a fetish. For instance, during the race riots in Detroit the white Americans, when all too infrequently prevented by the police from beating up their black fellow citizens, yelled at these police 'Gestapo.' After all, the intervention by the police was the infringement of their right as individuals to beat up the Negroes. At the same time this very individualism has produced in the U.S.A. some wonderful examples of what the free individual can do.

We in Canada, however, have from our very background of conservatism put the emphasis on the necessity of social order. Our nation was founded after the American Revolution by those people who believed in order. Or course our citizens must be free. Equally with the Americans we share the belief in the individual's inalienable and indestructible rights, which is the chief pride of Western civilization. Free, yes – but not so free that by his freedom he endangers the freedom of others and so disrupts the pattern of social order. Our inherent conservatism said order and self-discipline are a natural concomitant of freedom. In fact, if you don't have that order you will inevitably lose that freedom in anarchy. For out of anarchy the only natural reaction is tyrannous authority and the end of freedom. So throughout our history the pattern of that belief in order has gained and expanded. When the chips were down, we did not accept the disorder of Papineau[1] or Mackenzie.[2] We accepted Baldwin[3] and Lafontaine,[4] men who represented freedom, but freedom within the institution. Later, in the opening of the West, order went first from the centre in the shape of the RCMP, where in the U.S.A. it was created on the spot by posses and vigilantes. To-day in our life we have strong movements in Canada – like the cooperatives, the CCF and Social Credit – that want to impose order on the undisciplined money changers. Our respect for the law and for authority has by and large been a deeper rooted part of our life than in the U.S.A.

This essential conservatism and belief in order has been marked in most of the fields of our national life. In our education, for instance, up to the last few years, we have never gone in for those theories that learning was easy and soft and that the main quality to be sought in education was entertainment. We have produced, for the most part, an educational system rooted in the strict disciplines. The same has been true of our religious traditions. We have never (again, not until the last few years) been much for the lunatic fringe. We have accepted the sane and orthodox religions rooted in the past. The great majority of Canadians have been either Roman Catholic or Presbyterian, Anglican, Baptist or Methodist; all of these are orthodox religions stemming out of the great traditions of the past and none of them over excited by the limitless possibilities of the human species; all of them conscious that mankind, if it is to live successfully and freely on this planet, must study self-discipline. We have never been so prone to, or so excited by those unorthodox, wonderful, and fantastic religious beliefs of the sects as has been the U.S.A.

## III

The character of our country has been stamped because at every stage of the development of this country we have had at our disposal the mature wisdom of the older civilization. Western European civilization as embodied in France and Great Britain through the centuries has developed in experience a great and noble culture. And because we had never broken away, that experience was always open to us. Politically it meant that we developed in this country the framework of British parliamentary government, the most flexible and truly democratic in the world. It meant that in times of stress men like Durham[5] or Elgin[6] were on the spot with their traditions of political sagacity. It meant, in establishing our educational system, we could call on men from England and from France to bring us their vast experience. In religious matters, there has been a continual stream of men bringing the best of European theology to this continent.

Now it would be presumptuous to say which of these traditions – the Canadian or the American – was the finer. The individualism of the U.S.A. has meant that often they have had greater imagination, greater ability to progress. On the other hand, our conservatism has meant that in stormy days we have a sanity and stability that prevents us from losing our balance. But whichever is the worthier, they are different. And it is from that difference that Canada has been created. We both are North American. But we used our existence on this continent in different ways. We stuck more closely than the U.S.A. to the traditions of

Western Europe. And from that difference Canadians exist to-day – not as imitation Englishmen or Frenchmen, but equally (and let us not forget it) not as imitation Americans. We are in fact something in ourselves. Something that is distinctively ourselves. We are the blend that has been produced by British North America. In the name of the statute in which our nation was founded lies the character of our country.

Of course against this view of our nationhood is raised the cry of colonialism. Some writers say that the maintenance of our bonds with Western Europe in general and the British Commonwealth in particular makes us a colony. They proclaim that we should have broken with our past. How foolish that is. First and foremost of course, we are to-day a sovereign nation. In no way are we a colony. As to breaking with the past, why is that such a glorious proceeding? To maintain connections with the past isn't colonialism, it is plain common sense. The analogy of the family is pertinent. The son or daughter grows up and achieves complete autonomy (as we have within the Commonwealth). But that does not mean that he necessarily breaks away from his parents. Much mutual help can be derived from remaining in close connection. The son or daughter learns judgement, maturity, and balance from the longer life and maturity of his parents. The parents gain vitality and vision from the offspring. Clearly the same is true of our connection with Great Britain; both parties have gained much of mutual advantage.

The point is of course that now all danger of being a colony of Great Britain is past. It might have been true in 1870 or 1900. But this is 1945. And in 1945 the danger to our nationhood does not come from any colonial feelings to the British, but rather the danger of becoming a satellite of the U.S.A. Our sovereign nationhood is menaced from that direction. And strangely enough, these Canadians who in the past affirmed our nationhood and said we must never be a colony of the British now seem quite ready to destroy that same nationhood by making us a colony of the Americans. But if the latter should take place, we will lose our nationhood as actually as if we were a colony of the British.

For it must be categorically stated that Canada will only continue to exist as long as we represent something individual and special in ourselves. Deep within ourselves we must continue to believe in the validity of those values on which our nation was founded. We must continue to put them into practice and into greater and richer fulfilment. We must cultivate our own individuality. If we don't have that belief in our own way of life, if we don't continue to practise these values, we will soon cease to be a nation. If we cut ourselves off from our roots, we will die. We always have the alternative to being Canadians – we can become Americans. Unless we have our own national way, we will have the American way. If we bow prostrate before the culture of Hollywood; if in education we accept from the south the phoney precepts of so-called 'progressive education'; if socially we welcome in our Granite Clubs the Babbittry[7] of the middle west and the intolerance of the deep south; if economically we accept the uncontrolled individualism of American business and call it British freedom; if our entertainment criterion is Frank Sinatra[8] and philosophically and religiously we accept the materialist claptrap from the U.S.A. – then we will in effect have given up those values that are essentially Canadian and we might as well become part of Leviathan. Morally and intellectually we will have become a colony of the republic and should therefore ask for admission to the union.

No, if Canada is to continue to exist as a nation – in every sphere in our national life – we must expound those values and tradition of decency, stability, and order that have been the best basis of our national life. In education we must continue to recognize that self-discipline must be the central core of education. In economics we must recognize that individual freedom must be carefully balanced against social order. In entertainment we must build theatres and community centres to produce something of our own. In films we are already doing it in the National Film Board.[9] As far as law goes, we must expound that tradition that nothing is more vital than the dignity of law and an uncorrupted police force. Only if we can maintain these standards of decency in ourselves, and so see that what we have in ourselves is right, will we maintain our nation. If we are too lazy or too weak to build up our own values, then we will cease to exist. Inevitably will we accept those from the south.

## IV

But of course the question must be answered: Is there any reason to maintain on this continent two separate and diverse forms of society – Canada and the U.S.A.? Or should this continent be united into one state centred at Chicago and Washington [?] To those who feel deeply and instinctively the importance of Canada, that is almost the question of the traitor. To most Canadians, the existence of our society is so right, so true, that it is unthinkable that it should be swallowed up or destroyed. But yet to-day, as never before, the question must be answered. For in this country many Canadians (and in places of high responsibility and power) consciously or unconsciously are leading this country in a direction that can only eventually mean one thing – union with the U.S.A. Was, then, the philosophy of Macdonald,[10] Laurier,[11] and Borden[12] merely a foolish romanticism? Was the building of a Canadian nation an idle and useless dream? Is there any ultimate and valid reason for the continued existence of the Canadian nation? The answer comes back, 'Yes' – emphatically yes, and now as never before.

The first and prime reason is diversity. For the colour and glory of life are not found in uniformity, but in diversity. The fact that in Europe there are French and English, Dutch and Italian, Spanish and many national cultures has enriched the contribution of that continent to the world. Would this continent make its greatest contribution if it was all bedecked in the same raiment? No surely the diversity and colour that an independent Canada could give to this continent is our main ambition.

Our diversity will be particularly important in the field of social organization. For in the world that is with us now the great problem is going to be to what extent man will be able to organize efficiently the industrial society he has created and yet maintain his freedom. Where the U.S.A. in meeting these problems is going to emphasize individualism, we have already shown in all the platforms of our three major paries that we are going to employ more ordered means. Like the other British nations – the United Kingdom, Australia, New Zealand – we are going to embark on a series of social measures. We will be the compromise between the individualism of the U.S.A. and the extreme social order of the U.S.S.R. Also in a small country like Canada, it will be easier to work out the problems of democracy in the industrialized age than in the U.S.A., where the units of power are so enormous that only a Roosevelt can control them.[13]

Of course the greatest reason for our independence is in the field of international affairs. Here we are, an American nation, and at the same time a member of an effective world organization, the British Commonwealth. An organization that, when all is said and done, held the free world together in 1940. We have strong and vigorous connections with the rest of the world. If we stay in that position we can exert a continuous pressure to see that the U.S.A. takes its proper place in world order. If we throw our weight to the south, we can strengthen the U.S.A. in its continental isolationism. Here the choice is ours and it will be a choice that will affect the whole world.

If our national existence is so important, we in Canada must strengthen it. And of course, first and foremost, if it is to be strengthened, that strength can only come from within ourselves. It must be repeated again. Only if we can build up within ourselves a way of life that justifies our existence will we continue to exist. We must fortify and expand these values that have made Canada what it is and from which we have developed. Our nation has had a great past; only if we have stability and vitality in ourselves will we have a great future.

## Notes

1 Louis-Joseph Papineau (1786–1871), lawyer, seigneur, and liberal politician, was the leader of the Parti Canadien (later Parti Patriote) representing the interests of French Canada against the English establishment in the years leading up to and during the rebellion in 1837.

2 William Lyon Mackenzie (1795–1861), editor and publisher of *The Colonial Advocate*, mayor of Toronto, and member of the Upper Canada Parliament, was a leading voice of the Reform movement and the leader of the unsuccessful rebellion in 1837.

3 Sir Robert Baldwin (1804–1858). See note 11 in *The Empire: Yes or No?*, p. 125.

4 Sir Louis-Hippolyte Lafontaine (1807–1864). See note 11 in *The Empire: Yes or No?*, p. 125.

5 John George Lambton (1792–1840), first Earl of Durham, 1828, British statesman associated with the liberal wing of the Whig party, along with Lord John Russell drafted the Reform Bill of 1832. Known by the sobriquet 'Radical Jack,' he was made governor of the Canadas in 1838 by British prime minister Lord Melbourne. After only six months in Canada he completed his famous *Report on the Affairs of British North America*, in which his major recommmendation was to reunite the Canadas in order to accelerate the assimilation of the French Canadians. The union was brought into effect in 1841.

6 James Bruce (1811–1863), eighth Earl of Elgin and twelfth Earl of Kincardine. See note 12 in *The Empire: Yes or No?*, pp. 125–6.

7  In using the phrase 'our Granite Clubs,' Grant probably intended 'the clubs that count,' where the businessmen of the Canadian Establishment gather for lunch to make business contacts. They include the York, the Toronto, and the National in Toronto, and the Mount Royal and the St James in Montreal. The Granite Club, founded first as a curling club in 1875 with its prestigious early membership including Sir John A. Macdonald, had become an important gathering place for the social and athletic activities of wealthy, established families. Grant stood with a part of the older establishment that was loyal to the British connection and suspicious of the growing American presence among the powerful in Canada during the period between the wars. Following the publication of *Babbitt* (1922) by American novelist Sinclair Lewis, 'Babbittry' had come to mean materialistic, complacent businessmen like the novel's protagonist, George Babbitt, a middle-class real estate agent from the Midwest. In Lewis's novel, Babbitt tries to rebel but finds the price of non-conformity too great and resigns himself to the superficial values of his business culture.

8  Francis Albert Sinatra (1915–1998), American singer and film actor, started his long and highly successful career as a recording artist singing with the bands of Harry James and Tommy Dorsey on radio, becoming one of the most adulated teen idols. By the mid-1940s, he had rocketed to fame, and riots broke out among his audiences, primarily teenaged girls.

9  The National Film Board of Canada (NFB), established in 1939, became the principal focus for Canadian film during the 1940s under directors John Grierson and Ross McLean. The NFB pioneered uniquely Canadian developments of the film medium in social documentary, animation, and documentary films.

10  Sir John Alexander Macdonald (1815–1891), first prime minister of Canada (1867–73) and (1878–91), was a shrewd and ingenious Conservative politician and Canadian nationalist oriented to central control by Ottawa.

11  Sir Wilfrid Laurier (1841–1919), seventhth prime minister of Canada (1896–1911). See note 14 in *The Empire: Yes or No?*, p. 126.

12  Sir Robert Laird Borden (1854–1937), eighth prime minister of Canada (1911–20). See note 15 in *The Empire: Yes or No?*, p. 126.

13  Franklin Delano Roosevelt (1882–1945), statesman and thirty-second president of the United States for an unprecedented four terms, constructed a new rural–urban majority coalition for the Democratic party. He met the crisis of the Great Depression by launching 'The New Deal' for national recovery, involving controversial measures such as state intervention in the market and a Social Security Act. At the outbreak of the Second World War, he was able to modify U.S. neutrality to favour the Allied Forces.

# Review of *Canada and the World Tomorrow* edited by Violet Anderson

Violet Anderson edited and introduced the addresses given at the Couchiching Conference of the Canadian Institute of Public Affairs, 19 to 26 August 1944. *Canada and the World Tomorrow* was published at Toronto by the Ryerson Press (December 1944) with a foreword by 'Malcolm W. Wallace, B.A., Ph.D., LL.D., Principal Emeritus, University College, University of Toronto.' Grant's review appeared in volume 5, issue 6, of *Food for Thought*, March 1945: 40.

Reports of conferences are often deadly dull. The speeches that stirred the hearers so nobly when given from the platform seem dismally uninspired on the printed page. This report of the Institute of Public Affairs at Couchiching in 1944, is, however, a pleasant exception. It is not dull, nor, fortunately, does it try to be inspiring! It is full of useful fact and basic interpretation that will prove invaluable to those who are attempting to develop a reasonable judgment of what is happening inside Canada and abroad.

Above all, its main contribution is that it deals with practical problems in a reasonable way. Instead of embroidering vague hopes, it attempts to elucidate immediate issues. In the section on international affairs, for instance, Professor George Brown, in his usual lucid way, does not build up Utopias, but defines a commonsense basis for Canada's membership in the Commonwealth.[1] In two articles on cartels and one on Bretton Woods, the writers face some of the problems, on the solution of which a peace may possibly be built.[2] Sir George Sansome's report on 'Some Problems of the Far East' hits that rare balance of looking forward to a better future without minimizing past achievements or possible difficulties.[3]

In the section on Canadian affairs, the emphasis on the practical is also foremost. M.W. MacKenzie deals with the reconversion from war to peace.[4] G.F. Davidson discusses various health insurance schemes.[5] C.P. McTague and J.W. Buckley both deal with labour problems from the most useful basis, that of their own experience.[6] Particularly pleasant is it to read essays by two French-speaking Canadians, Senator T.D. Bouchard and Maurice Lamontagne,[7] and to find at the end an excellent description of a round table under the heading 'Canadians and Canadiens.'

I happened to pick up an old copy of the proceedings of that same Institute in 1936. Nineteen forty-four shows certainly a heightened maturity. In the early year, the speakers all talked of our rights in the international and Commonwealth fields, and propounded that amazing paradox that the less responsibility we took, the more adult we became. War is an agonizing and ghastly price to pay for maturity. But these 1944 proceedings certainly show that we are growing up.

The choice of speakers is good, they handle their topics in a sane and satisfactory manner, and the volume has been edited with care and discrimination. For those interested in what is happening in Canada and the world, this volume is indeed a worthwhile investment.

George Grant

## Notes

1  George Williams Brown (1894–1963), professor of history at the University of Toronto (after 1925) and editor of the *Canadian Historical Review.* Along with many articles he published *Readings in Canadian History* (1941) and *Canadian Democracy in Action* (1945).

2  Frank Albert Knox (1895–1976), professor of economics at Queen's University, Kingston (after 1924), delivered chapter 4, entitled 'The "Bretton Woods" Proposals.' Bretton Woods was the site of the international conference in New Hampshire that set up the economic system after the Second World War, leading to such institutions as the General Agreement on Tariffs and Trade (GATT), the International Monetary Fund (IMF), and the World Bank. It established a system of fixed exchange rates that lasted until the early 1970s. Corwin D. Edwards, Oxford-educated professor of economics at Chicago's Northwestern University, formerly the Consultant on Cartels, Department of State, Washington, delivered chapter 5, 'Is There Need to

Control Cartel Activities?' Vincent Wheeler Bladen (1900–1981), professor
of political economy at the University of Toronto (after 1921), delivered
chapter 6, 'International Cartel Policy.' He later presided over the 1950s and
1960s expansion at Toronto, became an adviser to government, and
founded the *Canadian Journal of Economics and Political Science*. He published
numerous articles and reports on the auto industry, university financing,
industrial organization, political economy, and Canadian economic affairs
and self-reliance.

3  Sir George Bailey Sansom (1883–1965), minister in the British embassy in
Washington from 1942 to 1947, where he made a valuable contribution to
the determination of Allied postwar policy towards Japan. He became a
meticulous student of all aspects of Japanese history and civilization while
a diplomat in the commercial department of the embassy in Tokyo after
1903, and published *An Historical Grammar of Japanese* (1928), *Japan: A Short
Cultural History* (1931), and *The Western World and Japan* (1950).

4  Maxwell Weir Mackenzie (1907–1991), a company executive at McDonald
Currie, and deputy chairman of the Wartime Prices and Trade Board in
Ottawa (1943), who later served as Deputy Minister of the Department of
Trade and Commerce (1945–51).

5  George Forrester Davidson (1909–1973), later President of the Canadian
Broadcasting Corporation (1970) and Under Secretary of Administration
and Management at the United Nations (1972), was Deputy Minister of
Welfare (1944) and formerly Executive Director of the Canadian Welfare
Council in Ottawa. A social worker active in the Vancouver area in the
Family Service Association and the Canadian Association of Social Workers, he produced reports on the Welfare Services of various regions of Canada in 1944 and published *Family Allowances, an Instalment on Social Security*
(1944) and *Issues in Social Security* (1951).

6  Hon. Mr Justice Charles P. McTague (1890–1965), chairman of the National
Wartime Labour Board (1943–4) and national chairman of the Progressive
Conservative Party (Sept 1944). He had been appointed to the Supreme
Court of Ontario (1935), served on the War Contracts Depreciation Board
(1940–3), and advised the Minister of Labour on industrial arbitration
(1941). John W. Buckley (1882–1958), strong left-winger and Canadian
nationalist, was vice president of the Trades and Labor Congress of Canada
(after 1943). He had served seven years as an apprentice wheelwright and
was active on the Toronto District Labour Council from 1929 to 1947. He
had been president of the Independent Labour Party from 1922 to 1924.

7  Senator Telesphore-Damien Bouchard (1881–1962), mayor of Ste-Hyacinthe
and Liberal MLA (1912–44), serving in the Tashereau and Godbout governments, delivered chapter 12, 'Social Change in Quebec.' He was a federalist
who spoke against L'Ordre de Jacques Cartier as a danger to Canadian soci-

ety and was appointed by King to the Senate in 1944. Maurice Lamontagne (1917–1988), professor of the Faculty of Social Sciences at Laval University in Quebec (1943–54) under Georges-Henri Lévesque, delivered chapter 10, 'Some Criticisms of the Current Proposals to Achieve Full Employment and Social Security.' The program at Laval was an important part of the liberal Catholic movement towards modernization and the democratization of Quebec labour and of Quebec society generally. Lamontagne later became a federal civil servant (1954), an adviser to Lester Pearson (1958–63), an MP (1963), and finally a senator in 1967.

# Letter to the Editor: 'Cheers and Jeers!'

On the inside back cover of April 1945 issue of *Food for Thought*.

The Editor,
*Food for Thought*.

Dear Madam:

Your editorial on 'Ideas and the People' in the March issue of *Food for Thought* seems to me to employ a time-worn and tedious device, that of putting up a dummy which has existence only in your own mind, knocking it down, and saying 'Ahah! that proves my case.' The dummy, of course, is the person who wants to teach ideas completely detached from life. I don't think there are any people left in Canada among the educators who want to do that. And by knocking down this mythical ivory tower educator you try and convince your readers that you have proven all the phoniest tenets of 'progressive' education.

The question between the 'progressive' educator and the sound traditional educator is not whether ideas are to be cut off from life or whether they are to be connected with life, but rather what is the best method of producing a child that can look at life clearly and effectively. The claims of classical education were not that they cut people off from life but rather that by their techniques they taught people to see life clearly. Classics, history, philosophy, were not taught in an effort to detach ideas from reality; they were taught so that people would have a strong, tough instrument with which to analyse reality.

The fallacy of progressive education is that so often it has believed thought was easy. The material it gave children to fashion their brains on was not tough enough. The result was inevitably sloppy thinking.

As a scientist remarked the other day, the trouble with progressive and pseudo-scientific education is not only that it fails to produce good human beings but that it does not even produce sharp enough minds to be truly scientific.

Finally, I would like to reiterate that the people who stand for the more traditional values of education in no way make the claim that ideas should be cut off from life as it is lived. After all, such great modern traditionalists as Sir Richard Livingstone,[1] President Hutchins,[2] Jacques Maritain,[3] have all shown clearly from their precept and from their conduct that they believe in education very much connected with life. Where they disagree with the Teachers' College, Columbia School, is how best this can be accomplished.

Yours sincerely,
George Grant

*[The original letter Grant submitted is in the CAAE archive. It contains the following passage at the end*: '(I don't really want this to be said but if Dr Corbett wants it I will say it.) Secondly, in your issue I would disagree with certain ideas in Dr Corbett's article. His emphasis on words like "mass education" and "adult education movement" seem dangerous. After all, the mass is only the sum total of the number of individuals and "movement" implies people finding their salvation in one narrow path, with everybody forced to take the same way. In stressing such ideas one is apt to forget the individual, or else to try and stereotype him into some preconceived pattern. The adult educator becomes an emancipated leader directing the unemancipated masses towards his own particular promised land.

Of course all Dr Corbett's work belies this and so does the rest of his article with its emphasis on people finding their own way. His emphasis [is] that the gate to salvation is very wide. But still, let us beware such phrases as "mass" and "movement." Under cover of the democratic sheep's clothing can be seen the authoritarian wolf.']

### Notes

1  Sir Richard Livingstone (1880–1960), British classical scholar and university administrator, championed the liberal arts curriculum. He delivered the Sir Robert Falconer Lectures at the University of Toronto in 1945 and published

them the following year as *On Speaking the Truth*. His works up to 1945 include *The Greek Genius and Its Meaning to Us* (1912), *A Defence of Classical Education* (1916), *The Future in Education* (1941), *Education for a World Adrift* (1943), and *On Education* (1944).

2 Robert Maynard Hutchins (1899–1977), American educator, president and later Chancellor of the University of Chicago (1929–51), and chairman of the Fund for the Republic. See Grant's review of Hutchins's *The Higher Learning in America* (1937) in which Hutchins criticized overspecialization and sought to balance the college curriculum and to maintain the Western intellectual tradition (pp. 6–8; see note 1 there for Hutchins's publications).

3 Jacques Maritain (1882–1973) studied under Bergson and then was converted to Catholicism in 1906, becoming a leading neo-Thomist philosopher. He taught in Paris (beginning in 1914), Toronto, Columbia, Chicago, and Princeton (1948–56). He wrote *Education at the Crossroads* in 1943. Other works up to 1945 include *Elements of Philosophy* (2 vols: 1920, 1923), *Three Reformers* (1925), *On the Christian Philosophy* (1933), and *From Bergson to Thomas Aquinas* (1944).

*Reviews: Oxford and Dalhousie 1948*

# Review of *The Philosophy of Francis Bacon* by F.H. Anderson.[1]

In volume 28, no. 3, of *The Dalhousie Review*, October 1948: 312–13. Anderson's book was published simultaneously by the University of Chicago Press and by W.J. Gage, Toronto. Grant's review was the first public expression of a conception of philosophy that was bound to offend many professors in the established philosophy departments, men like Professor Anderson at the University of Toronto. The attack on Anderson was the first in a series of difficult encounters between Grant and Anderson through the 1950s that culminated in Grant's resignation from York University in 1960. (See Volume 2 of the *Collected Works*.) Anderson was enraged enough about the review to try to get President Alex Kerr of Dalhousie (his alma mater) to censure Grant. President Kerr did not comply.

Today we are faced with the paradoxical situation where the mob accepts as its priesthood those men we call scientists, when at the same time this very priesthood leads the mob shouting to the cliff. It is therefore extremely provoking to read a study of the thought of Francis Bacon, who, as much as any other, stimulated men to that study of nature, which on the one hand has given us ether and penicillin, and on the other hand mass production and scientific war. One may be allowed to say in the present journal that it is especially interesting to read such a study by a distinguished graduate of Dalhousie.

Professor Anderson's study is not a popular essay for those who want to garner a few vague generalizations about Bacon. It is a careful and exact examination of all Bacon's writings. In the last chapter Professor Anderson describes Bacon's contribution to thought under three headings which are worth quoting.

(1) freeing science from learning and the privileges of the learned (2) separating completely truth which is humanly discoverable from the dogmas of revealed theology and (3) propounding a philosophy which is to be achieved by (a) a new sort of scientific organon (b) a 'modern' interpretation of nature and (c) the identification of metaphysics with a generalized natural science based on natural history.

Where one may criticize Professor Anderson is in his failure to judge the limitations of Bacon. The scholar is always called upon for a judgement of worth, and surely in the light of what we know today, the enslavement of Bacon to the optimism of the scientific Renaissance is worth considering more deeply than Professor Anderson attempts. For instance, under point (2) quoted above, what meaning is there in Bacon's attempt to cut off truth humanly discoverable from the revealed dogmas of religion? Its only implication is that the truths of religion are not rational but arbitrary. Therefore it leads to an exaltation of the truths of natural science, and such an exaltation, coupled with man's original sin, leads straight to the grinning mask of scientific humanism at Hiroshima. An even greater criticism of Bacon could be made at the ridiculousness of attempting an identification of metaphysics with natural science, however generalized. This book is a useful study of an earlier philosopher of natural science. It could have been an important one if Professor Anderson had judged how that philosophy had helped to bring us to the barrenness of today.

George Grant

## Notes

1 Fulton Henry Anderson (1895–1968), professor of philosophy and head of the Department of Philosophy at the University of Toronto (1945–63). In addition to this work Anderson published *The Influence of Contemporary Science on Locke's Method and Results* (1923), *The Argument of Plato* (1934), and another book on Bacon entitled *Francis Bacon: His Career and His Thought* (1962). He edited Francis Bacon's *The New Organon and Related Writings* (1960).

# Review of *The Pickersgill Letters: 1934–43* edited by George Ford

In volume 28, no.3, of *The Dalhousie Review*, October 1948: 313–14.
The Pickersgill letters were edited by George Ford and published by the
Ryerson Press. Grant's sister Alison had been a close friend of Frank
Pickersgill's. Frank's brother was John Whitney (Jack) Pickersgill, a histo-
rian who taught at Wesley College, Winnipeg, and a highly influential
public servant and Liberal politician during the King and St Laurent eras.

These are the letters of a young Canadian who in the war of 1939–45
worked gallantly for the French underground and was found at the
end of the war beaten and tortured on a butcher's hook at Buchen-
wald. They are the record of the pilgrimage of this North American,
from the easy hopeful years in the 1930s as a student at the University
of Manitoba, to his full decision for prodigious courage before the evil
and horror of the war of the 1940s. The letters are in the simple terms
one uses for letters home and to one's friends, so that much is left
unsaid. Yet through them and behind them, one can feel as they
develop the pulse of a man called by his conscience to a terrible agony.

The first letters are about Frank Pickersgill's life at the Universities
of Manitoba and Toronto. He was eager and ardent; yet like his generation cynical and bewildered, because of the depression and because he
did not know what to do with his life. He tells of his first trip to Europe
with the superficial admiration for the Nazis and his despising of the
French. He recounts his discovery that militarism was really wicked
and brutal and that in the solid love of the individual, as he found it in
the French, lay the basic hope for human beings. He writes to his family of his imprisonment by the Germans and his miraculous and exciting escape to England. The letters end with his decision to be

parachuted back into France, as an agent of the underground. Such a decision he took freely, swayed only by the desire to do what he considered the only right. He took it knowing deeply that it meant the probability of death. That death he met.

Moral courage such as Pickersgill's is a virtue before which one can only bow. There is only one greater – charity. That he had as well. It is the final condemnation of our epoch that he was forced to employ those virtues in the viciousness of war.[1] It is his glory that he did so employ them.

**Note**

1 The original review contains the following sentence at this point in the text: 'It is his glory that he was forced to employ those virtues in the viciousness of war.' Probably an error was made during the typing or typesetting stages. It seems highly unlikely, though not impossible, that Grant meant to include the sentence we have deleted. If that were the case, he might have been making the point that the truth that men like Pickersgill were forced to fight in the viciousness of war was both the condemnation of the epoch and the occasion of such men's glory, adding with the final sentence that Pickersgill rose to the occasion.

# Review of *The Function of the University* by R.S. Seeley[1]

Appeared in volume 9, issue 3, of *Food For Thought*, December 1948: 43–4. Seeley's book was published by Oxford University Press, Toronto, 1948.

This short book is both sensible and middle of the road. All the right and proper attitudes about universities are solemnly and solidly upheld. One may well believe that if one took a poll on education from university teachers, found its common denominator, and put it into pleasant literary form, one would be close to this book. The perplexing questions, general to all our universities, are carefully raised. How can the calibre of work be maintained, when the democratic community says that, on the one hand, all should be worthy of the opportunity of a university education and, on the other, proclaims the condition of that opportunity to be prosperous parents? What is the responsibility of the university for producing useful technicians, what for producing educated men? Is it possible to blend these two jobs? What is the responsibility of teachers to relate the knowledge they teach to certain dogmas without which decent life is not possible? These very real questions and many others are competently raised by Provost Seeley. Anybody who does not recognize them as problems will do well to read his book.

However, what makes this book disappointing to this reviewer is that it never asks the profounder question of what is possible for our Canadian universities, in this year of our ice-age 1948. It seems to be always a sign of a civilization's decline that the idealist proclaims his ideals with clarity, but outside the possible; while even more blindly the tough men of action pursue their petty self-interests, fooling themselves that it is realistic. This book is a clear statement of an ideal; but quite without any lucid or searching attempt to relate that ideal to the possible.

Take, for instance, the question of the government of our universities, which must surely be central to the possibility of any achievement. Provost Seeley talks pleasantly about the necessity for businessmen and professors to recognize each others' problems. But at no place does he mention the inescapable facts that Canadian universities are run by businessmen and that they serve a community where among all classes the ethic of material success is overwhelmingly predominant. Can either of these facts be doubted by anybody who knows the score? And they mean two things. First, that since the direction in which an institution is tending is set by who have final sovereignty, the direction of the university will be set by the businessmen. Secondly, that the community will welcome that direction. How then is Provost Seeley's ideal in any way possible? When the ends of the sovereign authorities will be respectability and, even more, technical efficiency, how can they also be something else? To put it practically, however much talk there is about the deeper spiritual realities at a university, one will be able to guarantee that the physics department will grow and grow, in relation to philosophy. Because he does not face these depressing problems squarely, there is a note of unreality about Provost Seeley`s book. It would be truly fantastic to write as if a University of Paris would be possible in a Russia governed by the Kremlin. It is only slightly less so to believe that a seventeenth-century Cambridge is possible in Canada today.

To sum up, this book is a clear and well-intentioned statement of an ideal which reconciles the best in all possible worlds satisfactorily for all concerned. It may be a help and an inspiration for some. It will only harm those who are convinced by Provost Seeley that his moderate ends can be easily achieved in this immoderate age.

George Grant

**Note**

1  Reginald Sidney Kingsley Seeley (1908–1957), Anglican priest (1932) and educator, came to Canada from England (1938) and became Provost and

Vice-Chancellor of Trinity College, Toronto after 1945. *The Idea of the University* contained the Hazen Lectures delivered at the Hazen Conference at North Hatley in June 1947. Seeley also published *The Sign of the Cross: A Meditation on the Place of the Cross in Human Living* (1945).

*DPhil Thesis: Oxford 1950*

# The Concept of Nature and Supernature in the Theology of John Oman

## EDITORS' INTRODUCTION

Grant's doctoral (DPhil) thesis, written in 1949 and 1950, is an important work because it establishes the point of departure of his thought. He chose the subject of the Scottish theologian and philosopher of religion John Oman (1860–1939), but Grant's thesis interests us not merely for the light it sheds on the Scottish thinker, but for what it reveals about Grant himself, just as his encounters over the years with Plato, Augustine, Kant, Hegel, Nietzsche, Heidegger, Ellul, Strauss, and Weil revealed as much about Grant as about the thinkers with whom he was engaged. In the theological context of his examination of Oman, Grant was posing his own questions for the first time, the questions he would raise in his classes, and later in the moral, political, and philosophical arguments of *Lament for a Nation* and *Technology and Empire*.

How did Grant decide on the topic of Oman? What can we learn about his relation to the European theological and philosophical traditions by looking at his examination of Oman? What was Grant's early theological position, and how did he understand the relation of his theology to the philosophical questions he was asking at the time of the thesis? And finally, how does Grant's work on Oman cast light on his lasting position – an agnostic believer, a moral egalitarian, a pacifist, an ambivalent critic of liberal modernity, and a Christian Platonist who argued the case for forgiveness not from the safe haven of eternal certainty but inside the doubt and despair of the modern world?

## I. Grant's Choice of Oman as Topic

Grant took up the topic of John Oman at the suggestion of A.D. Lindsay, the Master of Balliol. Grant said in a 1945 letter that he considered the topic 'a pin' on which he could hang his two years of reading Descartes, Plato, Aristotle, Calvin, Luther, St Thomas, Marx, Freud, and his favourite of the moment, Pascal.[1] The main body of the work was written after his first two years of teaching at Dalhousie University (1947–9), and he finished the writing in England during a leave of absence in the summer of 1949, when he was thirty years old. L.W. Grensted was Grant's supervisor, while Austin Farrer was an examiner and presided at his oral defence.

As indicated by its title, 'The Concept of Nature and Supernature in the Theology of John Oman,' the thesis contains an evaluation of Oman's 'philosophy of religion,' particularly as it is presented in his major work, The Natural and the Supernatural. In that book, Oman undertook nothing less than a comprehensive account of God, nature, and human beings, attempting to reconcile his traditional faith with the insights of the liberal theological tradition of Friedrich Schleiermacher and Albrecht Ritschl. Grant examined Oman's 'metaphysic' systematically, thereby commenting on Oman's treatment of a broad range of subjects, including science, history, art, morality, politics, nature, God, and human persons. According to Oman, human beings, in their encounter with nature, 'sense the holy' in it, 'judge it to be sacred,' believe thereby in a 'supernatural reality' that underlies it, and then act with 'moral reverence' accordingly. Oman thought about the way human beings, nature, and the supernatural belong to a unified whole.

Grant had turned to philosophy and theology to make sense of his experiences during the Second World War. He was trying to comprehend how evil (identified for him especially with the horrors of the London Blitz) could be reconciled with accepting the world as the creation of a loving God (as he himself had done, after his conversion). He sought in Oman's work a philosophy that would 'meet the cry of men bewildered by their period.' He counted himself among the bewildered, and believed also that his students at Dalhousie, while lacking his experience of the Blitz, were confused or uprooted from their religious traditions, and thus needed a philosophy that would respond to their confusion as they were drawn into mass secular society.

## II. Grant's Bearings in The Context of European Theological and Philosophical Traditions

Grant formulated the main questions that would inform his teaching at

Dalhousie during the 1950s, in part through a response to the philosophical and theological traditions of modern Europe. We can see him working on his own approach to basic questions as he examined Oman's encounters – with the British empirical tradition derived from Locke and Hume, with Kant, with the post-Kantian theologians, and with Hegel and the idea of history. Grant's thesis shows that Plato and St Augustine had become central figures for him. Their ideas provided a ground as he encountered the modern thinkers.

As he examined Oman, Grant began to lay the foundations of his critique of the British empiricist tradition derived from Locke and Hume. Oman had opposed the empiricists, or the 'naturalist' philosophers as they were called in the thesis, along with the scientists with whom they were allied. He had simply asserted a different experience of things. He argued that the 'naturalists' are not describing our actual experience, that they are sacrificing our true experience of nature in order to obtain the benefits of practical manipulation.

Grant pointed out that Oman came from the Orkneys to teach at Cambridge. There he was surrounded by the vigorous scientific and secular intellectual culture that had engulfed and overwhelmed the traditional faith and the simpler world in which he had grown up. His 'philosophy of religion' was an attempt to build a bridge between the two worlds. A man of faith was addressing the secular, empiricist culture on the issue of the validity of the religious vision of human beings in relation to their natural and supernatural surroundings.

Grant felt Oman underestimated the difficulties of making his theological case in a world firmly committed to scientific empiricism. The clash of the two worlds was deeper than Oman could see, ironically because he was a man of such exemplary faith and morality. When trying to communicate with secular people, one could not simply assume a different primary experience as a starting point. It was insufficient to defy the firmly established analytical empiricism by asserting an account of the experience of God or supernature as an indispensable part of a holistic, metaphysical understanding of things. Grant believed that we must find a way to understand God, nature, and human beings within a unified philosophy. But he saw the weaknesses of Oman's approach, and spent his years at Dalhousie trying to find more adequate ways to put the case to modern people. Oman, for example, was 'not rigorous enough in the sharpening of knives' when he attacked the sceptics; he often didn't bother to define his concepts properly, and so weakened his case.

Grant knew that secular civilization is committed to human autonomy without God, and to science, technology, and industry guided only by human purposes. Faith, he argued, has to engage this position head-on, while at the same time acknowledging how strong the modern experience and its arguments have become. Grant's thesis was a preliminary effort to address a problem facing a Christian philosopher such as himself. Could he put forward a Christian philosophy that was true to its principles and also communicate effectively to modern people whose starting point was not the Christian faith?

At the time of the thesis and during the 1950s at Dalhousie, Kant was easily the most important modern philosopher for Grant. He was drawn to him primarily because of his moral philosophy, the defence of duty and self-control, the supremacy of reason over sensuous inclination – the side of Kant compatible with Christian Platonism. (Later, in the 1970s, he would focus on the side of Kant whose teaching on human autonomy or freedom as self-legislation had dealt a death blow to the older tradition of virtue as obedience to a divine order.) At this stage, Kant was still the influential giant who stood behind nineteenth-century thought; who had set the scene for the Protestant theology and philosophy that followed him. Protestant theologians respected him because he established strict limits for both modern reason and traditional theological propositions. He argued convincingly that we are finite beings who cannot know nature as it is in itself through science because the categories of time and space belong to our minds and are imposed on nature. Nor can we know God or the infinite through pure reason. We do, however, know how to act morally, because we know that we are subject to duty. And thus we can know God through practical reason, from our own experiences of the moral law inscribed in the conscience of all human beings.

Is our human existence a moral one? And, if this is so, are we therefore religious by implication? Are we able to act morally only because we are religious? Or are we able to act morally even if we are no longer religious? Or do neither of these two positions do justice to our moral and religious existence? These questions became permanent points of reference in Grant's explorations in the 1950s. In his thesis, Grant agreed with Oman's attack on Kant's view of religion. Oman argued that human freedom as self-legislation could have no content without a religious starting point. To him it was clear: we have to be religious to have grounds for our morality. Nonetheless, Grant's teaching during the 1950s was deeply shaped by

Kant's moral philosophy; in the world as it had become in 1950, he found Kant more compelling for his students than Oman's insistence that morality must begin with religion. Kant allowed Grant to argue for absolute morality and practical reason to those students who no longer saw the world, and their place in it, from within a religious tradition.

Grant's response to the liberal Protestant theology of Schleiermacher and Ritschl, especially to their use of the language of 'persons' in defence of the experience of faith, shows that in the early years he agreed with their focus on free moral and religious individual beings. He speaks of the 'personalist categories of the Gospel' and sees the necessity of doing battle with the 'impersonalist categories of post-Renaissance philosophy and science.' And at this time he is also using Hermann Lotze's philosophical defence of non-scientific estimations of value which are thought to yield objective 'values.'

For those who know Grant's later work, it is surprising to find him identifying as much as he does with the language of 'persons' and 'personality,' and, closely related, with Lotze's language of subjective and objective 'values.' Grant claimed, for example, that a Platonic/Kantian position such as his own begins by asserting 'a hierarchy of values,' a phrase we cannot imagine him using in the 1970s. We know that he became a strong critic of the contemporary liberal use of 'persons' and 'values,' because he saw how well these words fitted into the technological paradigm he was opposing. A look back at the earlier use of the terms, however – a look back at the spirit that brought them forth – perhaps explains why Grant embraced them in 1950, and also why he would come to find them wanting.

Both the language of persons and the language of values were brought forward in nineteenth-century theology and philosophy to defend the experience of faith against two enemies which threatened to marginalize it. These enemies were dogmatic theology, consisting of propositions rather than experience, and, on the secular side, the growing conviction that enlightened human reason could solve all problems. The two languages were part of a movement which tried to articulate the experience of individual beings whose choices determine their destinies within the context of an eternal destiny.

A century later, however, advancing technology and the shattering experiences of war and class struggle would cause many theologians and philosophers to see the language of persons, by itself, as too private. And many came to see estimations of value as mere subjective preferences, rather than evidence of what is given. Viewed in that way, the terms could no longer do justice to the experience of moral duty, let alone to faith as the bridge to God. Grant himself would come to see the two languages as part of the world they were supposed to resist.

In the thesis, Grant was also beginning to work out his response to Hegel and the idea of history. He agreed with Oman's attack on Hegel and the Hegelians for submerging the individual in great historical movements. He also rejected Hegel's historical justification of the suffering of individuals as part of 'the cunning of reason' – a triumphal rationality which works itself out historically. At the same time, however, he criticized Oman's own understanding of history as inadequate. He thought Hegel's conception of history was better, in one respect, than the liberal doctrine of history as progress. Where progress assumed that science and capital were leading us to a paradise on earth, Hegel at least included a rejection of the immorality of the world. And history, for him, was driven by human beings seeking to overcome the evils of their situation.

A conception of history should honour the experience of free individual human beings (including their attempts to change the world) and hence recognize the threat to individual freedom posed by 'the mass age,' as Grant would come to call it in the 1950s. Without such an understanding, Oman, like many of the Christian thinkers of his day, was left by default with liberal progress. He ended up becoming too easily reconciled with contemporary liberal civilization. Grant saw a key component of his own philosophic task posed in that dilemma. On the one hand, he found the idea of progress wanting; on the other, he believed the alternative Hegel and Marx offered was wrong about individuality and faith, though morally and politically superior to liberalism on other grounds. The task of philosophy, therefore, was to find a new conception of history, one that could acknowledge the need to change the world, while at the same time constraining human freedom within moral limits.

## III. Grant on the Relation of Faith and Theology to Philosophy

Grant began to think carefully about the relation of faith and theology to philosophy while coming to grips with Oman's philosophy of religion. And he would continue to find the relation difficult through all the years of his teaching and writing because he was a Christian teaching in a secular university. He did not wish to forsake his faith, and yet he was not content to communicate only to a Christian audience. He was a Christian Platonist, as Oman was. He therefore accepted and lived by the principle articulated by Augustine and Anselm: *Credo ut intelligam* – I believe in order to understand. But at the same time he always tried to communicate to his students and readers in terms they could understand, faith or no faith. His students at Dalhousie were drawn to an engaged philosopher rather than to a theologian, though it was also true to say that his theological starting point was an essential part of his approach to philosophy. He did not put aside his faith in order to 'do philosophy,' or to teach philosophy professionally.

Grant argued that Oman's philosophy of religion could be understood only within the context of his faith, as expressed in his account of the crucifixion in the theological works. But Oman, he says, did not make this important truth clear in his philosophy of religion, that his starting point had been faith. Grant said that this 'failure of exposition, rather than of content' is the chief criticism he would make of Oman. This failure made Oman's case look weaker than it was. Clearly, Grant hoped he would be able to make faith the explicit starting point of his own philosophy. He was to find out just how difficult such an approach had become when he tried to put it into practice in the secular universities of the 1950s and 1960s.

Grant's thesis in 1950 is the only major early work (except for the shorter 'Two Theological Languages' in 1952) in which he discusses theological matters systematically. He provides an exegesis of Oman, but we are conscious of his own voice throughout. He evaluates Oman's strategies and methods, stating his outright objections to some of his positions. Reading carefully, we can also see where he is agreeing, even when he doesn't say so explicitly. By gathering together his positive and negative responses to Oman, we arrive at what we might call 'Grant's early theological position.'

Caution is required, however. Grant never claimed to be a theologian. Moreover his thinking about these theological questions continued to evolve over the years, and was certainly not fixed even at this early stage. Nonetheless it is fair to say that he always had theology in mind when he was teaching, or writing and talking on the radio. This is true even though in most works, theology is mentioned only in passing, and is not discussed extensively until 'Faith and the Multiversity' in 1986.

In the first paragraph of the abstract of the thesis, Grant suggests that Oman's philosophy of religion should be read within the context of his 'theologia crucis' or 'theology of the cross.' What did this designation mean? First, he did not mean that Oman used that term about his own work, but rather that he, Grant, thought the work deserved the name of the theological approach Martin Luther set out and defined in his Heidelberg Theses of 1518. Luther defended the theology of the cross there, against what he called 'the theology of glory.' The essential elements of his argument, for our purposes, are set out in Theses 19–24.[2] We know from Grant's letter from Oxford to his mother in November 1945 that he greatly admired Luther among the Reformers, perhaps partly because he, like Luther, had been near despair 'in a great tribulation,' searched 'with all his heart and soul and need,' and found 'a gracious God.'[3] The theology of the cross meant to Luther – and Grant – something broader than a reference to the crucifixion, or a doctrine of atonement. It meant that one could know the love and forgiveness of the gracious God only through 'faith,' that is, through receptive trust and openness to Christ's Passion as a revelation of that love. The theologians of glory believed that humans could reach the truth about God and his purposes in the world through speculative reason and human will. Luther, instead of this, insisted that they must start with an understanding of God that is seen through the suffering of Christ, so that when they turned to the power and glory of God in the world, they would not misuse 'the best things,' that is, human speculative reason and law, 'in the worst manner.' When Luther stated in Thesis 18 that 'it is certain that man must utterly despair of his own ability before he is prepared to receive the grace of Christ,' he had in mind the need to break the arrogant egos of the scholastic theologians and princes of the church. By overestimating human powers and the triumph of God in the world, they also underestimated evil and the great gulf between God and the world as it actually is.

Grant would often quote the 21st Heidelberg Thesis in later years: 'The theologian of glory says that evil is good and good evil; the theologian of the cross says that the thing is as it is.' The scholastic theologians made the mistake of claiming that evils are 'justified' as part of God's providential plan. Grant not only agreed with Luther's critique of these theologians; he carried the opposition over to secular believers in the doctrine of historical progress through human effort (along with their Christian allies). He hated the idea that the suffering that comes from war, for example, could somehow be seen as 'justified' for the sake of progress.

What then is the understanding of God that is revealed in the crucifixion according to Grant? He agreed with Oman that Christ, by the way he bore the cross, revealed how God's love and forgiveness had entered into the suffering and injustice of the world. Both argued that individual human beings can partake of this forgiveness and hence know God's world as good, albeit in a mysterious way that cannot be explained. They are saved from despair, and from what Luther called 'secret anger against God and hurt to oneself;' they see the world with its afflictions and joys as what it is.

Two central implications of this theology of the cross which stayed with Grant permanently deserve special attention. He agreed essentially with Oman about both of them. First there is the conviction that Christians must be 'agnostic,' and, second, the assertion that our inability to explain God is a necessary presupposition for a belief in moral equality. By the word 'agnostic' Grant and Oman meant to emphasize the doctrine that God's providence must be, for us, an ambiguous mystery, not a truth we possess and can define. The good is often not visible to us, and God's providence is inscrutable. Without such an honest agnosticism, we are led to trivialize evil, and to caricature God as a 'confederate of our petty adventurings.'[4]

The essence of the Gospel was for both Oman and Grant a firm basis for moral equality. Grant was not as inclined as Oman was to carry moral egalitarianism into secular politics and art. He was beginning to work out the position he later expressed in 'An Ethic of Community' (1960), that the principle of hierarchy which arises from the diversity of talents must be balanced against the principle of equality which arises from the absolute worth of each individual. Every human being is equal in God's sight, and salvation through loving forgiveness is open to all, regardless of their circumstances and their moral and intellectual abilities. Salvation, therefore, cannot be the special dispensation of the theologians, philosophers, or clerics in possession of true doctrine. Grant, incidentally, believed that classical philosophy had been wrong about equality and had been corrected by Christianity. He also found that some modern philosophers were superior to the ancients in this respect, in spite of other failings.

The strength of the cross, as Grant saw it, included the coming of forgiveness not only to the faithful but also to those in despair. Here he found Oman weak. He argued that Oman was not enough aware of the depth of the despair in Christ's cry that he had been forsaken, and thus also not enough aware of the extremity of modern despair and doubt; of the difficulty modern people have in accepting the leap of faith demanded by Christianity. A philosophy that seeks to reach modern people must be aware of that despair. The cross could help bewildered moderns, Grant argued, because it did not deny the desolation and doubt that have followed in the wake of the shattering experiences of this period. 'It is this failure to understand despair at its most terrible that prevents Oman from using that language about the Cross that sees it as a beacon in a world of darkness.' In his teaching Grant adopted the approach of plunging into the modern way of thinking with its doubt and despair in order to uphold the morality of Jesus and Socrates. He thought that the alternative approach – arguing from within the faith – was not as effective, though easier on the practitioner.

Grant stated that Oman's greatest work was written about 'strength through weakness.' He applauded Oman for his claim that such a stance is the best way to confront the evils of the world. Oman followed St Paul in arguing for weakening the arrogance of the human will to make way for the strength of God's grace. Grant thought Oman's pacifist students were justified in believing that he would recommend withdrawal from participation in the state when Britain went to war in 1914. They were right to be shocked when Oman did the opposite.

According to Grant, Oman's thought contained a conflict between what he (Grant) praised as 'quietism,' which, he said, should have led to a pacifist stance in 1914, and what he called 'liberalism,' which had actually won out in Oman's mind in 1914. The word 'quietism,' as Grant used it, does not mean a passive or apolitical withdrawal from the world, but rather a detachment from the purposes of the state when they were in conflict with Christian principles. The word 'liberalism,' used here in relation to Oman, could be misleading if we take it out of the context of nineteenth-century German theology, or early-twentieth-century English theological debate. Oman was not a 'liberal' in the more radical contemporary use of the word, referring to such men as Harvey Cox or the 'God is dead' theologians.

For Grant, the problem of Oman's 'liberalism' was defined by his acceptance of progress in The War and Its Issues. In that work, Oman argued that the war was necessary for the progress of Western civilization, and that his students should enlist and support the British state in its execution of the war effort. 'In the moment of decision,' Grant says of Oman, 'his quietism did not stand before his honest belief in the Christian's responsibility to the state.' Grant himself would continue to believe that strength through weakness was best, however difficult it was to live up to it.

As Grant worked out his differences with Oman, he was beginning to understand the difficult relation between his own religious convictions and the progressive liberalism with which he had grown up. In a letter to his sister Margaret in the early 1950s, he said, 'What Plato is teaching me is not that I disagree with the tradition of liberalism in which I was raised, but that the tradition in which I was raised hadn't sufficiently examined itself to find on what principles it did exist.' Grant agreed with Oman's insistence on the liberal principle of human freedom and responsibility. Human beings are dependent on God in a way that demands a kind of moral independence, though this independence differed from Kant's notion of self-legislation. But at the same time he thought that Oman should have made clear just how his liberal account of religion was governed, limited, and grounded by faith.

The strength of Grant's opposition to Oman's liberal Protestant Christianity (and also his continuing attachment to it) is shown in his stated reason for not publishing his DPhil thesis. In a 1986 letter to Peter Self, an old friend of his Oxford days, he wrote:

> I always refused to turn my thesis on a great liberal theologian into a book because I did not want to produce a book which patronized a tradition which is admirable but fundamentally failing because it did not face the profound division between Christianity and progressivism (in its best, its liberal form). I tried at one point to write something about a Canadian politician of the 19th century, Joseph Howe (because once both my father and grandfather had written lives of him), and yet when I came up to doing it I felt I could not write it without some ridicule of Howe's liberalism and I did not want to do that.

Arthur Davis

## ABSTRACT OF THESIS [GEORGE GRANT]

'Nature and Supernature' is the fundamental concept of John Oman's philosophy of religion. That philosophy, found in his book *The Natural and the Supernatural*, should be read within the context of his 'theologia crucis,' which is given in his earlier theological writings.[1] Oman's faith is that Our Lord on the Cross reveals the Father as Love, Who demands from men that they take up their crosses in forgiveness. The Father's Love and man's freedom to partake of it are the essence of Christianity. All else is but relative and changing.

In so embarking on a philosophy of religion that is regulated by faith, Oman is attempting to reconcile the challenge of the Gospel with its rationality. His certainty that its truth is not dependent on the approval of metaphysicians is combined with his consciousness that it is his duty to explain to the world in reasonable terms the character of that Gospel. For there to be purpose in discussing his philosophy of religion, tentative agreement must be given to the possibility of such an undertaking against those who believe in the corruption of all 'unredeemed' judgment, and against those who believe that the philosophy of religion should be based not on faith but on 'natural evidence.' In saying this it may be regretted that Oman does not make more explicit in *The Natural and the Supernatural* its dependence upon faith. Consequently it would not be difficult to overemphasise his debt to and connections with the traditions of European secular rationalism.

As a preliminary to the account of Oman's philosophy of religion, the bare course of his life and writings between 1860–1939 is described in relation to his involvement in the traditions of modern Europe. Without suggesting determinism about a man of Oman's originality, he may be seen more clearly in the light of the contrast between the Biblical faith of his Orkney childhood and the secular philosophy current in his day. Though he scorns the scholarly reference, his immense reading in the field of post-Kantian liberal theology may be seen in his debts to Lotze's realism,[2] Schleiermacher's theology of feeling,[3] and Ritschl's Christocentric scorn of metaphysics.[4] Oman's reaction against Hegelian speculation may be the better understood when it is remembered that he was a practising minister till his forty-seventh year. The change in his writings from the simple Gospel, addressed to those within the Church, to the philosophy of religion addressed to the world may be partly explained by his experience in Cambridge, where he spent the last third of his life. In this atmosphere he saw how deep was the necessity for a metaphysics which would show to men dominated by their visions of the world as 'things' or 'life' or even 'spirit' how the most real and important world was that of 'persons.' By his response to the European catastrophe of 1914 the practical substance of his ethics is clarified.

Oman's metaphysics is approached by describing his account of how the supernatural makes its appearance to consciousness. The fitness of this approach may be justified by Oman's belief that speculation must always necessarily proceed from an already held hierarchy of values. He does not believe it possible to assume only the self-evident. He lays down that men know the supernatural environment as meaning and that that meaning depends on the unique character of the feeling it evokes, which he calls 'the sense of the holy;' and on the absolute value men find in it, which he calls 'the judgment of the sacred.' The immediate conviction of a special kind of objective reality inseparable from this valuation he calls 'the supernatural.' Oman does not analyse or describe the far-reaching assumptions underlying these seemingly simple terms which he uses in his own particular way. The advantage of this failure to analyse his terms is that he takes the reader straight into his brilliant use of them; the disadvantage is the resultant ambiguity in his groundwork, some of which is later clarified but much of which is not.

With these terms Oman embarks on a profound discussion of the relation of religious dependence to moral independence, or what he calls in his theology 'the problem of grace and personality.' The sense of the holy, given with and through our contemplation of the natural, is the pioneer in presenting men with absolute values. Only, however, as the will responds to those insights by freely employing them in the natural, does our sense of the holy change from awe to reverence. He describes the interdependence of the two relations to the supernatural, action and contemplation. Rightness in action is described as 'faithfulness,' true contemplation as 'sincerity of feeling.' After disposing of the naturalist and Hegelian accounts of the moral judgment, the relation of the holy to the sacred is illuminated by a comparison with the Kantian account of the moral judgment. Kant's brilliant understanding of the categorical quality of ideal values does not save his ethics from legalism, consequent on his account of personality simply as an autonomy of volition and not also an autonomy of insight. Its weakness as criticism lies in its obscurity about the relation of ideal to natural values, as compared with the clarity of Kant's imperious duty.

Oman's account of the appearance of the natural to consciousness centres on his description of 'awareness' and 'apprehension.' Through these faculties we are given nature as it is in itself, as compared with 'comprehension' and 'explanation' which allow us to deal with nature for our own purposes. The rationalist epistemologies of nature fail to do justice to those elements of knowing in which children and poets excel. By sensitiveness of awareness we are given the natural in its dependence upon the holy; in sincerity of apprehension there flash up those ideal values by which we may deal with the natural. Nature is then the symbolism through which God speaks to us and by which we reply to Him. Its very mystery, however, must tell us that it is more than that. It is regretted that Oman's radically personalist conception of nature is not made sufficiently explicit in *The Natural and the Supernatural*, but must be [seen to be] implied from his other work and from the writings of his pupil Professor H.H. Farmer.[5]

Nature and supernature, so related and distinguished, cannot be conceived apart from one another. Equally they can only be conceived in relation to Oman's concept of man. With these three terms and their relationship, Oman passes beyond monism and dualism to give his account of 'prophetic monotheism.' Monism, according to Oman, whether religious or philosophical, is motivated by the attempt to avoid the conflicts of the world by sinking back into the undifferentiated sense of the holy. Thus the natural and persons are submerged in the supernatural. No proper place is allowed for the suffering and striving of the world. Such theology must either disregard it or despair about it. On the other hand, dualist solutions, whether explicitly as in Persia or incipiently in the philosophy of Kant, conceive personality as the performance of atomic acts of freedom detached from man's insight into the supernatural and his consciousness of the natural. So the supernatural is conceived as a Judge meting out rewards or punishments. Morality becomes a legalism without trust,[6] not the glorious liberty of the children of God. In the interplay of theory and practice the world becomes less and less conceived as all God's.

The prophets, particularly Hosea, first strove to overcome that dualism. They found that revelation through the natural and reconciliation to the natural were reciprocal. Thus they came more and more to understand that forgiveness in which the world could all be dealt with as the Father's. Our Lord's Life and Death finally reveals that prophetic monotheism in all its fullness. Our Lord's forgiveness of those who tortured and degraded Him reveals that God's Nature cannot be less glorious than that vision. Men can in that light find joy in the world by the knowledge that all can be redeemed. Dualism remains for all men a standing problem, but it need never be accepted as a solution. The conclusion of Oman's metaphysic is just the simple Gospel of the Father's Love and His children's freedom.

To understand what Oman means by the supernatural the attempt must be made to fathom what he makes of the concept 'history.' This question cannot be answered in terms of his classification of religions in *The Natural and the Supernatural*, for that is in essence the arrangement of historical phenomena in the light of an already held metaphysics, not a theology of history. It can be answered only in terms of the Christology found elsewhere. Oman will not define the Being of Christ beyond St Paul's phrase: 'God was in Christ reconciling the world unto Himself.' Simply because of the Passion, to which the Resurrection adds nothing essential, men can know the Mind of God and, therefore, trust that all history is to good purpose and will have a final glorious consummation. But no particular doctrinal statements about these matters is of the essence of the Gospel. Such a quietist trust is not ahistoric in any Greek sense, but it cannot affirm any scheme of history. Oman is here unclear about the relation between the consummation on the Cross and the doctrine of progress, acceptance of which seems often to be implied in his writings.

A practical theologian can fairly be judged by his theology of politics. Though Oman writes on no subject more voluminously than on the Church, his politics are not concrete. In his doctrine of the Church there is a practical contradiction between his assertion that the Church should be the fellowship of the saints, leaving all issues of power with God, and the belief that the religious life should be just the ordinary life well lived. This is partly determined by his interpretation of the relation between the thought of the Reformers and the men of the Renaissance and *Aufklärung*. Oman seems to underestimate the value and necessity of tradition. What he means by denial and possession of the natural is also complicated by his contradictory statements about the possibility of creative politics for the Christian.

In 1914 his liberalism triumphed over his quietism. Despite his criticism of Kant's failure to take account of the varieties of function, Oman gives no principles under which men can attempt to reconcile their vocations with the demands of the Kingdom of God, except his *'logique du coeur.'* Particularly in a practical theologian who is not greatly concerned with speculative cosmology, a failure of analysis at this point is to be regretted.

Oman's philosophy of religion is not, in the late Professor Laird's phrase, open to audit by reason alone.[7] Men do not know the Truth only by clearheadedness but also by sincerity of feeling and faithfulness in action. It is possible to say of Oman: here are failures of analysis, here exasperating silences, here opaqueness of style and a simple vocabulary covering obscurities. One must either accept or reject his central faith. From that acceptance or rejection one must consider the possibility of such a Christian philosophy of religion, dependent on faith yet appealing to the image of God in all men. Must a challenging and a rational Gospel be ever in complete contradiction? As that question is answered in the negative, Oman's philosophy of religion is judged a remarkable attempt to make visible the world of persons in Christian terms and in relation to other worlds. It meets the cry of men bewildered by their period. With a sensitivity that is strong and an individuality concerned with essentials, he holds consistently together his faith in the Majesty of God's Love and in the dignity of man to know that Love in autonomy of action and contemplation.

## THE CONCEPT OF NATURE AND SUPERNATURE IN THE THEOLOGY OF JOHN OMAN – A THESIS BY G.P. GRANT.

### CONTENTS

CHAPTER I

John Oman employs the concept 'nature and supernature' as the main instrument by which to expound his philosophy of religion, as found in *The Natural and the Supernatural*, published in 1931.* In analysing that concept it must be laid down from the start that Oman's philosophy of religion cannot be understood except within the context of his faith. The Augustinian and Anselmian formula of 'Believe so that you may know' Oman accepted not as a justification of obscurantism or as a denial of the value of intellectual activity, but as a realisation that for the Christian there is a necessary subservience of that activity to Christian experience.

Before proceeding therefore to the analysis of Oman's concept of 'nature and supernature,' something must be said about the content of his faith and how it regulated his philosophy of religion. Oman's faith centres on his vision of the Cross. In taking upon Himself the agony of Gethsemane and Golgotha and turning those events into the service of His Father's Will, Our Lord Jesus Christ reveals to us that even the bitterest of life's appointments are from the Father. Thus can men find the only monotheism that does not shirk the problem of theodicy. Because of Golgotha, men are not presented with the alternative of a dualist despair or a monist failure of compassionate imagination. The sublimity of Our Lord forgiving those who tortured and degraded Him, does not allow Oman, if he is to hope at all, to believe that God's Nature could be less glorious than that. Belief that forgiveness is the crown of all man's activity determines all that Oman wrote. In that vision, God is revealed as an infinity of care for each person, as He Who seeks us while we are yet sinners. The simple Gospel of the Cross[1] which is Oman's theology thus reconciles hope with demand, for in revealing to men the Father, Our Lord at the same time challenges men to take up their own crosses, to follow Him in that mystery of forgiveness of which there is no end. Oman is a practical theologian who calls upon men to recognise the supremacy of charity, and declares to those of weaker heart that as they choose to be reconciled the riches of God's grace will be revealed to them. The essence of the Christian faith is simply this forgiveness. All else – doctrine, Church order, and even sacraments – are not of the essence.

* See bibliography, Appendix B.

That Oman's 'theologia crucis' regulates his philosophy of religion must be stated unequivocally, because it is not made clear in *The Natural and the Supernatural*. Because he does not do so, there is a danger of minimising his reaction against secular rationalism on this issue, and so exposing him unfairly to that criticism of rationalist pretensions that has characterised Christian thought of the Augustinian tradition. From the assumptions as to method in *The Natural and the Supernatural* and the fact that its metaphysical conclusion is just the simple Gospel put in different language, the dependence of that work on faith may be confidently asserted. How unfortunate therefore that the clear statements of that dependence are only to be found elsewhere in his work. The following is one of these affirmations.

> And when we find one whose bearing was wholly right, in utter emancipation of soul from the blindness of worldly prudence and the fetters of evil desire, who with the absolute courage of faith walked ever in the unseen and eternal, theology thinks it has found its right beginning, the attitude in which it can hope to have good success, the freedom and the emancipation whereby it can interpret to man the higher realm of his possibility, which is essentially a world of freedom in larger truth and more far-reaching aspiration.*

Oman therefore in no wise affirms that human *scientia* must be the critique of all that God can give us to know. To speculate about the philosophy of religion must never be even to hint that the authenticity of the Gospel is at the mercy of the metaphysicians. The venturing saint knows more than another of God's grace. Nor is it possible in writing a philosophy of religion to push aside the visions with which the writer has been blessed for the duration of speculation. To seem to do so is dishonest. *The Natural and the Supernatural* is not concerned with 'natural theology,' if that contentious phrase is defined as cosmological speculation within the present state of logical and scientific studies, claiming agreement from men of clear intellect.

Yet the fact that Oman wrote *The Natural and the Supernatural* is evidence of his belief in the value of rational speculation about religion.

---

* Article 'Method in Theology,' 1923, from *The Expositor* [8th Series, p. 92]. See bibliography, p. ii.

He did not rest in the saintly practice of good works. He did not admit the criticism of those who call religion poetic mythology or an emotive call to action, and therefore reduce all philosophies of religion to descriptive psychology. Nor did he admit criticism in the name of the regulating insight that all human judgment is utterly corrupt. Whether for good or ill, Oman was not willing to accept secular rationalism or to dismiss the problems it raised because of impatience with its dogmatic intellectualism and moral caution.

At this stage it is not appropriate to justify by argument Oman's belief that the philosophy of religion was a 'useful' undertaking, either as against its critics from without or within what may be loosely called the Christian tradition. What are judged his general reasons for embarking on a philosophy of religion will be described briefly before proceeding to the description of that philosophy itself.

Reason, though not the source of revelation, must be constantly testing its claims. Though not emphasised in *The Natural and the Supernatural*, in his other writings Oman sees rational speculation chiefly as the means whereby the dignity of persons in their autonomy of action and contemplation may be guarded from the encroachments of religious tradition, as incorporated in legalist organisations. In this connection it may be remarked that Oman seems to assume, almost unconsciously, that the dominant tradition of any society will take the form of a religious legalism, rather than a secular rationalism or pagan irrationalism. Also his liberalism may justly be seen in his emphasis on the imperfections of any given tradition when compared with human reason's Idea of the Good, rather than on the fact that tradition sustains and enriches men, being nobler and more varied than any single person's poor partaking of it.

In *The Natural and the Supernatural* he is more concerned with chasing the phantoms of modern psychologisms and naturalisms and monisms than with religious tradition. Whatever else that work may be it is masterly in chopping off the Hydra heads of the naturalist monster. He uses reason to dispel those myths which in the name of things, or of life, or even of spirit, deny reality to the world of persons with its manifold predicates. He shows the assumptions on which these myths are based and illuminates the consequences of believing them in their manifold appearances. He considers it in the interest both of Christians and non-Christians to exorcise these demons, which particularly in an age of confused tradition bewilder the intellects and stultify the wills of good men.

Beyond this negative task, Oman affirms the value of expounding the Gospel in terms that relate it to men's condition. He does not believe that 'relevance' to the problems raised by philosophy, science, and all the varied activities of an advanced civilisation leads necessarily to Pelagianism or a surrender to the *Zeitgeist*.[2] Because in the last centuries men absorbed in these activities had shown contempt for the Gospel is no reason to meet contempt with contempt. To deny the capacity for revelation in all men, to believe that the *imago Dei* is destroyed in men not of the faith, are assertions impossible to Oman, because they make unanswerable the problem of theodicy. To meet that capacity for revelation it is necessary for certain Christians to understand in charity the traditions of modern scepticism and phenomenalism, and out of that understanding to expound an epistemology and metaphysic in which the range and subtlety of human experience is related in some systematic manner to the glory of the Cross. To assert that no useful purpose is served by such an attempt is to Oman to weaken the content of that phrase which rings through his theology – 'The redeemed who are the redeeming.' Though Oman is in revolt against systems of rational philosophy in the Hegelian sense, because of his profound intuition of the involvement of the intellectual in the finitude of ordinary men, he will not allow that the distinctive challenge of the Gospel is lost by an appeal from reason to reason. He defines religion as a practical relation to environment, and because men deal with environment by the understanding they have need of theologies.

This hope of a Christian approach to epistemology and metaphysics is important to Oman because he judges that much of the language of Christian apologetics has become so debased in the eyes of the secularist, and so accepted by the believer, as to prevent either from examining it. He therefore attempts to use, whether successfully or not, a new language to illuminate these problems.

The alternative for Oman is not between inferential arguments for the existence of God and the unargued preaching of saving faith. To describe and to discuss his alternative is the purpose of this thesis. For that to be profitable, some provisional assent must be given to the possibility of that alternative.

**II**

Before beginning the direct discussion of Oman's concept of 'nature and supernature,' some attempt must be made to follow the course of his life by describing briefly the full body of his writings, and to place his thought against the background of the European tradition he inherited. Under any circumstances a historical account may degenerate into an easy historicism which turns the thinker under discussion into a slave to his inheritance. In Oman's case such a danger must be avoided at all costs. For there is in him that prophetic autonomy which transcends inheritance and moulds it by judging it. Also the extent of Oman's scholarship makes the historical appraisal of his traditions difficult. Indeed any sophisticated European living as did Oman between 1860 and 1939 was heir to a tradition of remarkable complexity. In Oman's case long years of scholarship had made many areas of this field his own. The simple language and lack of scholarly reference in *The Natural and the Supernatural*, published when Oman was seventy-one, cannot prevent the reader from recognising the intensive and selected learning that lies behind each sentence.* Though the problem is too subtle for any accurate charting, some attempt at a historical introduction must be made.

John Wood Oman was born and bred in the Orkney Islands – that is, at the very periphery of European society. Those islands remained geographically and spiritually far from the new industrial world which between 1860 and 1939 spread its mass-production and community-less cities and scientific wars over most of Western Europe. The rhythm of the agricultural and fishing economy of the Orkneys was not much troubled by the new techniques. The Christian Church, particularly in its Presbyterian form, still held its sway. Men there were little touched by that drift away from Christianity, which had started in Europe as a revolt of the intellectuals but which in the mass industrial world became among the many little more than indifference. The depressing fact that in the eyes of many decent men Christianity became identified with the interests of the dominant economic class was not of impor-

---

\* I once asked a close friend of Oman's whether Oman had read any of the work of a school of modern German philosophers (a question for which there was no direct answer in his writings). The reply was, 'I do not know for certain, but have no doubt he did read them. He read everything.'

tance in the Orkneys. Oman's writings affirm how important a mediator of God was his childhood. Intimacy with his natural surroundings
gave him, from his earliest days, a knowledge and love of nature
which was vigorous and unsentimental. His life in a Christian farming
community gave him direct knowledge of the religious life of ordinary
people, and the realisation that any Christian theology, must, above all
else, be rooted in the possibility of salvation for all in the plain circumstances in which God has placed them. Despite his life as a scholar he
never forgot this Presbyterian egalitarianism.* The most evident guide
of his growing mind was the Bible, read continually as the living prophetic Word of God. Such a practice was the glory of the Presbyterian
tradition, both in Church and home.† Both his writings and the testimony of his friends tell of Oman's intimate knowledge of the Bible,
woven into the fabric of all his experience.

Without sentimentalising, one may marvel at Oman's good fortune
in that when he went forth into a world uneasy with all manner of disturbance and impregnated with false and soft doctrine, he carried with
him a secure faith in God, given to him through the sea and the fields,
his family and his community, his Church and his Bible. Though flexible enough to allow him to learn, this faith provided him with a steadfast citadel of prophetic theism, from which to interpret his experience.
Unlike so many men and women of the twentieth century, he did not
have to find his way back to God. This Biblical inheritance was of espe-
cial importance in an age when much philosophy was indifferent to
the Hebraic origins of the European tradition, and where even a Christian such as Illingworth could write as an Hegelian, with the Biblical
revelation almost, as it were, tagged on at the end.[3] Oman was inter-

---

* Oman's sense of the religious genius of men in their everyday callings is seen in his
  dedication to his Kerr Lectures in 1906 (*The Problem of Faith and Freedom in the Last
  Two Centuries*, see bibliography, p. i). 'To the memory of my father, a scholar only of
  life and action, but my best teacher.' Like so many Presbyterians in Scotland in the
  nineteenth century, Oman carried this sense of egalitarianism over into the realm
  of secular politics, where it may not be so necessarily valid as in Christianity. See
  Chapter 6.
† Oman's family did not belong to the Church of Scotland, but to the United Presbyterian Church. This body had broken from the main part of the Church in the eighteenth century, chiefly in protest against any close connection between Church and
  State. This tradition of ecclesiastical independence and of individualism certainly
  helped to shape Oman's theology. The broad lines of doctrine in his Church were still
  however that Knoxian Calvinism which characterized all Scottish Presbyterianism.

ested in the philosophic speculations of the classical and modern worlds, but for him they were regulated by and not regulative of the personalist categories he found in the Scriptures.*

Any disadvantage such a childhood may have had for a theologian of that period resulted perhaps from that very security. For the pain that men must undergo Oman had indeed an exquisite sympathy which runs like a river through his writings, never letting him depart far from the problem of theodicy. But at the same time one doubts whether he ever comprehended the full agony of the faithless. Compared with St Augustine, for instance, whose period is not unlike Oman's in its intellectual and moral chaos, there is little in Oman of the bewilderment of having partaken of that very decadence and the joy of being released from it. This made it difficult for him to sympathise with certain forms of the Christian consciousness that increasingly characterise the twentieth century. It may also be in part responsible for his greater admiration of the values of civilisation as compared with St Augustine. Oman ever maintained the islander's distrust of the grandeurs of civilisation, but that is a different reaction from the revolt of an Augustine born and bred within the privileges of that civilisation.

The strength of Oman's faith may be seen in the fact that at seventeen he decided to start his training as a minister of his family's Church. He took his Arts course at the University of Edinburgh and proceeded to the training college of his Church in that city.† Here, for the first time, he met directly and with growing understanding the varying forms of secular and semi-secular rationalism. He was being taught philosophy in the country of David Hume. His professor was Pringle-Pattison, who, though he criticised the impersonalism of the English Hegelians, was still of that speculative tradition.‡[5] Presbyterianism was ever a firm believer in education and therefore produced

---

* It is interesting to compare Oman's childhood with, for instance, the training of his contemporary A.N. Whitehead.[4]

† The chief source for the external events of Oman's life are the memoirs of him by George Alexander, M.A., and Professor H.H. Farmer, D.D., which are at the front of Oman's posthumous *Honest Religion*, see bibliography, p.i. See also *John Wood Oman* by F.R. Tennant, Vol. XXV. *Proceedings of the British Academy, London.*

‡ See Oman's account of Pringle-Pattison in his review of the latter's 'The Idea of God in the Light of Recent Philosophy,' *The Journal of Theological Studies* Vol. XIX pp. 278–279. See bibliography p. v.

men of curiosity to whom cosmological speculation was a necessity. Oman was touched by the German equivalent of these problems when in 1883 he went to Erlangen and in 1885 to Heidelberg. The influence of German liberal theology, philosophical idealism, and critical history was to remain with him always.

Oman would never succumb to the judgment that his native practical Protestantism and the best in the traditions of European rationalism were irreconcilable. In the course of the following chapters it is hoped to make somewhat clearer which aspects of those diverse traditions he made his own. Here only two points will be made about his reaction to the larger world into which he moved.

First, Oman disliked the attitude which many Christians in authority took to secular philosophy, scholarship, and science in the nineteenth century. He had no sympathy for the actions of a man such as Bishop Wilberforce.[6] The behaviour of the authorities in the Robertson Smith case appalled him.[7] His was a liberal's faith in the open forum of truth. He had a remarkable trust in the intellects of ordinary men and therefore little sympathy for the claims of ecclesiastical conservatism. Doubt was God's judgment on the Church for hedging itself round with external guarantees.

Secondly and more important (here must be touched the indefinable core of his personality), Oman's primary concern remained always with men's salvation so that much of the post-Descartian rationalism made little appeal to him. The question 'How shall a man live?' could never end in the rationalist insistence on certainty. Oman could not summon up interest in cosmological speculation abstracted from the needs of ordinary men. Bradley and Bosanquet, confident in the privileges of their community and cushioned from the barest level of ethical decision, produced systems that faced the needs only of a contemplative élite.[8] Therefore in the tradition of rationalist speculation it was to Ritschl and through him to Kant that Oman turned. Though their account of the moral judgment was rationalist they still recognised the primacy of conduct. This practical interest of Oman saved him from any deep worry about the results of Biblical criticism. The questions of evidence and interpretation, though a necessary activity, were not to him important as they did not substantially affect the question of how men shall find a gracious God. The Truth for Oman was essentially the Way and the Life.

In 1885 Oman was licensed by his Presbytery, and after short appointments at Makerstoun and Paisley in Scotland, he became a minister at Alnwick in Northumberland, England, remaining there from 1889 to 1907. In any account of Oman's life it must be remembered that he was a practising minister till his forty-seventh year. During his ministry at Alnwick he filled three theological lectureships, one in the U.S.A., and produced three books.*

The body of Oman's writing may be divided into two parts representing differing interests. The first of these are his theological writings, belonging mainly to the period up to the end of the first great war. The second are his post-1918 writings, in which his interest is fixed on the questions of Christian philosophy. In making such a distinction it must be remembered that Oman does not accept the division between natural and revealed truth, in its Thomist form, with the consequent tendency to detach secular metaphysics from theology, and that therefore in a Platonist such as Oman the above division of his work is one of emphasis not of principle. Moreover it would be quite inaccurate to say that in his early period he was unaware of the philosophic issues at stake or that in his later period his philosophy was not at the service of the simple Gospel.

This distinction can be most clearly made in considering to whom he was addressing his works. In his earlier books he assumed an audience of Christians who would share with him certain traditions and experiences and who would therefore be ready to follow him in at least certain minimal assumptions. To this audience he concentrated on expounding what he believed to be the essence of the simple Gospel. After 1918, he came to believe more and more that he had a prime responsibility to a non-Christian audience to whom, therefore, he must attempt to justify his assumptions with as little appeal to common traditions and experience as was possible. Only in that way could he even hope to expound to some non-Christians what the primary truths of Christianity really were and to convince men that only in terms of them could consciousness become more than a blight.

---

*  (i)   *On Religion: Speeches to its Cultured Despisers* by Friedrich Schleiermacher. Translated, with Introduction by John Oman, 1893.

  (ii)  *Vision and Authority,* or *The Throne of St Peter,* 1902.

  (iii) *The Problem of Faith and Freedom in the Last Two Centuries,* 1906. See bibliography, p. i.

Oman's first work does not in fact fall into either of these classes. It is a translation of and introduction to the second edition of Schleiermacher's *Speeches*.* He believed there was value in presenting this classic of *Religionsphilosophie* to the educated Anglo-Saxon public. Schleiermacher's chief value lies, for Oman, in his affirmation that the seat of religion is in the immediate experience of the supernatural, and that men know it 'by the intercourse of feeling as intuition.' Such an affirmation seemed to Oman a healthy reaction against the traditional natural theology which, when detached from revelation, had in the hands of the deists turned religion into arguments about the existence of God. Oman does not decide in his introduction whether Schleiermacher's system was really a Christian theism of persons or a cosmic pantheism.† In his introduction to Schleiermacher there appears once again that interpretation, so difficult to judge, of the thought of the Renaissance and of the Reformation as being in essence complementary.

Oman's first purely original work was *Vision and Authority or The Throne of St Peter*, which appeared in 1902.‡ This work is a discussion of the seat of religious authority, addressed to men within the Church. Negatively it is mainly concerned with the complete rejection of the Catholic approach to the Church, the sacraments, the priesthood, and doctrine. It is a discussion of the failures of religious legalism. The Catholic denial of the glorious liberty of the children of God involves for Oman the denial of the true Fatherhood of God. As God is the Father He will only choose to achieve His mysterious purposes through free and therefore fallible persons. The life and death of Our Lord is a revelation of God's care for each person's autonomy and, therefore, the ungodliness of anything that overrides that autonomy. The influence of Ritschl is seen in the direct appeal back across the centuries to the early Church. Though Oman is chiefly concerned with the refutation of the Catholic error, he includes under that error a criticism of the legalist elements in the Reformed Churches. Protestants must be willing to bear the full consequences of the original Lutheran declaration of the glorious liberty of the children of God.

---

* See bibliography, p. i.
† Oman continued to discuss Schleiermacher's thought at regular intervals for the rest of his life. He increasingly stresses his fears of the pantheist undertone in Schleiermacher's work.
‡ See bibliography, p. i.

In *Vision and Authority* Oman describes the essence of the Gospel as simply the call upon free men to follow the demand made upon them from the Cross. To that Gospel, which must regulate all else, Oman returns again and again. The difficulty of this work does not lie in what it says, but in what it does not say. The practical implications of the Gospel of Love are not developed. For instance, from that work it would be quite impossible to tell how that regulating Gospel should be applied to the relationship of Church and State or whether the Christian had any right to take part in secular politics.

Oman's next work was *The Problem of Faith and Freedom in the Last Two Centuries*, delivered as the Kerr Lectures at the Glasgow College of the United Free Church of Scotland in 1905 and published in the following year.* In these lectures Oman returns again to the problem of the Gospel and rationalism. How can the Christian assert his faith in the Father and yet affirm the duty of men to follow the truth wherever it may lead them? In the first lecture he formulates that question in language that he was to use for the rest of his life. 'The ultimate problem of the last two centuries I take to be the relation of Faith to Freedom, the problem of how Faith is to be absolute and Freedom absolute, yet both one.'† His own vision of this problem is expounded in an analysis of the attitudes of English, French, and German thinkers from Luther to Ritschl, with special emphasis on men of the eighteenth and nineteenth centuries. His method is to take some great figure, whom he judged to have emphasised some essential aspect of Christian truth, and to compare that thinker with others of his period who failed in such a recognition. Thus he compares Pascal's Jansenism[9] with the ecclesiasticism of Bossuet and the Jesuits,[10] Butler's axiological theism with the natural theology of the deists,[11] Kant's understanding of the categorical quality of the moral judgment with the optimism of Voltaire and the easy scepticism of Hume, Ritschl's theology of justification and reconciliation with the impersonal process implied in the critical history of the Tübingen scholars.[12] In dealing with Schleiermacher and Newman he departs from this method. Schleiermacher's thought he uses to illustrate the strength and weakness of German Romanticism, in its most religious representative. Newman, whom he

---

* See ibid., p. i.
† *Faith and Freedom*, op. cit. p. 2.

denounces more fiercely than anyone else in his writings, he uses to illustrate the weaknesses of Hegelian and Roman Catholic absolutism and the close relation between them.[13] Oman's concentration on the theology of the well-known does not, however, prevent him from illustrating his thesis by an intimate knowledge of relatively obscure German and British writers of the eighteenth and nineteenth centuries.

Oman's approval of Pascal, Butler, Kant, and Ritschl is evidence of how much he faces the problem as a practical theologian. As he wrote in an article on Ritschl about this time – his first of many contributions to *The Journal of Theological Studies*:

Our response to this revelation [that of Jesus Christ] lies not in accepting a body of doctrine or stirring up in ourselves a special type of feeling, but in fulfilling our calling, in meekness and patience in the tasks and burdens of life, and in living in love in the Christian fellowship.*

Even Schleiermacher failed to recognise this. In this work Oman's debt to Ritschl is evident as nowhere else. Ritschl had understood that faith and freedom could only be reconciled if revelation was received as each person's assertion of a judgment of worth. Ritschl's denial of the value of the impersonal categories of modern and indeed of classical metaphysics, his refusal to assert any natural ontology that would destroy what Oman called 'the individual frontier' and above all else his return to the documents of the early Church, were all profoundly in accord with Oman's temper.

It must be noted, however, that in the last chapter of *Faith and Freedom* Oman hesitantly questions whether Ritschl is not left with a dualism almost as unsatisfactory as he considers the Kantian system. Ritschl's acceptance of Kant's universalist account of the moral judgment left him with a morality pharisaical rather than victorious as in the prophets and Our Lord. Oman raises this question of dualism *à propos* of the vagueness with which Ritschl wrote about the Resurrection, wherein a division between God's Love and Majesty was almost implied.† These questions presage, though not systematically, Oman's

---

* *Journal of Theological Studies, op. cit.* Vol. XI, p. 473. Brackets the present writer's.
† It is interesting that this passage in *Faith and Freedom* (pp. 387–92) should be the only passage where Oman questions Ritschl's stand on the Resurrection.[14] For a further discussion see chapter 5.

attempt in *The Natural and the Supernatural* to seek some defined reconciliation of that overt dualism, by describing the interdependence of
religious dependence and moral independence. To do so he had to give
up his suspicion of metaphysics, in the stern form he had held it, and
assert a natural ontology arrived at by intuition.

*Faith and Freedom* is a work of theological affirmation rather than
philosophical analysis. Oman makes little attempt to relate such religious positions as eighteenth-century deism or nineteenth-century
monism to their background in the secular science and culture of their
day. He was clearly interested in Kant's criticism of the possibility of a
rational ontology, but does not discuss the question epistemologically
or metaphysically. All positions are judged against his own personalist
theism, but no attempt is made to justify that theism. In the seventeenth century he is interested in Pascal rather than Spinoza or Leibniz,
the great expositors of an idealism influenced by the new mathematics
and physics. He is writing for Christians, and the chief targets of his
criticism are ecclesiastical legalisms, not secular traditions. Always
there is the implicit assumption that the main revolt of Christians will
be against the inadequacies of organised religion. There is no sufficient
realisation of how much Christian traditions had become meaningless,
particularly among the educated classes in Western Europe. This may
be explained by the fact that he had not passed the last years among
the controlling classes of that society.

Oman's third book is *The Church and the Divine Order* published in
1911.* This work is a fine blend of scholarship and immediacy, arising
from Oman's ability to meet a practical question and yet refuse to
answer it except on the level of profundity. In his preface he raises the
contemporary debate between individualist competition and legal
socialism. Neither can be accepted by the Christian as a proper basis
for society, because an atomic individualism rooted in pursuit of material gain is opposed by a system that puts its trust in the coercive powers of the state to bring in the Kingdom of God.† To answer this
question the Christian must think clearly about what role the divine

---

* See bibliography, p. i.
† All this is so much the common coin of the present day that it hardly seems worth
  saying. [The year] 1911 was a different day. It is also worth noting that Oman's liberalism made him stress much more vigorously the corruptions of capitalism than the
  dangers of statism.

society – the Church – should play in the 'here and now' of history. Oman presents an analysis of Church history to illustrate the problem by showing how Christians have faced it.

That analysis is strict criticism carried out in the name of the Gospel of love rather than descriptive scholarship. He interprets Our Lord's and St Paul's visions of the Church as consisting of those who can live the life of love and leave all issues of power with God. The divine order must be an order of free persons. Any organisation that departs from the rule of love ceases by definition to be the organisation of the Kingdom of God – the fellowship of the Cross. Love is the sole mark of the Catholic Church. Its only influence on the world in general and the state in particular must be as an autonomous body which by the force of its example persuades the state to become less of an instrument of coercion. To Oman that principle is valid at all times in history. Indeed in a certain sense for the Christian there is no history, as the ethics of the Cross must always be the standard. This is as true when the Christian lives in a civilisation nominally Christian as when he lives in a society avowedly pagan. The Christian must not, because of this, fall into any stoic despair of the world, but recognise that it can only be redeemed by love.

*The Church and the Divine Order* is the high point of Oman's quietism. Indeed his position would lead one at times to believe that he is advocating a Tertullian isolationism. One might well expect the phrase *Quid Athenae Hierosolymis?*\*[15] The difficulty in this work is, however, the same as in *Vision and Authority*. A prophetic ideal of the Church is proclaimed, yet little is said about how that ideal is to be worked out in the imperfections of the world.

Two events had a profound effect on the course of Oman's thought in the last half of his life. The first was his move to Westminster College, Cambridge, in 1907, and the increasing influence of that university. The second was the Great War of 1914–1918. As the second of

---

\* In an article published in this period, Oman asserts that Tolstoi working on the land after his conversion is nearer the Christian ideal than the good-willed Christian socialist trying to reform the abuses of civilisation by state action. See *Dictionary of Christ and the Gospels*, article by Oman on 'Individualism,' Vol. 1, p. 818. See bibliography, p. ii. Also, I was told by Professor H.H. Farmer that in 1914 many of Oman's pupils expected him to declare himself a pacifist. In the light of *The Church and the Divine Order*, such an expectation is not to be wondered at.

these can be more directly traced in his thought, it will be discussed first.

To a man of Oman's sensitivity the storm of the first scientific war must have been appalling. Oman had never been one of those who put their faith in civilisation. Yet to see the sores of so great a civilisation laid bare must have been an awful agony for one who had inherited much from the optimism of Victorian days. A man who owed such a profound debt to German thought must have suffered from his belief that the prime responsibility for the conflict lay with that country. To repeat, many had expected him to be a pacifist. Oman was not a man to shirk responsibility, so in March 1915 in *The War and Its Issues* he stated unequivocally his reasons for believing that the British Christian should support the British state in its conduct of the war.*

What is remarkable in the effect of the war on Oman is that it brought to the surface his liberalism. This is interesting in view of the fact that the war was in no small measure responsible for many theological and philosophical criticisms of liberalism. As a prime example the theology of Dr Barth may be cited.[16] Oman had always a faith that went far beyond any mere immanentism and therefore when the war came he had to face honestly just what were the claims of civilisation on the Christian. In the case of others, hostile or indifferent to Christianity, the horror of the war made them face the emptiness of immanentism or a mere utilitarian phenomenalism. To say this is in no sense to imply that the war detracted from Oman's moral intensity – indeed to the contrary. What it did was to face him unavoidably and specifically with what he meant by love, and what he thought of the possibility of creative politics. In the moment of decision his quietism did not stand before his honest belief in the Christian's responsibility to the state. The word 'liberalism' is here more accurate than 'conservatism'. In *The War and Its Issues* – particularly in the second part dealing with responsibility for the peace – his optimism in politics puts him far beyond the Christian conservative such as St Augustine or Luther.

The influence of the war may be seen clearly in *Grace and Personality,* published in 1917, which is Oman's fullest exposition of his theology

---

* See bibliography, p. i. See also two articles by Oman in *The Elements of Pain and Conflict in Human Life, considered from a Christian Point of View,* 1916. Bibliography, p. ii. These articles are less directly on the war.

of persons.* Though the problems with which the work deals had been long in his mind, its style has a high intensity to be associated with the years of the war. Oman always cared too deeply for the autonomy of his readers to convince by simplification or false rhetoric. That work is, however, theology at its best when clearheadedness is combined with a noble personal intuition of the meeting of God and man.

Here Oman attempts to explain how religious dependence and moral independence – the two great facts of Christian experience – can be seen not in contradiction but as interdependent. His argument is that to deny man's autonomy is to deny that God is Love, and that to deny our religious dependence is to turn action into a proud and joyless striving and to have some deist conception of God as far less than the Ruler of all history. He analyses his concept of 'person' which he defines as an autonomy of volition of insight and of consciousness. Thus the concept 'person' is empty of content apart from its relation to God and His world. This is not to say that Oman's intuition into the essence of God and man [is that they] are one, but that they cannot arise apart from each other.

Oman's argument in *Grace and Personality* is a simple one. He hammers home the essence of the Gospel as the meeting of the Father and His children. Though he touches on the implications of this central fact upon some of the great problems of Christianity such as revelation and the Church, there is no attempt to expound a systematic Christian theology from this insight. Neither is there any attempt to relate his personalist intuition to the problems of metaphysics and epistemology. For instance throughout the work there are repeated criticisms of Pelagian ethical systems, in which without doubt Oman has Kant in mind, yet he never brings this out into the open by discussing the Kantian system. *Grace and Personality* is the summation of all that Oman had written previously. It is the maturest and clearest of those practical theological statements in which he drives home vigorously what he considers the core of the Christian faith.

In this connection mention must be made of the book of sermons, *The Paradox of the World*, which was published in 1921.† In sermons IX, X, XVIII, and XIX the stature of Oman as a great man of God can be seen as

---

* See bibliography, p. i.
† See ibid.

nowhere else in his work. Oman uses little of that rhetorical piety that so easily mars sermons. The way of the Cross is presented in all its hardness and actuality, yet as a great hymn of joy because men are called to so great a destiny. These sermons are the *theologia crucis* in all its sensitivity and strength. If out of all that Oman wrote in any field, one piece alone could be preserved, the present writer would choose Oman's account of St Paul in his sermon 'Strength Through Weakness.'*

The event responsible for turning Oman's attention from practical theology to the philosophy of religion was his move to Cambridge and his life there from 1907 till his death in 1939. He was first Professor of Theology at Westminster College. In 1922 he was appointed Principal, an office he held until his retirement in 1935. Oman's first obligation at Cambridge was to men training for the Presbyterian ministry and to colleagues who were ministers of that Church. He was not, however, a man to shut himself off from the world around him. As a member of Queens College, later as an honorary fellow of Jesus College and as a university lecturer in the philosophy of religion, he was thrown in contact with the general university community. Here he was among the intellectual and ruling élite of England, and that élite were in many ways more estranged from Christian thought and experience than any other class in the British Isles. For a wise and simple Presbyterian, it must have been parallel to an early Palestinian Christian moving to Athens. An outsider may be allowed to judge that educated nineteenth-century England was one of those rare and finely flowering civilisations that history so seldom produces. Particularly before 1914, in the midst of its Edwardian success, such a civilisation could scarcely doubt that it was an end in itself. Men who judged it by Jerusalem could hardly fail to be confident that the claims of Jerusalem were reconcilable to such a world of learning and beauty.

Two influences in that university may be singled out. Hellenism, with its tradition of rational speculation and the pursuit of beauty, permeated Cambridge in ways both varied and profound.† The prestige of

---

* *The Paradox of the World, op. cit.* pp. 247–61.
† E.M. Forster's exquisite biography *Goldsworthy Lowes Dickinson* (Arnold & Co., London 1934) gives a fine description of how much the ideals of the classical world were standards in Cambridge education.[17] Christianity is there treated as the barbarian and superstitious idea that threatens the order and tolerance of the world of the civilised contemplative.

natural science was immense at Cambridge, for the university was a centre of scientific renown. Thomson, Rutherford, and Eddington were making their discoveries during Oman's years there.[18] Russell and Whitehead were producing the groundwork for a revolution in logical studies.[19] The philosophies of Whitehead, Russell, and Moore, whatever differing merits they may have, would be difficult to label as Christian.[20] They had certainly rejected or ignored St Augustine's criticism of the pretensions of rationalist philosophy. Even Eddington, who called himself Christian, wrote philosophy with the categories of scientific idealism, and in no sense implied that those categories should be regulated by Biblical conceptions. Even several years after the first war, the extent to which science and secularism were the sources of Cambridge philosophy is indicated by the remark of one of its leading thinkers in a work on ethics:

> Still, people who feel very strongly about any subject are liable to over-estimate its importance in the scheme of things. A healthy appetite for righteousness, kept in due control by good manners, is an excellent thing; but to 'hunger and thirst after' it is often merely a symptom of spiritual diabetes.*

Even in those English theologies which attempted to buttress the faith by their Platonic philosophies, the categories used must have seemed to Oman far from the radical personalism of the Bible. Von Hügel and Father Tyrrell, Cook Wilson and C.C.J. Webb, William Temple and Edwyn Bevan use the categories of science and culture in a way that clearly implies little thought of dilemma between the interests of their civilisation and the vigour of the Christian religion.[22]

The traditions of modern secular rationalism did not come to Oman always in educated and pleasing forms. Though the naturalism of Huxley and Spencer had always been challenged in the scientific fraternity, they continued to exert a powerful influence, and it often became the dogmatic system within which new 'sciences' such as psychology, anthropology, and comparative religion were carried on in the Anglo-Saxon world.[23] It hardly needs saying that a work such as *The Golden Bough*, though supposedly an objective account of phenomena,

---

* C.D. Broad *Five Types of Ethical Theory*, Kegan Paul, London, 1930, preface p. xxiv.[21]

must have led to certain metaphysical conclusions in the minds of young men who read it. It is strange that after Kant's account of the assumptions and limits of natural science, trained men should have remained naturalists. It is even harder to understand how educated men could accept utilitarianism or the ethics of Spencer, after what Kant had written of morality. Men were, however, confident and busy enough to disregard or discard the past. Had Christianity ever produced as wonderfully tangible results as had the study of natural science? In training men to be ministers and in meeting senior and junior members of the university, Oman must have come across this naturalism in a wide variety of appearances.* Even the impact of Bergson's early writings only challenged the categories of mechanism in the name of biology, not in the name of persons.[24] As Oman remarked, Lloyd Morgan is only Spinoza turned biologist.†[25]

The mild-mannered liberal naturalisms of the intellect made their post-war appearance as pagan irrationalisms rooted in deeper levels of the personality than the intellect. How much more humane must be considered even the thought of Spencer or of Nietzsche, than the post-war daemonisms of Céline or Rosenburg or D.H. Lawrence.[26] It would be folly to make any comments on the long-term result of God's judgment on the Christian Church in Europe's self-destruction in the first world war. Certainly one of the immediate effects of which Oman must have been conscious in his years at Cambridge was the moral suspicion by young people of an institution which had seemed to stand merely as a passive confederate to national and secular adventurings. This revolt was related to and just as important as the intellectual one, the results of which are much easier to assess.

Before such influences the direction of Oman's thought could not but be modified. It was borne in on him just how closed honest minds had become to understanding the biblical personalist categories of thought that had once sustained so many. The breakdown of the Christian tradition in western Europe had not in Oman's mind come from any perverse retreat from God's appointed truth but by that very mys-

---

* It is worth noting that Oman never mentions that strenuous naturalism of the will – Marxism. This is probably due to the fact that Marxism made its appeal more to the simple man of action than to the intellectual addicted to naturalism in its contemplative forms.

† *The Natural and the Supernatural, op. cit.*, p. 160.

tery in man – the Imago Dei – which allows men to stand above any tradition and correct it.* According to Oman the old Catholic tradition had been shaken in its authority by men who were honestly endeavouring to surmount its limitations and its contradictions. But once that tradition was shaken, men could no longer find in it grounds on which to live. Therefore as in the Platonic age they turned for help to their other creations – their visions of the world as a concourse of atoms or as the flow of life to higher levels of complexity – hoping to find therein some solution to their dilemma. Caught in the grip of these other productions, men could no longer believe in the reality of the world of persons. Yet Oman never denied the honesty of that doubt or the reality of that dilemma. For him Christianity did not stand or fall with the Aristotelian natural metaphysics with its compromise between mechanism and teleology.

In a situation where men honestly sought grounds for their actions in worlds where they must of necessity be frustrated, there was to Oman a palpable necessity of making visible just how real the world of persons was and of relating it, as best he could, to the other worlds. From such an undertaking he expected no easy success, nor was he so proud as to imagine that there were no nobler and more important ways of making this world visible than by the activity of the intellectual. Nevertheless, that he judged to be his function and he stuck to it.

Gone then was the time when the theologian could be most profitably occupied by holding high the ideal of the Church before his fellow Christians. There were too many men who just could not understand what it meant to believe in a personal God who rules all history. What could grace mean to those who conceived man solely as 'Life' at the point of highest development (so far). What could such language as 'the salvation of sinners' mean to those who sought their grounds for action in harmony with *Deus sive Natura*. It seemed no proper application of the Pauline determination to know nothing but Jesus Christ and Him crucified, simply to present to unbelievers the old formulas (themselves inadequate descriptions of the promises of God). All systems were revealed as necessarily limited and contradictory by the

---

* For an example of how far the motives of these reformers of the tradition can be discredited as sheer bad intention, see Professor Maritain's account of Luther, Descartes, and Rousseau in *Three Reformers*, Sheed and Ward, London 1928.[27]

judgment of the Cross, but that did not mean there was no purpose in attempting them.

Thus Oman published *The Natural and the Supernatural.** That remarkable book is divided into four parts. In the first of these parts, 'Scope and Method,' Oman defines the field of enquiry, which is religion as a practical relation to environment and therefore concerned with the natural as well as the supernatural.† He then lays down a preliminary justification for that distinction. He discusses the appropriate method for dealing with such a problem. Finally he lays down three essential questions raised by experience, in terms of which the main problem will be discussed. Each of the three last parts of the book is concerned with one of those questions. The second part, 'Knowing and Knowledge,' describes how persons are given objective knowledge of nature and supernature. That is, Oman expounds a realist epistemology in which he attempts to hold the problem of 'knowing' and 'being' in indissoluble unity. In the third part, 'Necessity and Freedom,' he uses the concepts that have been so arrived at to expound a metaphysical position that does not rest in monism and yet transcends any acceptance of a dualist solution. Here he defines by what right men may use personalist categories of the supernatural and so expounds a Christian monotheism, in terms of nature and supernature, which is but a sophisticated account of the simple Gospel.‡ In the fourth part, 'The Evanescent and the Eternal,' Oman takes the phenomena of comparative religion and interprets them in terms of this prophetic mono-

---

* The length of this book and its concentration of style and content (though not the lucidity of its exposition) are evidence of how long it must have been in preparation. Further evidence is the fact that Oman published much between 1918 and 1931 which is but notes for the *magnum opus*. See his reviews and articles on the philosophy of religions for the *Journal of Theological Studies* between these dates. See bibliography. His articles for *The Student Movement* in 1922 show almost an outline of the later work. Bibliography, p. iv. Also his article 'The Sphere of Religion' in *Science, Religion and Reality* in 1926 defines his main terms. See bibliography, p. iii.

† In most of *The Natural and the Supernatural* Oman uses capital letters for those two terms. In this thesis that practice will not be followed except in quotations from Oman. Though nature and supernature carry personalist connotations in Oman's use of them, as the present writer will often use the word God, capitals will be reserved for that word and for His attributes.

‡ This is not to say that Part II of *The Natural and the Supernatural* is Oman's epistemology and Part III his metaphysics. With a position such as Oman's there can be no clear distinction between these studies.

theism. Thus he ends his work with an account of the faith of Our Lord and the prophets that clarifies and expands what he means by his tension between monism and dualism.*

Such a description of *The Natural and the Supernatural* may imply that Oman is mainly concerned with the systematic exposition and analysis of his own position. This is not the case. What he says positively emerges only slowly from the preliminary rejection of a multitude of errors in all fields he touches upon. Once again it is repeated that Oman recognises how deep and detailed is the confusion of his age and therefore sees that no metaphysical position can be asserted until a multitude of phantoms has been chased away. However necessary such an activity and however brilliantly undertaken by Oman, it must be admitted that it adds difficulty to the understanding of his position. Often what he himself asserts is described in a few cryptic sentences after a detailed and lucid criticism of other positions.

As this thesis will be primarily concerned with Oman's own position about the Christian's knowledge of God and His world, and only secondarily and by way of illustration with his refutation of other positions, it may be well at this point to describe what are the main metaphysical systems to which he returns again and again to criticise and so to transcend. These positions may be classified as three different types of modern rationalism: (1) naturalism, (2) spiritual monisms, and (3) Kant's incipient dualism between nature and reason. Oman's criticism forms a path leading from his scorn of certain positions, which seem to him so patently false as only to indicate the extent of modern confusion, up to those positions from which he learnt much, but which he still judges to fall short of the prophetic victory of Christian monotheism. As has been said, Oman is not so greatly concerned in *The Natural and the Supernatural* with his differences from other Christian metaphysics, such as Thomism, as he is elsewhere.

The beginning of Oman's critical journey is taken up with his battle against the naturalisms and psychologisms of his period. To the reader it appears as if the beast dies a thousand deaths, as Oman chops at the heads that spring from Humian atomic sensationalism, Darwinian biology, and modern species of phenomenalism. He attacks them as

---

* In this fourth part Oman does not discuss the problems of theological history. Such a discussion must be sought elsewhere.

they appear in a multitude of places, from Leuba's psychology[28] to Sir James Frazer's anthropology.[29] *The Natural and the Supernatural* must be considered a classic condemnation and refutation of these fallacies.

The second level of Oman's criticism is directed against the monist cosmologies of modern idealism. Oman includes under this classification criticism of men of such differing periods and varying terminologies as Spinoza and McTaggart.[30] The archetype of such systems is of course Hegel. He relates all these forms of modern idealism to similar religious attitudes in other periods, because of the similarity of their practical approach to environment. Thus from this point of view Neo-Platonic, Indian, and Christian mysticism[s] are closely allied with the rationalist monisms. The greatness of these monisms lies in their recognition of the primacy of spirit, their faith in the universe as wholly God's, and their earnest attempts to show how the contemplative can reach out to partake of the peace that passes all understanding. However, because they fail to proceed from an adequate intuition of the essence of personality – with its autonomy of volition and consequent sinfulness – the result is that man becomes ideally a passive mirror of the universe and sin an unexplainable failure to be such a mirror. The ideal in rationalist monism as in mysticism is the aristocratic contemplative who achieves salvation by practices not open to the ordinary man. Their attitude to the world can only be, if consistent, a detachment from it or a submerging in it, not a victory through it and over it. Their God is an abstract rational process which determines the reasons of the intelligent, but not a Loving Father Who seeks all His children, while they are yet sinners.

The third and highest level of Oman's criticism of modern idealism deals with Kant. In *The Natural and the Supernatural* Oman devotes more space to the theological implications of Kant than of any other thinker. For instance, the last three chapters of Part III of that work, where Oman moves forward to the exposition of his own prophetic monotheism of nature and supernature, are written against a background of a discussion of Kant's metaphysic of conscience. Here for the first time Oman goes carefully behind Ritschl to Kant.

To Oman the most admirable of modern philosophers was necessarily he who had recognised that ultimate reality was fundamentally ethical in quality, and who tried to preserve, whether successfully or not, the autonomy of each person in his idealism. How sympathetic to

Oman was Kant's criticism of any attempt to place the seat of religion in the assent of the intellect to propositions. Kant's denial of the possibility of natural theology had not been motivated by the sceptical denial that men can know, but by the noble faith that they ought not to know. It was an assertion that men must walk by faith not by sight. Oman never interprets Kant as in essence a phenomenalist or an Hegelian. Kant redirected theology by insisting that all its conclusions must be implications from the facts of our consciousness. He insisted on the central importance of what Oman calls the question of ideal values – that is, how individual finite minds in the flux of the world can justifiably assert absolute standards. Above all else Oman interprets Kant's greatness in terms of his attempt to relate the natural and the supernatural by some kind of moral victory. By such an attempt is the monotheism of any philosophy to be judged.

Because Oman owes so much to Kant's metaphysic of experience in setting the pattern for the exposition of his own, the points wherein he finds that philosopher unsatisfactory clarify what he is trying to expound positively in *The Natural and the Supernatural*. His differences from Kant illustrate how far the theology of persons must depart from the traditions of philosophic idealism. Kant's Copernican revolution is in Oman's opinion a magnificent attempt to maintain the autonomy of the person. It springs, however, from an intuition of personality as the performance of atomic acts of self-determination, detached from the autonomy of insight and self-consciousness, so that it leads to an exaltation of reason and its corresponding acts and to a distrust of the given. Thus is set up a disjunction between reason and nature.* Because of this inadequate intuition of the essence of personality Kant can only describe man's knowledge of nature as a series of appearances, and his actions as attempts to overcome the dread world of chaotic inclinations by negative commandments. Men can never know nature as their Father's house, nor can they act in it trusting it to be the means whereby the Father leads men to Himself. To use Oman's language, Kant can show men how they should deny the natural, but not how they should possess it. Because freedom is depreciated to a mere

* Oman never used the phrase 'a disjunction between reason and nature.' The writer attempts to interpret in his own language what Oman said about Kant. He is not here suggesting that Oman's system has not as many difficulties as Kant's.

consent to be determined by the rational, Kant's conception of God can only be an abstract Judge Who metes out the exact equivalence of action and award. It can never attain Our Lord's conception of the Father Whose infinity men know as His care for each one of His children. Kant's account of freedom as self-determination leads to a Pelagianism, which gives no account of the glories of grace nor can show how the highest form of action is always permeated with joy.

Oman attempts in *The Natural and the Supernatural* a description of the meeting of man and God which surmounts these difficulties. In a detailed account and analysis of human experience, he describes how the meaning and purpose of the supernatural is given through the contemplation of the natural and how by their intuitions of that meaning men are able in action to be reconciled to the natural. Thus men need accept no monism that disregards all dealing with the natural or calls that natural by the name of God. Thus as men recognise that reconciliation and revelation are reciprocal, they need never accept dualism as a solution though it must ever remain a problem. When persons can maintain a continuous relation to all the world through sincerity of feeling and faithfulness in action, morality becomes more than prohibitive rules and the peace of the Gospel more than the mystic's rest. Men know nature as that environment through which is mediated the immediacy of God's Love. Such a description provides no system for it calls men through mystery to a finer sincerity and through demand to a nobler faithfulness. It provides them with no natural metaphysics whose conclusions must satisfy sound reasoning. Rather it is the interpretation of all experience in the light of the Cross, as a journey of the mind into God.

After *The Natural and the Supernatural*, Oman produced one more work of consequence, *Honest Religion*.* Oman here returns to the expo-

---

* See bibliography, p. ii. *Honest Religion* was published two years after Oman's death. Mention must be made of *Concerning the Ministry*, published in 1936. These are his popular lectures to students for the ministry at Westminster describing his ideal of the practical minister. They are full of great charm and shrewdness. Mention must also be made of his two works on the Book of Revelation. See bibliography, p.i. These constitute an attempt at exegesis after attending a seminar of Professor Burkitt's.[31] As will be seen in chapter 5 of this thesis, Oman returned again and again to the problem of apocalyptic. These works, however, add nothing in principle to what he says elsewhere. The present writer is quite incompetent to make any comment on this exegesis and merely accepts the testimony of the experts that Oman's work in this field was not highly successful.

sition of the Gospel of the Cross as the only solution to the problem of faith and freedom. He adds nothing in principle to the position he had put forth in *Grace and Personality*. Certain points are, however, made with the exquisite emphasis of a man who knows this to be a final work. Also certain points in the Gospel of personal theism are clarified by relating them to the language of the philosophy of religion. Finally, certain specific issues of dogma are treated openly for the first time, e.g., the Virgin Birth. Oman faces, though not explicitly, the issues raised by the post-war reaction of Protestants against liberalism.

The chief difficulty in *Honest Religion* is that, though it is clearly intended for a wide audience, neither its style nor its content allows it that fate. Even when Oman writes simple sentences, there is behind them that depth of reference towards which the reader must strive. The strength of Oman's intellect never allows him to understand how difficult is his writing.

Despite this difficulty, *Honest Religion* remains a moving work of wisdom and imagination. Here at the end of his life stands a man of God. There is no cant or jargon about his theology. His characteristic openness with his readers, his appeal to them as dignified rational men, never fails him. All his maturity that does not lack intensity and all his strength that never fails in compassion are here to the full. Regulating all his thought shines his vision of man as called to accept in joy the way of the Cross. The last chapter in which he describes St Paul still praising the glory of God's Love through all disappointments and agony is the right conclusion to Oman's thought. In 1939 Oman died at Cambridge.

## CHAPTER II

The definition of Oman's concept of 'supernature' must be begun by describing how the supernatural makes its appearance to consciousness. This is necessitated by what Oman says about method in the study of religion. It has been regretted in the previous chapter that he does not say clearly in the first part of *The Natural and the Supernatural* that his philosophy is dependent on faith. Nor does he expound the nature of that faith as the simple Gospel of the Cross. This failure of exposition, rather than of content, is indeed the chief criticism that the present writer will at any time make of Oman. However, what he does say of method implies this dependence. From his strictures on method it becomes clear that the exposition of his philosophy of religion must proceed from an account of the appearance to consciousness of the supernatural.

On the question of philosophical method, Oman stands with the Platonic and Kantian tradition of beginning speculation from the assumption of a hierarchy of values as the most real and asserting its right of affirming an adequate ground for the same.\* Such a procedure, it must be admitted, does assume as solved the most difficult problem in philosophy. Oman would, however, maintain that such a procedure is a necessary consequence of the way in which experience is given to finite beings. To fail to make this explicit, whether in the interests of scepticism or of faith, is to be dishonest and to court muddleheadedness. To proceed with the discussion of Oman, assent to this assumption as to method must be given – at least provisionally.

This is to say that Oman starts from the premise that the determining factor in all our experience is our knowledge of the supernatural, regardless of how we suppose that we have come by that knowledge, and indeed even admitting that the attempt to analyse and to describe how we came by it must always be in terms of an imperfect inference. The recognition of this necessary irrationality from which all philosophy proceeds, whether it admit it or not, shows how far Oman departs from the dominant tradition of post-Renaissance philosophy. As he writes:

---

\* In the following description of Oman's philosophy of religion the present writer often prefers to describe Oman in language very different from that found in *The Natural and the Supernatural*. Oman never would have used such language as the above sentence. This procedure is believed necessary as Oman uses a vocabulary all his own which, though it often brilliantly illuminates by its individuality and its avoidance of jargon, also often obscures by its refusal to use technical terms.

There is a small difficulty in saying that Oman stands in the tradition of Christian Platonism. Oman rarely writes of Plato except in criticism. Indeed would any Christian doubt that Platonism cannot stand uncriticised in the light of the prophets and the Cross? Yet Oman's philosophy of religion remains indubitably Platonist. One wishes therefore that having written *The Natural and the Supernatural*, Oman had openly admitted that his Ritschlian contempt for Greek metaphysics could no longer stand and had acknowledged his debt to Plato in somewhat the way St Augustine did in his *Confessions* (vii, 9).

Theories of knowing are not first demonstrated, and then the nature of reality deduced from them: but philosophers, like other people, form their views of the world from their whole intercourse with it and according to their widest knowledge and highest knowing; and, like other people too, they only use their reasoning powers to test, and sometimes merely to maintain, what, on other grounds, they already believe. Hence their religious, or perhaps their non-religious outlook, is primary, and their philosophy, even when sincerely used for its true end, is only a touchstone of it.*

In the study of religion, assumptions cannot be confined to the self-evident (that is, where the terms are exhaustively defined through simple known relations). Religion is concerned with the supernatural environment and that environment has to do with 'the as yet unrealised.' Therefore it is quite vain, in speculating about it, to start from the self-evident and proceed by analysis. Rather it is necessary to work from intuitions and anticipations which are quite irreducible to simple modern relations.

Religion is not greatly concerned with interpreting experience as it is. It does not think it can be so interpreted. We must go as far as we can in understanding the world, because the better we interpret things as they are, the better we may see the higher world to be realised through them. Yet philosophy is only, as it were, the grammar of experience ... Even if we had an omniscient metaphysic of experience, philosophy would still not be religion, because religion would still be asking what God means to make of it all.

Theology, as the study of religion ought, therefore, to be of the nature of prophecy.†

Also it must be emphasised that Oman proceeds from sternly realist assumptions about this hierarchy of values.‡ Knowledge of 'environment' can only be given in the immediacy of experience. He asserts time and again that a proof of the ontological reality of any environ-

---

* *The Natural and the Supernatural, op. cit.* p. 149.
† Article 'Method in Theology' *op. cit.* p. 91.
‡ It may again be remarked that Oman would not employ a word such as realist in describing his own position.

ment cannot be reached by metaphysical inference from other premises.

> We cannot prove the reality of any environment while omitting the only evidence it ever gives of itself, which is the way in which it environs us. If this count for so little to us that we need to have its existence proved, it would not seem to matter much whether it exist or not: and in any case, no environment presents further testimonials besides its own witness. So far is reality from feeling obliged to meet all our objections that it only dimly unveils itself to our most sympathetic and far-reaching insight. This may be highly unphilosophical on the part of environment, yet the fact remains, and even philosophy can only accept it.*

Much modern philosophy had accepted as given the ontological status of the natural environment, because of the predominant interest in manipulating the natural, and because of the aftermath of the scholastic enthronement of the Aristotelian epistemology. Thus 'natural theology' attempted to argue from the natural as given to the inference that the supernatural existed. However, since the natural is also given to us in intuition, scepticism about its ontological status is on a plane with scepticism about the status of the supernatural.

> Thus the awareness of the reality of the supernatural is not something added ... from the natural world. The fatal misrepresentation is that, at this point, religion is identified with theology, and theology is hung up in the air without any world of its own to work in, so that it is expected to be its own reality, instead of being, like the other sciences, the study of a reality already given.†

Though Oman never writes of those European philosophers known as phenomenologists, his argument here is almost identical with theirs. Objects and values (aesthetic and moral) appear to consciousness as if

---

\* *The Natural and the Supernatural, op. cit.* p. 52.
† *Science, Religion, and Reality, op. cit.* p. 298. There is no evidence that Oman was greatly taken up with that brand of sceptical analysis associated with the Vienna school of philosophers. In his day it had not yet exerted its influence on the secular philosophy of England. For a discussion of what approach he would have made to the Vienna school see the final chapter of this thesis.

independent of consciousness. This appearance must be credited unless there are, from other sources, arguments against it. These arguments, if they are to be admitted, must in turn be able to show how the appearance of independent existence is so constituted. Thus Oman assumes that, though a strict proof of the 'objective reality' of environment is impossible, it is to be assumed so long as scepticism has no effective arguments against it. By what right does scientific verification assume that it is the criterion by which psychological impression is distinguishable from fantasy? When Oman uses about his work the term empiricist, he interprets the phrase quite differently from the English tradition of Locke.

It is this approach to the problem of ontology that sharply distinguishes Oman's thought from that of his contemporary and friend, F.R. Tennant.[1] As Tennant wrote in a review of *The Natural and the Supernatural*:

> It seems a great leap from the fact that we pass value-judgments, to the alleged fact that such absolute valuations bespeak another reality.*

Tennant sees that that alleged fact is self-evident to Oman, and as he cannot agree, he demands from Oman proof or at least reasonable grounding. Oman simply repeats his own position when he reviews the second volume of Tennant's *Philosophical Theology*. He writes:

> Is it not the essence of a really philosophical view to show that all enquiry is really only working backwards from the highest we know with all our learning and all our intuition, and that no enquiry, therefore, can legitimately call this higher world in question?†

This difference between the two writers is here made because their names are often classed together as 'liberal theologians.' Such a difference at this crucial point as to the possibilities of reason in theology makes any such coupling of their names inappropriate.

So important is Oman's stand on this matter that is will be illus-

---

* *Mind*, a periodical, London, 1932. See Tennant's review, pp. 212–18.
† *Journal of Theological Studies, op. cit.* Vol. XXXIII, p. 283. See also Oman's review of the first volume of Tennant's work, *Journal of Theological Studies, op. cit.*, pp. 403–7.

trated by his criticism of Descartes. In a period of intellectual uncertainty, Descartes had been motivated by the admirable intention of accepting no authority but the witness of reality to his own mind. However, because of his concentration on mathematical truth, he believed truth could be pursued from assumptions reduced not only to the self-evident but to the minimally self-evident. Such a method inevitably excluded the reality of the supernatural environment. By analysis all that could be deduced from such assumptions were mechanical explanations reached by alteration of the parts already given. Indeed, to set the whole system going Descartes had found it necessary to make use of the Platonist ontological argument, to show God as the ground of the existence of nature. That argument, however, had no valid place in his system. It assumes the reality of the principles of thought. How then can it be used to prove what it assumes?*

In comparison with any purely analytical method, one further description may be given of what Oman considered his own.

> It is never more than a pretence to start anywhere else than in the whole actual present, or with anything less than the conclusions of our experience. All we can do is to use the fullest capacity of mind which has been developed in us by the highest training of its powers, with all its knowledge and all its insight: and from the historical position in which we find ourselves, not to seek to empty ourselves of our convictions, but to be ready to revise them. That we can start from nothing and end with everything is plausible only because where we are to arrive is there all the time. Thus it is an illusion that we can work with any merely analytical method. Nothing is explicable about any environment except from the highest experience of it and the fullest knowledge of it we have. The only truly empirical inquiry works with all experience possible for us to have, and the other kind of empiricism, which is supposed to start with sensations, starts not from facts but from hypothesis.†

To many, such methodological assumptions will be indeed a scandal.

---

* Oman traces the influence of Cartesianism through the history of European secular philosophy down to Alexander, whose thought he believes to be still in the grip of the rationalist fallacy in a way that Whitehead's is not.[2] See Review of Whitehead's *Religion in the Making* in *Journal of Theological Studies*, Vol. XXVIII, 196–304.

† *The Natural and the Supernatural, op. cit.*, p. 117.

They do, however, clearly indicate that the account of Oman's concept of 'supernature' must begin with a synthetic description (which in no sense can be considered necessary) of how the supernatural makes its appearance to consciousness. Those who in the name of rational certainty call Oman a 'sixth sense' philosopher can but consider his thoughts mere poetic mythology. If the philosopher's task includes more than analysis, then in what follows he is performing a proper function.

## II

Oman begins his description of how the supernatural appears to men by stating:

> We know all environment, not as impact or physical influx but as meaning: and this meaning depends on (1) the unique character of the feeling it creates; (2) the unique value it has for us; (3) the immediate conviction of a special kind of objective reality, which is inseparable from this valuation; and (4) the necessity of thinking it in relation to the rest of experience and the rest of experience in relation to it.*

The unique feeling the supernatural evokes Oman calls 'the sense of the holy.' The unique judgment men make of its value he calls 'the judgment of the sacred.' The reality immediately apprehended as standing behind the holy and the sacred he calls 'the supernatural.' The activity of thinking [these] together he calls 'theology.'

In this paragraph many of the main terms and nearly all the essential assumptions of *The Natural and the Supernatural* are laid down. Immediately it must be admitted that Oman makes little attempt at analysing these assumptions and terms. For instance, 'we know all environment as meaning' is an ambiguous expression. What does Oman mean by it? At no point in the work is there an analysis of what this repeatedly used phrase means. It seems to mean that we know environment as objective value.† But it would surely have been better to have defined this in *The Natural and the Supernatural*. Also in the

---

* Ibid., p. 58.
† Oman in fact so defines it in his review of the first volume of Tennant's *Philosophical Theology*. See *Journal of Theological Studies, op. cit.*, Vol. XXXI, p. 404.

phrase 'a special kind of objective reality which is *inseparable* from this valuation' there is implied the enormous assumption that having value connotes objective reality. Such an assumption is necessary in Oman's system, but its central importance would be the better understood by the reader, if here it were analysed in relation to contrary positions. In the phrase 'the necessity of thinking it in relation to the rest of experience' Oman assumes a hypothetical unity of aesthetic, theoretic[al], and moral. As description proceeds it will be seen how the word 'feeling' is used in a different sense from the usual sense of his day and country. Should not this be made clear from the start and a justification of such a use attempted?

Oman's assumptions at this point are in certain cases clarified later in the work. To enumerate them here is not to imply any obscurity in Oman's mind. He is here laying down the basis for a philosophical theology which avoids those positions made untenable by the attack of modern scepticism on cosmological speculation. It is a very sophisticated paragraph. The objection is rather that Oman never makes public the private justification out of which this paragraph came. He begins his exposition almost at the point where a critical analyst such as Kant leaves off. The reason for this may be judged to be that Oman considered *The Natural and the Supernatural* as written for the educated layman who had not mastered the language of idealist analysis and who was more interested in the structure to be built on such assumptions. Oman's failure to analyse does however leave his work open to attack as leaving undefended his basic assumptions.

Leaving aside his silences, it is now necessary to describe in some detail how Oman uses his two terms 'the sense of the holy' and 'the judgment of the sacred.' What Oman had said in simple language in his theology about the meeting of man and God he now elaborates through the use of these terms. Here the two ontological relations to reality – action and contemplation – are described in relation to each other. Oman is at his most brilliant, not as an analyst but as a descriptive theologian with remarkable insight into the subtleties of man's consciousness.

'The sense of the holy' Oman applies to the unique feeling of reverence that certain ideas and objects evoke. The sense of the holy has its own unique quality as feeling, being a direct sense of a special environment. Immediately the difficulty arises of demonstrating its uniqueness. Feeling *qua* feeling is opaque to intellectual description. It only can be described by the apprehension of its *a priori* cognitive structure. It must therefore be emphasised from the start that Oman rejects the idealist account of feeling as the subjective appearance of judgment. Oman proceeds from a realist assumption as to the subject–object relationship. That is, the sense of the holy is a relation one term of which transcends consciousness. It is given within an assumed ontological structure. This makes it possible to describe the uniqueness of the feeling in a way that would not be possible in an idealist system. From the beginning we are given an object that makes a unique impression and so have some ground from which to proceed to mutual understanding. The sense of the holy can be isolated as unique in the hierarchy of our feelings because it is an appearance to consciousness always related to a particular form of valuing a particular environment.

This, however, leads to a further difficulty: the very ontological structure within which is demonstrated the uniqueness of the sense of the holy is only assumed at this stage in Oman's argument. It is neither carefully described nor substantially justified. It is necessary to proceed with the description without such a justification. The espousal of an untechnical language does not avoid the problems for which technical language was invented.

The sense of the holy can then best be described as the feeling stirred by that which we value absolutely. Because it is invariably connected with this absolute valuation, the feeling can be isolated from others that may seem similar when subjectively considered. For example, *qua* feeling it might be difficult to differentiate between the awe associated with magic and the awe of the holy. Yet they may be distinguished because the awe attached to magic always results in a natural valuing – that is, it is attached to values which are merely the convenient. But the sense of the holy always passes into a valuation to which our convenience must be made subordinate – that is, into a value that is absolute. Thus the mark of the sense of the holy is that, even at its most primitive, it is the ground of our moral reverence.

In a passage towards the end of *The Natural and the Supernatural*, Oman illustrates the progress of the sense of the holy from awe to reverence:

As reverence, the sense of the holy is the humility which is the fountainhead of all right and courageous independence in seeking truth, and truth only: as awe, it is a timid and even a shuddering fear of all enlightenment. As reverence, it is the graciousness, the sincerity, the high responsiveness which gives us deliverance both from the mere pleasing of the senses and the artificial tastes of our time, and makes us both small and great before the austere sublimity of true beauty of form and character: as awe, it is as a cloud of blackness upon the earth and of horror upon our souls, leaving us nothing in which to rejoice, and no spontaneity of feeling by which to appreciate. As reverence, it is the regard for our neighbour and our own souls which gives us independence of the canons of respectability and what we may call traditional divine jurisprudence, enabling us to exercise freely our own judgment of good in face of our own situation: as awe, it imprisons us in traditional rules and formal respectabilities.*

Thus, whereas the distinguishing mark of the sense of the holy for the purpose of description is that it always regards some idea or object as absolute, the mark of its historical development is that it is always becoming less the awesome holy and more the ethical holy. Thus when the appearance of the holy among primitive men is viewed with sufficiently sympathetic and understanding eye, even what seems its crudest manifestation is found always related to the sense of something absolute in value. At the same time, even in the highest reaches of morality there is a quality akin to awe. For as the sense of the holy must become ethical because it is sense of an environment which is essentially ethical in character, so morality for Oman is a religious development springing from our sense of the holy.

Thus from the earliest appearance in history the sense of the holy is an incipient moral reverence. The mark of development both in individual minds and in the progress of the race is that the holy becomes less fearful as it becomes more an evaluation of the supernatural environment as sacred. The possibility of a growing power of the rational over all our feelings at the expense of the merely impulsive lies in this interaction between feeling and value. A feeling is rational when it is proportionate to and dependent on the actual value it regards. Thus the sense of the holy becomes more rational as by regarding our absolute valuations it becomes an objective reverence for the supernatural

---

* *The Natural and the Supernatural, op. cit.*, p. 308.

rather than uncontrollable subjective emotion, overriding the autonomy of our personalities. It becomes instead an objective sense of an environment which calls upon us to respond as persons.

It may be remarked in passing that Oman does not explicitly distinguish between primary and secondary orders of knowing – that is, between the description of the appearance of the holy to his own consciousness and the inferences about its appearance among primitive men. This is matched by a failure to be explicit about the distinction between (1) the development of the holy in individuals from awe to reverence and (2) the same development in the progress of the race. As a man of his time he was naturally taken up with evolutionary and historical questions. It is perhaps picayune to ask him to make such a distinction. Yet in the light of much contemporary confusion about these matters one can but wish that he had been careful to make such distinctions openly.

Indeed the interaction of feeling as intuition and of man's valuations is in Oman's opinion a difficult matter to define clearly.

> On the one hand, the valuation may immediately follow the feeling, or, on the other, the feeling may immediately follow the valuation, though it is not, in either case, mere sequence. We value things because they appeal to our feelings, but we also feel about them largely as we value them. Yet, more frequently perhaps than any other feeling, the sense of the holy follows and depends on its value; and, on the whole, this becomes increasingly the case as the mind develops.*

Thus to sum up, at this point in the analysis all that can be affirmed is: (1) the sense of the holy can be described and its uniqueness deduced by the fact that its appearance is always related to an absolute valuation of some object or idea; (2) in the progress of individual men and in the progress of the race as a whole the sense of the holy is tending to become less predominantly awe and more consciously a sense of ethical reverence; (3) these processes take place as the feeling forgets its subjectivity and becomes an objective sense of an environment.

---

* Ibid., p. 66. Oman never made a clear or close analysis of how man's autonomy of insight carries over into volition. Perhaps that is to ask too deep a penetration of the mystery of personality.

The relation of the sense of the holy to man's capacity to make judgments of absolute value may be illustrated by a discussion of Oman's criticism of Rudolph Otto.*[3] For Otto, the holy is subjectively the sense of the numinous evoked by the object *numen*. It is the sense of a *mysterium tremendum et fascinans* before the sheer might of which the individual feels himself abased. In it the individual is given directly a sense of his creatureliness. This sense is a unique datum of consciousness, impossible to define rationally. As such, it is to be carefully distinguished from the intellectual and ethical activities of man. It is in fact related to these activities *a priori*; but it is given to consciousness as a continuingly separate experience, the individuality and independence of which must therefore be insisted upon. To use Oman's language, the *numen* is not an environment which men can know increasingly as ethical; but one that continues to be of might and power. The source of our knowledge of God is in this intuition of His absolute Might and our utter dependence on that Might. We add only by the process of schematisation all the rational predicates that we may attribute to Him.

The essence of Oman's criticism of Otto's position is that it does not distinguish rightly, nor relate rightly, the sense of the holy and the absolute valuation associated with it. Otto, in his use of the phrase 'the sense of the numinous,' includes under one term a feeling and a valuation, which should be distinguished. The result of his failure to recognise that he has thus included under one phrase two distinguishable activities is that he has then no way of drawing the distinction between the religious and magical. For once having included in the holy, albeit unconsciously, man's ability to judge objects as having absolute worth, the distinction between natural and absolute values cannot be used to differentiate the religious holy and the magical. In Otto's system, the value springing from the holy is as natural as that which results from the magical. Therefore there is no way of distinguishing these realms.

A cause of this identification is Otto's acceptance of the Kantian universalist account of the moral judgment. Thus he cannot properly relate value and feeling, because the rationalist account of moral judg-

---

* See Rudolph Otto, *The Idea of the Holy*, translated by J.W. Harvey, Oxford University Press, London 1926. For Oman's criticism of Otto, see particularly Article in *Journal of Theological Studies, op. cit.* 'The Idea of the Holy,' Vol. XXV, pp. 275–86. See also Oman's review of Otto's *Religious Essays: A Supplement to the Idea of the Holy, Journal of Theological Studies, op. cit.*, Vol. XXXIII, pp. 286–8.

ment can only be appended to the irrational sense of dependence by schematisation. Otto is left with an inescapable disjunction between the rational and the irrational in man. By identifying the religious with the irrational the possibility of a religion of persons is forever closed. His attempt to overcome that disjunction by stating that the rational and the irrational are connected a priori is no satisfactory solution. In Oman's opinion this is only to say that they are connected historically by reflection and that is a denial of what is true of every known form of mental development – namely, that what appears in the course of development can always be detected in germ long before it appears in separate or distinguishable form.

The central question at issue is whether the *numen* becomes an object to be valued absolutely through schematisation by ideas added from other spheres, or whether there is already in it a valuation that only needs to be more clearly understood to be known as ethical. Is not the consequence of accepting the first of these alternatives a denial of prophetic monotheism? For is it not to assume the existence of two supernaturals, one of which is realised through the irrational dread of the creature – whether man or beast – and the other in the autonomy of the children of God?

Oman appeals to the biblical tradition. What was the essence of that tradition but a growing realisation that God's Holiness was an ethical Holiness? How can that growing realisation be interpreted but as the gradual objectivisation of the sense of the holy through its valuations of an absolute character? Oman writes:

> One has an uncomfortable feeling that, with his views, Professor Otto, had he lived then, might not have had his present enlightened views about sacrifice, and that he would have regarded Micah as little better than a rationalist.*

He asks Otto how his position can be reconciled with the Gospel of Our Lord with its insistence on the infinity of God's care for freedom.

Oman illuminates his criticism of Otto's position by appealing to a particular experience of his childhood. Though this adds nothing in principle to what has already been said it is given here as[4] an example

---

* *Journal of Theological Studies, op. cit.*, Vol. XXV, p. 284.

of the force and individuality of Oman's approach to theology. He describes how as a child he had once ridden past a spot where in pre-Christian times there had been a place of worship. He had felt a strange stirring of awe and his horse had bolted. He addresses to Otto therefore the following question:

> As the feeling had probably not arrived at being religious for my horse and had ceased to be religious for me, it would be necessary to ask, what was the peculiarity which, without disrespect to his intelligence, I may assume my horse not to have attained and which, without excessive pride in my state of civilisation, I may assume I had passed beyond, which made it for primitive man religious?

In attempting to identify that experience of the primitive men and to relate it to the environment that had evoked it, Oman continues:

> And is not the essence of it that it is an order of absolute value which, when it escapes from its material form, is just the ethical sacred, the sense of the requirements of a Spirit in the world which is absolute and of a spirit in ourselves in its image which has its worth in accepting as its own these absolute requirements and refusing to bring them down to the level of our temporal convenience? It may only appear in an irrational material taboo, but, if man has said 'This is sacred and I would rather die than disregard it,' he is not only religious, but, by his religion, he has won a footing amid the sands of changing impulse and association. My horse, we may assume, had not reached this valuation, and I was at least learning to make it by less material ways.*

However, although the sense of the holy can only be described in terms of the values it regards, it is not simply the sense of moral reverence that accompanies our actions – that feeling which Kant maintained must be interpreted as respect for the moral law. To interpret the sense of the holy as merely consequent to moral action, is to misinterpret the central role that feeling plays in Oman's theology. To him, feeling is the only gateway to knowledge of reality; it is the pioneer in all our experience. He writes:

---

* *Journal of Theological Studies, op. cit.*, Vol. XXV, p. 283.

To be obtuse in feeling is merely to be wall-eyed before every kind of reality; and to have no keen sense of the holy would mean that, however we lived and moved and had our being in the Supernatural, we never could realise it.*

Whatever inadequacies he finds in the thought of Schleiermacher at other points, he is decisive in supporting him in this insistence on the central importance of feeling. The sense of the holy only becomes moral reverence because of the moral nature of the supernatural environment that evokes it. It is, however, the feeling which gives original experience of that environment. It is the root from which the value arises. 'The root lives and grows by its foliage, even while the foliage is wholly dependent on the root.'†

Because feeling plays so important a part in Oman's thought it is a pity that he does not analyse what he means by that word. He rightly rejects the rationalist accounts of the beautiful and the sublime as only allowing to 'feeling' what can be justified by the understanding. Perhaps it is then an impossibility to go farther than Oman does in his accounts of the norms of feeling. (See following.) But he uses the word to convey a cognitive activity that is not far from that 'intellectual intuition' which lies at the basis of all Platonic theologies and the possession of which Kant was at such pains to deny to men. One wishes that if this were so Oman had admitted that relationship and had attempted some discussion of the *a priori* nature of that faculty. As his thought stands, the term 'feeling' bears a heavy weight without sufficient discussion to support it.

The sense of the holy arises spontaneously in consciousness from the unity of awareness which underlies all perception of nature.‡ Oman uses the term 'awareness' to describe that state in which all the senses are active, but in which no particular object in the natural world has

---

* *The Natural and the Supernatural, op. cit.,* p. 79.
† Ibid., p. 66.
‡ In expounding a monotheistic system such as Oman's which seeks at all costs to avoid any dualism between nature and supernature repetition is difficult to avoid. Oman's conceptions of 'awareness' and 'apprehension' are the very basis of his account of how the natural is given to consciousness and will therefore be discussed at greater length in chapter 3. Here there will only be given what is necessary to the description of the sense of the holy.

been singled out for apprehension. It is a state of pure undifferentiated feeling. Because men only analyse their consciousness when they are adults and as adults all consciousness is permeated by the activities of the intellect, they can never return to this state of awareness directly. Nor can they ever reach back to that stage of consciousness, for recollection is only possible after the apprehension of some particular object. However, in the analysis of adult consciousness it can be recognised that such a state is a necessary foundation for the later, more intellectual forms of knowledge. Also by an analysis of the ways of knowing of the artist and of the child, both of which class of persons are more intuitive than philosophers or scientists, we can begin to understand the character of such a state. With this awareness there arises spontaneously the sense of the holy. Men are carried beyond the senses to a holy environment on which all the world of the senses depends. Thus all environment is felt as supernatural as well as natural. It is not a perceiving of the supernatural in the natural, but rather a perceiving of the natural as all in the supernatural. Men are given immediate contact with an environment on which they feel the totality of nature (themselves included) to depend.

In a long and beautiful analysis of his own childhood in the Orkneys Oman describes how the sense of the holy became active in him, just as his unity of awareness was first broken by individual apprehensions.

I had been to church. I think the preacher had been expressing the absolute difference between good and evil under the material forms of heaven and hell. I went down to the edge of the water alone, and stood, a very small child, with the full tide at my feet. Along the smooth waters of the sound a path of sunshine carried the eye out to the open sea. It flashed on me that, if I dropped in and floated out, with endless sea around, I should be alone for ever and ever.

The result was a consciousness of myself which set me thinking, yet not about myself. Instead it caused doubt about whether the world I saw was in the least like the world other people saw. I tried hard to find out, but words were like the measuring rods of the relativist – their use was regular, but this might conceal any difference of meaning.

Theoretically no very small boy should have any such notions: nor would he, if they were problems of comprehending and explaining. But the contention here is that they rise up spontaneously from the form of our awareness. This is what gives them their extraordinary intense character, quite different from our later days when, by understanding and explaining, we have reduced time and space from fascination to formulas, and ourselves, in the midst of them, as bearers of the same strange impressive quality, to an argument about the existence of the soul.*

The fact that the sense of the holy is never primarily applied as ethical feeling indicates its independence from judgment. It first appears in two ways: (1) as the undifferentiated holy and (2) as the particularising holy. The undifferentiated holy is the feeling of the supernatural as one absolute reality. Oman describes it in the following ways: It is like 'seeing the sunshine and not what it illumines.'† It is 'having a general sense of infinite force.'‡ It is the feeling of a bare empty form of unity so that all that exists is given as one universe. In it we are given immediately three unities: (i) a unity of the mind as one awareness, (ii) a unity of all environment as one and (iii) a unity of feeling connecting that one mind with the one environment. These unities are not to be confused with the ideas of reason reached by the intellect as necessary inferences of our scientific knowledge. The ideas of the reason are reached by speculation. These unities are given immediately in feeling and underlie all our activities. These unities are an example of the difficulty that reason must find in discussing Oman's philosophy. Here two metaphysical unities and a unity of relation between them are reached from the experience of a pervasive and unvarying feeling of reverence. That this may be so it clearly possible. Yet no account is given of how they are arrived at. They can in no sense be considered necessary.

The particularising holy is the feeling of holiness concentrated on one object. Oman describes this feeling in the following simile:

It is like running your head so hard against a brick wall that the wall seems to embody the whole power of the universe.§

---

* *The Natural and the Supernatural, op. cit.*, pp. 136–7. Though Oman asserts (and it is judged correctly) that Wordsworth's poetry is more deeply tinged with theory than the poet admits, he uses passages from 'The Excursion' and 'Tintern Abbey' to illustrate what he means by the sense of the holy.
† *The Natural and the Supernatural, op. cit.*, p. 61.
‡ Ibid., p. 64.
§ Ibid.

The sense of the supernatural is concentrated on one object of the world of the senses. So intense is the feeling of holiness about that object that men know it to be dependent on an environment of absolute holiness. To use language other than Oman's the particularising holy, at its best, is a concentration of the sense of holiness on one object of the natural world so that we intuit it to be a *vestigium Dei*.

Thus as the undifferentiated sense of the holy gives men the sense of the unity of all their natural environment as belonging to one supernatural, the particularising holy gives them the sense of the individuality of all objects of the natural world – a particularity which can result in the valuing [of] each object as having its own importance under its dependence on an environment of absolute holiness. The sense of the holy can therefore be either overwhelmingly exclusive in its concentration on one object or it can be the most diffuse of emotions in that it gives the bare empty form of unity which gives men the world as a universe. Though to a practical theologian such as Oman the problems of cosmology are not a matter of central interest, here answers to them are found in terms of the sense of the holy. The Aristotelian natural theology of sense having gone down before the attacks of the sceptics, it is replaced by an intuitive theology of nature.

As Oman bases his philosophy on an intuition of man as autonomous (not yet defined) the misuse of any faculty by men is always possible. The misuse of the sense of the holy may therefore change that sense from the gateway to reality to an obstacle holding men back from it. The chief misuse of any activity arises when men concentrate on it to the exclusion of other necessary activities. Therefore however disastrous for the misuser, for the philosopher attempting to understand man and his world, the analysis of these abortive misuses is helpful, for in them he can see certain activities both concentrated and isolated. Thus Oman attempts to understand the undifferentiated and particularising holy by analysing their misuse.

The undifferentiated holy is misused when men are content to abide in the very form of unity it gives and do not proceed to give content to that form from the challenging world of the senses and the duties of the world of action. Men so wrap themselves in the enjoyment of this bare form of unity that they fall into the illusion that by a denial of the importance of their senses and their moral intuitions – that is, by emptying themselves of all that makes them persons – they will come to know God. In denying their own personality and the value of the natural they deny the Personality of God; in denying the Personality of God they deny their own personalities and the reality of the natural. They seek the impossible, to know God above the categories of nature and history. This is Oman's definition of mysticism: 'There is a direct revelation of God which is not through experience of the world; and the presupposition of this type of mysticism is that experience is not a manifestation, but a veil which for moments waves aside and gives glimpses of reality.'*

Nevertheless, though the mystic's experience of resting in this form of unity reveals no reality, it is useful to the epistemologist in illuminating the form of feeling that underlies all our activities. It suggests the fact that the feeling of unity is the motive that drives us to seek harmony and peace in all our experience and the strength that sustains us in that search even when harmony and peace appear to our intellects to be absent. By an analysis of the mystic's activity we are able to isolate the central question about the undifferentiated holy – namely, what kind of unity should it challenge us to seek. 'We can sink back into its mere undifferentiated unity, or we may find it a challenge to seek an ideal which does not suffer us to rest anywhere in the effort to harmonise all our experience.'†

The particularising holy is misused when the concentration on one object remains fixed simply on that object and does not pass over into an ethical judgment. The feeling fails to be related both to the undifferentiated holy and to our general moral duties. Thus the particularising holy is the source of idolatry, whether that idolatry be the central factor or a more peripheral part in advanced religions.‡ As a general rule it

---

* *The Hibbert Journal*, Vol. XXVI, pp. 445–58 Article 'Mysticism and Its Expositors,' see p. 450. Bibliography, p. iii. An account of Oman's attitude to mysticism will be found in Appendix A of this thesis, under his classification of religions. It may be remarked here that so ineffable is the experience of the mystic that though one may sympathise with Oman's dislike of its esoteric quality, his certainty about the nature of mysticism is difficult to follow.

† *The Natural and the Supernatural, op. cit.*, p. 65. Oman distinguishes between those who shirk the challenge of the natural and of autonomy by a flight to the transcendent unity of the holy, and those who rest in its undifferentiated immanence. The former he calls acosmic pantheists, the latter cosmic pantheists. See further Appendix A.

‡ In *The Natural and the Supernatural* Oman generally takes his examples from ancient religions and therefore avoids those openly controversial criticisms of certain Christian traditions which characterise his theological writings.

may be laid down that the particularising holy is misused among ordinary men fulfilling the simpler functions of society; whereas the misuse of the undifferentiated holy is the vice of the esoteric aristocrat, freed from the particularity of manual work. Both abuses concentrate on the subjective quality of the emotion rather than on the objective environment given therein. The mystic basks in his own contentment with the given unity; the idolater stirs up his own emotions and those of the crowd. Psychological statements add nothing to a discussion of truth or falsehood, but it may be remarked in passing that Oman's deepest contempt is for the religious aristocrat who attempts to know God by ways not easily open to ordinary men; therein may be seen the abiding influence of Oman's origins with the strong sense of moral egalitarianism which characterises the Presbyterian congregation, so intricately and strangely related to its doctrine of election.

In the light of the misuse of the holy the norms of right feeling may be the better described. Oman returns again and again to the attempt to capture just what he means by right feeling. Some of these attempts are as interesting as anything he ever wrote.* He would in the end admit that only the lover of the beautiful can truly grasp his meaning. Clear definition of the norms of feeling is an impossibility. First, feeling is an ultimate in experience and as such its uniqueness cannot be captured by the categories of the intellect. Secondly and more important, feeling 'is the pioneer in all experience, and, therefore, the higher appreciation of its values is more continuously in the making.'† Oman believes that God leads men to Himself through this mystery of intuition and therefore its norms could only be accurately described if that journey of the mind into God were conceived as finite.‡

The two words that Oman uses to describe the qualities of right feeling are 'sensitiveness' and 'sincerity.' They apply to the sense of the holy which gives men the supernatural environment. 'Sensitiveness' is the right functioning of our senses as keen and active when our whole being is alert to appreciate all our environment. The joyful awareness of all that comes through the physical senses leads us to that upon which the

---

* *The Natural and the Supernatural, op. cit.*, pp. 140–3 and 209–12.
† Ibid., p. 212.
‡ In the description of the norms of feeling that follows, once again the reader must be referred ahead to the next chapter, where the importance of feeling in giving us the natural will be discussed.

natural depends. Here Oman is insistent that it be remembered that feeling is an activity and therefore must never be thought of as passive.

> The activity of the will proper, directed to possessions to be gained and evils to be escaped, is generally recognised, but responding to impressions justly and completely is as truly an activity as altering the world for our benefit.*

Thus sensitiveness is just the reaching out in sympathy to environment so that it can tell us of itself. Wordsworth had defined that quality of feeling as love. Oman accepts such a definition, if by love is meant the willingness to accept all that may be known and not the mere appreciation of any select part of our environment.

Of much greater importance for the right sense of the holy, indeed a concept of central importance in Oman's thought, is 'sincerity of feeling.' Sincerity is the right interpretation of what we are given by our sensitiveness. The regulating fact about sincerity is that the less aware [we are] of the feeling by which we know any environment, the more objective our knowledge of that environment will be. The same law holds good both of our sense impressions of the natural world and the sense of the holy that gives us the supernatural. The more the impression is objective witness, the less it is the subjective feeling. Sincerity is, then, the ability by which the subjective feeling is kept in proportion to the objective environment that evokes the feeling. Oman describes insincerity of feeling in the following terms:

> It is not a question of having 'inordinate affection,' but of school-mastering feeling to make it say what is desired, or turning it into sentimentality, divorced from all objective significance. True sincerity means having neither hard Stoicism, especially towards others, nor false sentimentality, especially towards ourselves. Lack of it is not concerned merely with ourselves and other persons. It goes to the roots of our whole perception of what is true and great in all our environment, natural and supernatural, being the essential and creative sincerity by which our knowing is wholly concerned with knowledge.†

---

* *The Natural and the Supernatural, op. cit.*, p. 204.
† Ibid., pp. 211–12.

Sincerity of feeling, as applied in the sense of the holy, is the proper use of our autonomy of insight into the valuable, in which men are given that hierarchy of values crowned by the Cross of Christ. It is Oman's description of that illumination of the soul by the Good, the miracle of which all Platonists have been at such pains to describe. To fall completely into Platonic language, if men possess that faculty they are given that system of subordination and superordination, by which they know that the Will of God creates both the principles of finite things and the finite things themselves. To use language at this point so utterly foreign to Oman is simply to remark how much a concept such as 'sincerity of feeling' belongs to the Platonist tradition of St Augustine and St Bonaventure.[5] The vision of the Cross takes men beyond the Platonic belief that knowledge of the Good is found particularly among the intellectual few, and opens to them a new joy in the created world. It is not, however, essentially at variance with that incipient idea of conversion, found in Plato, in which a doctrine of autonomy makes its hesitant appearance. Thus sincerity of feeling is that faculty whereby the supernatural, given to us as feeling intrinsically tinged with value, is rightly graded into a scale proportionate to the actual values of the environment that has evoked the feeling. Thus in Oman's system persons are essentially mediators of value. Sincerity of feeling is the norm of that autonomy of insight by which we reach out for the objective values of the given; our wills are the activity by which we freely choose between that given.

It is now possible to see more clearly what the sense of the holy should ideally be. 'It is not to be cultivated as overwhelming emotion till all things merge into its dazzling glow, but to be changed into an objective reverence, the witness to an environment of this absolute quality.'* It does not give men as philosophers a theoretical system so complete that it frees them from intellectual and moral struggles; it must not be supposed to give religious men that sense of peace that frees them from striving both in the natural and in the supernatural.

[The peace and harmony it gives] is not emptiness, but a world of infinite variety, harmonious to the feelings, like the poet's; a world challenging to understanding and in relation to one mind, like the philosopher's;

---

* *The Natural and the Supernatural, op. cit.*, p. 308.

a world to be explained on one consistent principle, like the scientist's; of one sphere of active victory, like the moralist's; of one reverence, like the religious thinker's.*

But before it can be seen how the above is possible, a description must be give of the way the judgment of the sacred arises in consciousness.†

The supernatural is given immediately to consciousness in the judgments men make of absolute or unconditional value. These absolute valuations Oman calls 'the judgments of the sacred.' It is the valuation of some idea or object as being of a worth that transcends comparison with what men judge convenient. 'The sacred ... means ... that which is of incomparable worth, and incomparable is not merely super-excellent, but what may not be brought down and compared with other goods. The moment we ask how this sacred value com-

---

* Ibid., p. 146.

† Before leaving the sense of the holy, mention must be made of Oman's debt to Schleiermacher and Windelband in his use of this concept.[6] In the first chapter has been quoted Oman's recognition of the importance of Schleiermacher in re-emphasising the central place of feeling for theology. In the same article on Schleiermacher, Oman defends him against the criticisms of those theologians who declare that in Schleiermacher's system 'The Word of God' is replaced by the relativity of subjective emotion. Much of the criticism of Schleiermacher is based on false interpretation of what he had written. 'One might gather that there is nothing objective about Schleiermacher's theology and that by feeling he meant sentiment and by absolute dependence mere mystical self-surrender, none of which goes with his persistent and well-grounded claim to be empiricist throughout' (*Journal of Theological Studies, op. cit.*, Vol. XXX, p. 401).

However, Oman believes that Schleiermacher fails to relate properly intuition to man's autonomy of volition. Oman also mentions his debt to the writings of Wilhelm Windelband. (See *Präludien*, W. Windelband, Tübingen, 1921, Vol. II. Essay, 'Das Heilige'; for Oman's comments see *The Natural and the Supernatural, op. cit.*, Appendix A.) However, the present writer is unable to see any real difference between Schleiermacher's and Windelband's positions except in (i) the use of the specific term 'the holy' in the latter's thought and (ii) Windelband's development of the implications of that intuition within idealist assumptions. He is therefore unable to understand just what Oman's debt to Windelband is.

The fact that Oman had been thinking in terms of the sense of the holy, so related to the judgment of the sacred, for at least twenty years before the publication of *The Natural and the Supernatural* is illustrated by a long note in his book *The Church and the Divine Order*. Here he approves the view of Kattenbusch that the difference between Apostolic and Catholic Christianity lay in the belief of the former that to be of God and to be morally holy are one, while the latter had taken over from pagan thought the idea of the holy as being in essence awesome rather than ethical.[7] See *The Church and the Divine Order, op. cit.*, pp. 121–3.

pares with pleasure or ease or prosperity, it ceases to be sacred.'* The fact that men are capable of such valuations is the primary intuition which regulates Oman's epistemology. To repeat, Oman also assumes the immediacy of the supernatural in that valuation. He does not, as Kant in *The Critique of Practical Reason*, proceed by inference from the appearance of absolute valuations among men to the inference of the existence of God.†

The appearance of the judgment of the sacred to consciousness stems from the sense of absolute dependence of the world upon the supernatural. As the sense of the holy arises spontaneously in men from the general sense of awareness, so the judgment of the sacred also arises spontaneously as men begin 'to apprehend' particular objects of nature within that general field of awareness. 'Apprehension' is that activity by which we isolate individual objects, but have not yet attempted to comprehend or explain them by the categories of the intellect. Thus in apprehension men contemplate the object as it is in itself. They do not distort the object as when they attempt to use it for their own purposes by comprehensions and explanations. Thus as men isolate some individual object of the natural world within the general sense of awareness, with that apprehension there flashes up in consciousness a value, which we judge as absolute. Initially, among children or among primitive men, that valuation is associated with the particular object in the apprehension of which it appeared to them. But gradually it is detached from that fixed association, and becomes a general judgment best described as the absolute value of the true, the beautiful and the good. Just as the sense of the holy changes from an occasional stirring of awe associated with some particular setting into an attitude of reverence underlying all experience, so the judgment of the sacred ceases to be a valuation associated with a fixed material embodiment and becomes a judgment of those sacred ideals by which men can determine their dealing with all environment. In converse with the natural world, felt already as dependent on that which is holy, men become increasingly capable of a general application of ideal values. Thus as in the sense of the holy a distinction is made between the

---

* *The Natural and the Supernatural, op. cit.*, pp. 65–6.
† It cannot here be discussed whether Kant departs from this position in his last work, the *Opus Postumum*; see for a discussion of this John Baillie's *Our Knowledge of God*, Oxford University Press, 1939, the concluding chapter.[8]

awesome and the ethical holy, so in the judgment of the sacred the distinction is between the material and the ideal sacred. It is never possible to free the sacred completely from its material embodiment, but continuously in individuals and in the progress of the race, men are becoming capable of associating the sacred less and less with such objects as beasts and birds, rivers and forests, and able to recognise that it is a general judgment of absolute value. The supernatural is always calling men to recognise it for what it is.

Oman does not accept what he considers the usual explanation of why sticks and stones have been judged of absolute value. This explanation insists that primitive men's scales of value were so different from ours that we cannot hope to understand them. But according to Oman, in even the crudest and most repugnant judgments of the sacredness of some object, it is possible to recognise, if we are sympathetic, three forces that relate them to our more general judgment of absolute value: (i) the affirmation of a reality of absolute value; (ii) the subordination of all else to it; (iii) a tendency to regard its nature less and less materially.

Oman accounts for this embodiment of the sacred in material form by distinguishing between what he calls 'free' and 'fixed' ideas. Fixed ideas are those fixed in one context, that is, they can only appear to consciousness with their whole experiential setting. On the other hand, free ideas are those that we can apply to any experiential context. But, as in Oman's system it is the sacred that determines our ability to transcend the flux of the natural and therefore gives us our ability to formulate free ideas, clearly men can make judgments of the sacred before they are capable of formulating free ideas. Therefore it is understandable why in primitive men and children the sacred is lodged in a material embodiment.

> Primitive man could no more conceive sharpness apart from a cutting instrument than sacredness apart from a material embodiment. Yet as he knew, in spite of that, what sharpness meant, so he knew also what sacredness was.*

The material sacred is then 'just an idea fixed in the particular material

* *Science, Religion and Reality, op. cit.*, p. 292.

conditions which stirred the sense of the holy and gave occasion for the valuation as sacred.'*

In his discussion of free and fixed ideas one wishes that Oman had been more specific in his vocabulary. The phrase 'in the context' could mean either the particular context when the idea is not yet grasped as such, of the specific context when the idea is grasped in a particular manifestation of it. Presumably he means that both 'sacredness' and 'sharpness' may be grasped not as ideas. But Oman is not clear whether here their similarity ends. For 'sharpness' has no meaning beyond its manifestations in a specific context. 'Sacredness' on the other hand – that is, as an idea of the class *a priori* – has an extension beyond objects in space and time. At least it must here be affirmed, that despite arguments to the contrary, ideas such as 'sacredness' have extension beyond space and time. Clearly such an assertion is of the essence of Oman's position.

Oman's problem seems to be that there was a common historical difficulty in reaching both empirical and *a priori* ideas. But was not there a further difficulty in isolating *a priori* ideas from material embodiment? He does not seem to make clear in his discussion the difference between ideas having extension beyond space an time and those that have no such extension. The result is that ideas like 'sacredness' and 'sharpness' seem almost to be identified as of the same level. But would not such an identification be disastrous for his whole position? The obscurity is once again judged to arise from his fear of traditional metaphysical language, i.e., his failure to clarify his use of the word 'idea' and his fear of such a term as 'a priori.'

Oman illustrates from the religion of Israel the development of the material into the ethical sacred.

> The prophets, just because their higher truths were sacred and required all their devotion, emancipated religion from material associations, in a way unparalleled elsewhere. These associations, which were sacred in the popular mind and were defended as such, the prophets denounced as idolatry, and found it the chief hindrance to the discernment of spiritual progress and what they regarded as the true sacred: but nevertheless even the prophetic religion had itself travelled through a stage at which

* *The Natural and the Supernatural, op. cit.*, p. 90.

the judgment of a sacredness about life had been embodied in material objects like the ark.*

The tendency of the material sacred to become a general judgment of ideals by which we deal with the natural is, then, that in which the progress of the race consists.†

By the appearance to consciousness of the judgment of the sacred we become in a true sense persons, that is, we are able to exercise our wills and our intellects. Only by the impact of the absolute value are we able to resist the determining impact of desire and association. Our wills awake to its incomparable demand so that we find ourselves autonomous beings. We find that consciousness of determining issues, that knowledge of our responsibility, those feelings of remorse which are the appearance to us of 'that deep and permanent essence of the soul,' our free wills.‡ We discover that we belong to an environment of absolute value and that we can only find our true selves by freely given loyalty to it. What has been given to us in feeling, our wills must choose to accept or to reject.

Through this absolute demand, intellectual activity becomes possible for us. For it alone has the force to free us from the dictates of passing association, without which freedom it would not be possible to order the impressions of our senses in a systematic way. Also, once it has arisen to consciousness, the judgment of the sacred is determinative of all our feelings. No longer is it possible to have merely natural or instinctive feelings, for they are transfused with the valuable and the rational.

Oman applies his intuition of the primacy of the sacred to the questions of theological history. He asserts that it was by making the judgment of the sacred that man became man. He examines four definitions

---

* *Science Religion and Reality, op. cit.*, p. 293.
† Oman does not in this passage seem to distinguish between the fixity of ideas among primitive men and their lack of clarity as to the content of the valuable. Also, Oman may be criticised, as he has been in the case of the holy, for failing to distinguish between the two orders of knowing. (i) knowledge of our own consciousness (ii) inferential knowledge about primitive man. It is perhaps pedantic to make this criticism once again, but he often writes of primitive men with just that certainty that he rightly found so repugnant in Sir James Frazer.
‡ *The Elements of Pain and Conflict, op. cit.* See Oman's first article, 'Human Freedom,' p. 70. For a further discussion of Oman's concept of personality see chapter 4.

of man, (i) man as a rational animal, (ii) man as a tool-using animal, (iii) man as a laughing animal, (iv) man as a religious animal. He clarifies the difference between the first and the fourth by defining rational as the ability to seek the true order of and relation between events, and the religious as the ability to make judgments of absolute worth. The common root of these definitions is in man's refusal to accept his environment as other animals do. But one of them must have been the stem from which the others arose. Oman judges that only the appearance of absolute values in consciousness was capable of giving that faith by which man arose above the flux of circumstances.

> He [man] obtained firm footing to deal with his environment the moment he regarded anything as sacred, because he could say 'No' and was no longer its mere creature. Without this foothold, no extension of his associations, no adjusting himself to his surroundings, no resolve to grin and bear it would have set him free: and without this freedom reason would not have gone beyond mere association, or working changes in his environment taken the place of mere adjustment to it, or laughter lightened grim endurance. But the moment he said 'This is sacred, this is not the realm of ordinary values,' even granting that it was said of what to us is the insanest of taboos, he had said to his world as well as to himself, 'Thou shalt not.' Forthwith he began to be master of himself, and thereby master in his world. Then, in some true sense of the word, he began to be free. Thus by the judgment of the sacred, man was set free from the leading-strings of nature, the nurse which, with the immediate values of the visible world, had hitherto nurtured all living creatures.*

This application of the primacy of the sacred to the problems of theological history raises in acute form the question of Oman's refusal to use traditional theological language in *The Natural and the Supernatural*. What kind of an answer is to be expected from such a question as 'What caused men to be men?' Because this passage is introduced quite without the traditional conception of 'Creation,' it could be interpreted as a circular argument. The assumed primacy of the sacred is used to prove itself the cause of our origin and then evolutionary

---

* *The Natural and the Supernatural, op. cit.,* p. 85.

theory is used to buttress the primacy of the sacred. Of course Oman is guilty of no such absurdity. What seems fair to say of him, however, is that in an attempt to touch the men of his age, who were so often intoxicated with evolutionary theory, he introduces an obscure passage unrelated to the theological dogma on which it depends. In his theological writings Oman avoids such difficulties as the doctrine of creation and confines himself to questions of practical import. It is therefore difficult to understand what he would have made of that mysterious doctrine. It seems likely that he would have accepted it. Here the dogma needs to be brought out into the open – that is, if this passage is to be meaningful. It may be remarked once again that the avoidance of traditional Christian language, in order to help non-Christians, often leads Oman into obscurity.

In the descriptions of the judgment of the sacred Oman insists on the absoluteness of ideal values and on the fact that they are given to men with the contemplation of the natural, and that the consequent judgment is always a dealing with the natural. Oman's position is that in converse with the world in sincerity of feeling one is given values both natural and ideal.*

Oman's position on the relationship of ideal to natural values will be approached by a discussion of what he made of Kant's account of ethics. As has been remarked in the previous chapter, Oman had a profound admiration for that account. In attempting to understand the problem of how finite minds are capable of making absolute judgments, Kant had never reduced the categorical quality of morality in the name of naturalism, nor had he attempted to preserve their absoluteness by defining the individual as a mere appearance in the process of cosmic reason, as the Hegelians. On the one hand, he had refused to reduce duty to passion; on the other, to reduce it to metaphysics.

As preliminary to what Oman does say, the remarkable similarity between his criticism of Kant and that of Max Scheler and Nicolai

---

* Oman's terminology may be criticised on a small point. In defining the sacred as that of incomparable worth he seems to be suggesting a lack of relationship between the naturally desirable and the valuable in general, which can only be defined as subordinate–superordinate. Would it not have been wiser to use some other noun than 'value' after the adjective 'natural'? This may still be said even though in Oman's position natural and ideal values never appear to consciousness in clear distinction.

Hartmann may be mentioned.*[9] Oman only mentions Scheler once and merely in passing and never mentions Hartmann.†Their relationship seems to have been the understandable one of differing men arriving at the same historical period at the same form of criticism. Hartmann develops in more technical language the ontological and epistemological implications of that realist criticism. He makes clear, for instance, as Oman does not, that quite a new meaning must be given to the term *a priori* than in the Kantian system. Oman, however, took much farther the theological implications of that criticism. Despite Hartmann's wide account of the phenomena of morality, Oman has a much deeper intuition into the moral predicaments of all sorts and conditions of men. Hartmann's technical use of language does sometimes clarify the implications of what Oman says.

Kant's belief that if the moral judgment is to be absolute it has to be derived from the form of the individual will, means that he defines the moral judgment in a general form that is empty of content. Defined as the necessary form of the wills of all rational beings, it can only lay down universal laws which cannot be related to the individuality of each person. The duties of the prince and the slave cannot be distinguished. The moral judgment, because of its universalist form is negative in quality.

> The essentials of the practical reason or conscience, which he so derives from the form of the individual as of sacred worth, may be thus summed up.(1) An absolute end: Treat every individual as an end in himself and never as mere means to other ends. (2) An absolute rule: What fulfils this end is a categorical or absolute imperative. (3) An absolute test: Test each judgment by its fitness to be a law universal, that is, for all individuals so valued. (4) Absolute independence: Our absolute worth confers as a right and demands as an obligation responsibility for our own beliefs and actions. (5) Absolute motive: Act only from reverence for this sacredness alone.
>
> ... its rules also are merely negative in spite of the positive form. They are: Do not treat man merely as a means; do not make your rule of life

---

* See M. Scheler, *Der Formalismus in Der Ethic und die Materiale Wertethik*, Halle Niemeyer 1916, and N. Hartmann, *Ethics*, translated by Stanton Coit, Allen and Unwin, London, 1932, particularly Vol. I, chapters XI, XII, and XIII.

† *Journal of Theological Studies, op. cit.*, Vol. XXXV, p. 200.

convenience; do not look at things selfishly; do not be merely an echo of other people; do not obey mere impulse and self-interest.*

Such an ethic is based on the fear that the given is an infringement of our autonomy and that therefore the supernatural environment is only inferentially given. In fact our intuition of belonging to it, through the sense of the holy, is a condition of the moral judgment.

Kant speaks:

... as though we could simply say, 'Reverence man as an end in himself,' and then conclude this to be the order of the universe; whereas man has only a right to this reverence, if already, by the order of the universe, he has a value in some form absolute in a world of this quality.

Though there is a sense in which we can because we ought, it is, therefore, obviously not in the sense that we can by mere fiat of will, it matters not what kind of persons we are or in what kind of world we act, do what we see to be right, or even put ourselves in the way of seeing what right truly is.†

Because in Kant's system moral action does not spring from our reverent sense of the holy, it can never become the glorious liberty of the children of God, joyfully striving after Their Father's Will. It can only be their attempt to impose order by law in a world of chaotic inclinations. Oman quotes the example of St Paul as a man who recognised the impossibility of the Law as a means of achieving righteousness. He writes:

Victory over ourselves herein is not possible by resolution, however courageous, but only by finding a better environment waiting to be possessed. Only as we seek a better country can we leave a worse, even though we must also be ready to go out, not knowing whither we go, as the way of seeking it.‡

The sacred is not then the bare form of the categorical imperative.

---

* *The Natural and the Supernatural, op. cit.*, pp. 319–20.
† Ibid., p. 302.
‡ Ibid., p. 304. For a discussion of how the Kantian account of morality affects the conception of nature and supernature see chapter 4.

Rather all our experience, all our striving and all our inclinations are intrinsically judged as of absolute and natural value. In as much as we are sincere in our feeling of the holy, absolute values appear to consciousness along with other values and the will is the arbiter between them. Sacred values arise from the sense of the holy just as colour arises as quality from the act of seeing. Thus Kant's conception of a chaos of inclinations that the will subordinates to its own order is quite denied. In Oman's ethic of intuition the will must constantly be active, responding in manifold individual situations that arise from this vast hierarchy of values.

Before leaving what Oman says about Kant's account of morality, several difficulties must be mentioned. The accounts of Oman and Kant have one essential difference – namely, Oman's assertion and Kant's denial that man is capable of intuition into the content of the valuable. This difference is of such importance as to make their systems difficult to compare. However, several comparisons will be made. Oman's system is clearer how moral concern comes into experience and also clearer how differing men fulfil the moral demands of their differing functions. It must be admitted however that in Kant's account it is clearer how the high universal ethical demands of the Cross are to be expected from each Christian. Oman in his Gospel proclaims the universal demand of love by the possession and denial of the natural. To use that language: though Kant is not clear how the natural is to be possessed, he is extremely clear about how it is to be denied. Oman's position, which as a *theologia crucis* must insist on denial, never makes clear how men are to judge when to deny and when to possess the natural.* His intuition of the supernatural in sincerity of feeling is less capable of definition than Kant's categorical imperative. As in most cases with Oman, it is a question of what he does not say, rather than what he does. If two points were more clearly described it would be easier to understand what he means. A closer analysis of how intuition passes over into judgment and a fuller description of what he means by the terms ideal and natural values would clarify his position.†

---

* For a discussion of this point in terms of the practical questions of the Church and the State see chapter 6 of this thesis.

† See Oman's section on 'Natural and Ideal Values' in *The Natural and the Supernatural, op. cit.*, pp. 204–7.

To proceed with the description: once it has been granted that feeling is the pioneer and that absolute values are given in the sense of the holy, we must recognise the importance of the will and even the importance of the negative criterion of the categorial imperative. Though our will can only become operative as an absolute value is presented to consciousness, we only become free as our wills freely choose to follow that absolute claim against the claim of some natural value. This may take the form of a decision between right and wrong in an overt action, and may be largely a refusal to follow the desirable. Thus the categorical imperative is a valid negative test whereby we set up our freedom as absolute, even though it cannot help us to live ever-increasingly in the supernatural.

Faithfulness in action is at least as important as sincerity of feeling for man's knowledge of the supernatural. They are both dependent on each other.

To sum up: through his use of the terms 'the sense of the holy' and 'the judgment of the sacred,' Oman has described the relationship between religious dependence and moral independence, which he had defined as the crucial question of the Christian life in *Grace and Personality*. For the purposes of description the sense of the holy can only be described by its relation to our sacred valuations and the reality that evokes them. Yet it is only possible to make such judgments because we have already entered the realm of the supernatural through the sense of the holy. Feeling, it must be repeated once again, is the pioneer in all experience. Yet it is only the pioneer. It depends for its continuance on the faithfulness of our wills. The vision of the Cross must mean that we take up our crosses and follow Him. In the final analysis, Oman makes faithfulness in action more the mark of the religious man than sincerity of feeling.

Everything that is sacred is in the sphere of religion, and everything in the sphere of religion is sacred. Unless dogmas express beliefs valued as sacred, they are mere intellectual formulas; unless rites are the worship of a power valued as sacred, they are mere social ceremonies; unless God Himself embody all we value as sacred, he is a mere metaphysical hypothesis. Only when the valuation as sacred accompanies the sense of awe and reverence have we the religious holy; and only a reality having this absolute value is the religious Supernatural. Therefore, if there be any one mark of the sphere of religion, it is this valuation of everything within it as sacred.*

'The supernatural' may therefore be defined as the environment that stirs our sense of the holy and demands to be valued as sacred. From the point of view of epistemology the sense and the judgment come first, as the reality of the environment is felt and valued in them. From the point of view of ontology the supernatural is primary for it is the reality in which those activities are grounded. Thus though the mark of religion is the sacred, the sphere of religion is the supernatural. In our daily lives we are concerned with what is and not with the analysis of how we know what is. Yet for the purpose of analysis and speculation the problems of Knowing and Being are inseparable in a system such as Oman's.

Thus, because we enter the supernatural environment as we exert our personalities by faithfulness in action and sincerity of feeling, we know in what sense we can call it personal.†

> Absolute values of truth and beauty and goodness are not dependent on our acceptance of them, yet they are not a mere divine ether, in suffusion in the universe and breathed into individual spirits as a sort of breath of life. They are true and beautiful and good only as they are chosen by persons; and their value is in the worth of the persons who in freedom choose them and are themselves thereby made true and beautiful and good. An order which is thus a realm of the free children of God, and not a theatre of even the most admirable puppets, and has its values in even the imperfect accord of their freedom, and not in the most perfectly correct opinions and gracious sentiment and impeccable behaviour imposed on them, is at least not better expressed by anything less than the mind of a person.‡

* *The Natural and the Supernatural, op. cit.,* p. 69.
† Oman's use of the term 'environment' with its impersonalist associations is to be regretted, since neither the natural nor the supernatural is conceived impersonally in his work. Its use is another example of his appeal to men trained in the impersonalist categories of post-Renaissance philosophy and science.
‡ *The Natural and the Supernatural, op. cit.,* p. 341. The Personality of God is the faith on which *The Natural and the Supernatural* is founded and for the demonstration and justification of which it was written. This demonstration must be delayed till further preliminaries have been described. See chapter 4.

Thus so far we have a distinction in consciousness between the sense of the holy and the feelings of the senses and between natural and ideal values. With this goes a distinction in reality between nature and supernature. At the same time we have a relation between the natural and the supernatural, because the sense of the holy is never given apart from the natural and the judgment of the sacred always results in a dealing with the natural.

> As the Supernatural is one thing if it is manifested through the Natural, and another if it is wholly apart and the Natural a mere temporal illusion, so the Natural is one thing if it manifests the Supernatural, and another if it is merely physical.*

We cannot rightly speak of the supernatural and exclude the natural; we cannot rightly speak of the natural except as God's world. Thus the central problem of Oman's philosophy of religion is this proper relating and distinguishing of the natural and the supernatural. This calls for speculation.

In Oman's insistence that religion must not be identified with theological speculation, he does not deny the value – indeed the necessity – of such speculation. The very character of the supernatural means that we can only live in it as free persons. Man, as he is free and therefore rational, cannot regard as real any environment that is not diaphanous to reason. Thus once we have achieved the use of free ideas, all our perceptions of the natural world and all our intuitions of the supernatural are increasingly transfused with those ideas. To this extent, all experience is determined by our theories and therefore, if we do not make a conscious effort to bring our theories continuously before the bar of our experience, the possibility of new experience will be more and more limited by the bounds of our theory. Though we can only reap in theology as we have sown in sincerity of feeling and loyalty of will, in the long run as we have sown in theology, we and others influenced by us will reap in sincerity and loyalty. We must pursue theology even though we know that its conclusions can never be stated in any final propositions.†

---

\* *The Natural and the Supernatural, op. cit.*, p. 205.

† A discussion of the relationship between Oman's view of theology and his doctrine of the Church will be found in chapter 6 of this thesis.

Once having so isolated the sphere of religion as the supernatural and having entered the pure air of theology, is not the enquiry at last free from the grossness and crudeness that have marked the holy and the sacred throughout history? However, as idolatry and sacrifice have marred the sacred and the holy, a confusion of dogmatic voices has marked the history of men's speculation. If we seek the depressing we find here the Tower of Babel and the Inquisition. Oman describes the way in which the supernatural has been conceived:

> To one it is an almost material force; to another a purely spiritual influence. To one it is indivisible unity; to another it is gods many and lords many. To one it is the most personal of all that is conceivable and the source and goal of all freedom; to another it is a fixed cosmic process of which the individual is merely the vehicle, and freedom is only compulsion from within and not from without. To one it is the meaning, goal, completion of the natural world; to another the natural world is a mere veil to hide it. To one it is a world to be entered by 'building up the pyramid of our individuality'; to another we enter it as we lose[10] even our identity. To one it has depths which we cannot, by any searching, find out and where our wisdom is faltering humility; another it makes omniscient enough to know that those who differ from him should be burned for the good of their souls. To one it is the immovable pillar of an unchanging world, secure in recognised authority and venerable custom; to another it is wholly concerned with worlds unrealised as yet, requiring heroic venture and the challenging of the obsolete and effete. For one it concentrates its fierce light on a single purpose and a few austere demands; for another, like the morning sun, it seems to turn muddy pools and common window-glass into flaming diamond.*

These confusions must in no way make us doubt the need of clear thinking about the relation of the natural to the supernatural, any more than shuddering dread and crude valuations should make us hesitate in our search for a nobler reverence and a better will. Before proceeding to the discussion of Oman's account of that relationship, some description must be attempted of how he believes the natural to make

---

* *The Natural and the Supernatural, op. cit.,* p. 70.

its appearance to consciousness. With that description the next chapter will be concerned.

## III

To conclude this chapter, Oman's dislike of the closed rational system must once again be repeated. Bergson might well have been thinking of Oman as a practical theologian and a great man of God when he made his last work an appeal for the open as opposed to the closed approach to religion and morality.*[11] For Oman finality in theology is the chief heresy as it denies the liberty of the children of God. Yet in attempting to expound Oman in reasonably consecutive terms his sense of mystery may easily be turned into a new finality. To do so, would be to lose[12] his partaking in the tradition of Christian agnosticism which recognises the unfathomable mystery of God.

> If we realise that absolute value is in our environment of the Supernatural, and that this is the realm of freedom, and that we are not free but only becoming free, with freedom as our goal and not our present achievement, we should not be discouraged from seeking a higher response to it in truer reverence, and a higher judgment of it in a truer sacred, or a nobler more adequate conception of the Supernatural, because what was once holy for men has become the ordinary, once sacred the commonplace and profane, once the Supernatural the merely rational or even the irrational ... Progress means that what once required high and sacred endeavour has become the ordinary and accepted both in the world and in human relations, while the holy and the sacred have moved on to a higher plane, with the still higher as both promise and power of attainment. The Supernatural thus creates ever greater freedom and is fuller environment for it: and, were we capable of fixing it at any point as universal determined laws, and so lose sight of the challenge to set up and pursue the infinite and eternal, we should no longer be in it. Wherefore the call is neither to faint nor grow weary, even were it certain that we are only a little farther on our way than the most primitive savage.†

* H. Bergson, *Les Deux Sources de la Morale et de la Religion*, Editions Skira Geneva, 1945.
† *The Natural and the Supernatural, op. cit.*, pp. 337–8.

CHAPTER III

In approaching Oman's concept of nature, it is once again insisted how much in his philosophy of religion he remains a practical theologian. Religion is always, whether admitted or not, concerned with a practical attitude to environment. Therefore the discussion of it can never consist in detached speculations about the cosmos. Therefore, Oman is not concerned, as was a contemporary such as Dean Inge, with a cosmological idealism that reconciles Christianity with the second law of thermodynamics.[1] He is interested in justifying by an epistemology what he already knows in faith – namely, that nature is a realm through which God speaks to His children and through which they do His Will. That is, he is interested in demonstrating in modern language his own dim partaking of that vision of nature which received the glory of each lily of the field and understood the meaning of each sparrow that fell and yet was able to pass beyond that love of nature to die upon the Cross.

Thus though Oman is not primarily concerned with cosmological speculations but in demonstrating a right attitude to the world, he cannot accept a monotheism that is not cosmological. Pascal's theology, tinged always with the fear that faith could only be maintained in despite of all that his intellect told him of the impersonality of the cosmos, is not possible for Oman.[2] This position is not, however, rejected, primarily because of the intellect, but because it must fail in that act of joy which to Oman is of the very essence of the Christian faith. Such dualism, even though Christian, must end in a morality that is not far from the Stoic. Thus though not concerned with cosmology as bringing Christianity 'up to date' with Einsteinian physics, he is interested in a demonstration to modern men of the personalist categories that must regulate the Christian's conception of nature.

So to present a conception of nature to modern men, Oman had to understand all those a priori insights – from nature as geometrical and mechanical system in Spinoza to nature as a great work of art in Goethe – which had imposed themselves so deeply on the thought of his time. He had clearly drunk deeply of a manifold of such visions as they had appeared in the art, the science, and the philosophy of modern Europe. Oman's glory is that he never surrenders to such partial visions and yet humbly tries to understand their real basis, so that they are not neglected or merely abused but shown in a scale of subordination under his prophetic monotheism. He does this by describing the visions of the saint, the artist, and the scientist, and arranging them into a hierarchy.

## II

Oman begins his analysis of how nature makes its appearance to consciousness by dividing our knowing into four distinct types: (1) Awareness; (2) Apprehension; (3) Comprehension; (4) Explanation. As unique data of consciousness these cannot be accurately defined, but only illustrated. He illustrates them in the following passage:

> While walking in a dreamy mood along a country road, we may have a vivid sense of all that is about us, without attending to anything in particular. Our knowing is then a general field of *awareness*, including scent and sound as well as sight. The more we are entirely in this state of pure awareness, the more all our senses are active, so that we may even have vague realisation of the taste of the apples in the orchards and the coolness of the waters in the streams.
>
> Something in this field arouses particular attention, say an object moving toward us on the road. If it especially interest us, as, for example, by being unfamiliar, we concentrate attention on it to see exactly what it is, seeking to *apprehend* it as one object by what appears to be its more relevant and important details. Let us say that we apprehend it to be a man riding a bicycle.
>
> Then, supposing we have none of the information we afterwards learn to include under the name bicycle, but have everything to learn about it, we try, as it approaches, to *comprehend* it. This we may do by considering the machine in relation to the man as a means of locomotion: and we think we comprehend it when we understand how it is the means for gaining this end.
>
> Finally, as it passes, we are faced with the problem that it seems to have no support from its breadth, yet keeps upright while travelling along a line. This singularity we must try to *explain*: and we do it with such general principles as the scientific knowledge we happen to possess provides.*

* *The Natural and the Supernatural, op. cit.*, pp. 120–1.

Several conclusions about our knowledge of nature, implicit in this division, point the proper way of reaching a valid concept of nature. First, as we proceed in our knowing from awareness to explanation, our interest is more and more concentrated and what is known increasingly limited. Secondly, as we proceed from awareness to explanation, our activity becomes less one of feeling and more of the understanding. The given element in knowledge becomes less important and our interpretation of that given by the categories of the intellect increasingly so. In the two former types the mind is mainly engaged in the contemplation by feeling of the objects as they are in themselves; in the latter types our interest is in manipulating the objects for our own free purposes. In awareness and apprehension we are perceiving nature; in comprehension and explanation we are using it. Thirdly, it must be borne in mind that all our comprehensions and explanations about objects of the world would not be possible if we had not previously apprehended objects within a general field of awareness. This fact may be forgotten by the practical adult living in a world he has to comprehend and explain, but it still remains a fact with which the philosopher must deal. From this data Oman arrives at the conclusion that if we are to know what nature is, we must start our analysis from an attempt to understand how it makes its appearance to us in awareness and apprehension. At the very least we must avoid the error of reaching our conception of nature only from what we know of it in our comprehensions and explanations.

To the criticism of this tendency Oman returns again and again. Those called to the activities of the scientist and the speculative philosopher are often the least suited to understand perception. Because they live constantly on the plane of the intellect, they forget just how perception operates through feeling and is received as particularity. Their theories of perception reduce it to a purely rational activity, with disastrous effects on the whole system involved. This tendency, operative in all periods, has been particularly evident in post-Renaissance philosophy. Men proud of their ability to control nature, equated knowledge of nature with control of it. Philosophers of this period conceived nature from inference based on the ability to control it by explanations. The result was that during this period such strange conceptions of nature arose as 'a mere dead abstraction called matter; then a kind of Divine speech, regular, but with no continuous reality; then a mere succession of impressions, with no link save custom.'* Men so taken up became blinded to the witness of nature in feeling, which is the foundation of all other relations to nature.

Through all his work Oman is objecting to that lack of humility among the intellectually gifted, in the name of the Christian understanding of God's revelation to all men. This pride is vouchsafed in the exaltation above all others of the truths of the laboratory and the study. Oman vindicates as against this the experience of the majority, the importance of which has been denigrated by rationalist philosophy. His egalitarianism is not as in Kant's case confined to an egalitarianism of action. It includes contemplation, whereby simple men in their practical callings may be given in and through nature the vision of God. It is the fear that the city will take from men the vision of nature in any terms save that of the tourist resort that makes Oman so fearful of industrialism.†

Therefore in his own attempt to expound an adequate Christian account of nature Oman proceeds from an analysis of awareness and apprehension.‡ For that purpose he attempts to isolate and to examine the experience of apprehending individual objects in a general field of awareness. He recognises that we cannot reach back to a state of pure awareness, because recollection does not become operative until there is some individual apprehension to recall and a context by which to recall it. Therefore, its priority must be recognised from the fact that our earliest remembered apprehensions are always given within such a general field. Even the task of isolating apprehension requires no mean feat of imagination for mature men who have long since lost the direct flame of their apprehensions, because of the immediate and continual calls to comprehend and explain their environment. If apprehension of

---

* *Method in Theology, op. cit.*, p. 88.

† Because of this fear, it is disappointing that Oman never develops the practical implications of his criticism of the scientific industrial civilisation. See chapter 6.

‡ Oman has been criticised by Tennant for not giving adequate space to the analysis of scientific knowledge and devoting too much to knowledge of nature given in awareness and apprehension. See Mind, 1932, op. cit. To say this is to infer that Oman is attempting in The Natural and the Supernatural to expound a balanced and well-rounded position. It is judged that this was never his intention. Rather that work concentrates on knocking the props under certain false emphases of modern thought and of re-emphasising certain positive intuitions of Christian truth. He is not concerned with a balanced synthesis, as for instance one finds in St Thomas.

the world is to be understood, the task is to transport oneself by imagination back to the world of childhood, when the light of pure feeling was untarnished and unbroken by the intellectual necessities of later life.

> We can ... recall a time when we lived in a continuous, lively awareness, with apprehension only as a brighter light always moving across its field, without ever keeping one object long in the foreground, and when comprehending and explaining did not trouble us.
>
> The rapidity, sureness, completeness and penetration of apprehension at this stage are for us, in later years, almost inconceivable. The objects of it still stand out uniquely in our memories, and what we now apprehend is vague in comparison, and, even so, is largely dependent on this youthful experience.*

The nature of awareness and apprehension is also illuminated by the study of those masters of perception – the poets. In any great poet we find a remarkable ability for perceiving concrete reality as it is. Oman chooses Shakespeare for his analysis.

> The difference between using Shakespeare in this connexion and, let us say, Hegel, is that while both are thinking about experience, Shakespeare's thinking springs spontaneously out of perceiving and is more likely to illuminate the process than Hegel's thoughts which are dialectically introduced.†

In beginning his analysis of perception by examining the work of a supreme artist, Oman conforms with all that he has said about the appropriate method for theology. Only by starting from the fullest and richest that the philosopher knows and working back from that to its elements can we hope to understand perception at its more ordinary. To Oman the Cartesian method of starting with the minimally self-evident is nowhere more unsuitable than in the question of perception. The application of the Cartesian method to perception resulted in atomic sensationalism, the foundation stone of modern scepticism.

* *The Natural and the Supernatural, op. cit.*, p. 123.
† Ibid., pp. 132–3.

Thus in one of the truly brilliant passages in *The Natural and the Supernatural*, Oman analyses the art of Shakespeare and his own childhood consciousness.* Though it is necessary to draw out in the following pages the epistemological conclusions of this passage, it must be admitted that in such a synopsis the flavour and originality of Oman's mind is lost.

The perception of the poet and that of the child are interfused by dominant intuitions of infinity. In both cases this intuition – because it is not grasped intellectually but is a baffled sense of infinity – is embodied in a symbol. With the child this embodiment took the form of an intuition of the endlessness of space. In the previous chapter the passage has been quoted at length in which Oman describes his childhood experience at the water's edge. Then as awareness was first breaking into acute apprehensions, there came to him a feeling of the infinity of space. In Shakespeare's perception the sense of infinity is embodied in an obsession with time, dominant throughout his imagery.

> With Shakespeare this burden of the sense of time has little to do with any idea of quantity, but is a quality which comes very near to what we have called the undifferentiated holy. He does not speak of ages. Ancient and modern seem to have little meaning for him. Three hours suffice to express it, as when the fool says very wisely 'it is ten o'clock, and but one hour ago it was nine and one hour hence 'twill be eleven.' It is this tale of our ripening and rotting, the tale of our terrible aloneness, which has in it the qualitative difference of the finite and infinite.†

Oman maintains that all great poets have some such dominant intuition of either space or time. Dante and Milton were obsessed with the idea of space.

This intuition of infinity interwoven in all true perception arises from the fact that in and with all our awareness there comes to us the sense of the holy. It is quite false then to talk of purely natural perception: from the first our perceptions are touched by the sense of something more than natural. We do not perceive the natural world as an independent entity which exists in its own right, but as a world depen-

* Ibid., pp. 128–43.
† Ibid., pp. 131–2.

dent on and transfused with the supernatural. As in general awareness we reach out in appreciation to nature there arises a feeling of reverence for that upon which nature depends.* Thus the child's and the poet's baffled intuitions of infinity are but attempts to embody and thereby begin to understand that sense of an infinitely holy environment, which has come to them in the clarity of their awareness.

> It is not a perceiving of the Supernatural in the Natural, but it is a perceiving of the Natural in the Supernatural in the sense of a value which could have no lower origin.†

It is in this childhood state then that persons are given those three unities which have already been described in the second chapter.‡ It is within these unities that all perception operates so that sense data are given rather as a langauge than as uncoordinated atomic sensations.§ The sense of the holy through these unities in effect solves for Oman all the main problems of what Professor Laird has called cosmological theism as opposed to axiological theism.¶ At the risk of repetition it must be regretted that Oman does not make clear just how imperfect is the inference by which these unities are derived from childhood consciousness. He makes no attempt to draw out his meaning at this point by comparing his position with any of the well-known idealisms. As has been insisted upon again and again, cosmological doubts do not seem to have plagued Oman's faith and therefore he is not greatly concerned with cosmological questioning in *The Natural and the Supernatural*. There is something almost cavalier, however, about the way these unities are introduced in relation to our knowledge of nature and used to solve quickly problems of the first magnitude. As imperfect inferences their validity could only be demonstrated in terms of the whole position of which they are a part. It can certainly be admitted that that whole position is a remarkable and convincing one. Yet for the slow

---

* Later in his work Oman identifies reverence more explicitly with the power to appreciate, see *The Natural and the Supernatural, op. cit.*, p. 211.
† Ibid., p. 212.
‡ (1) a unity of environment as all one, (2) a unity of our individual minds as a unique system, and (3) a unity of pure feeling relating our minds with environment.
§ For Oman's discussion of this point see later in this chapter.
¶ See J. Laird, *Mind and Deity*, Allen and Unwin London 1941, final chapter particularly.

witted, Oman could, at least, have included with the introduction of these unities a passage showing what a vast role they perform in his account of experience.

Thus despite all the individuality and concreteness of Shakespeare's perception we know that all he perceives is held together as belonging to one environment seen by the unique system that is his own mind, which has reached out to the world in one unified feeling of awareness.

So with the child:

> While my apprehensions of the countryside continually varied with sunshine and shadow, day and night, summer and winter, my general awareness of it was neither of a changing scene, nor of the aspect I preferred, nor was it of an average impression or of a composite picture, but of something one in all its moods and aspects, much like awareness of a friend ... This general, sustained aesthetic impulse, and not a series of individual impulses which had to be changed as attention moved from one object to another, caused the restlessly inquiring nature of attention.*

In the very intensity of his reverent awareness the child first reached some sense of himself as distinct from the world.

It must be repeated that these unities lying at the base of perception are fixed unities of feeling and as such distinct from the free unities we reach by reflexion. As we become free persons our intellects reach transcendental ideas or as Oman would call them, free unities of reflexion. However, it is by the fixed unities of feeling that we first know the world to be a sphere responsive to our activity.

Within this general field of awareness, 'apprehension' lights up the concrete individuality of the world. So Shakespeare perceived a world in which each thing and each person was its own unique self. His mind was untroubled by the abstractions and generalisations that dim the glass of vision. Everything and every person had 'a local habitation and a name.' His particular genius lay in apprehension.

> This interest in the vast variety of human nature sprang from the clearness with which he saw everyone as an individual and his value just as man. Working mainly with awareness and apprehension, he does not

---

* *The Natural and the Supernatural, op. cit.,* p. 135.

group men together by general conceptions and relations. His whole idea of tragedy depends on the sense that everyone is alone in the depths of his soul, with his own responsibility and destiny.*

So also with Oman as a child:

The most noticeable feature of my earliest view of the world is of how minutely, definitely, decisively everything in it was individual. My language being an advanced Aryan tongue, I had abstract terms, and no doubt made some use of them. But they were luxuries and not necessaries. That to their owner a flock was only sheep, which he did not know one from another, seemed to show an incredible blindness. The birds were too numerous and rapid and changing for personal acquaintance, but a flock of them was an object by itself, with its qualities of flight and grouping; and when birds were nearer and few enough for separate attention, they were always particular living creatures, each with some singularity of colour or form or behaviour. Life of every kind fascinated: and there was a different quality of apprehension of it which is lost when interests are in another direction and classification has to be used to save the trouble of individual apprehension.†

As we feel for individual objects we come to value them rightly, and to value them rightly is to know them for what they are. Thus whereas in awareness the essence of right feeling is sensitiveness in which we reach out in reverent appreciation to all our environment, the prerequisite of right apprehension is sincerity, that ability to feel each particular object of nature for what it is.‡

---

* Ibid., p. 130. Oman does not discuss here the difference between Shakespeare's knowledge of objects of nature and of other persons. Oman does not in fact in *The Natural and the Supernatural* concentrate on that difference between knowledge of natural objects and persons which has occupied much British philosophy since Cook Wilson, and which on the Continent has been more ably and imaginatively discussed by Professor Buber[3] than by anyone else. This is probably because he had always assumed that difference in a way that those trained in and surrounded by the primacy of natural science did not. Presumably in his system we are given in sincere apprehension of other persons in their proper value, so that if we follow that intuition in faithfulness in action we will come to know other persons as they truly are. For a brilliant mention of the subject see *The Natural and the Supernatural, op. cit.*, p. 340.

† Ibid., pp. 133–4.

‡ See previous chapter.

The chief quality of Shakespeare's art is sincerity. All else is subordinated to the overriding interest of seeing the world just as it is, of placing the appropriate value upon everything. This sincerity saves him from cultivating the merely pleasurable. Easy enjoyment or superficial beauty of form – the traps of the less sincere artist – do not tempt him from his essential task of seeing 'life steadily and seeing it whole.'[4] His sincerity of feeling creates objectively true works of art.

So equally with the child:

> ... I cannot recall any memory of attending to anything because I liked it or turning away from it because I disliked it. On the contrary, in particular apprehensions, the conscious purpose of gaining pleasure or shunning pain was conspicuously absent, or at least it was over-ridden by something of general import which was much more powerful.
>
> It may, of course, be argued that the only possible motives are subjective pleasure and pain, whether we recognise them or not; and that when we say they are not, we ought only to say that youth has not reached the time of reflexion. But this is to settle a question of experience by a general conclusion of comprehension, which is precisely what is here being challenged.*

Oman agrees with Goethe that we should ask the boys and the birds, rather than the philosophers or the scientists, how the cherries taste. And he adds that in their subjective apprehension of cherries would be found a truer objective description of cherries and their value in the whole scheme of nature than would be found in the categories of the plant biologist. Thus by apprehension we come to know

---

* *The Natural and the Supernatural, op. cit.*, p. 135. These descriptions of Oman's childhood cannot be passed by without once again comparing them to St Augustine's description of his childhood. To refer ahead to chapter 6 it does not seem inappropriate to remark that Oman remains agnostic about the dogma of original sin. The sincere and passionate decency that rings throughout his account of childhood cannot however be accepted as a universal phenomenon among men. In *The Office of the Ministry* (see bibliography, p. i) Oman remarked that man should keep his guilts and sins to himself. Perhaps it is just this motive that keeps him silent about the terrible side of childhood. This may be doubted, however, for in his accounts of adult life there remains this fine straight faith. In writing about forgiveness, as the crown of all human activities, his examples are of the need to forgive rather than of the need to be forgiven.

nature as it is in itself. We know it as a hierarchy of beings whose varied comparative values we can make some attempt to gauge.

With the development of apprehension our attitude to nature is
changed, for it is with apprehension that sacred values first make their
appearance to consciousness, and as our wills respond to them we
become free persons. From that moment, nature becomes less and less
a realm that we contemplate in feeling and which gives us its varied
comparative values, and becomes a realm which by free ideas we can
manipulate for our own purposes – be they of the sacred or of our own
convenience.

As we begin to apprehend objects, there flashes up into consciousness a vast hierarchy of values – the comparative values of the natural
given in feeling through the senses, and the ideal values of the supernatural given from the sense of the holy. By these we deal with the natural. It cannot be considered that in Oman's system there is any
discontinuity between ideal and natural values as they are given in sincere feeling. He explicitly affirms that the higher values of the natural
manifest the ideal. The discontinuity between them on which he has
based his most important distinction ('natural–supernatural') lies in
the response that the will makes to them. The ideal values are of a categorical obligation which demands allegiance from our wills at all costs
and above all bargains; the natural values are merely matters of expediency or convenience for our wills.*

In his account of awareness and apprehension, Oman is laying the
epistemological basis for that tension between duality and unity which
is the fundamental philosophic characteristic of his theology of persons. 'The unities of perception,' he writes, 'explain both the breaking
up of the Supernatural and the impulse never set aside of thinking it as
one.'† To Oman the unity of relation between mind and environment is
the abiding force that never lets us set aside the impulse to think all our
experience together as belonging to one holy universe – even at the
moments when the results of our misused freedom make that universe
appear a chaos. Yet in the very awareness in which we are given that
relation we are first given a dim sense of ourselves as persons, felt over

---

* In the discussion here of how apprehension gives us values by which we deal with
  the natural, what has been said about Oman's elusiveness on this subject in the last
  chapter must be repeated.
† *The Natural and the Supernatural, op. cit.,* Appendix C, p. 477.

against That upon Which we depend. As our wills become operative in apprehension, so we truly discover our own essence as autonomy and at the same time realise That upon Which we depend to be truly He upon Whom we depend. Thus through awareness and apprehension we are given both the feeling that binds us to dependence upon God and the unavoidable distinction in reality between our wills and God's. Once given both the unifying feeling of dependence and the discovery of moral autonomy, strait is the gate,[5] according to Oman, between two dangers. We may fall back into the safety of the pure feeling of dependence, in disregard of our automomy, so that the particularities of our natural appointments appear as illusion, or on the other hand, we may so concentrate on our independence as to interpret it as successive acts of atomic self-determination, so that we lose[6] the sense of religious dependence and nature becomes something to be proudly denied, not a realm in which we can live in joyful service of Our Father's Will. It is between this Scylla and Charybdis that Oman sails to bring home his prophetic monotheism.

With the appearance of sacred values, free persons are no longer in the position merely of receiving values from nature, but must impose values on it. Two questions as to the character of nature arise from this new relationship. First, what can we learn about it from the fact that we can manipulate it by comprehensions and explanations? Secondly, what do we learn about it from the fact that all our attempts at living by the sacred take the form of some dealing with the natural? Indeed, what must nature be if we only receive the highest revelation of it when we use it under the power of the sacred?

Comprehension and explanation can give us little information about the character of nature, as compared with awareness and apprehension. As has been said, this is because we are imposing our meaning on nature not trying to receive its own. To live at all we must do this. Yet nature appears to us as an endless variety of concrete phenomena. Therefore, we have to learn to select, omit, arrange, arrest the given, so that we can control it. The most important device of the understanding is the scientific law, because the ideas of quantity are both the simplest and most useful way of managing our environment. In the most abstract of all abstractions, number, in which all qualities of an object are excluded other than the bare fact that it is a unit, it must be remembered that we are isolating the object in our intellects in a

way that it is never isolated in our experience. Therefore, as scientific
law is determined by our finitude and its own purposes and not by
what is given, it is of little use in providing us with the information on
which to conceive nature aright.

> Science serves its purpose precisely by its limitation. Its justification is
> that it extends a process of arresting and stereotyping which has already
> begun in perception; that it enlarges man's practical management of his
> world by isolating quantity from all else, both the mind that knows and
> the varied meaning by which it knows; and that it goes behind all mean-
> ing the world manifests to find the means whereby we can make the
> world speak our meaning. Thus it is an effective instrument precisely
> because it is not fitted to provide a cosmology.*
>
> ... comprehension reduces an object to a skeleton of its purpose, and
> explanation reduces this to a formula of its forces. Only by recovering
> from awareness and apprehension what has been dropped by the way is
> there any return to the whole object in its whole setting, which alone
> manifests its meaning and value. Science being simply judgment and
> reasoning applied to the natural world, the result is the same reduction
> by the understanding of everything to a diagram and the explanation of
> it to a formula: and from this there is no way back to a concrete world.†

Oman is extraordinarily vigorous in his indictments of those who
seek in science the basis for their cosmologies. He traces out the influence of that tendency not only in the sophisticated rationalist philosophies but in the cosmologies of the popular mind. The way in which
nineteenth-century men took a useful practical instrument – the Newtonian law of inertia – and turned it into a determining cosmological
principle, he compares brilliantly with the way the men of the sixth
century B.C. isolated self-determination from all else and so reached a
rigid cosmological principle of 'the exact equivalence between action
and award.' To Oman these are examples of how speculation runs riot
by fixing itself on one aspect of experience.‡

---

* *The Natural and the Supernatural, op. cit.*, p. 257.
† Ibid., p. 251.
‡ Ibid., chap. XIII. For a further discussion of this comparison see chapter 4.

Like the notion of interpreting the order of the world by the idea of a perfectly equal bargain, this notion of interpreting it by the experience of exerting effort in proportion to the weight to be moved was so level to the common understanding that it penetrated to multitudes of persons whose knowledge of science never went beyond the encyclopedia and the popular text-book, and through them, to many more who knew nothing about science. As third-hand information is the *fides implicita* by which the atmosphere of an age is created, the verdicts of scientists came to be regarded as infallible; and the scientist, in spite of himself, was affected by this diffused influence of his own ideas and came to regard them as much more clear-cut than his science showed them to be. But as what is infallible must be clear-cut, what is clear-cut is apt to appear infallible. So the most modest scientist fell into the habit of speaking *ex cathedra*.*

In these days when so many have been awakened by the strident voice of atomic energy, such indictments appear from all sorts and conditions of men. It seems fair to Oman to remember that his attack on the pretensions of natural science was made twenty years ago and by a man who had been educated in the nineteenth century.

The fact of nature's transparency to the categories of the understanding does, however, teach us something of what it is in itself. The scientist omits and selects and arrests, but he does not do this at random but in respect of a given reality. As the categories are effective instruments for manipulating nature, they must correspond with something in the order of reality. Oman's belief is that the rigid quantitative scheme with which the scientist deals, belongs to the symbols behind meaning about which we can have knowledge.† If nature had not this fixed symbolic structure about which we can have knowledge it would not be possible for free persons to impose their meaning upon nature.

Thus as soon as we become persons we find that nature is no longer to be conceived as simply that realm through which we are given our intuitions of the true, the beautiful and the good, but as a sphere to be

---

* *The Natural and the Supernatural, op. cit.*, p. 232.
† For a clarification of what Oman means by the symbols behind meaning see later in this chapter.

redeemed by our faithfulness in action under those ideals. Faithfulness in action is as much a prerequisite of our knowledge of nature as it is of our knowledge of supérnature. Our knowledge of the supernatural takes the form of dealing with some given situation in the natural, as for instance our families and our work. Thus a true conception of the natural is only to be reached as under ideal values we can possess it in joy and yet deny its control in the name of the Cross. The final words of *The Natural and the Supernatural* are: 'Denying the world does not mean that we do not possess it in courageous use of all possibilities, but only that we do not allow it to possess us.'*

In faithfulness to the values of the supernatural we are able to reach the highest vision of the natural – as a sphere which God has given to His free children for their redeeming work. Such a conception of the natural cannot, or course, be static, for it is a view of nature ever-deepening as we make our journey into the mind of God. Also its corollary must be that as the natural is all dependent on God and also a sphere for our activity, when we try to manipulate it for ends contrary to the true, the beautiful and the good, it will be turned into a sphere of calamity. Yet that capacity to be calamitous makes more evident than ever God's care for man, in using nature to draw us back to Himself.

Oman in the optimism of *The Natural and the Supernatural* does not lay much stress on this corollary. One passage may, however, be quoted:

> With this independence, we do not return from the possibility of choosing the higher merely to the lower. If we renounce its victory, we fall back, not to the wise instincts, the unconcern and fitting action of the lower creatures, but to positive falsehood, and gross delights, and doings that are vicious, and the deliberate sacrifice of others to our passions and our greeds. In short, we return to the unnatural, not the natural. We only abide in the Supernatural as we choose it, but this shows that the Natural is one thing as steps upward, and another, even at the same point, as a glissade downward.†

Here two practical difficulties arise: Oman neither discusses the

---

* *The Natural and the Supernatural, op. cit.*, p. 471.
† Ibid., p. 291. See also a short remark about this on p. **CR**.

principles governing the tension between man's possession and denial of the natural, nor does he discuss the relation between the natural as a glissade downwards and the fact that men are given the natural as an environment already manipulated by other men.* Oman's criticism of the use of scientific knowledge for cosmological purposes is valid as far as it goes, but it does not touch the more difficult question of when the scientist's activity (or for that matter the artist's) of possessing the natural must be given up in the name of the Cross. As Oman does not espouse a Kantian position with its universalist rigorous morality, presumably the Christian must use his intuition as to when to deny and when to possess. Is this related to our judgments of given historical circumstances? If so, Oman gives no account of how that judgment operates in and towards those varying circumstances. It may be wrong to ask of a philosophy of religion principles governing such practical issues, but as Oman insists that religion is concerned with a right attitude to environment, his philosophy of religion does depend on just such a discussion of the operation of the practical judgment towards the natural. This lack is felt here because such a discussion is not found elsewhere in his writings.

## III

Oman's concept of nature may be further defined in terms of the analogy between language and perception to which he returns often throughout *The Natural and the Supernatural*. This analogy does not add anything in principle to what has been given in the four types of knowing. He uses it however not only to illustrate his own position but as the basis for his criticism of a wide variety of false theories of perception. It is clearly a useful analogy for one who is attempting to demonstrate through an analysis of experience why the Christian is justified in using personalist categories about the natural.

Before discussing this analogy, it must be remarked that in his main use of it Oman is more guilty than usual both of a failure to make explicit the dependence of his thought on faith, and of an elusiveness

* The second point is only mentioned here, as Oman's failure of understanding of man's corporate dependence will be discussed in chapter 6. The first point will also be discussed there in the larger context of what may be called functional and personalist ethics.

in exposition.* He introduces this analogy without making clear that it is dependent on a theology of persons; he concludes the analogy without clarifying how it in turn can enlighten such a theology. Indeed in *The Natural and the Supernatural* as a whole, only in the last chapters of the third and fourth parts does he properly use personalist phraseology about the natural. As these two chapters are at the end of two discussions, the introduction of personalist phraseology in them alone could easily lead to the implication that Oman is deducing the personalist character of nature from his account of experience, rather than showing what such a faith means. It is almost as if he were falling into that very Cartesianism which he so deplores. There seems an almost unconscious lack of frankness in these chapters, which is so foreign to the general spirit of Oman's writings. It also leads to much greater difficulty in the reader following his argument than can be considered a necessity of the subject. The reading of *The Natural and the Supernatural* may be compared to a journey in a boat down a river. At certain points the boat ambles past well-known and rather obvious country; then it dashes past exciting new territory so that the traveller gets only hints of what the country is about.†

Oman approaches the analogy between language and perception by way of a criticism of the thought of Berkeley. He judges that in Berkeley's work nature is considered solely as the language of God to His children. Oman writes of Berkeley's 'divine visual language.'‡ Therefore, in his criticism of Berkeley is seen the extent to which Oman believes that this analogy is valid. As far as agreement with Berkeley goes, he writes:

---

* *The Natural and the Supernatural, op. cit.,* particularly chap. X.

† It is not necessary here to repeat again Oman's motives for refraining from the use of personalist categories. His work at this point may be compared to Professor Farmer's *The World and God*, Nisbet and Co., London, 1935. In that work the relationship between this analogy and a theology of persons is carefully worked out. As Professor Farmer was a pupil, a friend, and a colleague of Oman's, the connection between the work of the two men is evident. It is perhaps not impudent to remark that Professor Farmer belongs to a generation more free than Oman from the great weight of awe about the language of the scientist that held men even when unrecognized. Certainly *The Natural and the Supernatural* would have been an even greater book if the categories of the Biblical tradition had been used more openly.

‡ *The Natural and the Supernatural, op. cit.,* p. 170.

Berkeley has not been shown to be wrong in thinking, as one of his critics expresses it, that 'sense experience has the intelligibility of a language whose conventions are one and all determined by a spirit akin to our own'; and his argument against a reality that is matter without meaning is valid to this day.*

Oman divides his criticism of Berkeley into three points. (1) The symbolism of speech may be entirely arbitrary, whereas the symbolism of perception is entirely fixed by the nature of things. As this is so, Oman asserts, but does not argue, that Berkeley has no right to assume that in God's mind the symbols may be as arbitrary as speech is in ours. (2) Berkeley overlooks the difference between the context of speech and that of perception. The context of speech has only to do with the context of thought, while the context of perception has to do with the consistency of our whole environment. Oman uses the words 'illusion' and 'thoughts imposed from moment to moment' as descriptions of what is implied in Berkeley's description of God's activity. He then asserts that God cannot be considered to act in this way. (3) Berkeley overlooks the fact that nature must be considered to have significance for itself apart from its meaning for us.

To criticise Oman once again, his remarks about Berkeley illustrate well the difficulties that arise from keeping the language of Christian theology so well hidden. For it is only in terms of the theological implications of his position that Berkeley's epistemology is exposed as inadequate. For example, Oman asserts that nature has significance in and for itself and that Berkeley's position does not take account of that fact. Yet in saying that, Oman makes no mention of the problem of theodicy. Is there any reason, however, apart from theodicy, why nature must be considered as having meaning in and for itself? In the same way Oman's use of the word 'illusion' about Berkeley's conception of nature has the ring of a naive realist, because it does not discuss the questions of error and sin against which such idealism must be criticised. This is not in the least to imply that Oman did not recognise the foregoing remarkably clearly. It is to criticise him once again for his silence. It is particularly disappointing in that Berkeley could have been used as the opportunity of bringing out into the open the irrecon-

* Ibid.

cilability of modern idealism with Christian theism, which is assumed throughout the work. It could at the same time have made clear what is slurred over in Oman's thought, namely that nature can only be given to men mysteriously, indeed arbitrarily, because God's purposes in creation are not confined merely to man. Oman could thus have related the necessity of nature being given to us in this arbitrary manner, and faith's concern with moral victory over nature, rather than speculations about it.*

Oman proceeds to the positive use of his analogy between language and perception. He asserts that because language and the senses (except for touch and its dependent taste) are similar in that they are both employed to give us knowledge at a distance, we may consider it likely that our power of interpreting symbols was developed first in perception. That is, speaking and writing developed from this ability. Therefore as we know something of the primitive development of language we can infer certain conclusions about perception. Such an indirect approach to explaining the character of perception is necessary, because the sheer 'givenness' of pure perception makes it a mystery.†

The central theory which Oman uses about primitive language is that primitive men had difficulty in using symbols freely. Symbols at this stage expressed a whole context of meaning. Primitive men found it difficult to isolate one aspect of that context from the rest. Man's use of symbols was determined by the fact that they could only operate within a fixed unity of feeling. So strong was this determination by the context of meaning that we find among primitive people that memories and imaginings are confused with perceptions, and even words with conceptual significance confused with percepts. Only as men

---

* Oman brings out this more clearly than anywhere else in a review of *Experience and Its Modes*, Michael Oakeshott. See *Journal of Theological Studies, op. cit.*, Vol. XXXV, pp. 314–16.

† At the risk of carping too often over small points, Oman does not make nearly clear enough that even if his major premise be granted (that language developed from perception) in his minor premise (that the development of language among primitive men followed such and such a course) he is on extremely tentative ground. Oman speaks about primitive language with an authority that for all his scholarship must be judged unwise. He switches quickly in his argument from direct knowledge to inference, seemingly without making any distinction. This justification of the unities given in the sense of the holy from the facts of anthropology indeed clarifies what Oman means by those unities. But the limitations of such a justification are not made clear. See particularly *The Natural and the Supernatural, op. cit.*, pp. 172–6.

developed free unities of reflexion by the use of free ideas could situations be analysed and parts of speech developed to express the results of that analysis. Only then was any sophisticated use of symbolism possible.

Assuming then that primitive speech is a gradual development from perception, from this analysis of primitive language we can tell something about how we perceive nature. Perception takes place in the same fixed context of meaning as does primitive language. It takes place within a context of fixed ideas. By fixed ideas Oman means ideas that cannot be taken out of the context in which they are given. That is to say, they are at once called up by a particular situation and in turn call up the whole setting in which they were first experienced, as well as other ideas associated with similar situations. As ideas they are fixed because it is impossible to perceive outside them. Man attains to free ideas when in action he explains his environment. With free ideas he can analyse his perceptions so that, for instance, he can isolate individual sensations from the general field in which they are given. It must be remembered, however, that when doing that he is no longer perceiving nature, but manipulating it by the intellect. Perception has ceased to exist. As soon then as we are manipulating nature by free ideas we are no longer receiving from it in contemplation the values it has for us.

Oman illustrates what he means by fixed ideas by the two most important of them – space and time. Space and time are the most fixed of all ideas because no experience outside them is possible. We cannot escape them, as we can other fixed ideas by dealing with our whole environment and thereby achieving free ideas. They arise from our perceiving as pure qualities of consciousness. They are forms of our awareness of nature. Only later as we achieve free ideas can we conceive them as quantities which we manipulate. Oman is particularly positive in criticising that theory of space wherein it is conceived as an abstract idea reached by generalising from the fact that each individual sensation is extended. Space is a fixed idea within which all perception and, therefore, all individual sensations are given.*

In dealing with the role of fixed ideas in perception Oman is obscure

---

* Oman returns to this point again and again in opposition to William James' and James Ward's psychologies.[7]

about one point. What is the ontological status of either space or time? He writes:

> Yet the enormous impressiveness of space, both for sense and imagina-
> tion, must represent a quality which belongs to the meaning of the
> universe.*

Twice he uses the phrase that fixed ideas are determined by the order of environment.† In discussing Kant's epistemology of nature he is always sternly realist in contradicting him. To Oman it is a necessity of his theology that we know nature as it is in itself and not as appearance.‡ He makes the comment, necessary for any theism, that space and time are not the matrix of reality, but that does not go far in dispelling agnosticism about their ontological status.§

To sum up, Oman uses the analogy between perception and language to clarify the way in which our perception of nature is given within the fixed unities of feeling in the holy. We do not perceive nature as isolated psychological events determined by we know not what, but as one coordinated stream of meaning coming from one ordered environment. All the vast and varied individuality of nature comes to us within a context of fixed ideas which are determined by the fact that nature is itself ordered. Perception can then best be compared to a dialogue into which we can always join, by good-will on both sides, though we have not known the beginning of that dialogue nor the end. Thus perception fits into Oman's personalist account of experience. It is the ordered way we are given nature, itself the mediator to us of the immediacy of the Father's Will.

In his account of the appearance of nature to consciousness Oman devotes much space to the discussion of sensation, not because what he says positively about it adds greatly to his epistemology but because he wishes to present an alternative to atomic sensationalism.

---

* *The Natural and the Supernatural, op. cit.*, p. 183.
† Ibid., pp. 155 and 183. It is difficult to see what he means by this phrase.
‡ See particularly ibid., pp. 152–5.
§ To refer ahead once again to chapter 5, it may be said that Oman is never much taken up with the idea of Christian history and therefore has none of that obsession with time that is found, for instance, in St Augustine. This is true, despite all that he alleges about Shakespeare's obsession with time.

The Humian account of sensation he believes to be the sheet anchor of most modern agnosticism. From atomic sensation, as a supposedly clear and distinct premise, is deduced mechanist cosmologies which deny even the biologist's teleology. Because sensation must be ever a mystery there is no refutation of such a position except by indirect means. To repeat, what Oman particularly dislikes about the meta-physical premise of atomic sensationalism is its pride in denying valid-ity to other visions of nature, such as the artist's or the saint's. Its claim to be empirical he considers nonsense, for how can we tell anything of the character of sensations without assumptions.

In reaching his own position on sensation, Oman begins from two assumptions that must be reconciled. On the one hand, he maintains that from what he has already said about perception it may be assumed that sensation is 'a particular aspect of the whole unified feel-ing responding to a particular aspect of a whole unified environment.'* On the other hand, it cannot be doubted that between the mind and its object there are both physiological and physical phenomena. Oman judges that from the present state of science both the physical phenom-ena of our environment and the physiological phenomena of our brain and nerves take the form of systems of vibration. The question imme-diately arises, what is the relationship between these two assumptions. What is the relationship between this double system of vibrations and the fact that we perceive nature as one continuous meaning? What is the relation between sensations and these systems of vibration?

Oman contends that sensations are not direct effects of these physi-cal vibrations but are interpretations of them within a system of mean-ing. Thus the physiological vibrations of our body are determined by this system of meaning and the physical system of vibrations in nature is determined by the meaning of nature as a whole. It must be repeated that Oman does not hope to prove such a contention – clearly an impossible task. He could give up believing that nature is a unified whole and fall back into a realism such as Bertrand Russell's; he could deny the reality of the system of vibrations and take up an idealist position – something like Kant's. But since, for theological reasons, quite outside the question of perception, he cannot accept either of these positions, he maintains both these assumptions.

* *The Natural and the Supernatural, op. cit.*, p. 185.

Oman's uncompromising realism is seen here in his attitude to the state of modern science. What is given by science he accepts as telling us of things as they are in themselves. Yet with that acceptance goes little discussion of the status of these physical vibrations in reality. Here Oman's practical attitude is once more evident. A discussion of the status of such things is not a deep concern of faith. Such vibrations are a necessity if the world is to be given to us as a reasonable environment, and that is all that concerns us.

Oman brings forward evidence which he considers can only be understood in the light of some such position as this. He first asserts as a fact that man develops sensations only in response to some interest. They are not automatically given. A particular sensation appears when man, interested in some aspect of his environment, develops the sense through which that aspect can manifest itself. For example, primitive man was so engaged in making a living that he had little interest in nature as beautiful and, therefore, had little appreciation of the colour blue, which has small practical utility. Evidence of this fact is that primitive people had no distinct word for that colour.* The second point is that sensations are not given to us as quantitatively measurable intensities of pleasure and pain, but as qualitatively distinguishable feelings. Indeed by means of the understanding, that is, by importing into them standards of measurement from the object that evokes them, it is possible to consider them quantitatively. But in so isolating them, they cease to be sensations as given in experience. Oman says this is a fact, but it is clearly as much theory as the Humian position. Moreover, this abstraction of sensations from their context interferes arbitrarily with the unbroken flow of time in which all sensations come to us. Oman does not labour this point that had been made so brilliantly by his contemporary Bergson. The third point is that the less sensations are considered as subjective emotions, the more they give us objective information. In pure perception we are not conscious of the sensation 'white' but rather that we are looking at a piece of paper. When we isolate the sensation 'white,' we cease to apprehend the piece of paper.

Oman asserts that none of these facts can be reconciled with an

---

* Since weather is presumably of importance in the lives of primitive men, it is surprising that the colours of sea and sky should not have been of great practical interest.

account of sensation as atomic events. They can, however, be fitted into his realism of the holy. Therefore he asserts the following account of sensation:

> Sensations have meaning because they are in a context. Thus even if the individual sensations have a more direct relation to their object than we know, the deeper reason why they have meaning is that they are in a system of meaning, somewhat in the same way as words are, and so are determined, not by pleasure or pain in themselves, but by an interest which governs their whole activity and makes them effective as response and not as subjective feeling.*

> If all perceiving be of this nature, at the frontier of the individual there is a system of symbols of vibration without and a corresponding system of sensations interpreting them within, and the significance of the individual frontier is that knowledge can pass it only as our meaning. Thus knowing is not knowledge as an effect of an unknown external cause, but is knowledge as we so interpret that our meaning is the actual meaning of our environment.†

## IV

To sum up it cannot be said that in *The Natural and the Supernatural* Oman embarks on the detailed epistemological analysis in terms of an incisive technical vocabulary, which marks the classical epistemologists of the rationalist school. His greatness is not in a deduction of the categories of our knowledge of nature, as they are given to us in the varying forms of consciousness, nor in relating that deduction to a unified metaphysical system. Even his denial that traditional idealism cannot be reconciled to a Christian theism only appears as a subsidiary conclusion of his main purpose. That purpose is to hammer home the right attitude of the Christian to nature – namely, that joy in the world that can praise God in His creation and yet is not so taken up with the world that it cannot recognise a purpose that transcends that Natural. Only in such an attitude can nature be seen as it is and only by seeing

* *The Natural and the Supernatural, op. cit.*, p. 199.
† Ibid., p. 175.

nature as it is can such an attitude be possible. Oman is concerned with demonstrating how the vision of nature as a 'school for immortal spirits' is given, and how with any less glorious vision our hope must be vain.*

As he puts it in the last chapter:

> The Natural need not all be personal. But only if it all have personal meaning and personal purpose, responding to us as we attain personal insight, personal values, personal independence of action, has the idea either of God or of man any content that would enable us to speak of God as a Father who cannot be separated from his children, or of man as having his hope in the love from which death cannot separate because life cannot.†

Indeed often that purpose is not made clear and its implications are not drawn out, but by and large the account of this vision is remarkable.‡

To show how reconciliation and revelation are reciprocal and how our knowledge of God and the world are inseparably bound together, Oman concentrates on reiterating the centrality of sincerity of feeling and faithfulness in action. Here Oman must be praised for the description of essentials that had been so often forgotten in the philosophy of his day. He does not consider *The Natural and the Supernatural* a subtle grammar of experience wherein details are worked out, but rather a prophetic reminder that these are indeed the essentials of the Christian life. To illustrate them in an age dominated by the visions of the scientist, he holds high the vision of the artist as an archetype of what is open to all conditions of men. He shows how the vision of the scientist and indeed of the artist must finally be subordinated to that of the saint. It must be insisted once more, however, he is not clear about the principles by which that subordination of insights in possession and

---

* Ibid., p. 460.
† Ibid., pp. 465–6.
‡ Oman for instance never makes the important point of the necessity of such an independent sphere if there is to be personal intercourse between God's Will and ours. Neither does he make enough of how a Christian theism can explain the arbitrary quality of nature in a way that idealist accounts cannot.

denial of the natural is to take place. In achieving his purposes Oman sweeps away much theory about nature that might corrupt men's vision of it.

Thus through his account of these insights and through his criticism of theory Oman moves forward to his own conception of nature. He expresses this better in a passage from *Honest Religion* than anywhere else in his works.

> Faith in the Father is the ground of our Lord's view of Nature.
>
> The uniformity of Nature is often taken to be the uniformity of indifference, behind which view lies the assumption that God should be a moral governor determining everything by exact material award according to merit and demerit. But to Jesus it is the uniformity of the wise goodness of a Father who sends His rain equally upon the just and the unjust, the evil and the good, and whose highest perfection it is to be kind to the unthankful and evil.
>
> This is not difficult to accept, either as fine sentiment or as the hard idea that whatever happens is good for us, Nature having a very large family and no leisure to coddle them. But our Lord's view is far nearer the poet's seeing, in the silent face of Nature, unutterable love. And when it is granted us to look for moments into her face with something of the poet's eyes, who then sees merely the dead processes of the laboratory? But, while One who saw the lilies of the field clothed more gloriously than Solomon did not lack the poet's eye; for him the way in which this faith can truly come home to us is by being perfect as our Father in Heaven is perfect, not in an austere and faultless morality, but in knowing no limit to the forgiveness of wrong, or prayer for those who despitefully [sic] use us and persecute us. When this is accepted, that the uniformity of Nature is a wise love can hardly be doubted. Anyhow, it is a matter of attitude not inference or argument.*

## CHAPTER IV

The attempt must now be made to understand how Oman conceives the supernatural – call it if you will God – in personal categories, and

---

* *Honest Religion, op. cit.,* pp. 76–7.

his justification of such categories.* This is the crown which all Oman's epistemological description is intended to bejewel. He holds before men the biblical 'philosophical theology' as a more adequate account of experience than the impersonalism which always seems to arise from thought detached from the Scriptures. As a preliminary to this attempt, an exposition of how Oman conceives personality in man must first be given. As should have been clear from the foregoing chapters, Oman's concept 'nature and supernature' is inextricably linked to his concept 'man.' For the purposes of exposition it was necessary to proceed from an undefined concept of 'the person' to whom all environments are related,[1] even though in the exposition of those environments the character of that concept must have tentatively appeared. To reverse the process, Oman's doctrine of personality will now be discussed directly, and nature and supernature only in relation to it.

To do this is in fact to relate the vocabulary of *The Natural and the Supernatural* to that of *Grace and Personality*. This is necessary because in *The Natural and the Supernatural* personality is not directly defined. *Grace and Personality* is, on the other hand, a careful discussion of his *a priori* intuition of man's essence and God's – distinct but inseparable as the ground of each other. So to bring in this new vocabulary must inevitably lead to yet more repetition, as the questions of personality and its environments are closely related. As has been said, Oman's writings as a whole do not cover a wide area but are the vigorous repetition of what he considers the simple basis of the Christian faith.

Here at the question 'What is man?' we are at the centre of Oman's thought. He stands in that great line of Christian philosophers – the greatest of whom is St Augustine – who, in periods in which rationalism has broken down an ancient tradition, criticise the claims of sceptical reason in the name of an intuition of man's essence, which shows

---

* On page 342 of *The Natural and the Supernatural* Oman writes: 'We can speak of God as a person who, if he is not the Supernatural, is manifest through it.' This is, however, the only place in his work where he employs this language of intermediaries or demiurges. At all other points it is implied that the supernatural is a synonym for God. Therefore the implication of the above quotation will not be discussed. Even though Oman's attempt to rescue the Darwinian term 'environment' from the clutches of the naturalist and make it serve a Christian purpose may not be considered worth while, the phrase [sic] supernatural will be used in this chapter.

the place of reason within a rounded account of man. St Augustine demanded from classical *scientia* a justification of the claims of reason, and attempted to show how those claims could only find their right place within the acceptance of Christian *sapientia*; so Oman asserts that the rationalists of modern Europe have detached reason from its proper role as a function of human personality, and therefore he attempts to reinstate in philosophy a more adequate account of man as a whole.* Nothing is indeed more attractive in Oman than the fact that all questions of philosophy are judged in relation to his imaginative and shrewd intuition of man's predicament. This may sometimes hold his thought back from certain detailed problems, but it means that his philosophy is always truly Christian in the sense that the problem of faith is primary.

This refusal, on the one hand, to reduce anthropology to an empirical science and, on the other hand, to detach theology from anthropology and so take 'a flying leap to the Word of God' is always typical of Oman.† Such a method has always been criticised for falling into contradiction. Indeed before this contradiction all traditions of thought (e.g., the medieval) seem to fall. The Christian philosopher must assert a knowledge of principles despite the evidently necessary incompleteness of our knowledge. Yet for the purposes of practice has the Christian any alternative? Must he not resort both to the method of clarifying his idea of God by holding it against an idea of his own limitations and understanding his limitations by holding them against the idea of God? At least it should be repeated that Oman does neither accept the 'anthropocentric' position that denies the possibility of the transcendental application of logic, nor the 'theocentric' position that succumbs to the judgment that human reason is utterly corrupt. Therefore the account of personality that follows may be considered a proper philosophic activity.

One caveat, however obvious, must be added. Since Oman uses the word 'personality' so much, and since it is so popular in much theol-

---

* In comparing Oman to St Augustine there is no intention to convey that their intuitions of personality were similar. They do not see the tragic in the same light. In mentioning St Augustine the present writer may be allowed to express a debt to his compatriot and teacher C.N. Cochrane.[2] Anything that is said is but a poor echo of the latter's *Christianity and Classical Culture* Oxford University Press, N.Y., 1944.
† Article on Schleiermacher. *Journal of Theological Studies, op. cit.*, Vol. XXX, p. 402.

ogy today, care must be taken that it does not become an Aladdin's lamp, magically producing what is wanted. There is nothing necessary in Oman's terminology. For whereas in his later work the term 'individual' is used to express an inadequate view of man failing to express his relation to nature and supernature, in an early work the terms are reversed, 'personality' being considered empty and inadequate, 'individual' appropriate and full. In an article published in 1906, Oman wrote that Ritschl contends 'not only against a catholicism which bears down the individual by the weight of the institution, but also against a mysticism which reduces all individuals to mere personality, upon which a Spirit, Himself mere personality, operates not as individual with individual, but as abstract spiritual force upon abstract spiritual substance.'*

## II

Oman maintains that man's essence is his autonomy.

> This autonomy appears in the essential quality of our experience, that it is self-conscious; in the essential quality of our aims, that they are self-directed; in the essential quality of our acts, that they are self-determined. Yet, we must beware of regarding these as separate autonomies, because much futile and misleading discussion arises from thus isolating the problems of mind. They are merely aspects of the one independence of a moral person.†

Oman would not stand with Kant in the belief that self-determination is to be inferred from 'the only fact' of ethics, the moral law. Consciousness of determining issues is the most immediate of all experiences. With it go two other experiences which can only be explained in relation to it; (1) our consciousness of responsibility for our actions and (2) our remorse for our actions. Responsibility is the more fundamental of these two, for how apart from it can we explain any continuous consciousness of self?

---

* Article 'Individual,' *Dictionary of Christ and the Gospels, op. cit.*, p. 816. It would be interesting to know what caused Oman to reverse the meaning of these words. No evidence as to this point has been found.

† *Grace and Personality, op. cit.*, pp. 42–3.

We stand with our faces toward our world and our backs toward ourselves, and only catch fleeting glimpses of ourselves over our shoulders;
and the continuous personal memory which gives continuity to our
experience, is not due to an unbroken vision of ourselves, but to uninter
rupted ascription of our doings to our own responsibility.*

Oman divides into three types those speculations which have
denied our self-determination: (1) the claim of the scientists that all
reality is explainable in causal terms; (2) the secular philosopher's
reduction of will to determination by motive and character; (3) the
theologian's denial of freedom in the name of the omniscience and
omnipotence of God. Though Oman throughout his works tries to
bring out the consequences of such positions, in fact the basis of his refutation is as simple as Dr Johnson's. What right has proud speculation,
in its desire to explain the world consistently, to deny what is evident
from the actions of all men (the speculators' included) and which
Oman himself finds immediately given?[3] Here Oman's position may
be once more compared to that of the modern phenomenologist.

Thus personality must primarily be considered autonomous will.
The mystery of that autonomy, the difficulties that it raises for speculation must not lead us to doubt its reality. Oman stands with the central
Christian tradition in affirming: *Quid nisi voluntates?* 'Will ... is one with
ourselves as no other possession can be identified with its possessor,
and there can be no personal relation with us except through it.'† In
another connection he writes:

Through all those changes, [life's vicissitudes] responsibility continues,
springing from a freedom which abides in some deep and permanent
essence of the soul, which the acts of freedom alone can alter.‡

In insisting upon that responsibility, the mystery of which may be
described in the traditional phrase 'the freedom of the will,' it is necessary to insist that our autonomy is not confined to mere self-determination. 'Freedom is not a succession of independent acts of freedom,

---

* Ibid., p. 46.
† Ibid.
‡ Article 'Freedom' in *The Elements of Pain and Conflict, op. cit.,* pp. 70–1.

but is a clearer, surer, more steadfast choice of the world in which we are free, in feeling as well as will.'* In stating that Oman conceives personality in terms of an autonomy of insight as well as an autonomy of volition, there is no need to repeat here what has been said earlier about the interdependence of the sense of the holy and the judgment of the sacred. According to Oman's firm realism, our sense of reverence gives us immediate insight into the mind of God.

Whereas in *The Natural and the Supernatural* the relationship between morality and religion is discussed in the cool air of epistemological language, in *Grace and Personality* the reconciliation of the two terms of its title is attempted by an exhortation to persons to find their proper end in the Christian life. It would not be true to say that Oman considered the Christian understanding of grace and personality as essentially paradoxical. For to use the language of paradox about Christianity must never imply that there are not graver antinomies about man in the secular account of pure morality. Though leaving men with mystery the interdependence of grace and personality allows them to understand facts about man of which secular morality gives no account. If the secular moralist denies these facts, Oman would simply appeal to those phenomena, and ask how apart from them man's destiny can be anything but despair. Oman's concept of man, like all others, is not only an exhortation to action but an appeal to what man has been.

The first fact is that human action is not only concerned with doing what is known already to be right but with an expansion of vision as to what is the right. The second fact is that the noblest reaches of moral action are always penetrated with the sense of joy.

> While rules may determine actions, and this, in certain circumstances, may be important, mere negative rules of 'touch not, taste not, handle not,' are not, as much experience besides the Apostle's shows, of any value against the disturbing clamour even of carnal appetite, and still less of what he calls 'coveting,' which is the real insubordination of ourselves to ourselves. And with these lusts of the eye and the pride of life, we must take the fear of reprobation and the desire for approval, and all that dominates us as individuals who are members of a herd. Victory

---

* *The Natural and the Supernatural, op. cit.,* p. 309.

over ourselves herein is not possible by resolution, however courageous, but only by finding a better environment waiting to be possessed. Only as we seek a better country can we leave a worse, even though we must also be ready to go out, not knowing whither we go, as the way of seeking it.*

Man can only understand these facts of his experience in terms of a doctrine of grace. Our actions are not concerned with creating a world but possessing the Mind of God. Oman compares this relationship with God to our friendship with other persons.

We know them [other persons] solely as they manifest themselves through our physical environment, but, through it, they manifest more than the physical, and this again we discern to be not so much a manifestation as the key to all the manifestations. All friendship is reaching out to the person, who is himself both the revelation and the prophecy of fuller manifestation. Is it not by something similar – something known by experience, but discerned as a revelation and a prophecy beyond it, which yet is the interpreter of all that is in it – that man sets up his ideals? And, however inadequate the description may be, have we any better name for what this manifests than a person?†

As we try to understand man's nature, we find it is of his very essence to be gripped by Something Other than himself. The essence of that Other we find to be Love. In the consciousness of being enfolded by Love is man's peace. Yet in no sense is that enfolding something that destroys our autonomy. Freely, in our contemplation, we must reach out to that embrace. The appalling difficulty of describing that meeting is seen from Plato to St Augustine, from St Bonaventure to Bunyan.[4] All that can be said here of Oman's attempt in *Grace and Personality* is that through three hundred pages he ponders upon the implication of the experience.

---

* Ibid., pp. 303–4.
† Ibid., p. 340. Though Oman devotes much space to the criticism of the Kantian morality, he never openly discusses Kant's criticism of a position such as his, namely that it must lead to hypothetical imperatives. Kant is answered indirectly in what Oman says positively about grace, but it would have added strength to his work to face it openly in its Kantian form.

Thus, it having been said previously that Oman's concept of super-nature cannot be detached from his concept of man, the reverse must now be said. Speculation proceeds from an intuition of man's autonomy as morally responsible to pursue his dependence upon God. Saying this[5] is but to repeat what has been said about the necessary procedure of Christian philosophy.*

Freedom cannot, however, be understood simply as self-determination in action according to the self-direction of our insight, for it must be remembered that freedom's only sphere of operation is the world of our self-consciousness. In using such language Oman is not intending merely to convey that every person is self-conscious, or that the possibility of knowledge implies a distinction between subject and object. He is insisting that all our acts and all our insights are in relation to the natural world, that that world can only be the sphere for our freedom in so far as it is brought into our consciousness and that this bringing of it into our consciousness is as much an autonomous activity as is any act of self-determination.

> Instead of finding a hostile or merely dead response [from nature], the more he is able to confer, the more abundantly he receives. Seeming chaos is turned to order, seeming menace to a smile to laugh with, seeming obstacles to a challenge to make them the means of victory. Then an environment, which was only pleasure and pain for the advancement of the animal life, becomes a joy, and it may be an agony, for the advancement of the spirit, both alike being seen to be good, if, with Ruskin, we do not wonder at what men suffer, but at what they lose.†[7]

---

* Oman never mentions Cook Wilson, who in saying the same thing to his students at Oxford evidently had a profound influence on such men as Professors Webb and Kemp Smith.[6] See *Statement and Inference*, J.C. Wilson, Oxford University Press, 1926, Vol. II. pp. 835 *et seq.* Neither do the above-mentioned philosophic theologians refer to Oman in their work. Though there is this similarity between Oman and Professor Webb's approach to Christian philosophy, the difference in their works is profound, because of their differing ethical tone. Oman has a much more vivid intuition of the gulf that lies between the demands of the Cross and the ethics of civilisation. Professor Webb is the gentle reconciler of Christianity with the best of the European tradition. Though it will be remarked in chapter 6 that Oman seemed to change his position as to civilisation, he never would have written about the presentation of Christianity to the modern world as did Professor Webb. As an example, see *Religious Thought in England since 1850*, C.C.J. Webb, Oxford University Press, 1933, pp. 186 *et seq.*
† *The Natural and the Supernatural, op. cit.*, pp. 340–1.

Again there is no necessity to repeat what has been said in the previous chapter about our knowledge of nature. Oman's account of personality as autonomy does not allow him to conceive nature given to us, as it were, automatically. We must reach out to that environment in an autonomy of self-consciousness. Therefore man cannot be conceived apart from his partaking of nature.

Thus Oman's metaphysic is always concerned with a triadic relationship between nature, supernature, and persons. If we attempt to understand the relationship between persons and supernature, we find that that relationship is always dependent on the intermediary, nature. On the other hand, the right attitude of persons to the natural can only be understood in terms of their joint dependence on the supernatural. Finally the true end of persons is only achievable as they rightly relate the natural to the supernatural. Inadequate theory about any of these terms must lead to inadequate theory about the others.

### III

Oman's metaphysical position with its three terms nature, supernature and persons must be seen in relation to his concentration on the question of theodicy. The conclusion of *The Natural and the Supernatural* is that only in the knowledge of God as Love can free men find that joy in the world without which they must rest either in despair or in a failure of compassionate imagination.* In *The Natural and the Supernatural* Oman's journey to that position is by way of his criticism of monism and of outright dualism.

In emphasising Oman's concentration on the problem of theodicy his account of the predicament of modern Europeans must again be considered.† Modern man's failures of faith cannot be considered as

---

\* What Oman means by the word 'love' must here be left. It is hoped that in the rest of this chapter and in the two following what he means by that difficult word will become clearer in quotations. One definition of that word may be given here: 'Love is fundamentally an estimate of man as an individual spiritual being whose own choice determines his destiny and whose eternal destiny is so great that no present affliction can be weighed for a moment against its attainment, and for whom death, however terrible in its pains and dread of unknown possibilities, is only the greatest of these purifying trials.' *The War and Its Issues, op. cit.*, p. 51.

† For an interesting account of this predicament see *An Outline of Christianity*, Vol.III, Introduction, 'Christianity in a New Age,' by John Oman. See bibliography, p. ii.

springing sheerly from revolt. All men strive, as the very image of God, for some abiding faith by which to face life's vicissitudes. The medieval framework within which men had found courage had broken because it could not face the implications of freedom. The medieval Church had lost the vision of the Father and His children by which the Apostolic Church had found its victory and joy. The revolt against Catholicism was a noble reaction, however barren that reaction became. Men can only rediscover the Word of God in the freedom to seek truth over the whole reach of experience. A theologian who places sincerity of feeling and faithfulness in action at the centre of his thought, cannot be said to eliminate the transcendent mystery from the Word of God. Oman always deplores that rationalist tendency in his teacher Ritschl which tends to eliminate the mystery from the act of faith. But, on the other hand, to put faith, in order that it shall challenge, beyond the bounds of rational reflection is to cloud it with the sense that its trust is an illusion. To ask openly how men can in all honesty and all imagination accept a theodicy is no Promethean revolt, but rather the assertion of the dignity of the children of God.

Without a firm willingness to accept the implications of our autonomy throughout all our experience, a theodicy is impossible. To Oman that fact is inescapable. His writing is at its most passionate in that assertion.

Were it the first consideration that there should be no divergence from what God knows to be true, and correct belief more essential than the right way of believing, or were action as God judges proper, anyhow done, better than truly conscientious behaviour which comes short of it, man's long groping amid error and evil would be a mere scandal of God's inefficiency. But if seeing truth is essential to its worth as truth, and deciding right to its worth as righteousness; if all spiritual possession, to be true possession, must be won by the soul that learns to be in accord with it; if this freedom is an essential relation to the Supernatural as well as the supreme possession of the Natural, not only religious history, but all history may manifest meaning and purpose, and its course be so confused only because a large part of it tells how men weary of the long and strenuous endeavour, and how the power who rules over men and societies never suffers for long any resting-place on this road. On this view of its goal, man's devious way has moral if not rational justification; while, if it is to be measured by the extent to which he is guarded from error and evil, it has neither.*

The way of freedom, though its final justification can only be its goal, at least saves life from being a dull as well as a ghastly nightmare, because, with it, there is a universe of living interests while, without it, there would be no more than a Punch and Judy show with conscious and sensitive puppets. And supposing an infinite mind contemplating it, could we expect him to be eternally interested in making it pirouette around him, however graceful and intricate he could make the performance? Calvin's predestinarianism, Leibnitz's monads, McTaggart's planetary system of souls are nothing more: and it is all as ghastly as it is dull. Nor does Hegel's process of Reason add anything to its cheerfulness: and his buoyant optimism naturally ended with Schopenhauer's pessimism.†

Though in the above quotation Oman identifies the Christian predestinarianism of Calvin with the rationalist monism of modern Europe, it is with the latter and its associate Indian religions rather than with the former that Oman is concerned in *The Natural and the Supernatural*.‡ All monisms, according to Oman, spring from one root. In the desire to find a faith that unifies all experience, men sink back into the bare form of unity which has been given them in the sense of the holy. So intense is the original feeling of unity in all men that it drives them to seek coherence. The monist is he who achieves coherence by turning his back on the responsibilities of the adult, which are

---

* *The Natural and the Supernatural, op. cit.*, p. 357.

† Ibid., pp. 290–1.

‡ Oman's identification in *Grace and Personality* of Kant with Pelagianism and Arminianism, and of Hegel with Augustinianism and Calvinism, cannot be considered a comparison of much value.[8] Particularly in a book such as *Grace and Personality* in which he appeals to a popular audience, that kind of comparison, quickly made and not carefully defended, could so easily lead to false conclusions. Surely even the identification of St Augustine's and Calvin's thought needs qualification. Though the present writer must admit his difficulty in understanding Hegel, and deplores easy attacks on him, an identification of him with the greatest exponent of the Christian doctrine of the will seems hardly appropriate. Also, St Augustine's criticism of classical rationalism is more radical than that of Hegel. Finally, those influences that St Augustine did admit from the classical world were from Plato; while Hegel clearly learned more from Aristotle than any other thinker. See *Grace and Personality, op. cit.*, chap. 3, pp. 18–26.

so hard to reconcile with unity. Thus in this great urge towards unity men use their reasons to develop speculative systems in which all reality is ironed out into a monism. Only Indian religion, according to Oman, is really consistent in using its intellect in the service of this desire for unity, and it alone denies everything except the All-one. In Hegel's writings there is much about a doctrine of the will and of duties. These are, however, denied in his system. As Oman writes:

> The charges are not made against Hegel. They are against the Hegelian categories, the schema into which he fits everything, and his view of the relation of the individual reason as mere pattern of the Absolute Reason.*

Or again he is willing to write of both Hegel and Schleiermacher:

> The weakness of both is that they had no real place for the individual, and, therefore, failed to give due place to the ethical nature of religion, and though both laboured hard to give a right place to the world, they did not really escape a pantheism which was acosmic mystical.†

In a desire to escape the duties of adult men in the natural, monism in the name of unity swallows up into the supernatural both nature and the person. The supernatural, as abstracted from our duties, is described in categories which express its bare unity and so is conceived ever less in terms of personality. By the interdependence of theory and practice, as the theory gets more impersonal so the practice gets less concerned with our responsibilities in the world. Thus we arrive at the extraordinary passive phenomena of Eastern religion.

Such a position cannot long remain optimistic when dominant in a society, but must degenerate into pessimism. Even if all awareness of other men has been destroyed, and however much we may deny the reality of ourselves, our own pain is so omnipresent as to lead us to that pessimism. Thus monism is either an optimism that fails to look out at the world or a general despair that corrupts all that it touches. It must be insisted that Oman's criticism of monism cannot in any sense be considered necessary. Indeed he will himself admit that within his

---

* *Journal of Theological Studies, op. cit.,* Vol. XXXII, p. 213.
† Ibid., p. 216.

account it ever remains a strong speculative position, for it begins with the overwhelming motive of achieving unity and therefore its systems are rationally coherent. What Oman objects to is its tendency to a passive morality and the way it is forced to choose between failure of compassion and despair. Clearly it is not in the name of reason that he condemns the attitude of despair or the lack of sympathy. It is in the name of his faith which has responded to the vision of the Cross.

An important difficulty arises over Oman's attitude to Buddhism. In his classification of religions he interprets all Indian religion in the way described above. Though the clarity of that classification is marred by his lack of examples, it is implied that Buddhism is included under the general heading of Indian religion.* Yet in Chapter XIII of *The Natural and the Supernatural* Oman places the origin of Buddhism in the isolation of our self-determination from our autonomy of insight into the supernatural, and our autonomy of self-consciousness towards the natural.† Buddhism is shown as the archetype of those positions that consider the final order of reality as an exact equivalence of action and award. Thus Buddhism is related to those religions that have dualist elements. Admittedly Buddhism under this account tends towards a rational monism by disregarding nature and supernature in its reduction of the world 'to sporadic acts of self-assertion.'‡ Yet it may be judged that in his dislike of the spirit of Buddhism, Oman gives it the worst of both possible worlds. In one, Buddhism originates from speculation motivated by the desire to return to the pure unity of awareness; in the other, it arises from speculation on our self-determination isolated from all else. Oman in his desire to demonstrate the uniqueness of the Christian Gospel and ethic, which alone maintain the right tension between dualism and monism, seems here to fall into contradiction. It may be that he does not mean Buddhism to be included under his general class of Indian religions, but if this is so his chapter on 'The Mystical' would need drastic cuts.§ Some account of the rela-

---

* See for instance p. 396, where he remarks that Buddha is consistent with mystic theory in forbidding his monks agriculture. See Appendix A of this thesis for an account of his classification.
† For a fuller account of this analysis see later in this chapter. See *The Natural and the Supernatural, op. cit.*, pp. 218–40.
‡ Ibid., p. 229.
§ Ibid., chap, XXIV, pp. 405–26.

tionship between popular Indian religions and Buddhism would also seem a necessity.

The difficulty in respect to Buddhism is matched by what he says about Plato and Platonism. Plato and indeed any of the Greek thinkers are but rarely mentioned in *The Natural and the Supernatural*. In his attempt to show the uniqueness of the categories of a Biblical natural theology, Greek metaphysics are avoided rather than criticised. He does say that Plato cannot be considered an acosmic mystic like Plotinus because of his active virtues and his interest in the world.* Would Oman have called the Platonic asceticism a dualism or an acosmic mysticism?

To return to the problem of theodicy: on one side of Oman's Christian metaphysic, there is the attempt to demonstrate that faith is only possible as men recognise the distinction in reality between our wills and God's and so reject all monisms. On the other, there is the insistence that only in Our Lord's revelation of the Fatherhood of God [do] we find a monotheism which allows us to exercise our freedom in the world, without being desolated by the threat of dualism. Here, in Oman's opinion, the important step is the transcendence of legalism, whether it makes its appearance in priestly Judaism, certain forms of the Christian Church, or the Kantian account of morality.

Oman sees the historic origin of legalism in what he calls 'the cosmological law of action and award.'

The central hypothesis of this cosmology was that all acts are acts of freedom up to the moment when actually performed, then they are awarded the exact equivalence of their merit. The origin of this view lay in the recognition of the fact of responsibility. From that fact it had seemed to follow that if there were to be rational consequences of action the ultimate reality of the universe must be a justice to award the good and punish the bad. Thus was exalted to the throne of the universe an exact equivalence between action and award.

Since the recognition of our self-determination is a *sine qua non* of civilised life, some such understanding of the universe must have been in men's minds at a time before recorded history. It was, however, in the sixth century B.C. that this intuition of our self-determination was turned into a cosmological principle. It appears in this century as such

* Ibid., p. 496.

a principle in India, Persia, Palestine and Greece. Oman has too subtle an intelligence to oversimplify the manifold and indeed contradictory elements that make up the religious positions of men and communities. Much may be believed in theory that is not practised; just as there may be practices that transcend or fall short of theory. Therefore, this principle cannot be said to dominate entirely the religious life of the period. However, its effect on men's thought and actions was immense.

As has been seen, Oman is always insistent that useful explanations have a tendency to solidify into formulas that restrict experience.

> A formulation is like the conception of the lever. Once we have found it, though the objects we use may have all kinds of other qualities, the more we regard it simply as a rigid bar, the more effectively we can use it; and, for practical purposes, we can ignore everything except rigidity and length. So any formulation which has been abstracted from our experience of reality, if it provide a specially successful lever for dealing with our world, by embodying some general manifestation of it, may be justified by its utility. But this does not justify reversing the process so that, instead of the principle being formulated out of experience, experience is formulated out of it, till it becomes like the interpretation of the forest by a sawyer in terms of planks.*

This tendency to limit experience by theory is operative in individual men and especially among the servants of an established order, the interests of which are served by conservatism. It was this tendency that hardened the intuition of our self-determination into a cosmological law of action and award.

Oman writes of the effects of that cosmology:

> In later Judaism the one God came to be conceived mainly as law working as action and award, in face of which devout souls had great difficulty in cherishing the freer, more gracious conception of the prophets. Among the thinkers of Greece one abstract rule of action and award tended to become an abstract destiny, and the common people, with increasing difficulty, gave it humanity from their more human pantheon.

* Ibid., p. 220.

The sixth century sees Xenophanes clearly expressing faith in one God, greatest of gods and mortals.[9] But how far does the belief go beyond the scheme of a justice conceived as the fixed apportioning of action and award? All the dramatists express the tragedy of this fated destiny. What more is even Plato's theory of the Good, and what are his eternal ideas but the pure pattern of it, of which the visible world is the changing, moving shadows? But even these shadows had some reality for Plato as a means of interpreting the real world: and, as in our day, much could be maintained in theory which was obviously not believed in practice.

Buddhism alone made the principle a complete cosmology and accepted it so entirely that it became a rule of life as well as a theory. Not only was it for Buddhism the measure of the universe, but, in the last resort it was the sole reality. Nothing exists but 'karma,' and karma is just the exact equivalence of action and award.*

The varying manifestations of dualism all spring from men's false attitude towards the natural. As the simple unity of feeling is broken up by apprehensions, men find that they are called upon to deal with the varying and bewildering situations in the natural. In this concentration on the form of freedom, the unity of feeling, which gives men the natural as all dependent on the supernatural, is broken up and nature becomes a detached environment that men must bring into subjection to the law. To repeat, the ability to determine issues is isolated

---

* *The Natural and the Supernatural, op. cit.*, p. 226. As has been said in the previous chapter, Oman makes a comparison between Karma and positivism. Both are the exaltation of useful hypotheses into determining principles by which all experience is judged. One particularly brilliant paragraph of that comparison is here quoted: 'Many fine ethical precepts are derived from this reference of all action to thought and of the quality of thought to desire, yet it is wholly a question of award: and in the end, the sole measure of award is pleasure and pain. Nor is there anything else it could be, for life is just the pleasure and pain of individual karma. Experience, being from it, means nothing except award in pleasure or pain. Nor can experience ever be more than a shadow in any universe reduced to a mere principle of sequence, whether moral or material. In Naturalism this principle has made us; and in Buddhism we have made it: but, in spite of the form of freedom in Buddhism, the world is left as meaningless, and all intercourse with it is made as much an oppressive unreality as by Naturalism. Just as a universe without freedom has no meaning, and without meaning no reality, so freedom, without a universe which is not its mere creation, has no meaning, and, without meaning, no reality. As the one reduces the world to a continuity of persistent motion, the other reduces it to sporadic acts of self-assertion. *The Natural and the Supernatural, op. cit.*, p. 229.

from our insight into the supernatural and our consciousness of the natural.

In this account of freedom as a series of atomic acts, morality comes to be considered as the obeying of laws that the supernatural lays down rather than the joyful service of the Father's Will. Nature is conceived as added to the supernatural, not transformed by its dependence. Thus it cannot be considered a realm through which the supernatural is revealed to us and which we are called to transform into a higher environment. Supernature is conceived as an order apart from us which rewards and punishes our actions as a Judge, but does not succour us as a Father.

> Laws are laws as they are impersonal, and a judge administers them as he is an incarnation of them in an individual and not a person ... the least adequate form of it [applying personal categories to God][10] is that he is one individual, standing over against each of us as other individuals; and the least adequate form of the relation is that we impose laws and he sees to their consequences.*

The reward and punishment consequent on our actions can only be thought of in terms of the natural. In early dualism these rewards and punishments are expected in this life. As that expectation is soon proved illusory, heaven and hell become material conceptions – heaven's blessedness and hell's misery being imagined in as absolute terms as the material embodiment will allow. Thus nature is ever more conceived as an environment for award and ever less as a realm the transformation of which into a higher environment is itself its own reward. Morality becomes the fulfilling of laws. The natural is thus more and more divided into two spheres – the secular and the sacred. The sacred becomes the sphere of religion while the secular is detached from the possibility of transformation by our activity.†

In the triadic relationship of nature, supernature, and persons, inadequate theory about any of these terms leads to less adequate theory about the others. Failure in practice leads to failure in theory and the theory in turn affects practice. Thus though dualism must be a problem

---

* Ibid., p. 335.
† See chapter 6 for a fuller account of what Oman means by this.

of all men's lives – out of which they must win victory into a prophetic monotheism – dualism as a solution (e.g., Zoroastrianism) is a disaster, as it stultifies morality into legalism and religion into the observance of rites[11] to maintain purity.

Oman shows much more sympathy for the dualist systems than for monism. However inadequately it faces the problems raised by freedom, it at least does not attempt to escape them. The Kantian position at least gives an account of morality which must incite men to striving; Hegel's account if taken seriously would eliminate all striving from morality.* Once again it must be stated that Oman's criticism of dualism is not based on evidence that all men must necessarily accept. It is rather that the various positions, openly or incipiently dualist, cannot affirm a confident faith in God and joy in the world and therefore cannot attain the reaches of morality possible to the Christian. Whether that joy is a great good and victory over despair a worthwhile attainment is clearly an assumption the truth or[12] falsehood of which reason cannot decide.

The Hebrew prophets were the first to transcend the view of supernature as a Judge. In their struggle to attain a righteousness that could find meaning and purpose in all the world, they were vouchsafed a vision of God as actively at work with men in history. It is only by understanding that struggle as we pass through it ourselves that we can begin to grasp what is meant by the Personality of God and achieve a true monotheism.

> Earlier and more vividly than others, the prophets saw the magnitude of the calamity of the fall of their civilisation. They bore their own fullest share and realised with the deepest sympathy the agony awaiting others. They never sought to shelter their spirits from the horror: they never comforted themselves with the thought that particular evil is universal good; they never took the individual personal sting out of their distress by generalising it into 'all life is misery.'
>
> But the more clearly they saw that the Natural, by itself and as man uses it for his appetites and desires, is all evanescent, and as he abuses it for his pride and ambition, all bad, the more they were taught to look for

---

* In including Kant with the dualist systems Oman interprets his thought as making a clear distinction between our wills and God's.

a deeper meaning and a more enduring purpose in it, which could make its defeats victory, its misery blessedness, its evanescence an eternal possession. Pleasantness and unpleasantness of sensation were thereby changed into perception of a higher world, manifest in the Natural yet above it, which provides values which make another kind of appeal and give another kind of joy in possession. Thus they were able to face physical evil as real and terrible, and moral evil as calamitous and perverse, and yet say that, by His own meaning in them and his purpose beyond them, the Lord God omnipotent reigneth. This confidence that no evil could hinder life from being one moral sphere, and experience from being one triumph of faith, was the essential victory of the prophetic monotheism, and is the sole ground still of any real confidence of one God being in all and above all.*

In that prophetic line Oman singles out Hosea more often and with greater sympathy than any other.† Hosea is always discussed as a preliminary to the account of Our Lord's ministry. Oman's passionate intensity is seen in his partaking of the life of Hosea.

Hosea had recognised, in the tragedy of his most intimate history and in the less immediate but equally terrible fate of his people, that although he could not wish that others should not face the consequences of their sin, he could not desire to mete out to them the reward or punishment of what they had done. He found he could only make his own life meaningful as he took upon himself the burden and agony of that sin. So he came to an intuition of the Fatherhood of God. How could that Majestic Holiness upon Which he depended be more limited in love than he, Its creature? How could the supernatural be less than an infinity of care for each person?

Oman writes of Hosea:

By his tenacious affection he interpreted the heart of God: and forthwith the idea of legal equivalent seemed wholly inadequate to God's rule, seeing that the last thing he desired for his erring wife was the just award of

* *The Natural and the Supernatural, op. cit.*, pp. 448–9.
† Ibid., pp. 445–7. See also *Honest Religion, op. cit.*, pp. 58–62, 97–8. To say this is not to imply that Oman disregards any of the prophets. For some of his finest writing about the subject see his book of sermons The *Paradox of the World, op. cit.* See especially his sermon about Ezekiel, pp. 236–46.

her evil life. How could a forensic righteousness, which would have been a poverty in his own spirit, be the righteousness of God? In seeing the calamity which follows sin to be for the deliverance of the soul, he found another key to the mystery of this sorrowful and perplexing world than legal equivalent. He made the discovery that it was in order to realise in his children their true worth that God has set life as the Valley of Troubling for a door of hope; and in this he found the reconciliation to the whole rule of God which is, in the full sense, monotheism.*

Oman illustrates through Hosea what he means by that mediated immediacy in which the revelation of the transcendent God is given to men with and through their apprehension of other persons.

Hosea did not say of his erring wife, this is a worthless woman in time, but I must think of eternity, and be gentle and loving and pitiful towards her and try to make her realise her situation as an immortal soul. He saw in her, just as she was, what made it impossible for him to be anything other than gentle, loving and pitiful, and, as he dealt with her situation in sincerity, he realised that no situation could ever take her out of his heart and his life. Then he knew also that the same must be true of sinful man and the mind of God. So, by the sense of the abiding worth of every person in the sight of God, he laid the foundation for the faith to which Jesus gave the final expression, that God is not the God of the dead but of the living, that in his heaven there is joy over one sinner who repents, and that his supreme purpose is to seek and save the lost.†

The faith of prophetic monotheism is only possible in its completeness through the revelation of the Cross. In Our Lord's meeting of all His natural appointments, His dealing with all persons and things and particularly in His bearing of the Cross so that it is triumph rather than defeat, we understand what it is to believe in the Fatherhood of God.‡ Oman's interpretation of the Cross is better epitomised in words from *Honest Religion* than anywhere else:

---

* *The Natural and the Supernatural, op. cit.*, p. 456.
† Ibid., p. 463.
‡ As the next chapter is concerned with Oman's Christology, no attempts will be made here to justify Oman's attitude to Our Lord, particularly against those who would find him guilty of the Socratic approach.

It has been said that Jesus was so great that His followers broke up the idea of God to put Him in. But the reason why He had followers at all was that their idea of God was broken and He brought it into one. Even the prophets had left unreconciled the bitter contrast between what they experienced in their own lives and saw in the lives of the godly and what they felt of God's mind and purpose in their own higher aspirations and their most spiritual fellowship. And for how many still is the great unresolved enigma why God's outward dealings should conflict so bitterly with his inward promptings. But the grace of Our Lord Jesus Christ, by victory over the darkest, saddest, most conflicting experiences through which men can pass, sets them in the light of God's infinite purpose of love and provides for us a spiritual fellowship, both Divine and human. Thereby it shows the world of our outward and inward experience to be alike from God and for ends for which in everything we may give thanks. Therefore, if man's world is to be renounced, it is that God's world should be possessed, which alone is the full recognition of one God in all and over all, of which mere abstract oneness of the Deity is not even the shadow.*

Thus it must be once more repeated that *The Natural and the Supernatural* is the justification of Oman's faith that the Cross regulates all experience. The epistemological description of the artist and the scientist, the examination of various modern metaphysics and ancient religions, is intended just to lay bare to other men that only in terms of the *theologia crucis* is any adequate theodicy possible. Only in the contemplation of the Cross in sincerity of feeling and the following of it in faithfulness in action can men affirm that God is Love, and make that affirmation without denying their own capacity for sin, or closing down their imaginations upon the suffering of the world.

One must hesitate at this point to remark how impossible it is to plumb the content that Oman gives to his concept supernature. For only as one dimly penetrates what he means by forgiveness can one dare to claim any understanding. What Oman does is to hold high the Gospels and say: 'This is what I mean.' He declares to men that as they start to scale that mountain of Love, strength will be given them for the scaling. Oman was a humble man and therefore through his writings

---

* *Honest Religion, op. cit.,* pp. 101–2.

he does not describe from his own life what forgiveness is. There is, however, in his work that note of reality – indefinable by the intellect – which gives the conviction that he is calling one to a territory into which he has indeed entered. This must be said, for when theology reaches this point it must shade off into poetry or preaching, where the tone is inextricably linked with the substance. To define Oman's concept of supernature must be simply to say 'Follow the Cross and you will understand what he means.' No boast of understanding can then be made.

Thus to Oman the uniqueness of Christianity is that it alone can make a victory out of suffering and so is able to find purpose in all of life.

> The distinctive element in the Christian religion is not any different[13] from other religions respecting the need of redemption from the world, except in so far as deeper moral insight may show more clearly the moral nature of the need, and so derive evil from sin and not directly from desire. What does distinguish it from all other religions is the kind of redemption it offers. In contrast to all ways of renunciation, its way of being redeemed from the world is reconciliation.
>
> This antithesis, thus baldly stated, might, however, mislead. Other religions, with the possible exception of Buddhism, also aim at reconciliation; and the religion which requires its followers to deny themselves and take up their cross and follow One whose obedience led to a death of shame and lingering agony, in a very high degree requires renunciation. But renunciation, in other religions, is first and for reconciliation; in Christianity, reconciliation is first and renunciation of value only as it is from reconciliation.*

It is by the Cross that men can understand the right relation between nature, supernature and persons. As has been seen in Oman's relating of the sense of the holy to the judgment of the sacred, all men are given that revelation of the supernatural by some reconciliation to the natural, which is made possible by realising in that natural the meaning and purpose of the supernatural. But over that reciprocity of

---

* *Grace and Personality, op. cit.*, p. 118. For a difficulty in Oman's use of the word 'redemption' see chapter 5.

revelation and reconciliation may so easily be cast the shadow of doubt which dims our intuitions and softens our wills. As we face the mature responsibilities of freedom, the primitive unities of dependence are broken up, and in the resultant demands upon them men ask if all the pain and suffering of the world can really come from that Holiness. So they can turn to doubt, or to the unity which disregards pain, or to the frustrations of dualism. But in Jesus Christ there is revealed to us One Who at the maturest and most painful level of responsibility is able at Gethsemane to decide to fulfil the Will of God on the Cross. Thus indeed all may be seen to be from the Father. Nothing is identified with Him, yet nothing excluded from His meaning and purpose.

In that vision the gulf between religious dependence and moral independence is bridged. Men find there a redemption from despair which calls upon them to become themselves the redeeming. There is made possible for men an objective, outward-turning morality, which seeks not reward nor self-fulfilment but which knows that all reward and all self-fulfilment are to be found in the love of other men. Oman recognises that any morality may be accused of eudaemonism, but he declares to any accusers that here the vision and the reward are one. Oman's supreme faith in God, and indeed in man, is shown in his lack of fear that the conception of God as a Loving Father will make men soft, for the vision and the demand are one.*

In the victory of the Cross it is possible to understand how persons need not be seen in opposition to nature, which opposition had led to so much of the despair of the classical world. It is not necessary to conceive nature anthropomorphically as standing opposite to man, as machine or soul. Man may live in the natural as a world he knows to be His Father's creation.

It is by the Cross that we can understand the full riches of the con-

---

* It must be said here in defence of Oman's position that certain theologies seem to keep the doctrine of the Divine Judgment as a means of making ordinary men good, rather than as a doctrine of how God in His Mercy will lead men to the Kingdom. See for instance, a recent publication by those in the Church of England who belong to the Catholic persuasion. *Catholicity*, Dacre Press, London 1947. There, in an historical analysis of the traditions of Christian Europe, a sharp disjunction is made by which 'Orthodox Protestantism' is opposed to 'Liberalism.' Ritschl is placed firmly in the second of these two classes and his insistence on the Love of God cut off from the Divine Judgment interpreted as a surrender to soft and easy ethic. See particularly p. 31.

ception of God the Father. It hardly needs saying here that Oman is entirely aware of the limitations of personalist symbolism about God. In *The Natural and the Supernatural*, written for non-Christians, when using that symbolism he nearly always breaks in with the word 'inadequate.'* In his works appealing to those within the Christian tradition he cannot be expected to qualify Our Lord's use of 'Our Father,' by arid little notes explaining that Jesus recognised the difference between creaturely fatherhood and the Fatherhood of the Creator. As has been said, Oman does not fail in that Christian humility that declares its agnosticism before the Holiness of God. As he puts it:

> Mystery is not nescience. It is the half-lifted veil of the sanctuary, through which all life's higher meaning shines, and which is the endless challenge to all our inquiries.†

He sums up the inadequacy of personalist categories in the following words:

> The idea of God as a person may be inadequate at best, an assertion only that he cannot be less than our highest way of dealing with him, and not that he is no more than we can conceive as the highest.‡

The alternative cannot be, however, to close our mouths and dry our pens. It is of supreme importance that we should write and speak about the supernatural. Men's understandings are in relation to God as much as their intuitions and their judgments, and the conceptions of their understanding influence their feeling and valuing. Personalist categories must be inadequate; when they become the formulas of corporations they are bound to become empty. But as we cannot know God above the categories of nature and history, we must be careful to conceive Him in terms of the highest, or we will cease to believe that forgiveness is the highest. In *The Natural and the Supernatural* Oman is less concerned with the ideas of legalist corporations than with the suprapersonalism of the English Hegelians. Such speculation empties

---

* See particularly *The Natural and the Supernatural, op. cit.*, pp. 330–43, chap. XIX.
† *The Natural and the Supernatural, op. cit.*, p. 213.
‡ Ibid., p. 335.

the idea of God of all content, and helps us to escape the awful responsibilities of the Cross.

Thus it is in terms of forgiveness that we best know the Fatherhood
of God. A quotation from *Honest Religion* says this better than anything
in *The Natural and the Supernatural*:

> It is God's dealing with the sorrow and sin of the world that gives the
> essential quality to the meaning of God as Father; and it is the place of
> His lost children which marks the essential quality of His dealing with
> all His children. The supreme revelation of His mind is in seeking and
> saving the lost; and the end of all reasoning with Him is the discovery of
> a patient pardoning love which makes sin that may be as scarlet, white
> as snow. This restoration to our Father and His family alone gives reality
> to pardon, which otherwise is mere condonation. It is reconciliation to
> the Father's mind and restoration to His peace, with an assurance which
> can face our whole experience, however distressful it may be. Its test is
> that, in everything, we are enabled to give thanks and that from every
> failure we can rise in hope, and from every transgression return to peace.
> It is not even a question of the pure in heart seeing God, but of the
> impure seeing the Father, wherein the unique significance of the life and
> death of Jesus while we were yet sinners most appears.*

## IV

A theology such as Oman's, that empties the idea of God of all elements of Justice and concentrates entirely on Forgiveness, must raise in
the reader's mind the question of universalism.[14] An antinomy must
arise at this point in a theology the main categories of which are 'love'
and 'freedom.' Oman meets this antinomy by leaving it open, indeed
only hinting at the question. In his silence may be seen much that is
typical of his theology.

In *The Natural and the Supernatural*, he is not interested in the details
of theology, but rather in writing a prolegomena to the whole subject.

> This inquiry is not a theology, even in this very general sense: but it ... is
> an attempt to lay a foundation for theology, by considering its method

---

* *Honest Religion, op. cit.*, p. 83.

and its problems. It does not aim at defending the theology of any religion, but its purpose is to discover what should be settled, before any particular question is raised.*

He does not however discuss the question in any of his writings.

Oman's reason seems to have been what may be called negatively his fear of system, and positively his sense of mystery. In a review of a work by Hastings Rashdall, he writes:

> When one compares him with St Paul, or even with Luther, one realises how little he cares to live in the half-lights, and how all the really creative souls have had to live there all their time.†[15]

Men must be concerned just with the Mind of God as given them for facing their appointments in the natural, and must recognise the mountain of His Holiness that will not allow them to fathom His purposes.

Allied with this sense of mystery goes Oman's belief that doctrinal systems tend to deny the freedom of all men to find in Christianity the way and the life. To nothing in his theological writings does Oman return so often as the simplicity of the Gospel. Nothing must be allowed to mar that simplicity. Speculation about universalism not only takes men beyond the bounds of responsibility, but it complicates that simplicity.

Nevertheless Oman's silence on this matter must be judged unsatisfactory. To the relation of God's Love and man's freedom he returns for chapter upon chapter. As is so often felt in reading Kant, to say less is not always to achieve clarity. Even if the issue had been left an antinomy, one wishes that it had been faced.

It is a deeper level than any desire for clarity, however, that one asks Oman for an answer to this question. A man who affirms his faith with such a note of joy must shirk no issue. Oman so constantly returns to those hymns of faith in which the agony, the defeat and the chaos of human life – all men being corporately involved – are seen as manifesting the Divine Providence. Such hymns, if they are to be saved from

---

*  The Natural and the Supernatural, op. cit., p. 98.
†  Journal of Theological Studies, op. cit., Vol. XXI, p. 270.

the note of pietistic complacency, need to be balanced by a ruthless discussion of the difficulties of faith. In none of Oman's writings is there that note of despair of himself and the world out of which the incipient dualism of a Pascal arises, and which makes men parade unflinchingly the doubts that hold back from faith. Oman is always able to believe that the Love of God rules all space and time, and to find in men the capacity to follow the destiny of the Cross. The vigour of that faith has indeed little note of ease. Coming to the faithless, however, it must come open to all questions.

What is Oman's position on this question in his later work?* In *The Natural and the Supernatural* the root of sin is made to lie in our self-direction more than in our self-determination. It is interpreted as hypocrisy rather than as individual acts of transgression. Oman writes:

> Sin, therefore, is used for anything which comes short of seeking the perfect order in absolute conscientiousness, or in other words the whole mind of God known or unknown. From it is distinguished conscious transgression. Yet it is sin, not transgression, which should determine our whole view of the question, because it places the emphasis, not on failing to do what our conscience demands, but on failing to respond to the whole call of aspiration and opportunity to be conscientious towards our whole higher environment and what may be realised in it.†

Or again:

> Thus sin can be used, as it is in the New Testament, for everything which comes short of the only blessed order, which is the whole mind of God; and what makes it really sinful be the insincerity which turns away from seeking it, called in the Gospels hypocrisy. This is the sin against the

---

* Once in a early work he mentions the problem: 'If as Ritschl maintains, the personality of God and man is individual and pantheism is wholly an abandonment of the religious problem which is how to maintain the spiritual personality against the whole material universe, through belief in the exalted Power that rules over it, it remains a problem whether evil can ever attain such power as to be able to blot out for God an individual.' See *Dictionary of Christ and the Gospels, op. cit.*, 'The Individual,' p. 816. Having stated the problem he does not attempt to answer it, except to say: 'There is a strange aloneness of the individual who has gone his own way, into which God Himself cannot intrude.'

† *The Natural and the Supernatural, op. cit.*, p. 329.

Holy Spirit, which is another name for every appeal of the sacred. 'It hath never forgiveness,' not because there is any sin that cannot be forgiven, but because it calls good evil and evil good, and so turns its back upon the manifestation of truth and the claim of duty, and not merely because it is radical evil, in Kant's sense of the breach of an absolute imperative. Such a breach, once committed, is really for Kant irreparable. Here nothing is irreparable except self-banishment by insincerity from the environment in which the spirit may recover purity and peace.*

It may be granted that such a view of sin by definition makes understandable the pardon of God's grace in a way that Kant's stern call to duty does not. But there is still something irreparable – self-banishment by insincerity. Presumably since Oman calls sincerity of feeling an autonomous activity, we can fail in it to the end. The annihilation of the insincere, the hypocrite, seems as difficult to reconcile with God's Love as the annihilation of anybody else.

The nearest Oman gets to any clear statement of the issue in his later work is the following passage:

If the essence of sin is estrangement from our true environment, there is at least the possibility of forgiveness, in the sense of what we mean by it in our human relations, which is neither overlooking nor condoning wrong, but the restoration, in spite of it, to the fellowship it has wronged. Then we can at least go forward to consider men's thoughts about it with hope: and if we find forgiveness a real and transforming experience, we shall be able to speak of God as a person with the certainty that we are not merely seeing the reflexion of our own faces, but know that our own forgiveness of others is a reflexion of the highest perfection which is kind to the unthankful and evil.†

As against Christian irrationalism, which denies man's right and ability to probe the questions of theodicy, Oman has affirmed the right and the responsibility of the Christian so to do. Openly, as against the secular rationalist he has insisted on the finitude of men and the neces-

---

* Ibid., p. 328.
† Ibid., p. 342. It is pertinent to the whole tone of Oman's theology to notice that his appeal is to our forgiveness of others, not to others' forgiveness of ourselves. This may well be compared to St Augustine's relations with Monica.[16]

sity of humility before the Word of God. His failure here, however, to make clear how Love and freedom must end in a mystery beyond our knowing is an example of a tendency in *The Natural and the Supernatural* to come too close, in the name of persuasion, to that rationalism which cannot understand the mystery and the leap of faith.


CHAPTER V

The personal supernatural, Who reveals Himself as an infinity of succour and pardon to all men and women, has revealed this nature in the course of time. Oman affirms what surely may be accepted by believer and unbeliever alike – that the belief that God is Love was not always self-evident even to those men with the keenest sense of religious dependence. Whether as truth or illusion, that belief appeared among men during the course of history. Believers assert, whatever differences there may be among them as to the definition of revelation, that God has revealed this to us at a certain period in time. To Oman it is indubitable that our knowledge that He upon Whom we depend is Our Saviour and not Our Judge 'dates from the day of His going in Galilee.' From such a belief must follow the questions of Christology and those of theological history, inescapably bound together. To understand what meaning Oman gives to the concept 'supernature' we must understand what his prophetic theism made of the term 'history.' How for the Christian can that fail to involve the intellectual questions that surround our Lord Jesus Christ?* In fact, only in relation to each other can any content be given to the words 'God,' 'Christ,' and 'History.' As we have already seen, the question of personality cannot be abstracted from the question of God. Equally as men are not solitary it cannot be abstracted from the question of history. And all are illuminated in Our Lord. Whether or not Oman likes such traditional language as the relation of Creation and Redemption, he is faced, as [are] all thinkers, with the same problems as arise from that formula.

The attempt to understand what Oman means by 'history' must

---

* Though this thesis is concerned with Oman's use of the concept 'supernature,' in the next two chapters the term 'God' will be more generally used. Not only is it the term that Oman uses in discussing these matters in his theological writings, but to state the most blatant of truisms it is a word that springs more easily to the mind.

involve turning way from *The Natural and the Supernatural* to his theological works. Indeed the last of the four parts of *The Natural and the
Supernatural* is called 'The Evanescent and the Eternal,' and deals with
the questions of history by classifying the great religions of the world
in terms of his natural–supernatural principle.* It must be granted that
this part is of positive interest as an illustration of his metaphysics and
especially as it shows the relation between modern metaphysical systems and the ancient religious beliefs. It is negatively brilliant in dispelling the many phantoms of naturalist comparative religion that so
often confused men's intellects. He does not, however, give any
remarkable account of the nature of historical knowledge, nor does he
tackle in detail the problems of God's rule over history. For example,
throughout that classification something very close to a Schleiermachian doctrine of the progressive moralisation of the race is assumed,
yet the relation of such a doctrine to the consummation of Cross is not
discussed. No attempt is made to define what is meant by history since
the Cross. The repeated insistence that Christianity is prophetic, in the
sense of looking forward, is not related to the fact that it looks back to
the moment when the Redeemer came.

The coupling in all Oman's work of 'grace and personality' and of
'faith and freedom' necessitate in the field of history that he hold in
unity the two terms 'discovery' and 'revelation.' In his classification,
however, he seems concentrated on the problem of 'discovery' and
does not relate it carefully to his concept 'revelation.' It has already
been said about other sections of *The Natural and the Supernatural* that
his meaning would be clearer if his philosophy of religion were placed
more clearly in its theological framework. In the early sections the relation is sufficiently evident, so that as his own position emerges its
dependence on faith is indubitable. Here in the question of history the
absence of a theological context is felt more strongly than anywhere
else. The rationalist alternatives to Christianity have always faced their
most trying problem in finding some place for that sense of the particularities of history which has been the glory of the Christian tradition.
When the scientific tradition seeks a philosophy of history it is likely to
succumb to the proud irrationalism of Marx. Is it not often the very
problems of history that force intellectuals back to respect Christian

---

* See Appendix A of this thesis.

theology, when previously they have seen it as a myth to keep the crowd in order? Therefore the absence of theological categories is more keenly felt in Oman's philosophy of religion when he deals with history than in other subjects.

To understand what Oman means by the term 'history,' attention must be focused on his other writings in which appear his Christology and his doctrine of the Church. It is hoped by discussing those works not only to clarify this term but to see his theology in greater detail. In a man as deeply Christocentric as Oman no account of his life from any point of view can be detached from his writings on Our Lord.

Again it must be insisted that by leaving the figure of Jesus Christ so much in the background till this moment, a grave scandal may be unwittingly imputed to Oman both as a thinker and a Christian. Is not this the imputation that Dr Barth brings against the theologians of 'liberalism' – namely, that Our Lord does not in the proper sense regulate their thought, but arises by implication as a secondary consideration? It would be, however, to misinterpret Oman utterly to suggest directly or indirectly that his thought is not Christocentric. The concretely real and suffering Jesus Christ is the fountainhead of all his thought, in a way that could not indeed satisfy Dr Barth, and which may not satisfy others intellectually, but so authentically that it is arrogant to deny it. Oman's thought, whatever difficulties it may contain, is above all else a 'theologia crucis.' Even when Oman distills his words to a fine simplicity, he has an accurate recognition of their implications. He is able to write: 'Christ is regulative of all revelation.'*

It must not be implied that Oman stands with those theologians who maintain that human science is the critique of all that God can give us to know. He must not be identified with his fellow Cambridge theologian, F.R. Tennant, whose writings give the impression of revivifying the 'antiquated' doctrine of the Incarnation by the precision of the Kantian philosophy. This thesis treats Oman primarily as a philosopher of religion and only secondarily as a practical theologian and a great man of God. In so doing nothing must be implied that would deny what is true for the Christian, that the practical theologian and indeed the preacher are nobler functions than that of the philosopher of religion. And whatever his function, the great man of God knows more than the intelligent

* *Journal of Theological Studies, op. cit.*, Vol. XI, p. 471.

of Love. Oman always returns with insistence to his doctrine of revelation to babes, and to the assertion that wisdom and understanding do not give men revelation but only test its claims and give us freedom over against tradition. All that is assumed in discussing Oman primarily as a philosopher of religion is that there is some value in what Christians of another era called 'spoiling the Egyptians.'

The insistence that Oman's thought is Christocentric is not a question of protesting too much, but of recognising a tendency in the present climate of Protestant theological opinion. Oman must be judged against the background of what may be called 'dialectical Protestantism,' which still exerts its influence on ministers of the Churches. There seems to be · a tendency in that school to pass over from criticism of theologians such as Oman for their failure to understand the immeasurability of the gulf between saving faith and all else – a criticism which, even if one disagree with it, one may still judge to be fair – to an imputation of a lack of moral seriousness in such writers. It is this passing over from intellectual criticism to the pride of incipient moral condemnation that makes Oman use the adjective 'abusive' to describe some of the writing of this school.* It is in this vein that a writer of this school falls into the naive half truth, the simplified historical judgment, of classifying Oman as a member of a school named 'bourgeois liberal.'† The philosopher of religion is a function associated so closely with what this school calls nineteenth century liberal theology, that in discussing Oman under this function the elements in his thought that are common with that liberalism may be too greatly emphasised. It is for this reason that the subservience of his philosophy to his theology of the Cross must be emphasised.

It would be wrong indeed to discuss the Christology of a man as deeply influenced by Ritschl as is Oman, without bearing in mind Dr Barth's repeated criticisms of the Ritschlians. Such a necessity presents, however, a dilemma to the present writer that must be made explicit. Dr Barth's emphasis on the discontinuity between man and God, and

---

* The influence of Dr Barth only became marked after Oman had written his chief theological works. Therefore Oman only once dealt openly with this influence. Also quite naturally as he grew older Oman became less interested in what may be called controversial theology. For that once see *Journal of Theological Studies*, Vol. XXX, pp. 401–5, an article by Oman entitled 'Schleiermacher.'

† *The Gift of the Ministry*, D.T. Jenkins, Faber and Faber, London, 1947, p. 105.

the glorious Love of God which overcomes that discontinuity, may be praised as a valuable reaction from the immanentism of an earlier generation. Christians may indeed glory in conversion. However, the present writer finds it quite impossible to believe that this experience is the only archetype of the Christian life, or to understand what it is to succumb to the position that all human judgment is utterly corrupt. Therefore he is excluded from understanding just what dialectical Protestantism means by 'saving faith.' Such a failure must according to this school prevent one from saying anything cogent about Christology, and indeed as Oman does not follow them in this doctrine, there is nothing cogent to be said. To count Oman out of the Protestant tradition is an impossibility, and indeed haltingly one must refuse to count oneself out. To be polemical, it may be said that a theology which by attacking the powers of reason excludes *ab initio* all criticism of itself, while maintaining the right to criticise violently the theology of others, may be intellectually forceful but hardly Christocentric. To say this is not to deny that such theologians have a knowledge of God of a character that one will never share, but rather to deplore the way in which humbler and perhaps less rich knowledge is excluded from the Christian tradition. Is it wrong to say that Dr Barth has little recognition of his meeting with Ritschl at the foot of the Cross?

Another milder *caveat* must be made about the following discussion of Oman's Christology. In viewing his writings chiefly in order to understand what he means by history there is a danger that his Christology may become a counter in an intellectual game, a dead body upon the laboratory table. This danger is increased when Oman's views are seen in terms of the history of theology. His debt to Ritschl or Harnack is mentioned and his faith is imperceptibly denigrated to the acceptance of an intellectual tradition, rather than a hope wrought out in fear and trembling.[1] Though it is not the purpose of this thesis to explore the beauty and sincerity of Oman's faith, it may be insisted that any of the last three sermons of *The Paradox of the World* or the last chapter of *Honest Religion* could not have been written by a man of superficial faith. These later works are singled out because in them Oman transcends his particular tradition and speaks with his own authentic voice. In *The Problem of Faith and Freedom*, for instance, the Christological position advocated is not in broad outline different from his later work. But in that earlier book, that which he inherited as a scholar and that upon which he staked his life do not seem to be integrated. He had not yet digested his debt to tradition and transcended it by using it. His later Christological writing has that quality that allows it to be compared without too great exaggeration to an art such as Bach's, where the benefits of a tradition are consummated in a unique personal statement.

## II

Christology for Oman proceeds from the intuition that all our existence must be judged in terms of the Cross. We cannot question that fact, we simply know it. Faith for Oman is that which we intuit in sincerity of feeling, and make our own by following in faithfulness in action. Indeed blessed by that vision, we have the duty to explain to others why it commands our loyalty, even though we know we cannot do so adequately. Some have the function to interpret all other experience in the light of that loyalty, for the sake of their own and others'[2] clarity. But to question that vision as the highest is impossible, and to understand why we have been blessed by it equally so.

To repeat what has been said in the last chapter, Jesus on the Cross, making the agony and pain of it into the triumph of the Son who does his Father's Will unto the uttermost, reveals to us God as does no other. Jesus on the Cross, able as he dies to commend His Spirit to His Father and to seek even then God's Love for those who torture and degrade Him, reveals to us in a way that is simply self-authenticating that Love such as this is the final order of the universe. For only Love such as this which faces reality at its most dreadful and uses it to good purpose can allow us to believe that the world is all God's.

As Oman writes:

> No one was ever so sure as Jesus of the Father's unlimited and unconditional forgiveness, with no one excluded unless by hypocrisy he shut his mind to God's mercy. Yet the faith which knows God's forgiveness to be real and transforming rests on Jesus because He lived and died setting this forgiveness in the heart of human experience and not merely proclaiming it.*

* *Honest Religion, op. cit.,* p. 122.

To repeat yet once again, the argument against Oman could be taken up by reason at many levels. At a level more superficial than the Spinozist, the optimist could simply assert that suffering and defeat are not self-evident phenomena about human existence, on the first level of consciousness, and therefore the Cross is not needed to make us pleasantly content with life. Presumably such a position is rationally possible if not likely in these days. In answer, Oman simply would say 'Look.' It would be also quite possible within the Christian tradition to deny the triumph of the Cross. Then despair may be affirmed, unless we look to the Resurrection. Oman never writes in any detail about Our Lord's cry of despair on the Cross, which clearly, with his opinions, should be of cardinal importance. As will be seen in the following pages, the triumph of the Cross is not for him dependent on the Resurrection. Presumably what he would say is that the cry of despair was consummated in the cry of fulfilment, and that even in the cry of despair the fact of Our Father is affirmed.

The foregoing places Oman in the position which was described by Kierkegaard as adopting a Socratic attitude to Our Lord – the view of Jesus as a moral hero.* It also shows how deeply Oman would reject that tendency in certain modern theology which seems to imply that the Cross would not have been much of an achievement if we did not assume that it was the very God upon it. Such a position glories in pointing out the large rate of crucifixions in the Roman occupation of Palestine. Oman rejects any substantial agnosticism about the Jesus of history.† He never deals with this subject except in short enigmatic sentences. Presumably it is a position so alien to him that he can see little reason to discuss it. His answer here would again be simply: 'Look.' Perhaps he would have felt as the present writer, that with every admission of the difficulties of evidence at many levels, when one turns from the three dialogues about the last days of Socrates to the accounts of Gethsemane and Golgotha, the moral gulf is as immeasurable as that between the ethics of the *Republic* and those of the Sermon on the Mount.

Thus all legalisms are nailed to the Cross. Our Lord reveals to us the inadequacy of any conception of the final order of the universe as a just

* For ridicule of this position see *By Faith Alone*, H.F. Lovell, Cocks, Clarke & Co., London, 1943, p. 94 *et seq.*
† For a gathering together of the evidence about this position see D.M. Baillie's recent *God Was in Christ*, Faber and Faber, 1948, London, see pp. 39–59.

equivalence between action and award. He reveals that God is Love, Who seeks us while we are yet sinners.

In this way Jesus Christ 'comes home to our business and bosoms' across the centuries. As He was reconciled to the Father, so is the Father revealed in Him and through that revelation the possibility of reconciliation is opened to us in a new way. As in our autonomy we are in some small way reconciled, so in contemplation of Him we may receive more deeply the revelation of the Father. The Cross, then, meets us here and now in our appointments. It demands from us more than any easy subjectivist reconciliation of feeling. It demands that we face God in all the grandeur and mystery of His Love. Oman is not afraid that in his insistence that the Gospel be 'relevant' he is falling into any submission to the *Zeitgeist*. For loyalty to the Cross takes us into the objective world of action where we can rest in no achievement. Oman once summed this up in expressing the central point of his agreement with Ritschl:

> Our response to this revelation [that of Jesus Christ] lies not in accepting a body of doctrine or stirring up in ourselves a special type of feeling, but in fulfilling our calling, in meekness and patience in the tasks and burdens of life, and in living in love in the Christian fellowship.*

In a noble sermon about St Paul, Oman illustrates best the relentlessness of his ethical literalism.† What had happened to St Paul on the

---

* *Journal of Theological Studies, op. cit.*, Vol. XI, p. 473. The brackets are the writer's. In understanding the historical background of Oman's ethical fundamentalism and his fear of dogma and mysticism, it is worth remarking that this is not only addressed to the 'Catholic' wing of the Christian Church. It must be remembered that he was brought up in a world where evangelical conversion and legalism were much more prevalent phenomena of Anglo-Saxon Protestantism than is the case in the present day. For an honest yet tragic example of the type of religion Oman feared, see the account of Pierpont Morgan's religion in F.L. Allen's *The Great Morgan*, Gollancz, London, 1949.

† *The Paradox of the World, op. cit.*, Sermon XIX, 'Strength Through Weakness.' As in the following pages Oman will be shown as calling on St Paul for support of his opinions, it seems best to remark that the present writer is unqualified to judge the accuracy of Oman's Biblical scholarship and, therefore, does not discuss it. Two points in this connection may be made. (i) Oman was not of a character to make any scholarly assertions lightly. (ii) His interpretation of the scriptures is prophetic rather than scholarly. He stands in the line of Kant, Kierkegaard, and Ritschl, in his fear of the pretension of the professors of exegesis. However, he never properly defines what scope he would allow to that vocation. As in most cases, it may be said that Oman errs on the side of distrust rather than over-confidence in the intellectual.

road to Damascus was indeed a cataclysmic revelation of God – or call it if you will, an intuition of the holy given in a moment of crisis. It was, however, a perfecting rather than a break with his previous nature. Oman's central theme in this sermon is that this first conversion was only a beginning of his understanding of the Gospel. Only after his stoning at Lystra and his reconciliation to that agony as all within God's purpose did he come to realise that the Gospel was in its fullest sense 'strength through weakness.' And despite all that Oman writes on other matters, he uses phrases in his account of that strength through weakness that are a most literal acceptance of the Sermon on the Mount.* What Oman writes of the Apostle so illustrates what he means by the Gospel that it is worth quoting *in extenso:*

> Even in his most argumentative speeches Paul aimed at true faith and never at mere intellectual refutation. But his earlier speeches could at the most have produced intellectual conviction. They tended to increase the danger of Christianity becoming merely one of the many movements of thought, which, at that time, were causing great commotion, but effecting little spiritual change.
>
> Even when Paul spoke of the Crucifixion, men would not necessarily discern that it was a new view of God and of life and of the true uses of the world. They could still have thought of it as a mere momentary triumph of wickedness in the midst of a revelation of might and glory, with its meaning the assurance that such moments do not last forever.
>
> But, in his suffering and weakness, Paul struck a deeper note. The faith in which his disciples were exhorted to continue could no longer be mistaken for faith in a glorious triumph of Divine power, but was now, beyond all possibility of misunderstanding, faith in a Kingdom only to be entered through much tribulation.†

As a corollary of this ethical fundamentalism Oman is always insistent that men should make no boast in the reconciliation they find in loyalty to the Cross. It makes possible no pride, it confers no privileges except to take up the Cross and follow Him. The redeemed are simply the redeeming and must bear with Jesus the cost of that redemption. If

---

* See chapter 6.
† *The Paradox of the World, op. cit.,* pp. 257–8.

those who know that faith can call themselves in any sense 'elect,' it is only as being elected to sacrifice.*

Oman's Christology is illuminated by what he says of the titles applied to Jesus in the New Testament – the Christ, the Lord, the Son. He is the Christ, the Anointed of the Kingdom of God, because by His Life and Death He has revealed to men the nature of that Kingdom, as the fellowship of those who find such joy and freedom in doing Their Father's Will on earth as there is in heaven. As it is through the sacrifice of Jesus that the Gospel of God's Love is made known to man, Jesus is the Anointed of that Kingdom. But as that Kingdom is made known through the Cross, it is a Kingdom of men called to the same redeeming work. Therefore though Jesus is the Christ, our task is no different from His.†

Indeed the Gospel of the Kingdom of God of which He is the Christ cannot be detached from the ethic of which He is the Lord. Here again we return to Oman's perfectionism. Jesus is the Lord in the sense that His way must be our way. Oman would clearly have disliked the distinction that Edwyn Bevan made at the end of his little book *Christianity* between Gospel and Ethic.‡ It also hardly seems worth noting in 1950 that Oman in dealing with Jesus as our ethical Lord makes short shrift of ideas such as Lawrence's and Nietzsche's that poverty of spirit means the morality of the slave. Presumably such ideas were more current among European intellectuals in his day than this.

Finally and most important for Oman, Jesus is the Son. 'It is as the Son that He is both Christ and Lord.'§ Jesus shows us the Father by being perfectly the Son, not by being Himself the Father. He is the Son because in Him we see reconciled the highest aspirations of the Holy

---

* As is so often the case in Oman's theology, the importance of this point in his thought is weakened by not saying it clearly and in not drawing out its implications. For a clear modern statement of what seems the crux of this matter, see Prof. L. Hodgson's *The Grace of God in Faith and Philosophy*, Oxford, 1936, particularly p. 97. It is perhaps their meeting on issues such as this which allowed Prof. Hodgson to write such high praise of Oman in his review of *Honest Religion* when they disagreed so deeply on other matters, see *Journal of Theological Studies, op. cit.*, Vol. XLIV, pp. 416–17. For the relation of this point to the possibility of rational theology, see the last chapter of this thesis.

† See *Honest Religion*, pp. 97–102.

‡ H.U.L.[Home University Library of Modern Knowledge] Oxford – reissued 1949.

§ *Honest Religion, op. cit.*, p. 100.

Spirit in us with all the antinomies of the world around us. Here again we may return to Oman's assertion that his theology is truly Pauline by quoting his description of the Apostle's views on the question of Sonship.

> The humanity of Jesus was as real for him as for Mark. On the physical side Jesus was of the seed of David, and shared the likeness of sinful man under the law; on the spiritual, He was God's Son by a spirit of holiness, and was exalted by way of loyalty, most conspicuously manifested on the Cross. Though undergoing the stern discipline which sin brings on His brethren, He Himself knew[3] no sin. Yet it was only because He knew no separation from the Father, not because He could know no temptation.*

Oman is never much concerned with the schools of contemporary theology, but several times he criticises the loss of the full humanity of Our Lord in the Anglo-Catholicism of his day. He writes of Bishop Gore:

> What human reality, for example, can be left in Christ's sufferings which could enable us to say, 'My God, My God,' even when we felt forsaken, and commend our spirits to our Father as the floods go over our souls, if, as Dr Gore supposes, He had the night before observed the eucharist proleptically in His glorified body?† [4]

Thus Oman affirms explicitly that it is in Gethsemane and Golgotha and not in the Resurrection that men must put their trust. Indeed he does not deny that the early Church was founded on the headship of the Risen Lord, but asserts that to Paul the Resurrection was God's mark of approval on the humility of the Cross.‡ As such it adds noth-

---

* *Honest Religion, op. cit.,* pp. 104–5. Oman maintains this thesis by considering the famous passage in *Colossians* (I, 16, 17) as an interpolation introduced to meet a later heresy. How, on Oman's presuppositions as to the historical Jesus, he is able to make any certain statement that Jesus had no experience of sin, is difficult to understand. All that surely he should be able to say is that our intuition of Him is as uncorrupted by sin. In this connection see his account of the fig tree incident in *The Paradox of the World* sermon.

† *Grace and Personality, op. cit.,* p. 152. See also his review of *Essays in Orthodoxy* by O.C. Quick. *Journal of Theological Studies, op. cit.,* Vol. XVIII, p. 246.

‡ *The Church and Divine Order, op. cit.,* pp. 55–6.

ing to the Cross, in which is the victory. How distasteful to Oman would be certain phraseology about the gloom of Good Friday.

On this point there is a small degree of uncertainty in Oman's thought because of a wavering in his position. In 1906 he affirmed that Ritschl's concentration on the Love of God at the expense of His Majesty leaves a grave uncertainty about the Resurrection. Though Oman does not expand the point he seems to be disagreeing with Ritschl.* But in an article, published four years later, though he still admits the vagueness of Ritschl on this point, he seems to have been in agreement with him. The fear of belief through miracle and the fear of any idea of exaltation that takes men away from the humility of forgiveness combine as reasons for this agreement.† In his last work he stands openly and squarely with Ritschl.‡

This is, of course, by no means to say about Oman, any more than it could be said of Ritschl, that he did not believe in the reality of the Resurrection. It must be remembered that Oman accepted the Moderatorship of his Church – a Church which affirms that Jesus rose from the dead. It seems difficult to believe that a man of Oman's honesty and one who was as little interested in place as he, would have accepted such a position if there had been anything in the Confession of his Church that he could not have repeated in good faith. Such a deduction from character in interpreting a man's thought may be weak and even dangerous evidence. In Oman's case, however, many wise men who knew him well admired him, particularly for his honesty. Therefore, such evidence may be allowed. Also in his work he says nothing that possibly could be interpreted as a denial of the Resurrection. Indeed he always stresses the sheer weight of testimony that must be overcome if it is to be denied. There is none of the clever iconoclast in Oman – he who finds a purpose in undermining the faith of the good and the simple. He has his own particular form of the Roman Catholic instrument of 'the economy,' with little of the pride often associated with that instrument.

What is important to Oman in the discussion of the Resurrection is to affirm that it is not a question of standing or falling faith. Leaving

---

* *The Problem of Faith and Freedom in the Last Two Centuries, op.cit.,* Lecture IX.
† See *Journal of Theological Studies, op. cit.,* Vol. XI, pp. 474–5.
‡ See *Honest Religion, op. cit.,* pp. 151–2.

aside the question whether he is right or wrong in this affirmation, with his position and his intuition of how many good men are held back from faith in Jesus Christ by just this problem, is he not right to affirm his *theologia crucis* in this way? He is always careful to say that a belief so central to Christian tradition and dear to many minds must be treated with careful humility.

Indeed in Oman's hesitations over the Resurrection, the central problem of faith and freedom can be seen better than in the more generalised problem of religious dependence and moral independence. He attempts to walk through the strait gate that lies between the cavils of Pelagian philosophers and the irrationalism that can say nothing to the faithless. Oman's view that God in revealing Himself never chooses to infringe our autonomy can only with the greatest care be reconciled with the Resurrection. He writes of Jesus Christ:

> Liberty of the children of God, as well as liberty of the enquiring spirit, forbids us to live under the authority of the past. Yet in practice it is impossible to come in touch with the spirit of Christ at all without realising something absolute, something which is precisely the rock on which we can stand in the flux of things and have the spiritual outlook which has a right to judge all things and be judged of no man.*

It is to maintain this liberty while insisting on the personal quality of the authority that, to preempt Luther's great phrases, Oman emphasises the *theologia crucis* while insisting on the dangers of the *theologia gloriae*. Throughout his work he is fearful of that view of Our Lord that sees in the Crucifixion the king in rags who will soon tear off his disguise and show himself in triumph.

## III

Before attempting to see what Oman's Christology means for his concept 'supernature,' and for the concept 'history,' two illustrations will be given of how he faces two Christian doctrines specifically dealing with history – his doctrine of Providence and his doctrine of the apoca-

* *Journal of Theological Studies, op. cit.* Vol. XXIX, p. 296.

lypse.* To write of his doctrine on these matters will not add anything in principle to what has already been said. Especially in describing his doctrine of Providence, there must be some repetition of what has already been said about his theodicy. But to repeat, Oman's writings do not cover a wide area, but return rather to a few problems which to him are the very essence of the faith. So often and at such length does Oman write about Providence, that it must be mentioned as an example of how he conceives God's Rule over history.

First, its importance:

> There is only one religious discovery of value. It is not that God is behind all events, for that may only make them more terrible and strange. It is that God is in all events, even when they are not of His causing but of our sins, and that, by His purpose and succour, they may all be turned to good.†

Yet such a doctrine cannot be knowledge if the word be interpreted as that upon which sensible men must agree. Oman is often preoccupied with the idea of Providence as held by men too easily. He returns therefore often to the attack on any such ease as vacuous and blasphemous. It is vacuous because it never faces the question of efficient cause, blasphemous because it can only be affirmed by men content with their lot and unimaginative about the lot of others. It is of the essence of the true doctrine of Providence to be the triumph of faith over difficulty.

It seems germane to the issue to remark that despite Oman's dislike of any belief in Providence not founded on Jesus Christ, in some parts of *The Natural and the Supernatural* the Cross seems so much in the background that there is an ease of faith that is almost natural religion.‡ Such a judgment is based on the tone of the work, not on specific words. In a theology of experience such as Oman's the atmosphere of writing is of the greatest importance, as in poetry. Also nothing surely can so harm the faith of others as writing on the doctrine of Providence that does not

---

* In *The Natural and the Supernatural* Oman uses the term 'apocalyptical' as a term of classification. See Appendix A. There the word is used in its most general sense of unveiling; here in its more specific sense referring to the glorious consummation.
† *The Paradox of the World, op. cit.,* p. 147.
‡ *The Natural and the Supernatural, op. cit.* See for instance parts of chap. XXVI.

make perfectly explicit the difficulties of that doctrine. Any such imputation to Oman is swept away by his theology. The title of his sermon on
Providence is *The Paradox of the World*, and therein the pain, the doubt
and the dilemma are well expressed.* There is no false piety in his theological writings. The Cross dominates all else. Indeed the last chapter of
his last work is a poem about Providence. Always halting, lest he should
override his readers with rhetoric, always careful, lest lack of qualification should distort or simplify a doctrine so implicitly dangerous, that
last chapter is the nearest thing to a hymn to God's Love as a style such
as his could produce.

Thus it is Jesus Christ who alone can make possible for us faith in
Providence.

> Even death, with every conceivable accompaniment of shame and agony
> and visible defeat, is turned into the doing of God's will and the revela-
> tion of His pardoning love and the manifestation and victory of His righ-
> teousness and peace. Having found there the good which alone is of
> incomparable value, we learn also that the worst as well as the best must
> serve it.†

Providence is comprehensible only through that reciprocity of revelation and reconciliation that *Grace and Personality* describes. It is as
men take up their crosses that they can dimly see how the evil will can
serve God's end.‡ Even at the dreadful moments in a declining civilisation, men can know that calamity is the manifestation of the Rule of
God. They can know that as God pulls down and uproots, it is only the
better to build and to plant.

By bearing his own cross St Paul could affirm his trust in Providence. Oman's interpretation of the Apostle is worth quoting again as
an example of his writing at its best.

> ... no doctrine of Providence is self-evident: and as a mere pillar of Natu-
> ral Religion it is little support, while just in loss and failure and distress
> Paul finds the greatest significance of Jesus Christ's revelation of the

---

* *The Paradox of the World, op. cit.*, pp. 110–25.
† Ibid., p. 115.
‡ Oman never takes up the problem with Voltaire at the level of natural event. Presum-
ably that calls on the same risk of faith.

Father. The Apostle had been so ill as to seem to have the sentence of death in himself, he was still in suffering and weakness, his plans had broken down and misrepresentation had followed, and he had to admit a change of mind leading to a change of purpose. But, he says, if my sole purpose is God's service, I am not changing if I alter my plans when I find they are not His. The Son of God Jesus Christ is never Yea and Nay, but always Yea, meaning that if we continue in His spirit, change itself may be consistency. Then come the somewhat enigmatic but far-reaching words: 'For how many soever be the promises of God, in Him is the Yea. Wherefore also through Him is the Amen, unto the glory of God through us.' (2 Cor. 1.20)*

What Oman believed of the relation between God and persons in history is further illustrated by what he wrote of Apocalyptic.† Here the same difficulty is raised as with the question of Providence. How can we maintain with certainty that history will witness the consummation of God's purposes, without denying man's autonomy?

Oman's position may best be approached by way of his criticism of Dr Schweitzer's famous writings on this subject.[5] To this criticism Oman returned for thirty years.‡ Dr Schweitzer's belief that Our Lord and St Paul were only concerned with an interim ethic because they expected an early end of the present order leads him to an arbitrary and material account of Apocalyptic. To Oman, the Gospel of Jesus Christ is of a Kingdom, essentially ethical in character, which men can enter voluntarily here and now by the worship of the Father. If all that Our Lord taught and did emphasises above all else the infinite care of the Father for man's freedom, is it possible to believe in a judge-like entry of God

---

* *Honest Religion, op. cit.,* pp. 189–90.
† See particularly *Encyclopedia of Religion and Ethics, op. cit.* Article on the Church. Also see *In Spirit and in Truth, Aspects of Judaism and Christianity*; see Oman's article 'The Abiding Significance of Apocalyptic,' pp. 276–93. Bibliography, p. iv. His interest in this subject is also illustrated by his already mentioned works on the book of Revelation.
‡ It sometimes takes the form of criticism of Dr Schweitzer's sins of omission and commission in Biblical exegesis. I must again state my lack of qualification to judge at this point. The issue at stake is, however, not in essence one of exegesis but of epistemology. Therefore exegesis may safely be avoided. It may be remarked, however, that a man of Lord Eustace Percy's moral sensitivity and scholarship recently interpreted St Paul as does Oman.[6] See *The Christian Congregation,* a lecture, Longman's, London, 1945.

into history in disregard of that autonomy? Oman states categorically that if there is anything in the records of Our Lord's life and death that leads to a contradiction between the spiritual and apocalyptic ideas, then it cannot be the former than must be sacrificed. For with any material Apocalyptic must not the Gospel of the Father be sacrificed?

> The prophets and Jesus and Paul may have cherished the idea of a near historical fulfilment, but this is a small matter compared with what is much more certain – that they were religious men of the deepest spiritual insight and the highest consecration, and not puppets pulled by the string of an obsession. While the very intensity of their faith in God's working in the world may have foreshortened their perspective of its full manifestation, they lived in a world of eternal realities which for them was already present and it was this that made them abiding moral and spiritual inspirations.*

In *Honest Religion*, written after his epistemological and metaphysical studies of *The Natural and the Supernatural*, Oman clarifies further his disagreement with Dr Schweitzer.† Looked at in terms of the history of thought, Dr Schweitzer, though in reaction against Ritschl's interpretation of the Gospel in terms of a rational ethic, has in that reaction accepted with Ritschl the Kantian account of the moral judgment.‡ Thus in Dr Schweitzer's position the religious and moral judgments are detached from each other. So he is able to write:

> Jesus accepts as true the late Jewish Messianic expectation in all its externality. In no way does he attempt to spiritualise it. But He fills it with His powerful ethical spirit.§

Oman writes of this quotation:

> If, however, there is anything certain about what Jesus did, it was to

---

* Article on the Apocalypse, *op. cit.*, p. 278.
† *Honest Religion, op. cit.*, pp. xxxv–xxxvi. This passage may be taken as an example of how his contemplation on the philosophy of religion illuminates for Oman the significance of Jesus Christ.
‡ See chapter 2 of this thesis.
§ Quoted by Oman from *Mein Leben und Denken*, see *Honest Religion, op. cit.*, p. xxxv.

work a moral regeneration by a religious one, and that His ethical spirit
was not of the Kantian order to be merely poured into anything.*

Materialist apocalyptic hopes were understandable among Our Lord's
followers but at variance with Our Lord's teaching. To believe in them
is wrong, for they deny both the Patience of God and the autonomy of
persons. One practical manifestation of Dr Schweitzer's position is that
he interprets Our Lord's life as too much a matter of alarums and
excursions. Once in maintaining to some fellow ministers the necessity
of contemplation in a busy life, Oman remarks that Dr Schweitzer
misses the peace and confidence of Our Lord's ministry.†

Yet in criticising Dr Schweitzer's position, Oman never denies the
apocalyptical element in Our Lord's Life and Death. His insistence on
the Patience of God is not a denial that history will culminate in the
achievements of God's purposes for His creation. His stress on our
autonomy of action and contemplation is not achieved by disregarding
the urgency of man's moral predicament. He quotes several times with
approval Bunyan's great phrase about his fear that the houses were
going to fall about his head. Oman calls his own theology prophetic
theism, and as such his criticism of Dr Schweitzer is not made in the
name of a rationalist metaphysics. He criticises a leading contemporary rationalist, A.N. Whitehead:

> Religion is concerned with reality, but its reality is not what the world is,
> but what God is to make of it: and that which is the ground of the possi-
> bility of achievement of what ought to be is as real as what is. This is the
> actuality of the kingdom of God. The importance of history for religion is
> connected with this, and what interprets it is not metaphysic but pro-
> phetic insight.‡

Oman affirms:

> The Gospel is not only the restoration of the individual soul to the love of

---

* *Honest Religion, op. cit.*, p. xxxv.
† *Office of the Ministry, op. cit.*, p. 12.
‡ *Journal of Theological Studies, op. cit.*, Vol. XXVIII, p. 301.

the Father; it is also the assurance that this love will one day have its perfect manifestation.*

Indeed some such doctrine is necessary for a thinker whose main antipathy is to those who attempt to commune with God above the categories of nature and history.† Yet it must remain fully a mystery of trust.

Oman believes that Our Lord has illuminated what the prophets had already dimly perceived – the necessary reconciliation of two facts. These facts were that the Kingdom of God is here and now to be realised by the free repentance and consecration of men and yet that only through the Finger of God can It come in Its fullness. This reconciliation comes by the understanding that man's evil lies in disloyalty to God and that his regeneration is achieved by true worship. Sin to Our Lord was a moral state, but determined by religious sincerity. In the act of living the life of love it is revealed to us that God's purposes will be fulfilled. Oman goes so far as to say that if we partake of that faith we can think that a change of rule might come at any moment by a change of worship. Thus he is able to agree on the rigour of the ethical standards that Our Lord preached without assuming that they were determined by His belief in a near eruption of God into history at the expense of men's freedom. 'There is a sense,' Oman writes,

in which all true morality is an interim ethic. It is not being in accord with any order that exists, but for one that ought to be. All increasing vision of what is required and all sacred obligation to follow it in reverence for the highest and in regard for one another, assumes in one sense the active presence of what should be now, and in another, has merely to do with what is an immediate call, leaving the manifestation of it wholly to God. This is the essence of Apocalyptic. It is that by the redeeming as well as the redeemed, God will in his own time and way manifest that the rule we live in is His Rule.‡

* Article on the Church, *op. cit.*, p. 619. In using this quotation it must be pointed out that this statement of a belief in a mystical consummation is only given once, while there are many quotations illustrative of the 'here and now' of the eternal Gospel.
† See Appendix A. Oman's main division among what he calls the higher religions is between the mystical and apocalyptic.
‡ Article on Apocalypse, *op. cit.*, pp. 292–3.

Apocalyptic expectation is then the trust of those who already realise the blessings of the Kingdom of God in their hearts and are thereby
assured that eventually it will come in Its fullness. Those in the Kingdom will consider it blasphemy to urge haste upon God. Such insistence on haste belongs in Oman's opinion among the stunts of
theology. Those in the Kingdom can 'disregard the whole question of
visible power, organise themselves wholly on the basis of love, and
leave all issues with God.'*

In this last sentence is the heart of the matter for Oman – indeed the
heart of his Christology and what it tells us of the meeting of man and
God in history. It is the declaration to persons in all conditions that
despite our finitude, at the moment of decision in contemplation of the
Cross we are able to transcend our particular civilisation and live now
in the Kingdom of God, and in so doing it is revealed to us that history
will have its glorious consummation. Nothing is made easy. The Cross
is ever before our poor freedom but in that freedom all men can find a
gracious God.

Such an approach to the question of Apocalyptic lays Oman open to
the charge mentioned in the last chapter of Ritschlian sentimentalism.
God is brought under our puny notions of love and all hold is lost on
the biblical category of judgment. Oman never recognises such criticism by argument about it. He admits often that there is a tendency in
men, particularly in easy circumstances, to turn love into a sentimental
category. The stern agony of the Cross militates however against this
tendency. Is there any solution in a doctrine of Judgment which is just
as easily brought under our puny notions as is Love, and which facile
men can use to bring the Majesty of God's care for each person down
to their own level? Oman is surely shrewder about the proclivities of
mortals when he believes that they can better understand the idea of
justice than the idea of love. The theology of the Judge is as anthropo-
morphic as the theodicy of the Father.

Before leaving this subject, a difficulty must be raised about Oman's
close association of apocalyptic hopes with the fall of any given civilisation. He asserts (surely a general Christian position) that no civilisation can be an end in itself. He also judges that the highest in any
civilisation never emancipates itself from its corruptions except by

---

* Church Article, *op. cit.*, pp. 619–20.

material calamity. In saying this it must be remembered that Oman understood the pretensions of civilisation before 1914. Events since then have made such understanding the current coin (often debased) of modern theology. One admires criticisms of civilisation made among the immanentism of 1900 more than its modern equivalents.

It may be granted as a psychological phenomenon that in these periods of catastrophe men's thoughts are turned to the glorious consummation. It may also be granted that in so far as the breakdowns of civilisations are indubitable historical events (leaving aside the appropriateness of such absolutist terms as 'breakdown' and 'fall') and so clearly fraught with grief and frustration for even the least guilty that, unless with Oman and Professor Toynbee men hold that God is revealing his Love through these calamities,[7] there can be no escape from the cyclical pessimism of Thucydides or Spengler.[8] The difficulty arises in trying to understand what relation Oman believes exists between these calamities and the coming of the Kingdom. Oman seems to make out that through the series of rising and dying civilisations God is bringing about His consummation.* Yet he is unclear about the relation between our knowledge of secular history and the theological dogma. He is indeed not clear what role civilisations play in the life of the Christian.†

## IV

At the centre of my faith is the conviction that God was in Christ (in a way I do not care to attempt to define) reconciling the world to Himself.‡

How does that agnosticism affect Oman's concept of supernature?

In a recent book on Christology, Professor D.M. Baillie maintains that those thinkers whom he characterises as content with the eternal

---

* Article on the Apocalypse, *op. cit.*, pp. 287–9.
† See chapter 6.
‡ This sentence comes from Professor H.H. Farmer. Oman wrote it for a leaflet preparatory to some services he and his students arranged at the end of the 1914–18 war. No copies of the leaflet are now available. However, Professor Farmer made a mental note of this sentence as typical of Oman. It is used here because it expresses in clear-cut form that agnosticism about the ontological status of Our Lord that is always present in varying degree throughout his writings.

God and the Jesus of history cannot give adequate Christian answers as to the character of God and the nature of history.*[11] Professor Baillie states (to paraphrase in a few words this section of an exquisitely wrought argument) that without the traditional doctrine of the Incarnation men are led a view of God as He who waits to be discovered, and a vague and uncertain view of history. What would Oman have made of these questions? To answer this some attempt must first be made to understand the grounds of his refusal to commit himself to a traditional Christology.

Oman's agnosticism at this point is determined by the question of faith and freedom. That problem is very much the problem of relevance. Oman's attempt to maintain the balance between a reasonable and a challenging Gospel must always leave him on the razor's edge between the rationalist and the irrationalist. As the use of the word 'relevance' offends the irrationalist, it is necessary here once again to emphasise that Oman never forgets the *mysterium Christi*. Indeed any relating of his thought to that of Ritschl must make the qualification that Oman understands the mysterious givenness of faith in a way that Ritschl does not.

Oman puts this beautifully in *Honest Religion*:

> Yet granting that the grace of Our Lord Jesus Christ thus unites the love of the Father over all with the fellowship of the Spirit as inspiration and guidance through all, and so makes God one for us in the unity of all experience without and within, does this not, you may ask, still go beyond honest recognition of the limits of our knowledge?
>
> And knowledge in the strict sense it is not. It is still mystery, in the proper meaning of mystery, as that which beckons us onward to know more by following what we see. It is a mystery of godliness, a mountain

---

* See *God was in Christ, op. cit.*, pp. 63–84. It is disappointing that Professor Baillie does not mention Oman or his pupils, Professors Manson and Farmer.[9] Presumably he judges Oman's work to be subsumed under his short treatment of Ritschl, Harnack and Herrmann.[10] Despite this fact, it seems worth while to hold Oman before the court of Professor Baillie's questions, for it is a court that really attempts to understand in charity positions close to Oman's. Though in disagreement, Professor Baillie's work shows a profound sympathy for the morality and imagination of those thinkers who raise the question of 'relevance,' and a charity in criticism of their answers. Questions raised in this spirit command attention in a way that a less charitable approach does not.

of God that rises on our vision as we fare forward climbing upwards, not a cloud in the skies of Church authority.*

Simply, however, to state – as I believe Oman would have been quite willing to state – the sheer mystery of the Cross, that they alone can know it whose eyes have been opened by means they know not of, that there is a cataclysmic division made for men by the belief that a cruci-fied peasant of Galilee reveals to us the very nature of God, and that to persuade men to that belief as the surest truth is indeed beyond all human rhetoric and logic, is all very well. But it does not face ade-quately the stern duty of the redeemed.

It is not that Oman wishes to bring *Das Wort Gottes* under the control of rational reflexion, but in the name of compassion to attempt to reach out to men wherever they may be. Granting the inadequacy of argu-ment as compared with other forces of love, certain of those who have been to some degree reconciled by Christ must through argument reach out to the world. As in the modern world the devil uses for some men the guise of 'what is the difference?,' charity cannot rest in the simple proclamation of the immeasurability of that difference. The dangers of anthropomorphism and debasing the Gospel are always present, but can they stop one from attempting to describe the 'benefi-cia Christi' in rational and everyday language? The proclamation of an abstract theory of the Majesty of God and a general theory of the cor-ruption of human reason can easily itself fall into the *hubris* of subjec-tivism. Men may achieve thereby an outward certainty to face the chaos of their age, but that certainty is not strength, for it is only achieved by cutting off the Church from the world, not in the proper sense of an isolation made necessary by the demands of the Cross, but in the sense of a cult proudly proclaiming the uniqueness of its esoteric experiences.†

Particularly does Oman stress the necessity of a relevant Gospel for he is deeply held by his historical intuition of the Church's guilt for the faithlessness of the world. Its deflection from the Gospel in the pursuit of other interests demands from it humility about the questions of

---

* *Honest Religion, op. cit.,* p. 102.
† The above description of Oman's position must be highly inferential for, as has been said, he only once deals openly with the theology of Dr Barth.

evangelism. It must rejoice rather than despair in the fact that God in His Love has swept away all external guarantees of the Gospel, thereby leading men back to the self-authenticating Cross. The Church must glory in the fact that it is now back in a period similar to apostolic times, with nothing to preach but Jesus Christ and Him crucified. To turn one's face from that fact in the name of some certain Gospel is for Oman to fall back upon stunts in theology that pass away leaving no spiritual impact.

It is typical of Oman that his sympathy for the predicament of the pagan is matched with little sympathy, indeed ruthless criticism, of what he calls ceremonial legalism in religion. Rational reflexion on the relevance of the Gospel is not only the duty of Christians to the world, but the weapon of liberation by which simple men can proclaim the simplicity of the Gospel against the pretensions of any priestly caste. Oman returns again and again to the fact that it was a priestly sacramental organisation and not the secular might of *Romanitas* that was chiefly responsible for the Crucifixion (at the level of efficient cause).

Oman's agnosticism about the Being of Our Lord springs from his fear that doctrines about it may so easily distract men from the essence of the Gospel. They may be used by men in their pride to deny the sheer egalitarianism which the Cross reveals. The tremendous joy of the Cross to Oman is that it reveals the Father Who seeks men in all their differing individuality; yet at the same time it reveals a salvation the attainment of which is open to all men whatever their circumstances. Oman always holds high that egalitarian revelation of the Cross against the aristocratic mysticism of the Brahmin, the pride of the rationalist contemplative and the subtleties of theologians.

Oman's radical interpretation of this doctrine of the simplicity of the Gospel, or of what he called elsewhere the doctrine of 'revelation to babes,' may be seen in the following quotation:

> To rediscover its simplicity, we must banish from our minds every thought about it except that it is just good news of God and nothing else. For Paul a ministry of reconciliation was the sun-kissed slopes of Olivet, near and friendly in the pure air; for his interpreters it has too often been the precipices of Sinai, wrapped in a thick cloud of dogma which echoes with the heavy rumbling of controversy. The words which to the Apostle were plain everyday speech have become remote and elaborate and

technical. 'God was in Christ' to him meant simply the felt presence of the Father in One who was perfectly His Son; to his interpreters it is a complex and mysterious doctrine of Christ's person. 'Reconciling the world,' which was simply turning men from enemies into friends, is expounded by perplexing controversies about prevenient grace. 'Not imputing trespasses,' which was simply the pardon which restores to fellowship in spite of offences, is turned into difficult and forbidding theories of justification. The result has been to change the simple gospel that God is a Father just because there is no limit to His love's endeavour to restore us to our place as His children, into a plan of salvation, which stands like a frowning precipice between us and God.*

Yet despite this concentration on the simplicity of the Gospel, this reconciliation of the paradox of faith and freedom in the stern ethical demands of the Cross, Oman is not ruthless about symbolism not his own. It must again be pointed out that he served the Presbyterian Church all his life and openly asserts that membership in any branch of the Christian Church is better than membership in none.† His tolerance of symbolism may be illustrated by his review of Hastings Rashdall's book on the Atonement.‡ After agreeing with Rashdall's criticism of substitutionary theories made in the name of the Kantian metaphysic, he still maintains that Rashdall is unable to express the sacrificial character of forgiveness as found in the Cross because of the limitations of his purely rationalist view of man. On the other hand, a theologian such as P.T. Forsyth, with whose intellectual formulations Oman disagrees profoundly, plumbs deeply the sacrificial nature of the Cross.[11]

Oman once writes of nineteenth-century European Christology that the strength of the German writers lies in their in their insistence on first principles, while the strength of the British writers lies in their moderation, their understanding of every day life and their willingness to live in the half-lights of truth.§ Oman tries to combine these two qualities. The refusal to say anything that would deny either man's freedom or God's Love, held closely together in unity, is com-

* *The Paradox of the World, op. cit.*, pp. 127–8.
† *The Office of the Ministry, op. cit.*, p. 19.
‡ *Journal of Theological Studies, op. cit.*, Vol.XXI, pp. 267–75.
§ *The Problem of Faith and Freedom in the Last Two Centuries, op. cit.*, p. 338.

bined with a humility about his own formulations and consciousness of the difficulties with which tradition has been forced to grapple. Unfortunately Oman never analyses the problems of theological symbolism in any systematic sense. Probably he would not have considered such an analysis of any great value. The result is however that behind his apparent simplicity there is a great subtlety and sometimes obscurity, both of which make it difficult to follow him.

A passage on Athanasian theology illustrates what Oman means by the simplicity of the Gospel, and his agnosticism about dogma:

> When we forget how much, to the ancient mind, the ideal was a sort of material reality, yet was not material, we take it to mean more than was intended. The Logos, Athanasius says, was at once in the bosom of the Father, ruling the world, and in Jesus Christ. Obviously he has no idea of a Divine which is absent from heaven when present on earth: and some in our day have found in this Logos an interpretation of science as well as faith. But, if it seems to you a materialising for materially-minded people, a useful simplification in face of fears of demonic powers and gods many and lords many, though honesty requires you to treat it with reverence, it also requires you not to carry it as a mere load upon your freedom.*[12]

In the light of this doctrine of the simplicity of the Gospel, what would Oman's answer have been to Professor Baillie's first question – namely, that without the doctrine of the Incarnation in all its paradox men reach the belief in an aloof or non-condescending God? As the Cross is given to men through their particular tradition, but accepted by individuals in a continuing reciprocity between action and contemplation in which one moment may or may not be decisive, they grow in the understanding that forgiveness is the final power in the universe. It is with the Mind of God that faith is concerned and only by inference with His Might and Majesty. Otherwise faith would be no venture and no triumph. Though creeds and confessions are useful and necessary, and the best of them hold more truth than any single man will be vouchsafed, no doctrine must be allowed to stand between the individual and the Cross. And such doctrines always tend to do so

---

* *Honest Religion, op. cit.*, p. 106.

– for example, the doctrine of the Resurrection or even of the Incarnation. Trinitarianism may be a noble attempt to explain the world, it may help certain men to find the Cross, but it is not of the essence of a standing or falling faith. We do not need it in order to know from the Cross that He Upon Whom we depend cannot be less than forgiveness, and so haltingly and stumblingly to take up our crosses.

> Sometimes it is said that God reveals Himself in grace and also in power. But grace is nothing if it is not the final power; and power is mere force if it is not grace. Wherefore, Jesus could say that all power was given Him of the Father: but it is in His own sense of all being for the rule of God as manifested by Him, and not in the sense of being Himself omnipotent. Though the fullness of the godhead which dwelt in Him in bodily form is a revelation of the nature and therefore of the true might of omnipotence, to turn what thus revealed the rule of love into mere might, and then transfer it to Jesus, is the same type of arguing from abstractions sent into the void as we have seen employed in other spheres. As in other spheres, it was a helpful, almost a necessary, simplification for a time.*

It would have been interesting if Oman had related theological passages such as this to his concept of the sense of the holy. From this quotation emerges more clearly what he means by the sense of the holy and its relation to the sacred. The sense of the holy gives us directly in feeling our sense of dependence. However, only as it passes from awe to reverence does it give us intuitions of the Mind of God. Though the sense of the holy gives us a cosmology of intuition, it cannot be complete. It is always a demand upon us.

What Oman means by faith being primarily concerned with the Mind of God is illustrated by a passage in which he compares St Paul with Calvin.† It must first be remarked that Oman repeatedly affirms his great admiration for Calvin as a thinker and as a man of God. St Paul and Calvin may be compared because of the intensity of their concentration on the Glory of God. But because Calvin found mystery in life but not in God's ordinances, his map of God's scheme of salvation

---

* *Honest Religion, op. cit.*, p. 95.
† Ibid., pp. 39–40.

tended to become a law and to cease to be a Gospel. He therefore missed St Paul's understanding of the mystery of God's purposes for men, even after Jesus Christ, which makes all faith a half-seen vision. As Oman writes of St Paul:

> Out of this comes the difference from Calvin in his conception of election. As touching the gospel, there may for reasons of human perversity and reasons beyond our knowing, be present failure; but as touching election, we can be assured of a love which does not accept failure. Thus the Apostle has no finalities of creed or conduct or organisation, any more than His Master, but those who live in the fellowship of the Spirit are led by him, while Calvin's are all finalities.*

More important and difficult is Professor Baillie's assertion that a position such as Oman's cannot give any adequate answer to the question 'what is history?' It is more difficult, because Oman in connection with Christology never deals with such questions directly but only by inference. In answering that question it become clear that Oman denies the validity of formulas about God's actions in history in the name of freedom. In Jesus Christ men can find reconciliation for the paradox of Providence – so knowing that all history serves the purposes of God – but they cannot assert any definite scheme of God's Rule over history. What Oman vouches for to the faithless is that if men face their appointments in the spirit of the Cross they will understand more and more of what God's care for all men means.[13] He cannot stand by any formulation of Creation and Redemption or say that the essence of the Gospel is a Covenant theology of the Old and New Israel. Indeed his agnosticism at this point asserts that we do not need to understand why that revelation of God's Mind is vouchsafed to us at that moment in history, or attempt to relate that fact to the rest of history. Simply we must make the act of faith that it is so, and take up the Cross and follow Him. Any more certain interpretation of history – that is, any Christian philosophy of history – if it go beyond that call to leave all issues with God, will soon become a law that infringes the glorious liberty of God's children. To sum up, it is therefore not necessary to define how God was in Christ or to relate that fact to the enigmas of the historical process.

* Ibid., p. 40.

This is not to say that to Oman there is no history, for we must trust in the infinite wisdom of God's plan. It is, however, to affirm a scheme something like the following. Hosea stood before God. Oman stands before God. In the intervening time Our Lord has lived and died and so changed utterly the given situation in which men exercise their autonomy. But because the Cross has changed the given situation we do not have to stand or fall by any particular attempt to conceptualise what the Cross means in the whole of the Divine plan for men. Oman uses such phrases as: 'My concern is with the eternally religious,'* and Christ 'challenges us in life and not merely in history.'†

The changing particularities of the historical process in which men meet their God hold little interest for Oman compared to men's ability to transcend these particularities and so face the eternal.

In Oman's concentration on the *hic et nunc*, he does not, however return to any cyclical view of history. Indeed it is quite impossible to read the European secular philosophers of the last three centuries and not realise how deeply the Christian idea of history stood explicitly or implicitly between them and any return to an ahistoric metaphysics. How much more deeply this influence must have played on Oman, whose chief inspiration was the criticism of rationalist thought in the name of the Cross. What must be maintained is that in his agnosticism about the ontological status of Jesus Christ there is an ahistoric element akin to Kierkegaard's reaction against Hegel.

A difficulty arises however when it is asked whether Oman is equally agnostic about other theories of history. What for instance does he make of the doctrine of the progressive moralisation of the race? Particularly in his classification of religions in which he discusses the development from primitive religion to prophetic monotheism he comes near, by implication, to a doctrine of progress. On the other hand, he makes clear that the categories of development are not easy to reconcile with the autonomy of persons. To the criticism of history conceived in Hegelian categories he continues to return. In his political theology however he often assumes a doctrine of progress. In *The Natural and the Supernatural* there is no attempt to relate the development of religion to the consummation on the Cross. The present writer

* Apocalypse Article, *op. cit.*, p. 277.
† *Honest Religion, op. cit.*, p. 75.

believes that if Oman had been openly asked about a doctrine of progress he would have affirmed his agnosticism, saying only that trust in God must involve the belief that God is making something of good purpose out of all the manifold we are given in the study of comparative religion. The difficulty is that he never makes this agnosticism clear, and often, moreover, seems to accept the idea of progress. Oman embarks on the study of the philosophy of religion to dispel the phantoms in metaphysics and epistemology which stand between man and a clear vision of the world of persons. Should he not have carried on that dispelling in a far more fundamental way among the metaphysical questions raised by history? To do so would have necessitated the introduction of many more theological concepts into *The Natural and the Supernatural*.*

With Oman's agnosticism about 'history,' a difficulty must be raised about his use of the word 'redemption,' particularly as it relates to his conception of the 'Fall.' Oman's position is that the open criticism of certain traditional doctrines that he does not believe to be of the essence of the Gospel can only result in purposeless argument that generates more heat than light, and in hurt to sincere men who find joy in such doctrines. Though one may sympathise one can still believe that he carries this principle too far in practice. His sophisticated simplicity about the Gospel which avoids problems can be very confusing for the simple. This lack of clarity appears particularly at the level of vocabulary.

It may be useful and unavoidable to preserve traditional language and there is pride and even ridiculousness in inventing new vocabularies unless one is a theological genius of the very first rank.† However, to continue to use traditional language, when it is not used

---

* In making this criticism of Oman in relation to Professor Baillie, I must admit that the weakness of Professor Baillie's defence of the doctrine of the Incarnation lies in the last pages of the book, where he draws out the Christian conception of history. In so doing he does not justify such a conception by relating it to the facts of the '*civitas terrena*.' It is easier to condemn the doctrine of progress than to elucidate a Christian conception of history that does not remove the Christian out of the hurly-burly of the secular world. Oman's indefiniteness must be judged in the light of the difficulty inherent in all accounts of history.

† Oman is at his most biting in his review of A.N. Whitehead's *Process and Reality* – see *Journal of Theological Studies, op. cit.*, Vol. XXXIII, pp. 48–52. He castigates Whitehead for his unnecessary invention of a new vocabulary.

traditionally, may disguise ambiguities that were better uncovered. This question arises over his use of the word 'redemption,' which he uses in all his works. All religions are religions of redemption.

Can it not be granted that at least since St Augustine the word redemption has been for the Western Christian inextricably linked with a conception of the Fall? It has been used as part of the phraseology to describe the Divine plan – a plan whose mystery has indeed been ever granted by those who affirmed it – but which in some sense involves 'a buying back' of man by God.

The question then arises whether it is wise for Oman to use such a word when he remains agnostic about that scheme of history. For Oman would use the word in a rather different sense. By seeing Jesus on the Cross men may be won back from the sins in which they have been involved. At this point care must be taken not to imply that Oman would cheaply fail to see that the agony and the sweat of the Cross were in the most sacrificial sense 'a buying back.' Neither must it be implied that he fails to see the cosmic significance of the Cross, in the light of which we cannot say of any person that he will not be saved. Again neither must it be implied that he whose trust is in God as the Ruler of history would not say with traditional Christianity that the free acts of Jesus and the action of God are mysteriously combined in the Cross. Nevertheless, what meaning has a word such as redemption for the Christian disassociated from an idea of the Fall?

What does Oman make of the doctrine of the Fall? He here maintains that sophisticated position of not denying the truth of that myth, yet of denying that it is of the essence of the Gospel. He writes in connection with a work of Otto's – a theologian whom he thinks too deeply tinged by the enthusiastic guilt that characterised some German theology after 1918, that:

> We inherit evil as well as good, and we have responsibility for both, but have we any more right to call the one guilt than to call the other merit?*

The fact that men are corporately involved in guilt is no reason to conceptualise the Divine plan in the scheme 'Creation, Fall, Redemption.' We can if we so choose, but it is not of the essence of the Gospel. If this

---

* *Journal of Theological Studies, op. cit.,* Vol. XXXIII, p. 287.

is his stand, is Oman wise to use such a word as redemption, without care over definitions? For all his attempt to penetrate the paradox of religious dependence and moral independence, is it wise for a theologian of freedom to make such cardinal use of the word redemption with its passive implications? For all the simplicity of the Gospel, has not the intellectual a duty to be careful over language in his discussion of mysteries?

It remains always a difficulty in Oman's thought how he conceives the relationship between 'supernature' and 'history.' This may, however, be further clarified by what he writes about the Church and the world.


## CHAPTER VI

Without affirming any narrowly pragmatic or even Marxian dogma, it may be admitted that a theology or philosophy is clarified by the attempt to understand what action is advocated therein. As action must always be political (using that term in its broadest sense), so must all theologies. It may be granted indeed that intelligent political action by the Christian demands a theology, though not necessarily in the concrete form upon which the Catholic would insist. Yet the terms of a theology can only become clear in the exigencies of a political decision. 'This primacy of the practical reason' may be seen even in the English Hegelians, the tone of whose writings sounds often as if speculative men are blessed by transcendence over the awful responsibilities of time. The interdependence between their desire that men should act to preserve that society with which they were well content, and their non-personal theology, has already been remarked upon. Greater men, such as St Augustine within the Christian fabric, or Plato without it, have been more aware of the dependence of speculation on decision and, therefore, more honest about it.

The judgment of Oman as a political theologian is clearly of crucial importance. As the Cross is in its essence a demand upon us to follow Jesus, the question must arise as to how we are to follow Him. A theology with a term such as 'the redeemed who are the redeeming' must have some account of how that redemption is to be carried out in the world. Oman's concept of God is based on the subordination of all analogies to that of forgiveness, therefore it must be seen how forgiveness can regulate all of man's other activities. Oman's theology is a description of the meeting of man and God. Yet as he believes that that meeting is a 'mediated immediacy' and scorns the mysticism that attempts to know God above the categories of nature and history, the concept 'supernature' cannot be understood apart from our involvement in mankind. A practical theology must be judged practically.

Oman's account of conduct must be taken out of the cool air of the judgment of the sacred. It must be seen what such necessary abstractions as the true, the beautiful, and the good can mean in a world of bodies and families, churches and civilisations. They must be defined in relation to a world in which (may it not be assumed as the starting point of argument) the claims of art and sainthood, of personal and functional ethics, of justice and love, of tradition and freedom, conflict. The dilemmas and antinomies which arise point the true emphasis of what he is saying about man and God, nature and supernature. The reconciliations of speculation appear less conclusive in the world of action. In this concrete field, moreover, how can men be tempted to treat the world of persons and its manifold predicates as unreal?

To repeat what has been said in an earlier chapter, Oman's concept of supernature is inextricably linked to his concept of nature. The natural is both the means whereby men are given revelation of the supernatural and the environment with which they must deal when reconciled by that revelation. Reconciled to the natural in contemplation and in action, men find a purpose in it by which they may possess it and a purpose beyond it by which they may deny it. Nothing in the natural is identified with God, yet nothing must be separated from His meaning and purpose. To use another language, it is in reconciliation to life's appointments that men begin to fathom the paradox of God Immanent and Transcendent.

A position such as this demands some answer as to how the Christian achieves this possession and denial of the natural. What kind of Christian fellowship best reconciles this contradiction? How do Christians take part in secular history so as to possess it and yet not be possessed by it?

In what Oman says about the Church as a visible continuing organisation, it is possible to understand his refusal to make doctrine of the essence of the Gospel and to judge the adequacy of that refusal. At the same point – namely, in his insistence on man's freedom over against tradition – his concept of man may be better understood. It is where his political liberalism – his assertion of the possibility of creative politics (the word used here in its narrower sense) – meets with the quietist elements in his thought, that the respective influences on him of Reformed and of liberal theology may better be estimated. The difficulties in his attempted reconciliation between a Kantian universalist ethic of reason and an Aristotelian ethic of function arise most clearly when he emphasises both that the religious life is just the ordinary life well lived, and also asserts that the Cross must mean for men literally strength through weakness. To put the same issue in a different way, he insists that the saints must inhere in the world and not escape their responsibilities for the law, and yet at the same time proclaims that the Church must leave all issues of power with God. What then does he mean by ethical reconciliation of monism and dualism and by a faith in the supernatural which allows possession of all the natural and which is not possession by it? To ask these broad questions is not to be so absurd as to believe that they can be answered. Nor is it to deny what is surely a paradox of the Christian life – namely, that to express Christianity in majoritarian terms has often meant that it is scarcely Christianity that is so expressed.

Before proceeding to seek Oman's answers to these unanswerable questions one limitation of his thought must be mentioned. This concerns the lack of concreteness in his positive political theology. On no subject does he write so voluminously as on the Church, but what he writes is almost entirely the reiteration of certain general principles about the relation of the visible to the invisible Church, and the negative implications of those principles. His negative statements are incisive enough for any man, but when it comes to positive political theory (that is, the clarification of what is meant by the Kingdom of God by defining its relation to concrete historical institutions) he has very little to say and that often vague. There is a strange dichotomy between his insistence on the practical nature of theology and his inability to be specific. This vagueness goes far beyond the understandable fear of being so concrete that his theology might become a programme to save others from thinking.

*Vision and Authority* may be cited as an example of his vagueness. This work, which examines the question of religious authority, is written to face the situation of his day. Admittedly immediate problems can only be properly judged in the light of general principles. Yet the general principles once expounded are never in that work applied to the world in which he lived. For instance, there is a discussion of the temptations of Our Lord and what they teach men about conduct. Oman asserts that they teach men to shun both materialism and other-worldliness. But what he means by these terms is left uncertain. From that discussion it is quite impossible to tell whether he believes the Christian may be a ruler or not. *A fortiori* what Oman conceives to be the proper relation between his Church and the twentieth- century British state is quite undetermined.

Oman's indefiniteness is no doubt part due to the very nature of the questions. It is also due to the extraordinarily conflicting elements in the tradition of political theory that he inherited. It does not necessarily lead to the acceptance of what may be shortly called Thomist politics, if some truth is seen in the standard Thomist criticism that since Luther an important element in Protestant theology has been a tendency to contract out of history. It is also possible to understand that liberal theology has its liberal politics, with optimism about political man, often not easily related to the Cross. Oman inherits much from both these traditions. The quietist influence leads him away from interest in the subtlety and intricacy of secular history in the name of the simple Christian. His liberalism, though necessarily more dependent on the appraisal of the facts of secular history than quietism, leads him to look for such appraisal in Macaulay and Gladstone rather than in de Tocqueville or Marx.* Such oracles must have been increasingly hard to square with the realities of his day. Both his liberalism and his quietism and the conflict between them may be judged to have produced that characteristic note of vagueness and lack of interest in the particularities of the historical process.

Oman's keen intuition of the breakdown of the intellectual traditions of western Europe is not matched by much understanding of the related social, political and economic difficulties. For instance, when before 1914 he upbraids the Protestant Churches for the growing gulf between them and working men, he writes almost as if the industrial

---

* See *Concerning the Ministry*. Throughout these lectures Oman gives examples of his reading outside theology.

proletariat of the twentieth century were not much different from the fishermen of the Orkneys or the Palestinians of Our Lord's day. Such an ahistorical attitude is possible for the Tertullian isolationist or for a Kantian whose ethics are universalist, but difficult in a thinker who is concerned with man's dealing with the natural.

In the light of this obscurity about political issues, it will be the purpose of this chapter to maintain that the essential difficulties in Oman's theology do not arise at the speculative level, but in his discussion of man's corporate life and dependence on continuing traditions and institutions. To go farther, it will be maintained that his criticism of other theological positions – for example those of Calvin and St Augustine – is weakened by the fact that he does not choose to discuss these very problems in the interests of which such men were often forced to be paradoxical.* Is it not better to risk the contradictions of being specific, than to avoid them by being vague?

## II

The description of Oman's political theology must start from his conception of the Church as the ideal fellowship of the Kingdom of God. As he believes man's essence to be his autonomy, and that the natural self must be viewed as subordinate to that essence, so his membership in secular organisations such as the state must be regulated by his freely chosen membership in the Church. Our membership in natural organisations is prior in time, but the Church is first ideally. Also, in order to be specific about the conduct that Oman advocates, it is easier to start from the ideal where difficulties are less obviously present. And as has been said before, Oman writes more voluminously about that ideal than about any other subject.†

---

* In no way must the above be taken to imply that Oman's weakness in this direction was caused by the fact that he did not have to face the exigencies of responsibility in a way that Calvin did. After all St Thomas faced no graver responsibilities than Oman and must be judged an able political theologian.

† For Oman's writings about the Church see all his books except *The Natural and the Supernatural*. Also see articles included in the bibliography. *The Church and the Divine Order* must be singled out for mention for in that work there is an examination of the doctrine of the Church in Christian history. As was said of that book in an able contemporary review, it is not '*Dogmengeschichte,*' but prophetic history. (See *Journal of Theological Studies, op. cit.* Vol. XIV, p. 301, review by A.S. Duncan Jones.) All sacerdotal

Oman's doctrine of the Church is determined by his radical interpretation of man's autonomy, and the New Testament conception of Love as excluding all other Biblical categories. Repeatedly he pours scorn on what he calls prudence in theology — that is, the attempt to reach a moderate position by balancing conflicting claims. As he writes:

> I knew a little the late Baron Frederick von Hügel, whose writings some
> of you may have read, and I shared with many a deep esteem for him.
> Yet I am quite unable to follow him in his view of Catholicity as a sort of
> Peter's sheet in which is let down from heaven and kept from spilling
> separately into the void, something of authority and of freedom, of the
> institution and of individual piety, of mysticism and of rites, of morality
> and of spirituality.*

Truth is not reached by eclecticism, but by following our highest insights to their final conclusion, even if that mean discarding much that would seem to be of the essence of the biblical tradition.

Oman repeatedly affirms the obvious necessity that if there is to be clear thought about the Church there must be clear thought about our use of the terms God and salvation. As Our Lord's view of God is of the Father's infinity of care for each person's autonomy, our doctrine of the Church must be determined by the glorious liberty of the children of God. The Church is the society of the Kingdom of God and the King-

elements in the Church are ruled out *a priori* and sacramentalism made subordinate. However, even in prophecy fairness about facts is of some importance. What can be said of Oman as a scholar in this work? The present writer must admit his inability to judge of certain subjects, e.g. the Greek Church or the thought of Hooker;[1] in connection with the Greek Church, however, even the amateur may wonder how Oman could expatiate on the completeness of its modern decadence without mention of Dostoevsky or Soloviev.[2] In the case of St Augustine, moreover, where the present writer is on more familiar ground, it must be judged that Oman's criticism goes beyond disagreement to the point of misinterpretation. From Oman's work it might seem as if St Augustine had learnt almost nothing from the antinomies of the Constantinian experiment. Oman never comes to grips with the immediate cynicism and ultimate hope that led St Augustine to his view of the relationship of the two commonwealths. In criticising St Augustine's view of Church order, none of the wonderful passages are quoted about the episcopate as an office of service. For the above criticism of Oman, the writer must again refer to the interpretation of St Augustine in *Christianity and Classical Culture*, op.cit., the last three chapters.

* *Office of the Ministry, op. cit.*, p. 35.

dom can only be entered freely. Love is an attitude only possible for the free person. As the Cross has allowed men once and for all to repudiate the idea that the relation between man and God is either that of slave and Master, or the judged and Judge, those conceptions have no part to play in the Christian Church. The chief quality of the Father's Love is Patience and by that Divine Patience must the doctrine of the Church be regulated. The idea that any particular identifiable organisation is the uniquely inspired vehicle of Divine Truth gives man a false means of escape from the cross of freedom. And why if God put His trust in anything less than each man's poor bewildered freedom did He not go all the way and make His creation less fraught with sin and suffering? Over all Oman's writing on the Church, brood the events that had taken place in Rome in 1870.[3]

It is impossible to overestimate the individualism of Oman's theology and in his doctrine of the Church it is best manifest. The decisive meetings between man and God are only possible in our aloneness. In his philosophy of religion it has been shown that his criticism of rationalist monism and of mysticism is directed against its loss of the concretely autonomous individual. In his political theology his chief purpose is to condemn any ecclesiastical encroachments on the individual's autonomy and ultimate aloneness which may be made by the various types of ceremonial legalism. Oman rises in wrath against the exclusive distinction made by apologists for the Church of Rome between membership in their organisation and the alternative of Humian philosophic individualism. This is to confuse the false atomic individualism, impossible for the Christian who knows he is not created to serve his own selfish ends, with the true ecclesiastical individualism which is not self-regarding but knows that the Gospel can only be received as a truly personal possession.

The Church is then the only organisation whose ideal is its essence. It is the consciously created fellowship of those men who have chosen to follow the vision of the Cross, so far as they have been vouchsafed it. It is the society of the saints who live the life of love and prophesy by their actions the consummation of the Kingdom of God. All else in the society – its doctrines, its order, its sacraments – are but relative and changing, subordinate to the decisions of the fellowship as reached in love. Legalism has been nailed to the Cross, therefore the Church is a society in which legalism is shown to be redundant. A 'fellowship' is a society in which a completely different standard of relations between persons is possible. Any ecclesiastical organisation that treats its members as subservient to the interests of visible unity, by that very act shows itself to be a secular organisation. The 'saved' are not necessarily sinless, they are those who in all sincerity are trying to live the life of love – that is, to live in this fellowship of free unity.

To quote again a passage that is typical of Oman:

> It [the Church] rests on the conviction that the true Divine order is ever ready to break into the world, if men will only suffer it to break into their hearts. It is the society of those who already realise the blessings of the Kingdom of God in their hearts – pardon, grace, joy – and are so sure that it will come in fullness that they can live as if it actually were come, and so can disregard the whole question of visible power, organise themselves wholly on the basis of love, and leave all issues with God.*

Oman indeed affirms that the Church is of the essence of the Divine plan for history. It is not an addition to faith in the Cross. It is a divinely inspired organisation standing above nature and secular organisations. He agrees with Ritschl's criticism of Schleiermacher's famous dictum. Schleiermacher is wrong in his affirmation that Catholics come to Christ by way of the Church, while Protestants come to the Church by way of Christ. The true difference is through what kind of Church they come. The only mark of the Church of Jesus Christ is the mark of love. Only in fellowship, however small, is love possible. Wherever it is sincerely striven for among a group of persons, there is the apostolic Church. Neither numbers, nor doctrines, nor sacraments but the spirit of love is the mark of Catholicity.

Oman's appeal to justify the perfectionism of this doctrine of the Church is typically Ritschlian. In an act of the imagination we can sweep away the accretions of the centuries, by contemplating Our Lord's earthly life and death and the early days of the Church as found in the works of St Paul. All the metaphysicising, the concessions to the expediencies of power, the legalisms of proud priests fade away and we see the ideal Church. It is typical of Oman that in this backward look he should affirm in his articles for scholars (who he perhaps

---

* Article on the Church *Encyclopaedia of Religion and Ethics, op. cit.*, pp. 619–20.

thought were too prone to the ethics of the solitary) his certainty that Our Lord intended the Gospel to be incorporated in a separate society; while in his popular books intended for fellow churchmen, his argument is always of Our Lord's denunciations of legalism.

Our Lord's view of the Church is best symbolised for Oman by His choice of St Peter as the rock on which it will be built. St Peter is the epitome of fallibility, simplicity, and enthusiasm. His very errors and changeableness are redeemed by the strength of his love. He has the simple man's understanding that what really matters is conduct. He has the proletarian's distrust of all kinds of authority.

Two quotations illustrate how Oman attempts to partake of the mind of Our Lord about His Church.

> That He expected this idea (that of God the Father) to be embodied in an earthly society is plain, for the beginnings of it arose in His lifetime. But it was to be a very singular society, in which none was to exercise authority on the one hand, and none to call any man master on the other.
>
> Nothing can reconcile this with the ecclesiastical embodiment of it in all ages, wherein the true succession has been placed in the officials, who determined not only action but belief, and who have penetrated further into the inner sanctuary of the individual life than any earthly government that ever existed.*
>
> ... the most perfect community organised on the only divine, the only permanent basis, the rule of God which is love ... may seem a very unreal dream, but, as Loisy says, Christ's dream was his project [4]... the society Christ founded was to be made one solely by being one with the Father through faith in Himself, whereby the power of the world to come should be so present in this life that all events in it should be found of His wise love and all demands of it the assured way of victory and peace. A society with the power of the world to come thus working in it, naturally could not be served by any bond of visible authority.†

Oman also invokes the authority of St Paul. St Paul better than any other man shared Our Lord's understanding of the true character of the Christian society. In him the apostolic Church's understanding of

---

* Article on 'Individualism,' *Dictionary of Christ and the Gospels, op.cit.*, p. 818.
† *The Church and the Divine Order, op. cit.*, pp. 51–2.

itself was epitomised. The Church was based entirely on the conviction that the risen Christ was its Head. But always St Paul's view of the Resurrection was as the sign of God's blessing upon His Son who had borne the sweat of the Cross in the spirit of forgiveness.* The Church was the fellowship of the Cross. It was the fellowship of those who understood that strength lay in weakness.† The scope of the Church was determined by the meeting of men in His name – that is in the spirit of forgiveness. It needed no external order for it was knit together by love. The office of elder or bishop had for St Paul no kind of legal authority. The unity of the Church lay simply in the self-authenticating nature of the truth of the Cross. Oman rejects entirely the idea that St Paul was led to a more externally guaranteed view of Church order, as he meditated in prison at the capital of the great worldly imperialism.

## III

Granting the sturdiness and indeed at times the sheer nobility of Oman's exhortations to the life of the saint, it must be admitted that these general principles do not take the reader beyond negative criteria as to what the Church is not. They do not take one far towards answering the question how the Christian fellowship lives the life of love amidst the imperfections of history. Without such definition love is an empty concept. To repeat, for that definition to be possible two types of question must be asked. The first group centres around the needs of the Christian fellowship for continuity and its relationship to the external religious institutions of the day. The second group deals with the relation of the fellowship to the world of natural and historical organisations other than itself. This division is an arbitrary distinction made for the purposes of exposition, as the two types of problem are closely

---

\* There is no need to repeat what has been said in the previous chapter of what Oman thought of the Resurrection and Apocalyptic, though clearly they have bearing on the present issue.

† This phrase 'strength through weakness' Oman uses several times about St Paul. It can, however, be easily attacked as one of those necessarily general paradoxical phrases that convey such a variety of meanings to different people as to be of little value. If asked what it meant Oman would presumably have said, 'Contemplate the Cross and you will see what it means.' It could easily be objected that weakness is not a happy word, as meekness is not weakness, nor is creative suffering easily achieved.

interrelated. These two main types of question must now be broken down into a series of smaller questions so that what is being asked of Oman may be clarified.

In the first type it must be asked, what is the relationship between the Church strictly so called and the Church generally so called. (The distinction 'invisible–visible' has been such a whipping boy in the past years that it is better avoided.) To express the obvious in its minimal form, some men in some parts of the globe are born into families who belong to differing organisations commonly known as Christian Churches. All men in western Europe are born into societies where organisations of this sort exist. What then are the duties of the saints to such organisations if they are brought up in them? It would be an equivocation to avoid stating that Oman considered certain of these organisations more Christian in character than others – e.g., English Congregationalism than the Church of Rome. What then is the right of the saint to leave one organisation for another or for none at all? To ask these questions is really to ask them about the situation in which Oman lived, that is, about British Protestants in the early years of the twentieth century.

To pass to more fundamental questions about the Church, it must be asked what Oman makes of the necessity of continuity among Christians. To put the question in an openly conservative way, what does Oman make of the fact (surely to be assumed) that men do not exercise their freedom in any isolated sense, but are exalted and controlled by a spiritual tradition which is more rich and varied than any individual's partaking of it, and also that man's autonomy is nurtured within a pattern of biological continuity? To put the same question in its radical form, what is Oman's attitude to this tradition since it must appear but the meanest shadow when compared with our ideas of the Good or with the fact of the Cross? As to Oman the Christian life is just the ordinary life well lived, what place do sacramentalism, Church order and dogma play in such ordinary life?

The second set of questions has to do with the saints and the world. Presuming that in some dim sense it is understood what Oman means by the fellowship of the saints, what is the relation of that fellowship to men and institutions other than itself, in all the wide variety of possible situations – that is, from those in which the world is mildly friendly to those in which it is actively hostile? More difficult, what should be the attitude of the saints to their common membership with others in organisations which, at least on the superficial level, must be considered necessities of history? For example, what is the relation of the saints to their membership in nations or empires which (again may it not be granted) must perforce depart from the life of love if they do not choose to commit national or imperial suicide? What must be the saints' relationship to states and rulers, in a world in which states would cease to be states, if there were not punishments, and rulers would cease to be rulers if they had no guile? Would Oman use such language as 'the Christian nation' or 'the Christian state'? To be quite specific, can the saint be a governor? If not, for what reasons is he excused from the terrible responsibility of government? Put in the language of another era, what responsibility for justice have those who have seen the idea of justice transcended on the Cross? What in fact does possession and denial of the natural mean in terms of the Christian's attitude to families and states?

It must be granted again that these two sets of problems are the obvious formulations of unanswerable dilemmas. They involve those insoluble problems, the openness to which Professor Jaspers has called the noblest mark of the European spirit.*[5] The combination in Oman, however, of vagueness in political theology with rigorous criticism of men who were less vague leads one to present him with such insoluble problems. To ask is not to expect answers, but to hope that thereby Oman's concepts of 'man' and 'nature' and 'supernature' may the better appear.

## IV

First, then, what does Oman think should be the relation between the fellowship of the saints which is the Christian Church, and the official organisations known as churches, which in his opinion are all tinged to varying degrees with legalism? For fear of misinterpreting what he says on this issue, it must again be insisted that he served his church faithfully for his lifetime. For all his despair about the organised religion of his day – and 'despair' is the only appropriate word – Oman never says anything that would contradict the categorical statement he

---

* Professor Karl Jaspers, *The European Spirit*, S.C.M. Press London, 1948, p. 61.

makes that 'with all defects, there is no branch of it (the Church) to which it is not better to belong than to none.'* For all that his bitterest attacks are reserved for ceremonial legalisms and particularly when those legalisms attempt to become theocracies, he never doubts that the Gospel calls for visible religious institutions. However much he may indict whole periods of Christian history, he feels himself joined to that long tradition. He is not the isolated secular scholar who stands outside the Church berating it for its imperfections. Yet in saying this in praise of Oman, it is possible at the same time to wish that his repeated expositions of the failure of organised religion in his day were more often combined with words about his own involvement in that failure.

Oman's attitude to the Church 'generally so called' can best be seen in his explanation of why the vision of Our Lord faded and the Church became another legalism. With his view of the apostolic Church, such a question is necessarily important. It seems best to use Oman's own words on this subject. First the description of what happened:

> The sense of the Father who is mightier than all sin and evil, and who works a spiritual deliverance through relating us directly to Himself and His purpose of love in Jesus Christ, gave place to a fear of sin and evil greater than the sense of God's might to overcome them. The apocalyptic hope was no longer the sense that the meek shall inherit the earth, but became material, and finally disappeared before the hope so to serve God as to merit heaven at last. God was mainly Ruler and Judge, and Jesus primarily a Saviour from hell to the bliss of heaven.†

Oman describes why this happened in the following way:

> This result is neither mysterious nor discouraging. The same process which had been required for the few to understand Christ is also required for the many. Thus there must be an ever-recurring discipline of the Law, because, though every believing soul is from the first under the

* *The Office of the Ministry, op. cit.,* p. 19. From conversations with men who knew Oman in the flesh it is possible to say that his despair about the churches was stated more forcibly in conversation than in the printed word.

† *Encyclopaedia of Religion and Ethics,* Vol. III, *op. cit.,* pp. 621–2. It is not the business of the present writer to change Oman's use of capitals.

influence of the Spirit, for the perfection of His work every soul also needs a 'fullness of the time.' The leaven, therefore, has to disappear into the meal until the whole be leavened. The fellowship of believers founded on Christ, governed only by love and nourished by helpful interchange of spiritual gifts, did not vanish from the earth, but has remained as a leaven working in all the various legalisms that have arisen – the early Catholic, the Orthodox Eastern, the Roman, the Protestant ... The natural man ... still likes material guarantees, and would rather not trust anything to God that can be managed by man. The essence of it is that an institution with official rule seems a better security than a fellowship with Divine gifts. So long as that continues, man needs and introduces for himself what Paul calls the schoolmaster of the Law a thing that may be lower, but is continually necessary.*

Oman justifies this interpretation of history:

The really depressing view is that Christianity kept all right for three centuries, and then proceeded to the developments which led to the present confusion. Whereas, the view that the long preparation of Judaism had provided a few who could receive the Gospel in its fullness, but that in the task of working out the Kingdom of God in the world, a new discipline of the law in some form or another is always necessary, and that as time goes on this discipline becomes more spiritual, and the Gospel itself more powerful, is full of hope and can justify even the sad necessity of our present divisions. The real question is whether the Incarnation was sacramental or ethical.†

This understanding of the relation of law to grace must be the guiding principle governing the actions of western European Christians in their dilemma over the shattering of ancient traditions:

Against this veiling of the truth in flesh it is vain to be angry. Till man is wholly spiritual it will be God's necessary way with him. We may not even despise, neglect, or fail to serve the organisation. At the same time it must ever be held, like the body, as subject to the soul, something that

* Encyclopaedia of Religion and Ethics, Vol. III, op. cit., p. 622.
† Journal of Theological Studies, op. cit., Vol. XI, p. 476.

must ever be dying, that the soul may live. Hence we have to recognise the significance of God's providential dealing in once more breaking down the discipline of the Law by division, criticism, and even unbelief. Out of this ferment a new phase of the Church's life must surely issue, and a new vision of the Gospel, and then possibly a new and, we trust, a more spiritual incarnation of it in outward form, one in which there will be at once more freedom and more spiritual power.*

This description of the saints' relationship to the official churches is clear as far as it goes. Live quietly the life of love inside the churches. Revolt is only advisable at the greatest provocation. Oman gives no criterion of how one judges the respective merits of legalisms or where to draw the line between revolt and stagnation.

It is still, however, not easy to see what Oman expects the life of the saint to be. On the one hand, he describes it as just the ordinary life well lived, and, on the other, he asserts that the saint must take up his Cross. Is it possible for the saint to accomplish both these undertakings? Indeed in his earlier work Oman seems to be making a distinction between the spiritual and the physical, smacking almost of Manichaeism, which is completely incompatible with the religious life being the ordinary life well lived. However, in all his later work he disavows this distinction, and by this later work he must be judged.† Yet the question remains as to what form the life of the saint is supposed to take when Oman asks from him both perfectionism and an inherence in the life of the world.

What is meant by the affirmation that the religious life is just the ordinary life well lived? As soon as this question is asked the difficulty of commenting adequately upon Oman becomes clear. For this affirmation is related to his historical judgment that both the theology of the Reformers and the thought of the men of the Renaissance and the

---

* *Encyclopaedia of Religion and Ethics*, Vol. III, *op. cit.*, p. 623.

† *Honest Religion, op. cit.*, p. 112: 'Neither spirit nor flesh is part of his (St Paul's) division of human nature. Man is mind in substance and body in form. But he lives in contact with two worlds – spirit and flesh: and he may draw up mind and body into the eternal – the spiritual; or sink mind and body into the corruptible – the fleshly.' It is interesting that these words of Oman are almost identical with what A.S. Duncan Jones wrote in criticism of Oman's tendency towards Manichaeism thirty years before. *Journal of Theological Studies, op. cit.*, Vol. XIV, pp. 301–5.

*Aufklärung* asserted this fact. Oman indeed puts forward the view that the Reformers and the men of the Renaissance were thinking in complementary rather than contradictory directions.* He rejects the opinion that secularism was in part a reaction against the Protestant concentration on the doctrine of our Redemption. Such a significant interpretation of the history of thought takes one to the centre of Oman's theology. Does he interpret the Reformers rightly? Does he estimate properly the relation of their thought to the Renaissance and to eighteenth century rationalism?

As soon as these questions are asked – in the light of which the range and depth of Oman's thought can alone be judged – an obvious hesitancy must be expressed. How, outside many volumes of scholarship, could comment on these issues add anything to what has already been said by great men? To face but a corner of these problems would be to embark, for example, on a careful exposition of the relation of the idea of the *Beruf* to the doctrine of *sola fide* in Luther's thought. It would be to face the opaque problem of what all the various forms of Protestantism (Lutheran, Calvinist and Anglo-Saxon Puritanism) made of the claims of secular life in general and secular philosophy in particular. To comment in a few words leads inevitably to a superficial Hegelian sergeant-majoring of history in the interests of one of the best known theological positions. Should one accept the traditional Catholic interpretation of this history that on the one hand Protestantism led to a secularising of life because it was not sufficiently sacramentalised, and on the other hand to a retreat from secular history because it read the doctrine of the Redemption out of the context of the doctrine of Creation? Should one echo Dr Barth's indictment of the corruption of the Protestant world by liberalism?[6] That would give one an historical criterion, but it would not make one much clearer how the Christian should face the secular world. Or should one agree with Oman that the best of rationalism and of Protestantism are easily reconciled? To judge the historical tones and quantities underlying Oman's thought is not undertaken in this thesis, except in the most superficial manner.

Within the context of this failure, it must still be asked what conduct it is that Oman wants from the saints, when the simple gospel is the

---

* See particularly *The Natural and the Supernatural*, *op. cit.*, Appendix D, 'The Origin of Modern Science.'

following of the Cross, and at the same time the religious life is just the ordinary life well lived. If Oman means by the ordinary life, the natural life, it is easy to grant that the saints should as a general rule live simple lives, earning their own livings and not pursuing any esoteric activities? But beyond that admission do not difficulties arise? Does not the way to the Cross have a tendency to come into conflict with certain human activities, e.g., art and metaphysics, which are difficult to exclude from the term 'the natural life'?[7]

Is not a belief in the need for Church government common among 'natural men,' however much the saints have transcended that need? Oman does not indeed seem to recognise the difficulties (almost one might say the contradiction) involved in one institution combining the role of an historic corporation that penetrates and uplifts all parts of society with the role of a prophetic community which openly transcends the values of that society. Can it not be assumed as a fact that the more the Church does its duty of inhering in the life of society, the greater difficulty it has in proclaiming a unique Gospel? Most of his writings state the Churches' task to be the prophetic one of proclaiming a unique Gospel and practising a standard of conduct that quite transcends the possible norm of any society – even the high standard of nineteenth-century Great Britain. Yet at other times he writes as if the prophetic remnant could be a national Church.* Nowhere in his writings is there a discussion of the contradiction between these two ideas. As a practical point, it may be granted to Oman that the saints should eschew any isolation of themselves that might turn them into a complacent coterie. But will not a certain isolation from the ordinary life of their society be *de facto* forced upon them by the very uniqueness of their Gospel and the nobility of their ethics? How will it be easy to remain in the legalism of their day, when the Gospel they proclaim must be a transcendence of that legalism? Do not the ethics of the Cross (men having only so much energy at their disposal) exclude many forms of the ordinary life? It is not easy to understand what conduct he is asking from the saints.

---

* Oman never discusses the meaning of the concept 'nation' for the Christian. He just accepts it without definition. Presumably he accepts it with the connotation it has had for Europeans since the French Revolution. The fact that it is nearly always used in a favourable context is an example of how much nineteenth century secular liberalism was accepted by Oman as *fides implicita*.

To state that Oman fails to recognise these difficulties does not mean that he openly asserts any Rousseau-like expectation that the road to virtue can easily be the way to the majority. He agrees with Sohm that the religion of the 'natural man' (a phrase he evidently approves) is Catholic, whatever its name.*[8] There is, however, much in his writings that has the ring of the Benthamite almost as much as the Christian hope.

The question of whether Oman recognises sufficiently how difficult it is for the saint to take part in certain form of the ordinary life may be raised in connection with his view of the function of the artist. In *The Natural and the Supernatural* it is declared that the highest contemplative activity for the Christian is art. Such activity is a true ascension to God through the natural, while the mystic fails in that ascension because he attempts it by a conscious pushing aside of the natural. Oman indeed went so far about the glories of being an artist as to say of Shakespeare:

Who but the Master Himself ever so loved the kindly race of men: and is not that religion?†

Here not only is a great artist of secular subjects placed higher than one of Christian subjects such as Bach, but, if this remark is to be taken seriously, Shakespeare is above St Francis or St Paul in the hierarchy of Christian function. However much the phrase is watered down, it shows at least how strongly Oman was influenced by the Schleiermachian tradition with its glorification of the aesthetic function.

Such a judgment raises the question of the possibility of the artist being a saint (however wide is drawn the meaning of that word) and of the saint being an artist. It may be granted that Shakespeare so transformed the ordinary life by the intensity of his vision that he gave many men a truer vision of the world. But in what sense can he be said to have loved his fellow men? Can the activity of the artist be called love, if that word is generally associated in Oman's thought with for-

---

* *Encyclopaedia of Religion and Ethics*, Vol. III, *op.cit.*, p. 622. Even this statement implies an optimism about standards below which a society will not fall, that would not be as easy to assert today as at the beginning of the century.

† *Office of the Ministry, op. cit.*, p. 12. Any man must be allowed his 'off days' and exaggerations in speaking, but why in cold blood commit them to print?

giveness, even unto the Cross? Is there not a great gulf fixed between the aloof contemplation necessary to the artist if he is to master his craft, and the man who cares for his neighbour as himself? Oman writes as if the artist were solely engaged in the direct and simple intuition of the beautiful, and does not mention how much the artist must take the content of those intuitions and mould them in terms of form, the knowledge of which comes largely from tradition. For the latter activity the artist must be a concentrated craftsman detached from the world. Oman's simplification of this function would make it easier to reconcile the possibility of the artist being a saint. But that simplification may be judged untrue.

Despite the above exaggeration about Shakespeare, Oman with his *theologia crucis* could not fail to recognise that there were nobler activities than that of the artist. He would have agreed with Father Hopkins' statement of the value of beauty:[9]

> What do then? How meet beauty? I Merely meet it; own, Home at heart,
> heaven's sweet gift; I then leave, let that alone.
> Yea wish that though, wish all, I God's better beauty, grace.*[10]

This is implied in what he once wrote of Whitehead:

> The ultimate importance of the personality of God concerns an order of
> freedom and not a mere aesthetic order.†

It is seen in his recognition of the inadequacy of Schleiermacher's theology to understand the categorical quality of morality.

All the same, does Oman sufficiently understand the conflict that exists between the practice of art and of a morality of forgiveness? Let it be granted to the men of civilisation that art is the noblest possession of the natural, but does it produce men who are able to deny the natural in the name of the Cross? At the worst it may often be carried on in scandalous disregard of even the simplest duties. It is all very well to

---

*   This quotation has been typed as prose. [Editors' note: Grant may have mistaken
    Hopkins's vertical bar-lines for line-break indicators. See Hopkins's account of his
    techniques in Letter XVI and author's preface in W.H. Gardner, ed., *Gerard Manley
    Hopkins: Poems and Prose* (London: Penguin 1953) 7–11, 187–9.]
†   *Journal of Theological Studies, op. cit.*, Vol. XXVIII, p. 301.

speak of Our Lord's appreciation of the lilies of the field as preceding the journey to the Cross. To admire beauty is, however, a different activity from devoting one's life to the disciplined production of it – an activity, it must be repeated, that excludes many others. Simply to judge historically, art of outstanding merit does not seem to have been often produced in the simple perfectionist Churches, but rather by members of those Churches which have become settled corporations living in close communion with the general life of their societies. Oman's partaking of nineteenth-century liberal theology's glorification of the artist and his doctrine of the simple Church of the saints are difficult to reconcile.

This argument could be duplicated over the saint's relation to metaphysics.* If the saint is to inhere in the ordinary life, surely metaphysics must be an activity of that life. At the least, it is possible to agree with the late John Laird that there is in men a natural curiosity about the universe of which they are a part.† Yet a tension remains between metaphysics and the practice of the morality of the Cross. Metaphysicians, however useful their function, can rarely have the time for outstanding charity. Again it surely is historically true that the Churches of the saints have not been admirers of metaphysicians. The argument might be raised yet again at the topical level of the scientist and the saint. It cannot be difficult in these days to see the possibility of conflict here. In the light of all this it must either be believed that Oman does not recognise the depth of these conflicts, or that he means by the ordinary life something very different from any interpretation that the present writer can imagine, or else that he means by the saint something quite other than what he implies when writing of the Cross.

The present writer must admit his inability to understand what visible form Oman believes the Church should take. On the whole, it would seem as if he expects the saints to remain inside the religious organisations of their societies, but ever bringing them nearer to the Gospel of the Cross. If this is so, what does he make of the value of tradition? After praising Oman as a theologian of freedom and mystery and courage, Professor Hodgson writes that Oman does not understand 'the necessity and value of those forms and institutions which,

---

* See final chapter.
† John Laird, *Mind and Deity*, London, Allen & Unwin, 1941, see final chapter.

by enduring from the past through the present into the future, preserve the element of identity.'*[11] If Oman believes the Church should be a historic institution penetrating all parts of the national life, then this criticism is entirely valid, as he seems to give little place to those instruments of continuity and enrichment by which that task can be accomplished. Do the saints depend on the legalism to which they belong for the continuity of tradition?

If, on the other hand, Oman does believe that the Church should be a separate organisation of the saints, and therefore a quietist organisation, Professor Hodgson's criticism still stands. For even a quietist Church has need of doctrine and organisation and sacraments in a manner that Oman does not seem to allow. Let Oman's negative case against Catholicism be granted; namely, that officials, doctrines, and even sacraments always have a tendency to enslave men; that in some periods of history they have so distracted the Christian congregation from its primary purpose, the life of love, that the Church has become a congregation of Satan; that the Church so organised forgets its own doctrine and moves towards theocracy (the most odious form of government). Because of these phenomena Oman concludes that the interests of continuity must never be allowed to make idols of any form of Church government, any intellectual phrasing of doctrine, or even any particular pattern of sacramental life. Therefore none of these activities are of the essence of the Gospel, as Catholicism affirms them to be. They must die that the Gospel may live.

Having granted this, however, it must be said that Oman does not face the question of what positive part sacraments, doctrines and order are to play in the congregation of the saints. He writes as if continuity were to be maintained only by the adult recognition of the vision of the Cross. As in his discussion of grace, Oman's concentration on autonomy is so ever-present that there is little understanding of such channels of God's love as the warm life of the family nurturing the child in habit; so in his discussion of the Church he gives little place to the means whereby a spiritual tradition is incorporated and within which children develop their freedom to choose or not to choose to be Christians. He often writes as if sacraments and creeds were to be understood by spiritual insight rather than as a noble means to produce and

* *Journal of Theological Studies, op. cit.*, Vol. XLIV, p. 116.

maintain it.* Are not even the saints in need of being upheld by such instruments?

At the risk of too simple an historical judgment, it may be said (to use Oman's own language) that so great is his fear of ceremonial legalism that he does not face sufficiently the dangers of paganism. In his insistence that legalism leads to an increasingly rigid distinction between the secular and the sacred and therefore to a dualism of practice if not of theory, he does not seem to have faced how easily ordinary men may be possessed by the natural if they do not employ a diversity of instruments to prevent it. A man such as Oman, bred in a society permeated by Christian traditions, however imperfect, may almost unwittingly accept it as a minimum below which men will not fall, and therefore concentrate his attention on the imperfections of that society and its religious organisations without fully recognising its greatness. In saying this the opposite tendency may be noticed – namely, that Christians appalled by paganism are only too willing to accept the stern discipline of legalism as an alternative. Oman's early life was passed in a society still in no small part regulated by Christian traditions and where widespread paganism was not present. The imperfections rather than the ancient wisdom of the Church attracted his attention. Only in his later life did he face the growing paganism of European society, which thought it could dispense with that wisdom.

To sum up: In dealing with the question of what visible organisation will allow the Christian fellowship to maintain the proper balance between possession and denial of the natural, Oman seems to underestimate the contradiction between the saint's possession of the ordinary life and his following the Cross. Because of this failure, it is not clear what form he believes the Christian fellowship should take, and therefore it is difficult to understand in concrete terms what he means by the paradox of possession and denial of the natural. Secondly, whatever he may have thought the Church could be – a small quietist band of saints or a national corporation – he underestimates the place of sacraments and doctrines and even order, as the means whereby the Church can inhere continuously in the historic and natural orders. This makes it

* In *Honest Religion* Oman wrote of the creative purpose of creeds in a way that he never had done elsewhere.

difficult to understand what Oman means by a faith in the supernatural that is a possession of all the natural.

## V

The dilemma of what Oman means by possession and denial of the
natural is also raised in questions about the relation of the Christian
fellowship to natural and historic institutions other than itself. The
issue arises in its most difficult form over the relation of the members
of the fellowship to the state. Therefore discussion will be limited to
that institution.*

The question of the Church and the state will be raised in connection with the possibility of the Christian taking part in secular politics.
This can best be discussed by an attempt to understand Oman's work
*The War and Its Issues,* which was published in March 1915. It may
appear unfair to judge his opinions on politics on the basis of a work
that must have been hastily written to meet an emergency. Should a
serious contemplative theologian be made to stand by his polemical
writings? The present writer answers in this case 'yes.' Here at the
moment of decision – and for Europeans what has ever been a more
crucial moment of decision than those months? – Oman declares himself on an issue of major consequence and thereby the essence of his
political theology is laid bare. As nowhere else in his work does he face
so specifically and positively the questions of Christian political ethics,
much is here illuminated that elsewhere can only be guessed at.

Here was a man who had ended his previous work with a subordination of all categories – biblical and otherwise – to the activity of for-

---

* The institution of the family does not seem to have presented difficulties for Oman.
Although he quotes Our Lord's remark about the subordination of the family to the
Kingdom, he never defines the circumstances under which the family should be
denied. The disciplined Christian family is for Oman the proper form of denial and
possession of the natural in this sphere. The vocation of celibacy would be to him
*prima facie* suspect as an improper denial of the natural that had not passed through a
true possession. Oman's attitude is seen in his single discussion of sex: 'Sex is the
most obvious way in which spirit and flesh meet. Hence it may be the lowest or the
loftiest manifestation of human nature. The very word 'love' may either have the
grossest sensual meaning or be the poet's highest symbol of the noblest and holiest.
As this depends on whether its well-spring is in the flesh or the spirit, no other
human interest is so responsive to a religious valuation of one another." *Honest Religion, op. cit.* p. 185.

giveness. He had asserted that trust in God meant leaving all issues of power with God. Here was a man who had never viewed his particular civilisation with a bewitched eye, but with that of a sceptical Orkney farmer who understood its imperfections and prophesied its downfall. After remarking that Our Lord never trusted in the state, he had written:

> The usual way of avoiding this difficulty is to say He could not be expected to look to a Pagan state as we are justified in looking to the Christian state. But is the state ever Christian?*

He had affirmed that Tolstoi working on the land after his conversion was nearer the Christian ideal than the good-willed Christian socialist who attempted to reform the world by influencing the activity of his state.† In 1914 the saint had to face the claims of the imperfect in all its imperfection. God's demand for justice could not be avoided. To repeat, any thinker can in imagination hold, as it were aesthetically, each differing position successively, without counting the cost of contradiction. In action he is faced with a world so much more real that in committing himself the balanced alternative can no longer stand.

It does not seem redundant to remark that whatever the limitations of *The War and Its Issues*, whatever contradictions it may contain, the admirer of Oman cannot but be glad that it was written. All that he had written previously faced him with grave responsibility to commit himself in 1914 and he faced that duty in all its consequences. That this work was produced so quickly after the outbreak of war shows how deeply he felt his responsibility.

Oman states emphatically that the British Christian should support the British state in its prosecution of the war. He begins his argument with some statements about the past and the present that show him to be a political liberal:

> Would the preparation for Christianity have been as favourable had the Greeks been defeated at Marathon? Would Christianity have developed as effectively had Charles Martel failed at Tours? Would the religious

---

* *Dictionary of Christ and the Gospels, op. cit.*, Vol. I, p. 818.
† Ibid.

history of Scotland and Holland have been the same with smaller sacrifices for national independence?*

This statement does not by itself commit Oman to political liberalism,
for it could be interpreted as the statement of a Christian conservative,
who sees no creative possibilities in politics but recognises their negative necessity. But with the following judgment of the war of 1914
Oman is committed to that liberalism.

> Are we not right to think that we are witnessing one of the great strug-
> gles for a freer and a juster world, one of those wars for which religion
> has often been invoked and of which religion has been the spring and
> the stay, one in which it might well seem that the sole duty is to come to
> the help of the Lord against the mighty?†

Having rejected any note of Tertullian isolationism, how far does
Oman go in the opposite direction? As a preliminary he asserts the
Christian must be in touch with the pulse of his society in its moments
of great enthusiasm:

> It would be far indeed from praise to say that we (the Christians) main-
> tained our independence of mind by closing it to this great and deep cor-
> porate emotion.‡

However guardedly that statement be interpreted, it shows how far
Oman would go towards the Church being secularised in a world
where corporate emotions are of the kind they are, and induced in the
way they are. His description of the saint is here very different from his
other pictures of the lonely prophet. To refer back, this is the type of
statement that leads one to believe that Oman saw the Church of the
saints as a national Church.

---

* *The War and Its Issues, op. cit.*, p. 14.
† Ibid., p. 13. Even accepting Oman's assumptions, this is no place to estimate the accuracy of such an historical judgment. Clearly in 1914 there were English liberals who
agreed with Oman, as also there were those such as Morley who disagreed.[12] Liberalism is clearly dependent in its ethics upon historical judgments of this sort. Neither
here nor elsewhere did Oman discuss the nature of historical knowledge adequately.
‡ Ibid., p. 12.

More important than this preliminary is the question of the Christian's duty to this state. Oman proceeds from the general principle that the Christian's membership in the society of the Kingdom of God does not mean that he is not also involved in the earthly kingdom. He states that the magistrate does not bear the sword in vain. He points out that the acceptance of the protection of the state in peacetime is closely related to the duty of supporting that state by arms when it is in need of defence.*

Oman affirms the doctrine of the just war:

Does not the right to oppose one's country in an unjust war involve the duty of supporting it in a just one?†

Such an affirmation must help one to understand what Acton meant in calling St Thomas the first Whig. It is interesting that Oman's Gladstonianism is forced close at this point to a Thomist position despite all his critical remarks about scholasticism in his speculative theology.

Before continuing with the description of how Oman conceived the state, it seems germane to risk an interpretation in psychological terms of his stand in regard to inherited traditions. Until 1914 he had expressed his ethical fundamentalism within the framework of certain inherent liberal assumptions. Despite his attacks on the pretensions of the state (themselves at a certain level typical of the liberal as well as of the perfectionist) he had nevertheless assumed a certain political optimism. It is permissible for an outsider to remark that such optimism about politics was particularly understandable in a member of British society, part of whose genius had been to compre-

---

* In the case of the British side of the 1914 war the question of the state and its aggressions may be considered not to arise. In *The War and Its Issues* Oman declared that he did not believe the Boer war to have been just. This is another example of his liberalism as opposed to conservatism. The conservative surely could but support his Empire in the enforcement of peace within its bounds. It also shows that trait of the liberal in trusting those secular organizations known as nations while distrusting empires.

† Ibid., p. 20. There is no need to comment on the second part of *The War and Its Issues* at any length. It deals with the political and religious aims for which those Christians not caught up in the actual conflict must strive. Here Oman's political optimism is chiefly evident. This is illustrated by the fact that in 1915 he should insist that the British state must on no account infringe the liberty of the individual by invoking compulsory military service in its fight against tyranny. *Sic transit gloria mundi.*

hend the real basis of liberalism as religious and to develop it as a great political form. When the quietist elements in Oman's thought were challenged by the exigency of a call to defend the liberal society he admired against one he did not admire, the allegiance to his liberalism triumphed over his quietism.

At this point may be seen the complicated strands of thought that underlie Oman's tradition. What is of such interest in the main stream of Anglo-Saxon political liberalism is that it originates both from liberal theology, with its insistence on man's continuity with God, and from the Puritan variety of Calvinist theology, which views politics as the call to serve the glory of God in the world. Oman several times uses the argument, so frequent among Anglo-Saxon Calvinists, of the superiority of Calvin's political theory to Luther's. He inherits that strange blend of theological liberalism and the vigour of Calvinist determination that has done much to produce the pattern of modern democracy in Great Britain and North America. From such a union a new democratic blend of natural and revealed theology must arise. Perhaps the enthusiasm of the former Master of Balliol, Lord Lindsay, for Oman's thought may be partly based on their common sharing of this political position.*

At the same time Oman is deeply influenced by the quietist elements that have characterised German theology since Luther. The perfectionist tendency, seen in Kant, is even more noticeable in Ritschl, with his attempt to return to the simple apostolic Church. In some of Oman's writings there is the fear that escape from the literal interpretation of the ethical demands of the Gospel is to deny the Gospel.

Without judging of the respective merits of ethical perfectionism and of Christian liberalism must one not admit that they make strange bedfellows? Political morality must always be an insoluble problem for the Christian, but with such a contradiction of traditions it is no wonder that there seem to be deviations between the various parts of Oman's thought. *The War and Its Issues* is the triumph of his optimism.

To continue the description of what Oman says about the Christian and the state, he writes:

* The present writer knows no place where this mixture of Calvinism and liberalism is better exemplified than in Lord Lindsay's numerous writings on political theory. For Lord Lindsay's review of *The Natural and the Supernatural, Journal of Theological Studies, op. cit.*, Vol. XXXIII, pp. 385–8.

> The Church as a society of the perfect order of God's Kingdom which rests on nothing except personal insight into truth and the determination of all duties by love, must no more consent to live for less than that order because of a war, than a teacher for knowledge because a boy is whipped, or a benevolent society for the appeal of kindness, because the police have had to be called in. But that does not determine what each individual may have to do in the way of helping with the whipping or with calling in the police.*

Love does not exist to destroy the law but to fulfil it. Oman defines love of other persons in such a way that it does not exclude the right to coerce them in their own best interests.

> Love is fundamentally an estimate of man as an individual spiritual being whose own choice determines his destiny and whose eternal destiny is so great that no present affliction can be weighed for a moment against its attainment, and for whom death, however terrible in its pains and dread of unknown possibilities, is only the greatest of these purifying trials.†

The activity of love must be turned towards the transformation of the state. The state is part of that natural order which in Oman's opinion cannot be set aside in any easier way than by transforming it into a spiritual order. The members of the Church must strive to make the state a spiritual organisation. The consummation of this process will be the disappearance of the Church into the state. Here one can only assume that Oman is more deeply influenced by the doctrine of progress than he chooses to admit. It is this process that the rise and decline of successive civilisations is witnessing. The Christian's duty in this development is accomplished by using his influence to modify the methods of the state and to limit its sphere of activity. Beyond these generalisations Oman does not go. He once more lays down the principle of denial and possession.

> The task for the religious man is how to be in the world and yet not of it;

---

* *The War and Its Issues, op. cit.*, p. 43.
† Ibid., p. 51.

how to live as a stranger and a pilgrim and yet with the assurance that all things, the world as well as Cephas, things secular as well as sacred, are his; how to have as it has been expressed, a joyous use of the present with a self-denying outlook upon the future.*

The difficulty is that nowhere in his writing does Oman lay down any general principles of how men should judge whether at any particular moment the state is to be possessed or denied. When does the time come, and how do we know that it is come, for the material interests of a given civilisation to be denied in the interests of a 'higher religion' and a 'purity of morals'? Oman indeed makes the sensible practical remark that when the state leaves the Church alone then the Christian fellowship should not lay down laws about the Christian and the state, but leave it to the differing individual judgment. So pacifists and soldiers can live together in the Church. But the appeal to individual judgment surely does not save him from the elucidation of general principles on this matter. Oman seems to assume that the state will leave the Church alone. But what when it does not? It is all very well to write of modifying the state's methods and limiting its sphere, but when do we judge that the state has so declared itself to make this impossible? What does the Christian do about anti-Semitic laws, or for that matter about anti-negro laws? Oman gives no principles to serve as general guides to decision on such matters.

The issue may be carried farther by describing what Oman says about Our Lord's attitude to war. He goes so far as to say that Our Lord was not a soldier because he was a Messiah and because He was not living in a free society. He asks the question:

---

* Ibid., p. 115. See also a quotation from *The Natural and the Supernatural* where the denial of natural organisations is more clearly stated. 'We are dependent on natural relations, like neighbourhood, family, tribe, for any moral relation in which we realise our freedom, yet mere natural relations may be in the sharpest antagonism to any right moral relation, and only as we deny them may we have any right relation to our fellows or any power to fill rightly our sphere and use our opportunity ... So also with civilisation. Throughout all history we find a constant antagonism between the material interests of civilisation and religion, and between their allurements and the purity of morals: and the antagonism is the sharper the more the civilisation is elaborate and the religion higher and the morals enlightened.' *The Natural and the Supernatural, op. cit.*, p. 305.

> Had He, like Socrates, been a citizen of a free state which had to defend
> against barbarism a higher civilisation which was to bless humanity,
> might He not, like Socrates, have participated in the task?*

As far as our duty to the world goes Our Lord should determine for us
(I) our own vocation and (II) its subordination to the Kingdom of God.

Leaving aside the tangled question of how Our Lord helps us to
determine our vocations, what does Oman mean by the subordination
of our vocations to the Kingdom of God? Under what principles does
this subordination take place? Here the relation between possession
and denial of the natural is raised in what seems its most essential
form – how the Christian solves the conflict between the ethics that his
function in the world demands e.g., as ruler, soldier, employer, etc.,
and the personal standards demanded by Our Lord. That such a conflict does exist must in the present argument be assumed. It will be
taken for granted that Christian ethical systems can only avoid this
contradiction either if they cease to believe that the Cross is a demand
upon them and equate the Sermon on the Mount with the Ethics of
Aristotle, or else if they contract out of history and so exclude themselves from any of the controlling functions in a society.

To repeat what has been said in an earlier chapter, Oman criticises
Kant because the latter's ethical system gives no place to the varying
facts of function. For example, it cannot show how the duties of the
subject and the ruler are different. Kant does not apprehend the differing individualities of God's children, so beautifully understood by Our
Lord.† It is well nigh impossible to compare the ethical systems of Kant
and Oman. The latter maintains what Kant denies, namely that intuition gives us an *a priori* insight into the content of the Good. Oman
believes that it is through nature that we are given such intuitions. He
makes no such rigid disjunction between reason and nature as does
Kant. Such different assumptions make comparison difficult. What can
be remarked, however, is the result of their assumptions. Oman's ethical intuition given through nature, and enabling us to deal with nature,

---

* *The War and Its Issues, op. cit.*, p. 45. Oman's Presbyterian egalitarianism is seen in his
  insistence that Our Lord would have been a private soldier and not an officer. As
  his decision against pacifism is based solely on the principle of responsibility, why
  should Our Lord not have been a general?
† *The Natural and the Supernatural, op. cit.*, pp. 319–21.

can account for the wide variety of human experience by which men possess the natural, in a way that the Kantian ethic cannot. On the other hand, Kant's imperious practical reason does give a simple and necessary account of how the ordinary man may deny the natural.

Oman would presumably have affirmed that the right proportion between the individualist 'ought' of function and the universalist demand of the Kingdom of God is achieved when each person cultivates the ethics of his vocation without neglecting his universal duties. The only principle he enunciates to achieve that reconciliation is the contemplation of the Cross in sincerity of intuition.

There can perhaps be found no solution, definable in rational terms more adequate than this *logique du coeur*, which does not drastically curtail the wide variety of ethical phenomena to be brought under the principle. The present writer must admit his own agnosticism as to how universalist and individualist 'oughts' may be reconciled. Two points may be made clear about Oman's position however. First, that despite his criticism of Kant, Oman's sincerity of intuition cannot vie in clarity with Kant's account of duty, in showing how the natural is denied. Secondly and more important, whatever the difficulties of this question, Oman does not take his analysis of it nearly far enough. A theology that scorns speculative metaphysicising and concentrates on the problem of relevance, is dependent for its clarity on a careful examination of the moral judgment. Oman asserts that the antinomies of speculation are only reconcilable as we deal with the natural. We can only understand the true character of Christian monotheism as we recognise how we must deal with the natural in denial and possession. It is disappointing therefore that in his attempt to clarify what he means by this paradox Oman never discusses Aristotle's ethical system, surely the greatest statement of the ethic of function. Dismissal of Greek metaphysics still does not save him from facing the problems with which that metaphysics dealt. Neither does he discuss the Thomist compromise between an Aristotelian ethic of civilisation and the Sermon on the Mount. However certainly he would have rejected these accounts of ethical behaviour, that very rejection, balanced against his criticism of Kant, would have made much clearer his account of the ethical judgment. It would have clarified further what he meant by denial and possession of the natural. As it is, that concept, so crucial for an understanding of what he believed the relation of nature and supernature to be, remains undefined.

## VI

After the doubts and hesitations of this chapter, it seems worthwhile to return to what Oman thought man to be. To repeat what has been said in the fourth chapter, Oman's theology is a view of man as partaking of the environments of nature and supernature. His theology may be conceived as a poetic description of man's existence in relation to those environments. Indeed implanted in that poetry is the development of the rational implications of his central vision, but that vision itself is in no way necessary. It is the assertion of intuitions that men may either accept or reject. In the light of his political theology, it is now possible to state his concept of man in greater clarity.

Oman's concept of man in relation to his environment is, of course, written within the Christian tradition. Therefore, most of what he says, as in all theologies, is but another version of the great Christian affirmations about man and God – affirmations to which Christians of varying subsidiary traditions would all subscribe. Therefore this account will concentrate on what is particularly individual in Oman's interpretation. To say individual is not to imply that other men have not concentrated on the same aspects. It is rather to search out the quality of Oman's unique vision.

Such an attempt will in no sense appear a proper philosophic activity to those modern philosophers who are insistent that the only questions which should be asked are those for which there are tidy answers. Leave, they would probably say, such imaginative descriptions of man to the novelists and the religious poets. They do not belong in rational thought. Enough has already been said to show how deeply Oman would have scorned that tradition of certainty. Surely the Christian must agree with him that to fail in a sense of necessary mystery and paradox is to end up content with the teaching of grammar. Then the great questions are left to those who have no respect for reason. The present writer would claim that he can in some small way better understand himself and other men from his study of Oman. Therefore the attempt to understand the tone of Oman's concept of man seems a proper activity.

Oman's view of man is above all else the view of the prophet. That is to say, his anthropology is hardly at all a scientific or speculative one. He is not particularly interested in observing and commenting on all the wide variety of ways in which men do in fact live. He is rather calling upon them to act in a certain way. Therefore to use the phrase 'Oman's concept of man' is not to say that this is what men have been, are and probably will be. It is to say that this is what men could be and ought to be. Therefore Oman is not concerned with a comprehensive definition that will cover all the phenomena, but with Christian man. Such a description must indeed take into account what men are, for a practical theologian who is calling men to certain actions must speak to their condition. As has been said at the beginning of this chapter, Oman often fails in that realism. But such failure is not of great importance to his work for it does not mar the primary task of the practical theologian. A speculative or scientific view of man is not possible for Oman, not only because it is not the function of the theologian, but also because the taking of such a view would be failing to judge man in terms of his essential activity, his autonomy.

Enough has been said already of Oman as a theologian of freedom and joy. One conclusion of that fact must, however, be stated. His theology is for the strong and he assumes in men a great capacity for moral strength. In making his main division between the higher religions, the distinction mystical–apocalyptic, Oman writes that the difference is between those who make of religion a great mother complex and those who decide that they will come back bearing their shields or borne on them. This remark epitomises his concentration on man's strength and his failure to sympathise with his weakness. Oman's view of what man should be has much in common with Kipling's Scot in McAndrew's Hymn.[13] His belief in man's capacity for courage may be seen in his account of the pain of human life. His sermon on Ezekiel shows that he did not underestimate the agony that men must endure, but there is always the sense that it is not too difficult for them to face that grief by girding up their loins and being courageous.* There is little sense of the nearness of defeat, and therefore of those aids to which men cling in order to avoid that defeat.

Oman's strength and confidence in shown in his remark that he is 'not greatly edified' by St Augustine's Confessions or by Bunyan's Grace Abounding.† He just does not share that sense of overwhelming guilt and the consequent sense of the miracle of salvation that has been the

---

* The Paradox of the World, op. cit., pp. 236 et seq.
† Office of the Ministry, op. cit., p. 12.

experience of certain of the greatest Christians. One could not go so far as to say, in terms of William James' distinction, that Oman is 'once born' rather than 'twice born.'[14] But it can be said that his temptation was not that of despair, and therefore his theology cannot easily speak to the despairing. To quote Father Hopkins once again, Oman could never have written:

> I am gall, I am heartburn. God's most deep decree,
> bitter would have me taste. My taste was me.[15]

He would probably have said that such lines were egocentric and that the writer should turn in reason to his objective duties in the world. It may well be asked of Oman how men are expected to turn from their despair. It is this failure to understand despair at its most terrible that prevents Oman from using that language about the Cross that sees it as a beacon in a world of darkness. It is this optimism about man that makes him concentrate on *Christus in nobis* rather than *Christus pro nobis*. It is perhaps his expectation that man can and will use his freedom that makes him stress the manhood rather than the Godhead of Jesus. This is no sense to indict his whole theology as corrupted by optimism, but to say that it speaks more to certain conditions than to others.

Oman's confidence in man's strength is seen in his trust in the powers of reason. However much he reacts from the aridity of a certain type of rationalism and insists on the role of feeling in the ethical judgment, his appeal is always to the power of reason. His comments about psycho-analysis are revealing in this respect:

> To be hunting out the worst kind of motive, and ascribing to complexes what I should meet by an appeal to reason and conscience, to worry about one's own inside perpetually when I should prescribe open air, or about other people, when what seems to be necessary for them is to live objectively in life's interests – is not an occupation spiritually profitable either to the physician or the patient.*

---

* *Order of the Ministry, op. cit.,* p. 26. It is interesting to note that one of Oman's closest friends was a pioneer in the relating of psychoanalysis to the Gospel. Oman was forced in his respect for this man to admit almost unwillingly that such activity might be an activity of love. See *Personal Freedom through Personal Faith,* a memorial volume for William Fearon Halliday; bibliography, p. iii.

Whatever may be said of the dangers of a non-Christian psycho-analysis, this statement shows a lack of understanding of the atavistic in man and the difficulties that prevent him from following the Gospel.

Nevertheless nothing must be said that denies how great a glory is Oman's sense of joy and strength and hope. His passionate under-standing that the crown of all values is that forgiveness which strives to see all men as God sees them, makes his theology in the noblest sense a telling of good news. Men need not despair, for they live in a universe where it is not necessary to choose between weathering the storm in a proud virtue that can find no peace, and a ruthlessness that must cast aside all intuitions of the Cross. At the same time, Oman's Gospel of joy offers men no ease of moral relation. Faith for him means no unimaginative rest, for it is presented with the Majesty of Christ's Love, the mystery of God's transcendent Demands. Whatever has been said about contradictions in applying the Gospel, nothing is said to deny that here is the good news by which all men's lives are regulated. To raise difficulties as to how men are to deny and to possess the natu-ral is not to doubt the glory of Oman's statement of the destiny to which men are called at the summit of the journey of their minds into God. It is the life of love, which by denying value to no part of the cre-ated order lives out that divine tenderness and patience by which alone the Christian knows the Kingdom can be consummated.


CHAPTER VII

To use the late Professor Laird's fine phrase, Oman's accounts are not open to audit by reason alone.* To say otherwise would, for instance, in the case of Oman's criticism of idealist monism, imply that many of Europe's greatest intellectuals could not properly use their intellects. That presumption must be avoided. Oman's metaphysical mono-theism of nature and supernature is based on the faith that only in the vision of Calvary can men in honesty see the pain of the world and still be able to say that the Father is over all and in all. But of course it is possible for an imaginative and reasonable man to look at Calvary and

---

* See the first chapter of the first volume and the closing chapter of the second volume of Professor Laird's *Gifford Lectures, op.cit.* Reason is used here in the Kantian sense of the understanding without the Kantian limitations.

to despair. It cannot be said that suicide is by definition irrational. Moreover, reasonable men are not of necessity graced with compassionate imaginations. All men live in some disregard of the crosses that others bear and therefore accept theologies that in some measure disregard the Cross of Christ. Oman may be right in asserting the historical phenomenon that in societies where monism is accepted by groups of men it tends to become increasingly pessimistic, but that may be 'in the long run' when the monists in question are themselves dead.[1] The change from Hegel to Schopenhauer was not determined by the superior intellect of the latter. Also are there not rational contemplatives who seem to perceive the consequences of the Cross, but who prefer their joyless certainty to its demands? There are rational and imaginative men of action, such as Colonel Lawrence, whose fear that joy is an illusion holds them from the Christian faith.[2] It hardly needs saying that a theologian of mystery and freedom such as Oman recognises to the full the variety of faiths open to rational men.

The following quotation from a letter of Dostoevsky's illustrates the mystery of faith. In it there is much that is remarkably akin to Oman's doctrine of the simple Gospel. Yet in all its weakness and all its strength, Oman could never have written it.

> I want to say to you about myself, that I am a child of this age, a child of unbelief and scepticism, and probably – indeed I know it – shall remain so until the end of my life. How terribly it has tortured me (and tortures me even now) – this longing for faith, which is all the stronger for the proofs I have against it! And yet God gives me sometimes moments of perfect peace; in such moments I love and believe that I am loved; in such moments I have formulated my creed wherein all is dear and holy to me. This creed is extremely simple: here it is: I believe that there is nothing lovelier, deeper, more sympathetic, more rational, more human and more perfect than the Saviour; I say to myself that not only is there no one else like Him, but that there could be no one. I would even say more: If anyone could prove to me that Christ is outside the truth, and if the truth really did exclude Christ, I should prefer to stay with Christ and not with the truth ...*

* Quoted from *Fyodor Dostoevsky*, John Middleton Murry. Martin Secker, London, 1923, pp. 77–8.

The beginning and the end of this quotation are quite unlike Oman's faith, while the middle is close to him. Oman's concept of the sense of the holy is useful in making explicit to men why it is possible for them to unite their axiological with their cosmological theism. It does not, however, explain why men such as Pascal and Dostoevsky find always that act of uniting one of aching difficulty, while men such as Oman and St Thomas find far less. The present writer is quite unwilling to say that that difference is due to greater rationality on either side, or for that matter greater sincerity of feeling or faithfulness in action. All that he is able to say is that in maintaining the tension between monism and dualism the Christian community has need of Jansenism to save it from complacency,[3] and Oman's strength to preserve in the act of faith the note of joy. But to say that the act of faith must always include this joy is to iron out Christian experience into one pattern.

So to insist on the dependence of Oman's metaphysics upon faith is to return to that question at which this thesis began. A provisional assent for the purpose of discussion was given in the first chapter to the proposition that philosophical theology was a possible undertaking. In trying to judge the value of *The Natural and the Supernatural* the issue must be reopened. For if the question is answered in the negative, then no more need be said. Does Oman fall before the attack of the secular sceptic, who would deny that propositions about religion have any place in philosophy, and would turn them over for examination by the empirical psychologist and probably the abnormal psychologist at that? How does he stand before the assertion of the Christian irrationalist that the philosophy of religion is not a proper activity for the Christian, who should confine himself in the intellectual field to preaching and dogmatics? Some answer to these questions must precede any more specific estimate of the value of *The Natural and the Supernatural*.

## II

To stand Oman before the court of secular scepticism is a fair undertaking, for *The Natural and the Supernatural* does not confine itself to addressing Christians. He explicitly lays open his philosophy of religion to criticism from outside the Christian community. It is in a certain sense unhistorical to hold Oman before the scepticism of 1950 because the 'Vienna school' was not of great influence in the years he was writing his philosophy of religion. The tradition of philosophical scepticism he must have encountered at Cambridge was of the gentler variety of Lord Russell. Yet it will be attempted because this modern scepticism, by ridding itself of the irrational niceties that men of Russell's generation still maintain, makes clear the extent to which it disallows traditional philosophy. Oman is so great a thinker that he must stand against the most hostile court.*

In comparing Oman with the modern sceptic, it must be remarked how far he goes in their direction. He ever maintains the place of the irrational in religion, yet without assuming that Humian contempt for it which remains, itself irrational, in the sceptic. His concentration on 'relevance' comes from that Kantian criticism of traditional metaphysics, to which the sceptic's concentration on 'verification' owes so much. His metaphysics are written with a high consciousness of what the sceptic has to say of their emptiness. Oman would grant indeed as a starting point that ethical and religious notions are the least permeable to human understanding of all man's mental equipment. The question is whether they are in any sense permeable.

Clearly the main difference between Oman and the logical positivist is on a question of fact. Oman would affirm that reason has an Idea of Spirit (so many different vocabularies might here be used) and with that Idea so much content as always to pass beyond the known or the possessed – very much in the way that scientific knowledge always

---

* In discussing modern scepticism it is presumed that it is unlikely to be Christian. This is not necessarily so. It is quite possible for the modern positivist to be a Christian. He must however be either a dialectical Protestant, a Roman Catholic who denies the possibility of Thomist natural theology or else Christian in the sense that the ineffable mystic calls himself so. If he stand with Christian irrationalism, his position will be discussed later in this chapter. In this connection it is worth remarking how similar in their approach to reason are the modern sceptic and Dr Barth, however different the practical aims for which such cynicism is employed. For a useful account of this similarity see M. Jarrett-Kerr C.R. 'Scepticism and Revelation,' a review of W.F. Zuurdung's *A Research for the Consequences of the Vienna School for Ethics*. See *Theology* – a periodical, London, Vol. LII, No. 353. To remark on this relation is in no sense to imply the same degree of respect for a position which (however inadequately and indeed almost uncharitably) holds high the Cross, and for men who believe that the philosopher has fulfilled his function in demonstrating the irrationality of all grounds for action.

points beyond itself. Therefore, though conclusions are not so readily confirmed in this field as in the sciences of nature, men are able to correct conservatism and yet avoid mere radical denial. Such a differing view of man's equipment must indeed make argument difficult. The sceptic enamoured of certainty finds this claim quite unsubstantiable. The Platonist (Christian or otherwise) must first and foremost simply assert his indubitable knowledge that man is so equipped. Reason can also appeal to the consequences of denying this capacity to man. In so doing the burden of proof may fairly be cast upon the sceptic. So often the sceptic appeals to common sense. Yet the consequences of denying this capacity force him into positions which hardly seem commonsensical – if that difficult word connotes what is practical for most men.

This seeking of consequences might be taken up at many levels, as for instance, the problem of the self. However, as all men – not only metaphysicians – must of necessity be interested in conduct, the issue is raised at that point. Indeed to raise it there is to be able to say no more than the amazing analysis of the consequences of ethical irrationalism which is the glory of the first books of the *Republic*. All that can be done is to dress that argument up to meet the modern sophist, and to see how that lesson is intensified by the Cross.

The division by modern scepticism of meaningful propositions into those which can be verified by an appeal to sense data and those which are the necessary tautologies of logic and mathematics leaves the account of those propositions traditionally considered ethical to be explained as statements of command or expressions of emotion. It clearly is not possible here to trace in great detail the results of such a description. If ethical statements are emotional expressions, then the statement by a man bred in a cold climate that he dislikes the heat of the Southern U.S.A. is of the same class as the expression of his disgust at seeing a negro beaten up in that area. It hardly needs saying that theoretically and practically the consequences of such a joint classification are no less than prodigious. As most Hebrew, Greek, and European writings use language only understandable by assuming the opposite, nearly all our tradition is presumably vitiated by grave misapprehension. The joint classification of the command 'Shut up you liar' and 'Thou shalt not bear false witness' does not need to be followed out in all its consequences – for instance, in the bringing up of children. Evidently men are capable of accepting such consequences in the interest of denying the possibility of metaphysics. It cannot be said that they are irrational so to do.

As, however, it seems impossible, though not irrational, to accept such consequences, one is led to believe that ethical statements are open to rational discourse. Then, however great may be the difficulty of understanding the relation of reason to conduct, and however much one's observation of oneself and the world must continue to plague one with doubts about that relation, some attempt must be made to delineate reason's operation in conduct. At this point some form of axiological metaphysics must at the least be allowed. Then as against the sceptics, *The Natural and the Supernatural* must be considered a proper undertaking of reason, whatever may be said of its conclusions. To accept this minimum – an axiological metaphysics – is not to close the question whether that minimum is all that is possible.

To turn to the Christian tradition is to face the tension that has always existed in that community between those who have affirmed the possibility, and indeed the value, of a philosophical theology or Christian philosophy of religion, and those who have denied it. Philosophical theology has seemed to many within the community a diffusion of energy better spent elsewhere. That such disagreement does exist and will continue to exist unreconciled is here assumed. To ask this question about the possibility of philosophical theology in connection with Oman is not to presume to question whether in this or that set of circumstances a man is right to embark on this activity. To judge other men's actions is not the purpose of speculation, and in Oman's case it would be the gravest impertinence. Rather it is to ask the theoretical question whether such activity is at any time possible for a Christian. Indeed the distinction here may be compared to what Oman says about dualism as a standing problem and dualism as solution. There is a standing problem for all Christian thinkers as to whether they are well employed in such speculative endeavour amongst the pain of the world, and one can well admire Dr Schweitzer. But it is another matter to accept the solution that philosophical theology is never possible.

Indeed to repeat what has been said in the preceding[4] chapter, Oman never makes clear how deep is the tension involved in this standing problem. One wishes indeed that in the light of his pre-1914 writings on the simplicity of the Gospel and the pretensions of Greek metaphysics he had in *The Natural and the Supernatural* justified philo-sophical theology as against the fundamentalist. That is not, however, to deny that he is right in principle.

To ask the question in principle is to bring Oman yet once more before the court of Dr Barth. As in the case of the positivist, it may be judged that it would be more historical to compare him with the evan-gelicism of a earlier age. But though the Mennonite on the prairies may be more consistent than Dr Barth in making his retreat from the world actual as well as intellectual, Dr Barth by remaining in the world has sharpened his weapons against it. So root and branch is his denial of 'unredeemed' man's capacity for revelation that the question is raised in clearest principle.

The disagreement between Dr Barth and Oman, as in the case of the positivist, is a disagreement as to fact and therefore of great difficulty to argue. Dr Barth denies what Oman affirms, namely that human rea-son has an Idea of Spirit with sufficient content always to pass beyond the known or possessed. Despite all visions of men as broken – not what they ought to be – it must be admitted that to someone brought up in the liberal world, the *imago Dei* is such a basic assumption that Dr Barth's theodicy is impossible to conceive imaginatively. Yet the ques-tion of theodicy cannot be the point of disagreement, for as has been said in an earlier chapter, Oman's theodicy of freedom must end in as great a mystery as any. All that is possible is to try and see clearly, and as fairly as can be, the consequences of denying the *imago Dei*. Only thus can be justified the denial that the unredeemed judgment is utterly corrupt. Certainly, if there is truth in Dr Barth's clear distinction between the elect and the unelect, the present writer would choose (though not able) to resist the Majesty of God's election.*

What seem the consequences of denying the *imago Dei* in all men? (1) What are the consequences of such a denial for the organisation of the Church? (2) What are the consequences on the relation of the Chris-tian to the world? All argument will here appear vain to those who hold the contrary view but it must be attempted.†

---

* See the Book of Exodus, Chapter XXXII: 31–2.
† The argument with continental fundamentalism has been carried on compassion-ately by British theologians in the last years, so it is almost redundant to repeat it once again. See for example professor J. Baillie's *Our Knowledge of God* particularly chapters I and II. It seems however germane to any assessment of Oman.

The present writer cannot see how the denial of the *imago Dei* in all men can fail to mean in practice that the lay members of the Christian congregation will be at the mercy of the ecclesiastical organisation. Theoretically, Dr Barth would affirm that only God's grace can save from such legalism. But what seems inconsistent in his theory is that although he is so vigilant in doing God's work in saving the Church from Promethean revolt, he leaves it to God to save the Church from the binding hand of tradition. That tradition – particularly in the intellectualist form Dr Barth conceives it – must be administered by some officials. Empirically, history does not make the layman confident that safeguards are not necessary.

Turning to the attitude of Christians in the world, it is possible to sympathise with Dr Barth's reaction from the nineteenth century identification of the Church with the world.* Yet that need not lead to agreement over theory. Dr Barth's insistence that God not only provides the miracle of revelation but by His grace gives also the capacity for revelation seems to lead to an ethical irresponsibility about the world that hardly seems Scriptural.†Though Dr Barth would deny that men can know anything of the Jesus of history, if one asserts that claim does Dr Barth's attitude stand up before that tender reaching out to all men that is found in the Gospels? Is it practically possible to maintain the deepest levels of charity towards other persons if they are not known (all of them) as bearing that autonomy that will not allow them to be manipulated? Does not such a denial set up a division between the two commandments of Our lord, making the second but a subsidiary inference from the first? How can this doctrine of election, in men less dedicated than Dr Barth, fail to lead to a pride among Christians, a note which is hardly present in the Gospels? To state these conse-

---

* That danger is ever present to the mind of one brought up on the North American continent. For there the identification is more complete than in Europe.

† See *Natural Theology*, a translation of a discussion between Drs Barth and Brunner; Bles London 1946.[5] Dr Barth writes: 'In my experience the best way of dealing with "unbelievers" and modern youth is not to try to bring out their "capacity for revelation," but to treat them quietly, simply (remembering that Christ has died and also risen for them), as if their rejection of Christianity was not to be taken seriously. It is only then that they can understand you, since they really see you where you maintain that you are standing as an evangelical theologian: on the ground of justification by faith alone' (p. 127). This passage is quoted as it seems the most balanced of what Dr Barth says about the matter.

quences is not argument. It is just to mention why it is impossible, despite all abasement before the Cross, to deny to reason its Idea of Spirit.

Once the *imago Dei* has been affirmed in principle, a Christian philosophy of religion must be considered possible. To say this is not however to place great value upon it. It is not to put scholarship higher than saintliness or to accept the immanentist view of civilisation that so often characterises those who write the philosophy of religion. It is just to say that certain Christians can reach out through reason to explain the challenge of the Gospel by showing other men how inadequate are all their ideas of 'things' and 'life' as grounds for action and by relating the world of persons to those other worlds, the reality of which men are so constantly aware.

Yet once the possibility of philosophical theology has been granted, Oman's position must be compared with those who interpret that activity very differently from him. The distinction is drawn between those who proceed to such a philosophical theology from 'natural evidence' and those who deny the possibility of such 'objectivity.'*The Natural and the Supernatural* may here be compared with the late Professor Laird's *Gifford Lectures*.* Laird's work is singled out because it is judged that his lectures maintain the balanced rationalist tradition in a way for instance that Tennant's *Philosophical Theology* does not, and in a way that metaphysicians of the Thomist persuasion do not, despite their distinction between natural and revealed religion.

Laird expresses his contempt for pulpit theism and soap-box atheism. Philosophical theology is the attempt to search out the truth guided only by the motive of aloof curiosity, and accepting only that evidence which may be called natural, that is, agreed on by men of common sense. Is this the only proper method for any theology that has the right to call itself philosophical? Laird's great difficulty is the question of 'natural evidence.' It is judged that in his volumes there is not one piece of evidence about which some tradition of thought has not expressed its scepticism. Of course Laird would admit this. But is his a possible position for the Christian? The Christian may be thankful that there are in Europe men who are free to pursue such activities, but he is not in their position himself. He cannot put aside for the duration

* See the first page of this chapter.

of speculation facts that he knows to be true. For instance, because some men affirm that intuition only gives reason the data of the senses, can he proceed from such an assumption knowing as he does that intuition gives men more – whether they admit [it] or not? It is such a false appearance of certainty that Oman again and again calls dishonest on the part of the Christian. As is said so often these days in philosophy and theology alike, the Christian is in no position to be disinterested. Oman is surely right in affirming that truth reveals itself to the interested not the disinterested. The present writer is unable, however, to go so far as to say that the position of disinterest is impossible for men other than Christians. Much of the supposed disinterest in the Aristotelian tradition does indeed seem quite unreal when allied to faith. Though men capable of disinterest may be rare, and the price they pay enormous, they do occasionally appear in a long and settled tradition such as that of European liberalism. Enthusiasm for a man such as Laird arises from the fact that in him disinterestedness seems in truth honest.

Therefore agreement must be expressed with Oman about the character of a Christian philosophy of religion. It can never be about the adequacy of argument from facts that themselves are considered 'natural evidence.' It is argument from the given of faith, by relating that faith to other experience and so discussing it that there emerges for reader and writer a clearer understanding of the character of the Christian Gospel. Indeed the Christian Platonist must face the question of evidence as much as the Aristotelian – for the mystery of man's knowledge of the Good and its relation to our other forms of knowledge is not easily clear to himself, or a fortiori to others. Yet in so doing he has no alternative but to maintain at one and the same time the challenge of the Cross with the knowledge that in all men there is the capacity to respond to that challenge, and grow in the understanding of how it regulates all experience. Humbly to hold discourse with other men about that regulation, by seeing faith in a wide variety of relations, is the duty of the Christian philosopher of religion. That this is a strait[6] gate cannot hold men from seeking it.*

---

* Such a justification of Oman's method may seem little more than an admission that the present writer has been convinced by Oman.

**III**

Having accepted for these very general reasons *The Natural and the Supernatural* as the embodiment of a proper human activity, one may pass to the questions of its detail. Recapitulating what are judged its weaknesses and its strengths is but to sum up what has been said in earlier chapters.

The primary failure of that work is that its dependence on faith is not stated with sufficient definiteness. The result is that the radically personalist assumptions are not as clear as they should be. As has been said, it is assumed that the reason for this failure lies in Oman's fear that much of the language of Christian apologetics has become a worthless coinage to the honestly zetetic secularist who can no longer penetrate to its content. Oman therefore seeks a language that will not offend unnecessarily. At the same time he seeks one which will force the Christian reader to abandon any of the complacency of the initiated and think through the faith under fresh conditions. Enough has been said to make clear that that motive seems praiseworthy to the present writer and involves no necessary surrender of the challenge of the Gospel.

In applying this principle, however, Oman often uses terminology that is far from personalist (e.g., 'environment'). The failure is more than one of vocabulary, and could have been avoided if in the first section of his work, where he deals with method, he had stated beyond the shadow of a doubt the dependence of his thought upon faith, and had described that faith. As the work stands, from the concluding chapters of Parts 3 and 4 its dependence on faith cannot be doubted. But it would have avoided criticism had that been stated at the beginning, and had language been employed throughout that related more clearly his metaphysics and epistemology to faith. Particularly in the fourth part where he is dealing with the question of history, this hiatus between his theology and his philosophy of religion makes what he says about the problems less profound than it could have been.

The second flaw within Oman's philosophy of religion is its lack of analysis at certain crucial points. Enough has been said to make clear that the present writer does not believe that the philosopher's function is limited to analysis. The sharpening of the knives is not enough, Oman in speculating from a given hierarchy of values is in the good company of Kant and Plato. Yet his primary instruments do need a more rigorous examination. This difficulty is partly due to his refusal to use traditional philosophic language. In this connection part of the first paragraph of chapter 5 of *The Natural and the Supernatural* may once again be quoted. Therein is laid down the core of Oman's metaphysical position in seemingly simple words:

> We know all environment, not as impact or physical influx, but as meaning: and this meaning depends on (1) the unique character of the feeling it creates; (2) the unique value it has for us; (3) the immediate conviction of a special kind of objective reality, which is inseparable from this valuation; and (4) the necessity of thinking it in relation to the rest of experience and the rest of experience in relation to it.*

Here are accepted a multitude of assumptions, some of which are later discussed and partially clarified but many of which are not. For instance, the phrase 'we know as meaning' with all its ambiguities and possibility of interpretations is never clarified. Apparently it means 'we know as value,' but that is not to carry clarification very far. 'Feeling' is used very differently and given a much wider connotation than in the rational psychologies of Oman's day and country (e.g., in the work of McDougall).[7] Yet the alleged cognitive element, though brilliantly described in terms of the consciousness of the artist and the child is not carefully analysed. Particularly because of the place of feeling in the idealist tradition, he should have made clear how radical is his departure from that tradition. Similarly, the phrase 'the necessity of thinking together' is capable of several interpretations, and is not clarified.

To criticise this key paragraph is not to deny that it is highly sophisticated – indeed to imply the opposite. Oman in *The Natural and the Supernatural* is attempting the exposition of a metaphysics which avoids those positions that in his opinion have become untenable in the light of the Kantian and post-Kantian criticism. This paragraph gives an epistemological basis for a metaphysics which can avoid criticism. It would be foolish to deny that it is the product of subtle analysis. What is regretted is that he only makes public the results and not the path to those results. He starts his speculation almost at the point where a critical analyst such as Kant leaves off. Oman, who is radically

---

* *The Natural and the Supernatural, op. cit.*, p. 58.

questioning the idealist assumptions common in his day, takes his reader with a leap to assumptions that must be very foreign and which by their unexplained foreignness may easily confuse. The relation of his realism to idealism needs more discussion.

This question may also be discussed in regard to those to whom *The Natural and the Supernatural* is addressed. It is certainly not a popular introduction to the philosophy of religion. Oman seeks a level of writing directed to the educated man who has not mastered the vocabulary of European idealism and its offshoots such as positivism. Indeed it may be granted that technical language may become so detailed and take so long to develop that the subject of interest to most men is never reached. A leap such as Oman's into the centre of the problem however does avoid those questions with which the professional philosopher must be concerned. His lack of analysis lays him open to criticism from such philosophers. Admittedly to say this is to look a gift-horse in the mouth. It is to ask from one book not only that it should be based on years of analysis of such subjects (which it is) that it have a magnificent personal intuition of the meeting of man with God (which it has) but also that there should be a careful and technical analysis of its instruments (which it has not).

Two other important failures of analysis must be mentioned. With Oman's concentration on the interrelation of religion and morality one could wish for a more careful discussion of the way in which intuition or feeling passes over into judgment. That activity, crucial in his system, is left so undescribed as to make it difficult to follow him. Secondly, he does not make clear relationship between ideal and natural values in consciousness. His vagueness here makes it difficult to follow his criticism of Kant. Indeed, this criticism is made more difficult throughout by his refusal to use the technical language of philosophy, so that his attack appears often a series of individual points rather than the root and branch departure that it is. Oman's work needs here to be read with a similar realist criticism of Kant such as Nicolai Hartmann's, who brings out the principles on which his criticism is based in a more systematic manner. To call in Hartmann, however, must in no sense imply that his positive metaphysics or his account of human personality has anything like the range or depth of Oman's.

A third criticism of Oman's philosophy of religion touches his failure to admit his debts to the traditions of pagan metaphysics, and to earlier Christian philosophy. This is not to question the wisdom of his remark in the introduction to *The Natural and the Supernatural* that he does not intend to fill the book with evidence of his erudition. Yet so great is his fear of tradition as enslavement that there is a note in his work that would almost imply that all pre-Kantian Christian philosophy was obscurantist. His failure to be fair to St Augustine in *Grace and Personality* has already been mentioned. In *The Natural and the Supernatural*, what may be asked for is a statement of his debt to Christian Platonism. What a Platonist work that is, with its implied acceptance of the ontological argument. How much it follows in the tradition of Christian Platonists such as St Anselm and St Bonaventure. Yet in holding before men the uniqueness of the Hebrew tradition with its own theology of creation, Oman never implies that he owes much to the Platonic tradition of epistemological and metaphysical analysis. His one remark in praise of Plato is the hardly overwhelming compliment that he was not a neo-Platonist mystic. Even admitting how much the Cross makes necessary a criticism of Platonism – its tendency towards an intellectualist ethics, its inability to find joy in God's world, its incipient dualism – Oman's conception of 'intuition' makes him deeply indebted to Platonism. The fear of Greek metaphysics cannot stand when one has turned out to the world in the speculation of *The Natural and the Supernatural*.

## IV

How unimportant do these criticisms seem when one turns to consider Oman's greatness. As a philosopher of religion that greatness appears in the way all problems are taken up into his own powerful individuality, and yet by his concentration on essentials that unique interpretation brings out the universality of the questions. Thus his originality is saved by that intuition of essentials from being merely esoteric and touching only the peripheral and the different. The essentials are illuminated by the freshness of his individuality so that the ancient Christian problems are seen as alive and present.

This combination may be seen in the conceptions of his epistemology –'awareness' and 'apprehension.' The directness of his mind penetrates behind the rationalist tradition of European epistemology and sees the problem of knowledge in a new light which in its very simplicity and freshness cuts right down to the central assumptions about man and how he knows. So much epistemological analysis seems but a technique learnt in the schools, adding nothing essential to what the masters of one tradition or another have said. Yet Oman by reaching back into his own life escapes from those traditions that in his period bound European philosophy with a dead hand. How simple it all sounds when one comes to describe it but how far reaching in its implications. 'Sincerity of feeling' is not an adjunct to decorate other epistemologies, but a concept which shows how the contemplative vision of God is open to all men. Then, as Oman describes how in mature men this autonomy of contemplation becomes interdependent with the strength of our wills to follow what we reverence, he has developed through the archetypes of the saint and the artist a concept of man so different from the traditions of his age. He has transcended the idea of 'rationalist' man yet has maintained all that that tradition has to say about the possibility of knowing the truth in dignity and hope.

This concentration on essentials is seen in the very ramblingness of *The Natural and the Supernatural*. That work spreads itself with all Oman's varied scholarship into a myriad of different subjects, touching upon the assumptions of the biologist and the physicist – both Newtonian and Einsteinian – relating the assumptions of differing rationalist systems to their essential religious hope, seeing the Christian faith in relation to other religions, connecting theories of perception to the moralities that go with them. Yet through it all the work flows on with a masterful consistency – not easy to see but always present. All is bound together, the relation of sincerity to faithfulness, of the sense of the holy to the judgment of the sacred, the tension between monism and dualism, the proper conceptions of the natural and the supernatural, the reciprocity of revelation and reconciliation, all are bound together to make clear the essence of the simple Gospel of the Father and His children.

The reality of Oman's sense that all men are the children of God is seen in his account of our knowledge of God. All his writings – whether of mysticism, of metaphysics or of the Church – are bound together by his unwavering conviction that Christian salvation is for all men or is nothing. Oman and von Hügel are in many ways alike in their account of nature and grace, their epistemological realism of joy and their concentration on the relation between religion and morality. Yet it may be said in humility before von Hügel's genius, that at one point he falls short of Oman. His writings are so often a beautiful appeal to the fine and sensitive products of a great civilisation. Oman always transcends that note and in his account of experience reaches out towards that universality that holds the Love of God before all men.

The firm union in Oman's work between the Father's Love and His children's dignity is seen above all in the way that the strength of his faith reaches out tenderly to the despair of others. Previously it has been said that Oman is not greatly touched by his own guilt and therefore does not use the symbolism springing from that guilt. To say this, however, is not to take away from his exquisite sensitivity for the world's pain and other men's dilemmas. His very faith in the Majesty of God allows him to understand why others cannot believe. He recognises what a tremendous step faith must be. It is this which never allows him to attempt any purely rationalist metaphysics or arguments for God's existence from the facts of 'natural evidence.' For Oman, a metaphysics must be a theodicy, because suffering and the nearness of defeat are more real facts to men than sense data.

And the theodicy is made possible through his vision of Jesus Christ. The Cross as triumph is to Oman the Word of God. Some may say that his vision is unreal because it is detached from tradition; others that it is no better than seeing his own face at the bottom of a well. Yet in it subjectivity and objectivity are bound together, so that certainty must depend upon demand and faith and hope upon charity. Through his personal statement we pass to that unique moment in time. Oman calls men to that strength which is forgiveness and in that call affirms the Gospel that 'all manner of thing shall be well.'[8]


APPENDIX A
OMAN'S CLASSIFICATION OF RELIGIONS

The following account of Oman's classification of religions is added as an appendix to this thesis rather than included in the main body of the work for the following reason. It does not add anything to the essence of the metaphysical position he expounds by the use of the concept 'nature and supernature.' This is not to say that in applying that concept to the interpretation of comparative religion he does not helpfully illustrate what he means by that concept, and also illuminate such subsidiary concepts as 'the holy' and 'the sacred.' Especially in the last chapter, where he interprets the work of the prophets and of Our Lord under the title of prophetic religion, he reveals that faith for the description of which nature and supernature are but instruments. Quotations from that magnificent chapter are found throughout the body of the text. But this fourth part of *The Natural and the Supernatural* does not add to his metaphysic by expounding his attitude to 'the theology of history.' That must be sought among his Christological writings. Indeed, in his classification of religions much is said which illuminates what he would make of such terms as 'revelation' and 'discovery' and their relation, and so throws light on that theology of history. But the main task of this classification is to view the wide variety of religious life that has appeared in history and bring it into some order. As such, it serves the negative purpose of dispelling many phantoms associated with the study of comparative religion, and the positive purpose of an interesting intellectual illustration of a metaphysic. However, it adds less to Oman's position than the other three parts of *The Natural and Supernatural.*

Oman indeed devotes a chapter, preliminary to the classification, to a discussion of historical knowledge and its interpretation. Here as usual he turns in two directions, first against the traditional interpretation of history (that is, as it is found among religious legalisms), and secondly against the modern naturalist and Hegelian interpretations of historical knowledge. As against the first of these what has already been said in Chapter Six of this thesis may be repeated here. In his discussion of the use and abuse of tradition, Oman is always more fearful of its abuse than optimistic about its virtues. Though he maintains that the sacred is always given to men in the form of tradition, he constantly insists on the imperfections of that sacred as it is given, and the need of prophetic insight to stand against that given and judge it in the light of the Good. He lays little stress on the function of those who conserve that tradition and much on the fact that tradition by asserting the authority of an imperfect sacred, may be a weighty force in holding men back from the truth.

Oman criticises naturalism under the title 'anthropological theories of history.' There is no need to repeat here his general criticism of the naturalist view of man and his environment. Oman tracks it to its lair as a theory of history with his customary incisiveness and cynicism. Its main confusions are its identification of origin with the beginning and its use of the word 'fact' to describe its dogmas about man's determination by nature. Two quotations not only clarify what Oman says but also show his style at its best.

> Supposing that religion had this low beginning, to argue that it must remain the same is like denying that there may be good fruit on a good tree because its roots were first planted in rotting manure. Obviously the result depends on the life of the tree itself, and of this the evidence is the fruit it produces.*

Or again:

> A man is not necessarily honest because his ancestors were Lowland farmers who bred their own cattle, nor dishonest because his ancestors were Highland reivers[1] who appropriated them from others. Superstitions are superstitions and truths are truths according to what they in themselves are: and this is not to be determined either by their origin or by their development.†

In the world of the nineteen-twenties and nineteen-thirties, the exorcism of naturalisms in the fields of history must have been of crucial significance. Again it is interesting to note that Oman is not concerned with what may be called the naturalism of the will (as compared with those of the intellect) – namely, Marxism. It would be interesting to know what he would have made of such 'prophetic naturalism,' with its Messianic undertones and its comparative social realism.

Oman proceeds to deal with the school of historical interpretation he calls the 'Religious–historical.' By this phrase he means generally those thinkers who pursued their historical studies within the general framework of the Hegelian dialectic (though he includes as a subsidiary category those who used biological categories for the purpose).

* *The Natural and the Supernatural, op. cit.,* p. 351.
† *The Natural and the Supernatural, op. cit.,* pp. 351–2.

This school of thinkers had the merit of a great interest in history compared with the ahistorical rationalism of the eighteenth century. They were at least learned and serious, and with their use of the categories of spirit and the absolute gave more weight to religion than did the crudities of naturalism. Oman admits the practical utility of much of the work done under the Hegelian inspiration. His criticism of Hegelian monism need not be repeated again. It interpreted history as an impersonal process of the Absolute Reason. Thus it fell prey to an historicism that allowed no place for creative autonomy. In the study of religion this Hegelianism went particularly astray by treating it as mainly a concern with dogma or theology. It therefore saw the fossils that time preserves rather than the living faiths by which men have sought so to live in the supernatural as to have victory over the merely natural.

Oman calls his own position as to the interpretation of history the 'prophetical.' He applies his conception of personality both to what history is as an object and to the consequent method of the historian. He says many useful common-sense things that were often forgotten in the age of a scientific history whose tone had been set by Ranke.[2] The historian cannot look at the world from any absolute standpoint. All historical knowledge must ultimately be related to practical judgments. In writing of history as object it must be remembered that one is writing of persons and therefore the categories applicable to persons must be employed. Many of Oman's points are more and more becoming the common coin of the new personalism. If today a great historian, Arnold Toynbee, can still sometimes write as if history could be interpreted by the categories of biology, à la Bergson, how much more important was it to insist on this personalism twenty years ago.

Despite Oman's common-sense personalism about the nature of historical knowledge, two criticisms must be made of what he says about that knowledge and of his classification of religions. The problem of historical knowledge and its relation to other forms of consciousness is not discussed in any detail. He remarks that men are related to tradition both as enrichment and enslavement, but never attempts to analyse how that relationship functions. It was certainly a useful service to state the problem in a personalist way, but he does not take the reader into a discussion of personalism and history. To refer to Chapter Six, it was remarked there that there is conflict between Oman's liberalism and his quietism. If he is a quietist then the problem of historical knowledge does not arise in any difficult form. If he is a liberal in politics, then clearly it does. What would Oman say as to the way that men learn from history?

This may be related to another criticism of Oman's classification and its method. What did he think was the purpose that this classification served? At the minimum it may be granted that it is a pleasant intellectual pastime so to classify religions. To mount the scale of utility, it is clearly useful to show men how the modern myths as to primitive religion are not mainly fact but dogma, and how other personalist interpretations seem more probable. The difficulty however arises when the relation of this classification to a theology of history appears. What is the relation of this scheme of development to the consummation of history on the Cross? In the fifth chapter, it was remarked that Oman remained agnostic about the questions of Christ's Being partly because he was willing to be agnostic about all schemes of history – whether traditionally Christian or progressive. But at times in this classification he seems openly to be affirming a doctrine of progress. If he does so, then the relation of the Cross to such a doctrine arises in clear cut form. Yet Oman never attempts to reconcile these two ideas. Whether such a reconciliation is possible the present writer would not hazard a guess. At the most it is possible to say that there seems a contradiction between Oman's liberal account of the development of religion and his Christology. At the minimum, here is another example of that failure to bring out the relationship between his theology and his philosophy of religion. Oman's refusal to use the traditional categories of Christian theology raises more difficulties than usual when he faces the problems of history.

Before elaborating his own classification, Oman briefly describes and rejects several other methods. These are:

(1) (a) The Pre-Romantic quantitative valuation of truth and falsehood in terms of orthodoxy.*
(1) (b) Hegel's and Schleiermacher's attitude to comparative reli-

---

* Oman seems to consider all thinkers before the *Aufklarung* to have been obscurantist. He may not mean to be so sweeping, but his words certainly lead to an almost Comteian interpretation.[5]

gions, both based on the idea of reconciliation – Hegel's on intellectual harmony with the universe, Schleiermacher's on artistic harmony.

(2)    A Kantian interpretation (elaborated by Tiele and Siebeck) which judges religions in terms of ethical legalism, with universality as the standard of its imperatives.[4]

Oman's criticism of (1) (a) and (b) was that these interpretations do not understand religion as a practical relation to environment, nor in their intuition of 'reconciliation' do they allow that reconciliation to the natural must be active, that is, a victory over life's evil and evanescence. His criticism of (2) would follow his general metaphysical criticism of the Kantian morality, namely that it cannot transcend law, as does the Gospel.

Oman himself prefers to classify religions according to their conception of the relationship between the natural and the supernatural. What truly marks a religion is the faith on which it bases the conduct of life (in other words its attitude to the natural rather than to the supernatural in any isolated sense). In the realm of conduct, however, the distinction between the two is in a sense artificial, for man has never acted as though the natural were his sole environment. But the relation and distinction between the two environments is the central significance of a religion, by which its quality may best be determined. Since the problem of all religion is redemption from the evanescent (i.e., the natural as isolated from the supernatural), the test by which to judge a particular religion is 'the worth of its view of redemption, measured both morally and theologically.'* Thus this form of approach allows Oman to maintain his attitude to the interdependence of religion and morality with which so much of his theology is concerned. Religion should not be regarded as creed nor morality simply as conduct. It has too often been held that the only relation of religion to morality is to provide rules of conduct and motives for following them. This is to Oman the natural masquerading as the supernatural. What religion really provides, and all it provides directly, is a sphere of absolute valu-

---

* *The Natural and the Supernatural, op. cit.,* p. 367. Refer to the end of chapter 6 of this thesis where Oman's use of the word 'redemption' is criticised.

ation and obligation. Without that sphere there would be no morality. To maintain this relationship in the study of comparative religion is of the greatest importance. The natural-supernatural classification allows this.

Oman classifies in terms of five kinds of redemption.

(1) The Primitive: Redemption by seeking the abiding in the natural through faith in an animistic force indefinitely many and vaguely one.

(2) The Polytheistic: Redemption as the management of the natural by faith in the supernatural conceived as individual spirits who rule over various parts of the natural.

(3) The Mystical: Redemption either by accepting the natural in its wholeness as the supernatural, or by excluding the natural wholly from the supernatural as illusion. Such acceptance Oman calls Cosmic Pantheism. The rejection he calls either Acosmic Pantheism or Acosmic Mysticism. It is with this rejection rather than with acceptance that he is chiefly concerned in this classification.

(4) Ceremonial-Legalism: Redemption by distinguishing sharply in the natural the secular from the sacred, and in the supernatural the power of good from the power of evil.

(5) The Prophetic: Redemption as reconciliation to the natural by faith in one personal supernatural, who gives meaning to the natural and has a purpose behind it.

These five distinctions include two separate types of development that lead Oman to make a subsidiary classification. This is: (1) The Primitive and the Mystical both seek the eternal in one unchanging reality which the natural, being illusion, hides. (2) Polytheism, Legalism, and Prophetic Monotheism seek the eternal in the meaning and purpose of the natural itself. Thus one group views the natural as the veiling of the supernatural, the other as the unveiling. One seeks the

'undivided and undisturbed primitive awareness of awe and sacredness,' the other seeks 'the eternal by a higher possession of the evanescent, not by escape from it.'* This subsidiary classification Oman calls
apocalyptic-mystical.†

### (1) *The Primitive*

In attempting to understand religion at its most primitive, the scholar
of the philosophy of religion must be particularly cautious. As primitive man's response both to the natural and the supernatural is 'from
environment to minds akin,' the scholar is left with inference and intuition and must be careful that his own prejudices are not hidden in
those inferences (e.g., Sir James Frazer). Here it is a question of stretching intellect and imagination back beyond recorded history and dealing with men very different from ourselves. Deductions cannot
properly be drawn from what are commonly known as 'primitive religions' still extant since these are often merely stagnant rather than
primitive. With this caveat about his own and others'[5] conclusions in
this field, Oman continues.

Primitive religion is sometimes called the religion of nature, and it
has two aspects which make such a description appropriate. The first is
the fact that redemption is looked for within the natural and not from
it. The second is that in primitive religion man's mind is working
mainly at the level of fixed unities of awareness.[6] These are the two
characteristics which mark a religion as primitive – not savagery,
which may be the result of stagnation or retrogression.

Oman would agree with Ankermann that primitive religion is an
emotional response to immediate situations.[7] But to say this is not to say
that the ideas of 'sacred' and 'profane' are simple developments from
those of 'dangerous' and 'safe.' All knowledge of any environment –
natural or supernatural – can only arise in terms of practical interest. But
this interpretation of the origin of the sacred does not explain how the
sacred could ever have developed its absolute connotations. Agreement
upon fact must not allow the acceptance of naturalist inference.

---

* *The Natural and the Supernatural, op. cit.,* p. 404.
† What follows will be mainly descriptive. Particularly in the first two religious classifi-
cations, the primitive and the polytheistic, there is little that concerns Oman's metaphysical conclusions.

Oman interprets the primitive mind as enclosed in its fixed unities of awareness, thereby excluding all that does not fit into its pattern and accepting environment as destiny rather than as challenge. Its unity is a world by itself, with the focus of attention at the centre, and an awareness of the undifferentiated sacred as its universe. This awareness is the source of animism and magic. It must be admitted that Oman does not make clear how this inferential interpretation is reached.

Since the primitive mind cannot achieve unities of reflection, and therefore is not capable of reasoning, it is probable that the conception of a soul arose mainly from a direct consciousness of life (*à la* Bergson) turning gradually into a free valuing of the sacred. At first, Oman suggests, although the world was felt to be one, each object on which attention focused was imputed a soul, because the felt unity of the world could not be taken out of its context and the variety underlying it recognised. This, he believes, is how animism arose.

In the practice of magic, barbarous as it was, one can at least begin to see a possibility of progress. For magic ritual stages situations to give effective fixed context for its operations. In this staging some kind of effort is made to impose a pattern on situations, to manipulate them instead of remaining passive before them. This freedom to arrange the situations was probably the first stage in developing an attitude of mind which could become scientific. The staging may easily, however, become mere routine tradition, and although 'tradition is man's first equipment for progress,' it may also be 'his supreme device for evading the labour of it.'[*]

Thus although magic ritual gives an opening for the emergence of free ideas, it only fully displays fixed ideas. Oman, in an interesting comparison, calls it 'mysticism in the fetters of fixed idea.'[†] By this he means that both magic and mysticism work 'with the sense of the holy as awe-inspiring in itself, as an infinity of undifferentiated feeling and not as it manifests a varied reality.'[‡] He goes so far as to draw a parallel between the drugged medicine man or whirling dervish, and the Yogi or the Christian contemplative, because they both practise strange devices in order to preserve 'a shell of sheltering unity, and prove the

[*] *The Natural and the Supernatural, op. cit.,* p. 384.
[†] Ibid.
[‡] Ibid.

power to exclude everything disturbing.'* These mortifications and other practices, whether of the savage or the sophisticated mystic, 'are all regarded as religious for the same reason that they are an exalted dismissal of the conflicts of life.'† As has been stated in Oman's sub-classification of religions, it is this attitude to the natural that Primitive religion and Mystical religion have in common – both attempt to escape from it into an undisturbed unity of awareness.

The working of the primitive mind, as seen in animism and magic, throws some light on what has been called primitive monotheism. Oman admits the evidence for some limited kind of monotheism, occurring mostly in simple communistic societies. He places its source in the primitive sense of unity of environment, which is an awareness and not a reflexive unity. So it is not marked by that victory over environment which is the mark of true monotheism.

The last aspect of primitive religion that Oman discusses is how it serves to illustrate that interdependence of religion and morality which is his chief interest in the study of all religion. However far one goes back in the study of primitive religion, the sense of the holy is always more than mere awe. It is always passing into some judgment of the sacred, however fettered in the material, and so there is some sanction of the supernatural, however beclouded by magic. Because there is no natural divorced from the supernatural, even in the most primitive times there is neither purely natural religion nor naturalist morality. There is even then a dim sense in man that he is dealing with that which manifests ideal values.‡

### The Polytheistic

Oman begins his description by stating that the origin of polytheism has always been considered an easy problem of deduction. Either it

---

* *The Natural and the Supernatural, op. cit.,* p. 385. Such a comparison must be left unquestioned and will be expanded when what Oman says about mysticism in general has been described.
† Ibid.
‡ Though it is judged that Oman's theory illuminates[8] primitive religion, this section suffers from the fact that there is no single example from any particular religion to illustrate his points. Though examples in this field may be so easily used to prove what one wants, his argument would have been clearer if some had been used.

was imputed to man's vanity, or else to his desire to explain phenomena simply in terms of cause and effect. Oman describes this interpretation of polytheism's supposed development in the following words:

> From a polyzoic or lowest animism, or animatism, through a more individual polydaemonism, to a therianthropic polytheism, in which, if the likeness was still to four-footed beasts and creeping things, the god behind was conceived in the likeness of man, until, finally, we arrive at anthropomorphic polytheism, or polytheism proper, with reverence for beings in human form, but above human power.*

This kind of interpretation derives the individual personal polytheistic deity from the vague *numina* that are found in quite advanced religions. These *numina* are manifestations of 'one mysterious awe-inspiring diffused potency.'†

Oman distrusts this account of the origin of polytheism, for three main reasons. First, there is no evidence that belief in *numina*, prevalent as an element in so many religions, ever existed as the sole religion. Secondly and more important, an intellectual inference from cause to effect is most improbable at the primitive stage under consideration. Thirdly, it is not likely that the higher deities were compounded out of these vague *numina*. 'How this vague unity of awareness, which was felt as a whole at every point of interest, as space at every point of perception, came to be broken up into powers corresponding to a wide range of organised interests and graded values, is a question as difficult as it is important.'‡

Rather than a rationally constructed explanation to provide a clear-cut theory of development Oman prefers parallels to help the imagination. First, he uses the analogy of a university, whose original medieval unity has been broken into the variations of its modern specialisation. Then he uses the analogy of that stage in the individual's mind when 'life divides into many varied interests, each a unity of imagination, which break up the whole awareness of life, yet raise problems which, if they are faced, may in time effect a harmonious unity of reflection.'§

---

* *The Natural and the Supernatural, op. cit.*, p. 390.
† Ibid., p. 391.
‡ Ibid.
§ Ibid., p. 392.

Polytheism as a stage in the development of the race is parallel to this stage in the development of the individual.

In polytheism, to use Oman's main terms, the sense of the holy is still awesome rather than ethical, and the judgment of the sacred is still well imprisoned in the context of material associations. Unity of awareness turns each particular sacred interest into a closed universe. Man's power of reflection is however growing, and as it grows he is more and more able to face life's concrete distracting problems as a concrete distracted individual. This allows in higher polytheism for some degree of what Oman calls 'possession of the natural.'

This growing self-realisation finds its expression in the fact that with polytheism there develops the institutions of private property. Although material possession may become a ghastly idolatry, and needs in any case to be transcended by the discovery of higher possessions, it does on a lower level provide a sphere of rights and responsibilities in which the individual may exercise his freedom. This is a great advance for man as it gives him a sphere for moral or immoral action.

Because the primitive unity of awareness has been broken up, polytheism leads to great progress in civilisation on many fronts. The interrelation of polytheism and civilisation is admitted by all leading scholars. Which was the cause and which the effect is more arguable. As usual, other presuppositions determine the historical judgment. Those who believe that social order and harmony can be achieved without the existence of ideal values may be able to see the whole supernatural structure as a later decoration. Yet once again Oman lays bare the naturalist assumptions of such an interpretation, particularly here in its relation to psycho-physical parallelism. Oman in his own position would reverse the determination. Only by living in the higher environment could man recognise the higher possibilities of civilisation.*

The polytheistic managing of the world is clearly related to the rise of agriculture. In contrast we find Buddha's refusal to let his monks engage in this activity. Such work not only led men out of the unity of awareness, but prevented the deliberate return to a primitive paradise which Oman sees as the psychological aim of mystical religions.

---

* It is not necessary to raise again the difficulties in understanding what Oman conceived to be the relation of Christianity to civilisation. See chapter 6. In his classification he is much nearer the liberal's 'good life' than the quietist position.

It may well seem that polytheism led more obviously to material than to spiritual advancement. But to say this is, in Oman's opinion, to put the cart before the horse. If we take the idea of evolution seriously, instead of assuming it to be an automatic process, we see that civilisation could only be produced by ideas and ideals. These, however imperfectly embodied in the natural, are of the supernatural. Therefore though history shows us mainly the material gains of polytheism, the spiritual insights are primary.

Polytheism's contributions to civilisation were the following: the first Oman defines thus:

> Polytheism gave a greater freedom of mind, which was a call to adventure upon wider and higher environment and a sense of security in following it.*

He illustrates this spirit of adventure by the spreading of the Aryan race in so many directions over the globe. They are thought to have located their principal god in the sky, the only place that would not disappear when they travelled far afield. The word 'Day-Father' is found in many Aryan languages far apart from each other, which suggests that the conception of the god preceded the venturing forth and dividing up of the race. A faith by which to travel had already been won. This Aryan concentration on one of their gods might almost be regarded as a kind of monotheism. Because all polytheism had this dim sense of the unity of the supernatural, it always had a potentiality for progress.

The second benefit conferred by polytheism, Oman described in the following words:

> Polytheism, by setting free higher sanctions from local limitations, made possible the formation of a state with universal laws.†

Oman admits that political conquest accounts in part for the fusing together of the gods of conquering and conquered tribes. But this only happens when the victors are already highly civilised, as were the Babylonians and the Romans. The Assyrians meted out savage treat-

* *The Natural and the Supernatural, op. cit.*, p. 398.
† Ibid., p. 399.

ment to the religions of their enemies. Oman does not, however, believe that political expediency or civilisation by themselves could account for the transformation of a collection of subject peoples into a larger state with equal laws. Oman is difficult to follow at this point. Neither his interpretation of this development nor his imputation of it directly to polytheism is clear. The ease with which the Romans fused their gods with those of defeated enemies does not seem evidence of great religious fervour, especially among the patricians. Oman's statement to justify this approach, that it is a fact that 'no law ... works merely by the will of the majority, but only as it seems to be established by some absolute quality of righteousness'* is so vague as to what is meant by 'works' as to be meaningless. It may be repeated that when he deals with the ethics of the ruler he seems at his weakest.

The third benefit Oman discerns in polytheism is intimately connected with the second. It is the rise of the family as a moral society, as well as a blood and bread and butter relationship. Necessarily he takes up his position from an *a priori* insight and does not give nearly enough evidence to show what he means by this interdependence.

These three main elements of 'progress' are according to Oman balanced by three limitations. The first is the failure in respect of a wider environment. 'Polytheism arose with the beginning of reflective unities, but when reflective thinking was carried farther, polytheism entirely failed to meet its needs.'† It either becomes completely irrational as in Egypt, or is criticised out of existence as in Greece. It could never develop a systematic theology, because essentially it 'presupposes the absence of thinking things together in one unity.'‡

The second failure of polytheism concerns its relationship to civilisation and the state. Polytheism has the power to create civilisation and has no quarrel with it. But when the particular civilisation disintegrates, the religion must decay as well, having no idea of a higher value. We see this in Babylon, Egypt, India, Greece, and Rome. Polytheism never could rise above what Oman calls 'the imperial idea of the Supernatural.'§

The third limitation which Oman singles out concerns its relation-

---

* Ibid., p. 400.
† Ibid.
‡ Ibid., p. 401. It is a pity that Oman does not discuss the breakdown of polytheism before the attack of the sophists, and the rise of Platonism from that attack.
§ Ibid.

ship to the family. Though polytheism had done much to establish the family as a social unit, it did not see that such natural organisations could be transformed by the vision of the supernatural. Not only was polytheism too weak to stem the tide of licentiousness, consequent on the rise of a successful material civilisation, it was even made the occasion and the justification for sensuality.

The problems of polytheism, being those of the natural, can never be solved in its own terms, since it is too little concerned with the supernatural for a true possession of the natural to lie within its reach. As men recognise the weaknesses of polytheism, they may either avoid its problems altogether by attempting to escape from the evanescent by means of mysticism, or they may continue to face it by seeking a higher possession of the natural in legalism or in prophetic monotheism.*

### The Mystical

With the mystical we come to more controversial material. When man becomes capable of unity of reflection and so can think his unities of reflection together, he needs to express his religion in terms of a theology. There are two main kinds of theology to which he may turn. Neither springs essentially from reason and speculation though they have to be worked out in terms of them. They are rather dependent on man's attitude to the natural. Therefore the issue at stake is not which argument is true, but which attitude is right.†

The distinction between the two main roads is the one already described by Oman's subsidiary classification, mystical–apocalyptical. The mystical sees the natural as illusion to be escaped by absorption into the one unchanging supernatural; the apocalyptic attempts to possess the natural by discovering in it the meaning and purpose of the supernatural. It is with the former of these attitudes that Oman here deals.‡

---

* It would be interesting to know what Oman would have made of the modern recrudescence of polytheism.
† This is yet another example of how little Oman stands with the traditions of rational theology. See chapter 7.
‡ Oman has previously distinguished cosmic pantheism from acosmic pantheism – that is, the distinction between those who reject the natural and those who submerge themselves in it. In his chapter 'The Mystical' he devotes himself to those who reject the natural. Spinoza is only mentioned in passing in The Natural and the Supernatural.

Oman first describes some of the ways in which mystical and apocalyptical religions can be distinguished. He judges pantheism as an artificial return to primitive religion, the main difference lying in the fact that it is the product of the reflective mind, working consciously with the unity of awareness, which the primitive only knows as feeling. By going back a step, as it were, pantheism avoids the problems raised by polytheism, with which it is the task of apocalyptical religions to deal, and to which the prophetic monotheism of the Cross can alone give an adequate answer.

In wishing to escape from the natural, the mystical religions according to Oman throw overboard at the same time the concrete individual with all his rights and responsibilities, in direct contrast to prophetic monotheism, which exalts the value of each person.*

Another contrast is the negative nature of mystical morality, the goal of which is Nirvana, as compared with the emphasis on active positive righteousness found in other religions.

These differences all spring from a different conception of the natural. Therefore again it may be said that the proper question on which to judge them is the right relation of man to the natural. Sheer speculation might indeed seem to favour pantheism because, proceeding from a given certainty of unity, it simply imposes unity on all things. This imposition of unity on all experience does not mean that thereby all things are brought into unity. More than anything else, Oman's dislike for these mystical religions seems to be based on his intuition that they are not compassionate and somehow disregard the sin and suffering of the world.

Oman proceeds to discuss Indian religions. He claims that as they alone embrace mystical pantheism wholeheartedly and consistently, they will be his main concern. In fact they are not. The position he clearly distrusts the most is Christian mysticism, to which he returns again and again. His general criticisms of mystical religion will therefore be postponed till his discussion of mysticism's appearance among Christians.

---

* It hardly needs saying that a theologian, one of whose chief terms is 'the sense of the holy,' makes quite clear that by mystical he does not mean religious intuition given in contemplation, but the cult of contemplative ecstasy in which the self is submerged in union with the Divine. He uses the German distinction *Mystik–Mysticismus* for this difference.

Oman first discusses the change from the primitive polytheism of the Rig-Veda to the cult of the pantheistic Brahma. This development is an example of how the change from polytheism to the mystical is not really an advance but rather a retrogression, though decked out in a more sophisticated dress. Whereas the gods of the Rig-Veda were many and the attitude towards them indeed utilitarian, they were at least in some sense transcendent, working in answer to prayer and sacrifice and controlling men's actions. Higher ethical ideas began to have some place as in Varuna, 'who is strict against sin while showing mercy to the penitent.' Brahma, on the other hand, could be actually controlled by the magical practices of the priestly caste, who were even allowed to use black magic. To control the natural under the guidance of the supernatural is all very fine – but to control the supernatural is going a little too far.

This change is partly accounted for according to Oman by what was once an objective and accurate language, made permanent in sacred writings, becoming the tool of subjective and dialectical minds. The traditional archaic ritual is used to arouse the sense of the undifferentiated holy, which lies at the root of all mystical religions. This kind of point may well make one hesitate, for how would Oman say that the vigorous and objective Aryans developed minds 'subjective and dialectical' enough to use their traditions as a tool?

Oman, above all, attributes this return to the primitive to the fact that the Hindus lived an aristocratic and irresponsible sort of life, with no responsibilities and with superiority to hard work. 'Any class which has freedom from the challenge of life's tasks and problems has a primitive mind.' Those 'who were in a position to provide their own discipline for their bodies, instead of being indebted to life's battle for enough of it' are likely to take a false attitude to the natural.* All such monisms, having no place for striving and achievement, cannot long remain optimistic, but must degenerate into dreadful pessimism. Feeling, driven in on itself, becomes predominantly an awareness of pain.†

Oman's assertion that the false attitude of Indian religion is largely determined by the fact that it was a product of a ruling class detached

---

* *The Natural and the Supernatural, op. cit.*, p. 415.
† Compare with Oman's remark that rationalist monism in Europe degenerated from Hegel's hope to Schopenhauer's despair.

from the problems of the natural cannot pass without comment, for it raises once again his liberal political assumptions. First, simply as a question of fact, can it be said that a class that imposed its rule and maintained its authority over most of a sub-continent can have been as unaware of the problems of the natural as Oman makes out? They had organised their world so that others were responsible for growing their food. To say that is not to say they were released from natural responsibilities. Secondly, the question of theory: let the failings of Indian mystical religion be for the moment granted (indeed, religious failings seem common to ruling classes that remain dominant for any length of time), but what is implied as to Oman's positive position by this general determination? In it we come back to what Oman thought about the possibility of the Christian ruler. If he accepted the position that the Christian ruler is a contradiction in terms, then this account of Indian religion would be understandable. But as has been seen in Chapter 6, he does not. His ideal rulers seem then to be a body of Jeffersonian farmers, not cut off from the duties of earning their bread and ruling their communities in their spare time. This Orkney egalitarianism is indeed a fine Christian ideal. But it must be asked whether such societies are likely to produce the art and science that Oman so admires. In the past, such societies have not been noted for these accomplishments. Oman seems to want it both ways. This matter must be raised as his account of Indian religion as the product of a soft ruling class may be a partial truth, but in making it the way he does, Oman raises unanswered questions about Christian political theory, both as to what is right and what is possible.

In discussing Indian religion, Oman compares the three forms of Christian salvation by works, by knowledge and by love with the three unities of form with which mysticism works.

> One is the world as one magical potency; one is the self as one knower including all knowledge; one is the feeling which is one all-embracing yet empty emotion.*

Thus the essence of all Indian religions is acosmic pantheism, however different are their methods.

---

\* *The Natural and the Supernatural, op.cit.,* p. 419.

All work with the abiding as mere undifferentiated unity, and all come to the same result of a feeling which has no objective meaning and victory, of a self that has no difference of quality or profit from experience, and of a universe which has no meaning or purpose in its changes.*

The present writer must admit his inability to judge the content of what Oman says about Indian religion, for despite attempts at reading its sacred writings their terminology is so foreign as to convey little to him. Certainly when put in the language of the west by its European exponents, it entirely lacks the victory of the Cross. On such evidence it cannot however be judged. The form however of what Oman says can be criticised. One may well sympathise with his desire to be freed from any of that relativism that damned so much of the study of the philosophy of religion. And since Oman's faith is in the Cross and not in the Resurrection, his insistence on the difference between Buddha and Jesus Christ is necessary. However, his work lacks that charity which he demands from the naturalist. As has been said, he criticises von Hügel as an eclectic, but his account of Indian religion would be the stronger for the tolerance of the latter. Surely the sternness of the prophet is better employed indicting his own civilisation (the activism of which had just passed through a bloody war) than in an indictment of another civilisation which he had never visited and in whose languages he was not a master. In view of his insistence elsewhere on the need of understanding religions as living attitudes, it seems a pity that he does not mention Tagore and Gandhi in all their virtues and failings.[9] This section on Indian religion is the least judgmatical of any in *The Natural and the Supernatural*. Is it even a useful polemical attempt to prevent intellectuals from espousing empty creeds?

Oman's account of Christian mysticism is mainly an account of 'undiluted' mysticism in general, rather than the particular Christian manifestations. He discounts the mysticism of St Augustine, St Gregory, and St Bernard as being neither essentially mystical, nor of the essence of their respective faiths.[10] The later Christians whose contemplation has more features in common with the East – visions, ecstasies, etc. – are the particular object of his attack. He does not, however, analyse any particular man or woman. When the mystic way is carried to

* Ibid., p. 420.

its ultimate point of ecstatic union with the Infinite, the adjective 'Christian' can have no bearing as all ideas of personality are lost.

Oman criticises undiluted mysticism for its failure to shoulder responsibilities in the natural. By concentrating on the undifferentiated supernatural the mystic, in the words of William James, is guilty of 'taking a perpetual moral holiday.'[11] Oman denies that the 'true' mystic has any wish for his experience to bear fruit in practice. 'Because the mystic's flights into the empyrean of ecstasy have exhausted him he must return to the world to recover energy for a higher flight, but this is not regarded as the natural fruit of energy and inspiration received from his ecstasy.'* Though one may agree wholeheartedly with Oman's attack on irresponsibility, is this a fair description of fact? St Catherine of Siena, St Teresa of Avila, St John of the Cross, and Jacob Boehme do not seem well described by these words.†[12] If Oman then defines mysticism as excluding the above figures, then surely he is falling into that error he criticised in others of so concentrating on the worst aspects of politics or religion as not to understand its proper functioning. No doubt it is a fact that certain mystics have been guilty of neglecting their practical duties. Perhaps, even, mysticism does not aid men to fulfil their duties. But Oman's sweeping generalisation that no true mystic can fulfil his practical duties seems invalid.

Oman attacks mysticism because it is esoteric – the religion of the aristocrat, not open to ordinary men. 'The mere fact of being esoteric is itself primitive.'‡ Religious experience which is not open to all types and conditions of men is to Oman a kind of blasphemy. Certainly it may be granted that much mystical practice seems far from the Gospels. Yet along with the accusation of esoteric practices, Oman makes the suggestion that the mystic's experience is easy of attainment. This is implied in innumerable words and phrases that occur whenever the subject is mentioned. A few examples even out of their context make this clear: 'to sink itself in bliss,' 'peace in quiescence,' 'primitive para-

---

* The Natural and the Supernatural, op. cit., p. 500.
† Oman says of St Teresa that she could have been better occupied than organizing girls into cloisters. See for a balanced dissent from Oman's account of mysticism J.K. Mozley's review of Grace and Personality in Journal of Theological Studies, op. cit., Vol. XXI, pp. 349–52.
‡ The Natural and the Supernatural, op. cit., p. 415.

dise,' 'the supreme Mother-complex of humanity,' 'relief from struggle,' 'The apocalyptic religions ... do not find it so simple.' Even though
peace be the end of the road, the earlier stages of the mystic way do not
seem to be in any way relaxing. Whether Oman is right about the
essence of mysticism, his description of it is freighted with quite irrational antipathy.

These points, however, only touch the periphery of the subject.
What is essential is Oman's account of the content of the experience.
'The suggestion has already been made that it has its source in real
forms of unity ... If so, it is just the attempt to have the forms without
being troubled by their harassing, conflicting, and not always manage-
able content ... The fact that mysticism works with real, and even fundamental, elements in experience, does not prove it to be revelation,
because, while empty forms may be real subjective experience, they are
not experience of objective reality.'*

Oman denies *a priori* the possibility of knowing God above the categories of nature and history, and therefore rules out the mystic way as
illusion. It is acosmic pantheism.† In withdrawing from the challenge
of the natural and of the concrete individual, the mystic refuses to face
life on the terms that God has given it. He despises the categories by
which God has ordained that He shall be known. He evades both the
Cross and the Crown. Far from rising above the idea of a personal God
which was incipient even in polytheism, they fall far below it.

As Oman writes:

> Are we to find the eternal only in what is unchanging, and the sole ulti-
> mate reality to be the All-one, into which we enter as we discard the
> empirical self? Or are we to seek the Supernatural as the Father of our
> spirits and him in whom all fullness dwells, as what gives meaning to
> the world and a purpose beyond it which assure that to be called accord-
> ing to his purpose is to find it all working for good?‡

It may be granted that mystical experience, defined in Oman's care-

---

* Ibid., pp. 423–4.
† Oman never mentions Eckhart's *scintilla animae, increata et increabilis*.[13]
‡ *The Natural and the Supernatural, op. cit.*, p. 425.

ful limitation of that term, is not of the essence of the Gospel, for it is not a knowledge of God open to all His children. So ineffable however is the experience of the mystic that the present writer would remain agnostic about whether it has any cognitive content. Oman's certainty and heat at this point do not seem necessary to his position.

### The Ceremonial–Legal

Ceremonial-Legalism falls into the second class of Oman's sub-division – mystical–apocalyptical. Throughout he uses the word 'apocalyptical' in its literal and more general sense rather than in the specialised meaning of eschatology. In fact, nevertheless, the more specialised sense of apocalyptical does apply to all the religions he discusses under that word except Mohammedanism. The essential quality of these apocalyptical religions is that they seek an unveiling of the supernatural in the natural. They do not seek to escape the problems of the natural as do the mystical religions. Zoroastrianism and Hebrew religion, for instance, arose in periods of physical hardship when men had to fight to get a living from the soil. As Oman writes:

> In such a conflict the negations could not be the virtues, nor the affirmations the vices.*

The person is not identified with the evanescent but is seen to serve some purpose that is of the Supernatural.

On the other hand, Ceremonial-Legalism does not attain the faith of prophetic monotheism. It cannot achieve the trust by which the natural may be all possessed. There is a double estimate of the natural as being tragically far from the absolute worth to which it points. Morality is judged in terms of material reward and so life becomes more and more the observance of ritual and ethical laws. The distinction between sacred and secular is conceived materially rather than morally. This involves a dualism which cannot understand the world as all God's. Thus Ceremonial-Legalism carries the problems of polytheism one step further, but cannot solve them.

* Ibid., p. 428.

Ceremonial-Legalism must not, however, be entirely cut off from Prophetic Monotheism. Not only do they overlap historically, but the legalisms are penetrated with prophetic elements, because often they have had prophetic founders such as Moses or Zarathustra. When these leaders taught a higher religion than their followers were able to assimilate, their teaching was incorporated into the popular religion in the form of ceremonial law. Often the prophetic spirit was so crushed by this shell of legalism that it could only be saved by the destruction of that shell. The higher the prophetic faith, the more elaborate must be the shell. One has only to consider, for an illustration of the process, the way in which Our Lord's rejection of the old Law was gradually turned by his followers into a far more elaborate Ceremonial-legalism than was ever Judaism. This does not imply that Oman believes that the Prophetic is the earlier form historically. The Law absorbed the prophets because it is deeply ingrained in natural man.

The characteristic of Ceremonial-Legalism with which Oman is chiefly concerned is its dualism. His discussion is mainly of the difference between dualism as a problem and dualism accepted as an explanation. The difference is seen in Zoroastrianism and Judaism. Zoroastrianism found in dualism its final theological solution; Judaism, though always concerned with dualism as a practical problem, kept it out of its theology.

Just as in India the heat and the ease had favoured the development of mystical religions, so in Persia the harsh climate and more dangerous life prevented men from unduly neglecting the Natural, and called forth the virtues necessary to deal with it.* In this situation Zoroastrianism had two great achievements. First it transformed the sense of the holy from mere awe into something close to reverence. Zoroastrianism could maintain 'Thou shalt seek the good thou dost seek only from the Good Power and never by any dealing with the lie or any favour of the might of evil.'† The awe thus concentrated solely on the Good Power

---

* Here Oman's writing may clearly be compared with Professor Toynbee's theory of 'challenge and response' as the governing factor in history. As in Professor Toynbee, this explanation of history is not related to the theological dogma of God as the Ruler of history. Oman uses the phrase that 'in principle' the faith is first. But it is difficult to see what he means.

† *The Natural and the Supernatural, op. cit.*, p. 437.

could pass from fear to reverence. To have given up appeasing the powers of evil involved also confining oneself to lawful means in obtaining one's desires. Thus though the good remained highly eudae-monistic, it still led to a higher standard of morality. The second achievement was the formulation of the law. The very formulation implied some kind of universal validity, and the law-givers themselves came under that universality. As Oman writes:

> Laws which are a revelation from Ormuzd to Zarathustra are very different from the unknown, uncertain, uncanny doings of the medicine-man.*

Despite these two elements of progress, Zoroastrianism was pre-vented from spiritual advance by its acceptance of dualism as a theo-logical solution. Righteousness was so clearly associated with the idea of material prosperity, and sin with worldly misfortune, that it was impossible to believe the world to be all of God. The good principle had created the world, but the evil principle had entered in and spoiled it. The chief means of self-preservation was in punctilious observance of Ormuzd's laws.

> Moral good is thus inextricably confused with ceremonial circumspec-tion about material good ... as every evil could be explained as neglect of the sacred, there was nothing to raise question about dualism as a com-plete and final solution.†

The decline of Zoroastrianism was above all caused by this dualist atti-tude to nature. This prevented it from reaching true judgments of value. The natural so interpreted as the pleasant and the unpleasant could not lead to objective judgments of the supernatural.

The Hebrews faced very much the same kind of external situation. The difference between them is seen in the fact that to the end the Per-sian considered the difficulties of agriculture to be caused by the pow-ers of darkness, while the Israelite saw that God had created the earth

---

* Ibid.
† Ibid., p. 439.

with its grudging response for man's own sake. The idea of good is no longer rooted in the material but has become moral, and thus dualism has been rejected as a final solution. Evil as well as good could be related to God, and affliction in the world could be seen not as ceremonial pollution but as some kind of moral failure. Once having spurned dualism as a solution, the problem of evil was always an open one to the Hebrews. However, they could not grasp the answer to which all the prophets pointed and which Jesus revealed on the Cross.* Since the Hebrews did not, as did the Persians, interpret the natural in terms of the pleasant and the unpleasant, they could be the vehicle for ever deepening insight into the supernatural. Thus though in Judaism all the elements of Ceremonial-Legalism were present – the appeal to the awesome holy and the material sacred, moral and ritual legalism, the division of the world into sacred and secular – the elements for the transcendence of legalism were also present. In the fullness of time, the Gospel was to fulfil the Law.

### The Prophetic

Enough has been said, particularly in Chapter IV of this thesis, about Oman's conception of prophetic religion, so there is no need to repeat his account of the Hebrew tradition, culminating in Our Lord. It is the faith by which men know that the Father is in all and over all, as they take up their share in His redeeming work. Once more the difficulty in Oman's use of the conception 'prophetic' may be mentioned. It is of the essence of prophetic religion to be looking forward to the 'as yet unrealised;' yet it is consummated on the Cross. It is not clear how these two aspects are reconciled.

---

* This account of Hebrew religion leads to a better understanding of the Book of Job than an earlier remark about that work in *The Natural and the Supernatural*. Oman says earlier in criticising Otto that: 'What Job is summoned to do, in face even of the most terrible works of nature, is, in repentance and humility yet in boldness, to gird up his loins like a man, not only to hear God but to answer him.' *The Natural and the Supernatural, op. cit.*, p. 60. The end of the book of Job seems far from a demand to answer God but rather indeed the most irrational law-giving of a tyrant. If Job is an authority, Otto's account of the holy is much truer than Oman's. However, in this account of Hebrew religion, the Book of Job may be seen as a noble statement of the problem for which the answer is inadequate.

## APPENDIX B
## BIBLIOGRAPHY ON JOHN OMAN

(Acknowledgments for this bibliography are made
to the library, Westminster College, Cambridge.)

### I. Major Works of John Oman

*On Religion: Speeches to its Cultured Despisers,* by Friedrich Schleiermacher.
Translated, with Introduction, by John Oman. Kegan Paul, Trench, Trubner &
Co., Ltd., London, 1893. pp. 287.

*Vision and Authority, or The Throne of St Peter.* First edition, 1902. A new and
revised edition by Hodder and Stoughton, 1929. Eighth edition with a new
Introduction by T.W. Manson, D.D., F.B.A., Hodder and Stoughton, London,
E.C.4., 1948. pp.352

*The Problem of Faith and Freedom in the Last Two Centuries.* Hodder and Stoughton, London, 1906. pp. 443.

*The Church and the Divine Order.* Hodder and Stoughton, London, 1911. pp. 338.

*The War and Its Issues: An Attempt at a Christian Judgment.* Cambridge: at the
University Press, 1915. pp. 130.

*Grace and Personality.* Cambridge: at the University Press, 1917. Second edition
revised, 1919. Third edition revised, 1925. Fourth edition revised, 1931. (American edition by the Macmillan Company, New York, 1925, with Introduction by
Nolan Best). (Third edition, pp.313)

*The Paradox of the World: Sermons.* Cambridge: at the University Press, 1921.
pp.292. (Cheaper edition 1936).

*Book of Revelation: Theory of the Text: Rearranged Text and Translation: Commentary.*
Cambridge: at the University Press, 1923. pp.168. (a published address).

*Office of the Ministry.* Published by Student Christian Movement, 1928.

*The Text of Revelation.* Cambridge: at the University Press, 1928.

*The Natural and the Supernatural.* Cambridge: at the University Press, 1931.
pp.500.

*Concerning the Ministry.* Student Christian Movement Press, London. April
1936. pp. 243. (Harpers Bros. Publishers, New York and London, 1937).

*Honest Religion.* Cambridge: at the University Press, 1941 (With an introduction by Frank H. Ballard, M.A., and a Memoir of the Author by George Alexander, M.A., and H.H. Farmer, D.D.) pp. 195.

## II. Articles, Chapters, etc., written by John Oman

[Editors' note: Grant included two articles not written by Oman in this section, presumably because they appeared alongside Oman's essays in the books cited in the section and were also discussed in the thesis.]

'Individual,' 'Individualism,' and 'Individuality' in *Dictionary of Christ and the Gospels* edited by James Hastings, D.D., with the Assistance of John A. Selbie, D.D., and (in the reading of proofs) by John C. Lambert, D.D., Vol. I (Aaron-Knowledge) T. & T. Clark, 38 George St., Edinburgh, 1906, pp. 814–821.

'Church' in *Encyclopaedia of Religion and Ethics* edited by James Hastings, M.A., D.D., with the Assistance of John A. Selbie, M.A., D.D, and other scholars. Vol. III (Burial-Confessions), pp. 617–624.

'The Presbyterian Churches,' Lecture III in *Evangelical Christianity: Its History and Witness*. A series of Lectures Delivered at Mansfield College, Oxford, in the Hilary Term, 1911. Edited by W.B. Selbie, M.A., D.D., Principal of Mansfield College, Oxford. Hodder and Stoughton, London. (Date not given). pp. 55–79.

'Human Freedom' and 'War' in *The Elements of Pain and Conflict in Human Life, considered from a Christian Point of View*. Being lectures delivered at the Cambridge Summer Meeting, 1916, by Members of the University. Cambridge: at the University Press, 1916. pp. 56–73 and pp. 157–172.

'Method in Theology,' in *The Expositor*. Eighth Series, Vol. XXVI. Hodder and Stoughton, Warwick Square, London, E.C., 1923. pp. 81–93.

'The Apocalypse,' in *The Expositor*. Ninth Series, Vol. IV. Hodder and Stoughton, Warwick Square, London, E.C., 1923. pp. 437–452.

Article on 'The Idea of the Holy,' in *The Journal of Theological Studies*. Vol. XXV, Oxford: at the Clarendon Press, 1924, pp. 275–286.

'Christianity in a New Age,' and introduction to *An Outline of Christianity*, edited by A.S. Peake and R.G. Parsons, Waverly Book Club, Vol. III, 1926, pp. xiii–xxii.

'The Sphere of Religion,' in *Science, Religion and Reality*. Edited by Joseph Needham. The Sheldon Press, Northumberland Avenue, London. 1926, pp. 259–299.

'The Ministry of the Nonconformist Churches,' in *The Problem of a Career Solved by 36 Men of Distinction.* Compiled by J.A.R. Cairns (of the Middle Temple, Barrister-At-Law. One of the Magistrates of the Police Courts of the Metropolis). Printed by J.W. Arrowsmith, Ltd., Bristol, 1926, pp. 127–132.

'Mysticism and its expositors,' in *The Hibbert Journal.* Vol. XXVI. A Quarterly Review of Religion, Theology, and Philosophy. Edited by L.P. Jacks, M.A., D.D., LL.D., D. Litt. and G. Dawes Hicks, M.A., Ph.D., Litt.D., F.B.A. October 1927–July 1928. Constable & Co., Ltd., London. pp. 445–458.

Introduction to *Ideas and Revelation*, by F.W. Kingston, Cambridge. Cambridge, W. Heffer & Sons, Ltd., 1928. pp. vii–viii.

'Schleiermacher,' in *The Journal of Theological Studies.* Vol. XXX, Oxford: at the Clarendon Press, 1929. pp. 401–405.

'The Roman Sacerdotal Hierarchy,' Chapter X (pp. 230–256) in *Why I Am and Why I Am Not a Catholic.* Part I, 'Why I Am a Catholic' by Archbishop Goodier, S.J., Father R. Knox, The Reverend C.C.Martindale, S.J., Hilaire Belloc, Sheila Kaye-Smith. Part II, 'Why I Am Not a Catholic,' by The Bishop of Gloucester, Professor A.E. Taylor, D.Litt., Professor H.L. Goudge, D.D., The Reverend W.E. Orchard, D.D., Principal John Oman, D.D. Cassell & Co., Ltd., London. 1931. (Chapter IX, 'Why I Should Find it Difficult to Become a Roman Catholic' by The Rev. W.E. Orchard, D.D., pp. 204–229).

'In Memoriam William Fearon Halliday,' *Personal Freedom Through Personal Faith.* A Memorial Volume, William Fearon Halliday, edited by J.R. Coates. Hodder and Stoughton, London 1934. pp. 39–46.

'The Abiding Significance of Apocalyptic' in *In Spirit and In Truth, Aspects of Judaism and Christianity*, edited for The Society of Jews and Christians by George A. Yates, M.A. With a Foreword by The Dean of Canterbury. Hodder and Stoughton, London, 1934. pp. 276–293. (Also an article, 'The Place of Jesus in Modern Christian Thought,' by C.E. Raven, pp. 263–275.)

Series of articles in *The Student Movement* (The organ of the Student Christian Movement of Great Britain and Ireland) edited by Tissington Tatlow. Vol XXIV, October–June 1921–22. Nos. 1–9. Student Christian Movement, 32 Russel Square, W.C.1, London. February 1922, No. 5. I. 'Looking Round our Position,' pp. 98–100. March 1922, No. 6. II. 'The Mathematical Mechanical Order,' pp. 124–125. April 1922, No. 7. III. 'The Evolutionary Historical Process,' pp. 153–155. May 1922, No. 8. IV. 'Mind as the Measure of the Universe,' pp. 171–173. June 1922, No. 9. V. 'The Sacred as the Measure of Man,' pp. 194–195.

## III. Book Reviews by John Oman

[Editors' Note: All the book reviews are published in *The Journal of Theological Studies* in Oxford, at the Clarendon Press. Volume numbers, page numbers, and dates appear in square brackets at the end of each entry.]

*Ritschlianism: An Essay*, by John Kenneth Mozley, M.A.,(James Nisbet & Co., London, 1909) and *Faith and Fact: A Study of Ritschlianism*, by Ernest A. Edghill, M.A.(Macmillan & Co., London, 1910). [Vol XI, 1910, pp. 469–76]

*Principles of Religious Development, A Psychological and Philosophical Study*, by George Galloway (Macmillan & Co., London, 1909). [Ibid, pp. 594–6]

*Group Theories of Religion and the Religion of the Individual*, by Clement C.J. Webb, M.A. (George Allen and Unwin, Ltd., London 1916). [Vol. XVIII, 1917, p. 244]

*Nature, Miracle, and Sin: A Study of St. Augustine's Conception of the Natural Order*, by T.A. Lacey, M.A., being the Pringle Stewart lecture for 1914. (Longman's, Green & Co., London 1916). [Ibid, p. 245]

*Essays in Orthodoxy*, by Oliver Chase Quick. (Macmillan & Co., London 1916). [Ibid, pp. 246–7]

*The Idea of God in the Light of Recent Philosophy*: The Gifford Lectures delivered in the University of Aberdeen in the years of 1912 and 1913, by A. Seth Pringle-Pattison, LL.D., D.C.L. (Oxford: at the Clarendon Press, 1917). [Vol. XIX, 1918, pp. 278–9]

*The Idea of Atonement in Christian Theology*. Being the Bampton lectures for 1915, by Hastings Rashdall, D.Litt., etc., (Macmillan & Co., London, 1919). [Vol XXI, 1920, pp. 267–75]

*A Short History of the Doctrine of the Atonement*, by L.W. Grensted, M.A. (Manchester University Press, 1920). [Ibid, pp. 275–6]

*The Ministry of Reconciliation*, by J.R. Gillies, D.D. (A. & C. Black, London, (no date). [Ibid, p. 277]

*L'Évolution religeuse de Luther jusqu'en 1515*, by Henri Strohl (Librairie Istra, Strasbourg, 1922) and *La liberté chrétienne: étude sur le principe de la piété chez Luther*, by Robert Will (Same Publishers). [Vol. XXIV, 1923, pp. 211–14]

*A Faith that Enquires:* The Gifford Lectures delivered in the University of Glasgow in the years 1920 and 1921, by Sir Henry Jones. (Macmillan & Co., 1922). [Ibid, pp. 214–17]

*Philosophy and the Christian Experience:* Being the Pringle-Stewart Lectures for 1921-1922, by Wilfrid Richmond, Hon. Canon of Winchester (Basil Blackwell, Oxford, 1922). [Ibid, pp. 445–6]

*Religion and Modern Thought,* by George Galloway, D.Phil., Principal and Primarius Professor of Divinity, St Mary's College, St Andrews (T. & T. Clark, 1922). [Ibid, pp. 446–9]

*An Introduction to the Psychology of Religion,* by Robert H. Thouless, M.A. (Cambridge: at the University Press, 1923). [Ibid, pp. 449–50]

*Psychologie der Religion,* by Georg Runze (Ernst Reinhardt, Munich). [Vol. XXV, 1924, pp. 202–4]

*Outlines of a Philosophy of Life,* by Alban G. Widgery, M.A., (Williams & Norgate, London, 1923). [Ibid, pp. 204–5]

*The Design Argument Reconsidered:* A Discussion between the Rev. C.J. Shebbeare and Joseph McCabe (Watts & Co., London). [Vol. XXVI, 1925, pp. 87–8]

*Religion et Réalité,* by Charles Hauter (Strasbourg, 1923). [Ibid, pp.88–91]

*L'épanouissement de la pensée religieuse de Luther de 1515 à 1520* by Henri Stroh (Librairie Istra, Strasbourg, 1924). [Ibid, pp. 91–2]

A review of six books. (see notes). [Ibid, pp. 409–20]

*Le culte: étude d'histoire et de philosophie religieuse.* Tome premier: *Le caractère religieux du culte,* by Robert Will. (Strasbourg: Librairie Istra, 1925). [Vol. XXVII, 1926. pp. 183–4]

*Miracle and its Philosophical Presuppositions:* Three lectures delivered in the University of London 1924, by F.R. Tennant, D.D., B.Sc., Fellow and Lecturer of Trinity College, Cambridge. (Cambridge University Press, 1925). [Ibid, pp. 184–5]

*Traité de philosophie,* by Gaston Sortais, S.J., Cinquieme édition revue et augmentée. (P. Lethielleux, Paris, 1923). Tome premier: Morale, Esthétique, Métaphysique, Vocabulaire philosophique. [Vol. XXVIII, 1927, pp.187–8]

*De Kant à Ritschl: une siecle d'histoire de la pensée chrétienne,* by H. Dubois. (Secrétariat de l'université, Neuchâtel, 1925). [Ibid, pp.188–9]

*Les contradictions de la pensée religieuse: Recherche d'une méthode dogmatique,* by Jean de Saussure. (Georg et Cie, Genève, 1926). [Ibid, pp. 190–2]

*Religion in the Making,* by Alfred North Whitehead. Lowell Lectures. (Cambridge: at the University Press, 1926). [Ibid, pp. 296–304]

*The oldest Biography of Spinoza*, edited by Prof. A. Wolf. (George Allen and Unwin, Ltd., London, 1927). [Ibid, pp. 425–6]

*The Philosophy of the Abbé Bautain*, by William Marshall Horton, Ph.D.(New York University Press, 1926). [Ibid, pp. 426–7]

*Notes on St John and the Apocalypse*, by Alex. Pallis. (Oxford University Press, 1926). [Ibid, p. 427]

*The Nature and Right of Religion*, by W. Morgan, D.D. (T & T Clark, Edinburgh, 1926). [Ibid, pp. 428–30]

*Adventure: The Faith of Science and the Science of Faith*, by Burnett H. Streeter, Catherine M. Chilcott, John MacMurray and Alexander S. Russell. (Macmillan & Co., London, 1927) [Vol. XXIX, 1928, pp. 290–6]

*The Christian Experience of Forgiveness*, by H.R.Mckintosh, D.Phil, D.D., Professor of Theology, New College, Edinburgh (Nisbet & Co., Ltd., London, 1927). [Ibid, pp. 296–9]

*Systematic Theology*, by Wilhelm Herrman, translated by Nathaniel Micklem and Kenneth Saunders (George Nelson & Unwin, Ltd., London, 1927). [Ibid, pp. 299–300]

*Studies of the Psychology of the Mystics*, by Joseph Maréchal, S.J., translated by Algar Thorold (Burns, Oates & Washbourne, London, 1927). [Ibid, pp. 300–2]

*Rationalism and Orthodoxy of Today*, by J.H. Beibitz, M.A. (London: Student Christian Movement, 1927). [Ibid, pp. 302–3]

*Philosophical Theology*, by F.R.Tennant, D.D., B.Sc. Vol.I. *The Soul and its Faculties*. (Cambridge: at the University Press, 1928). [Vol. XXXI, 1930, pp. 403–7]

*Georg Wilhelm Hegel: Samtliche Werke*, Herausgegeben von Georg Lasson: Bande XII–XIV, *Philosophie der Religion* (Verlag von Felix Meiner, Leipzig, 1930). [Vol. XXXII, 1931, pp. 211–17]

*Le problème de Dieu*, by Édouard Le Roy, membre de l'Institut, Professeur au College de France (L'Artisan du Livre, Paris, 1929). [Ibid, pp. 217–19]

*Process and Reality: An Essay in Cosmology*, by Alfred North Whitehead: Gifford Lectures, delivered in the University of Edinburgh (Cambridge: at the University Press, 1929). [Vol. XXXIII, 1932, pp. 48–52]

*Le culte: Étude d'histoire et de philosophie religieuse*, by Robert Will (Tome Deuxième: Paris, Librairie Félix Alcan, 1929). [Ibid, pp. 52–4]

*The Philosophical Basis of Biology*: Donellan Lectures, University of Dublin, 1930, by J.S. Haldane, C.H., F.R.S., M.D., LL.D. (Hodder and Stoughton, London, 1931). [Ibid, pp. 216–18]

*Philosophical Theology*, by F.R. Tennant. Vol II. *The World, The Soul and God* (Cambridge: at the University Press, 1930). [Ibid, pp. 281–3]

*The Philosophy of Religion based on Kant and Fries*, by Rudolf Otto, D.D. Translated by E.B. Dicker, M.A., with a Foreword by W. Tudor Jones, M.A., Ph.D. (Williams and Norgate, 1931). [Ibid, pp. 283–6]

*Religious Essays, A Supplement to the 'Idea of the Holy'*, by Rudolf Otto. Translated by Brian Lunn, M.A. (Oxford University Press, 1931). [Ibid, pp. 286–8]

*Schopenhauer: His Life and Philosophy*, by Helen Zimmern. Completely revised throughout (London, George Allen & Unwin, 1932). [Vol. XXXIV, 1933, pp. 98–101]

*An Introduction to Schleiermacher*, by J. Arundel Chapman, M.A., (Oxon.), B.D. (Lond.). Professor of Systematic Theology, Wesley College, Leeds (The Epworth Press, London, 1932). [Ibid, pp. 213–14]

*Das Kommende: Untersuchungen zur Entstehungsgeschichte des Messianischen Glaubens*, by Martin Buber, Professor der Religions-wissenschaft an der Universität Frankfurt am Main. Band I. Königtum Gottes (Schocken Verlag, Berlin, 1932). [Ibid, pp. 214–16]

*An Idealist View of Life*, by S. Radhakrishnan, being the Hibbert Lectures for 1929 (George Allen & Unwin, Ltd., 1932). [Ibid, pp. 216–18]

*The Logic of Religious Thought: an answer to Professor Eddington*, by R. Gordon Milburn, formerly lecturer in Logic and Philosophy to students of Calcutta University (Williams and Norgate, London, 1929). [Vol. XXXV, 1934, pp. 197–9]

*Imago Christi: Beiträge zur theologischen Anthropologie*, edited H. Bornkamm (Alfred Töpelmann, Giessen, 1932). [Ibid, pp. 199–200]

*Experience and its Modes*, by Michael Oakeshott (Cambridge: at the University Press, 1933). [Ibid, pp. 314–16]

*The Idealistic Conception of Religion: Vico, Hegel, Gentile*, by Aline Lion, D.Phil., with a Preface by Clement C.J. Webb (Oxford: at the Clarendon Press, 1932). [Ibid, pp. 404–5]

*La pensée intuitive II: Invention et vérification* by Édouard Le Roy (Boivin et Cie, Paris, 1932). [Ibid, pp. 405–7]

# Notes

## Editor's Introduction

1 Letter to his mother, dated 3 November 1945, *George Grant: Selected Letters*, ed. William Christian (Toronto: University of Toronto Press 1996), 122.

2 19. That person does not deserve to be called a theologian who looks upon the invisible things of God as though they were clearly perceptible in those things which have actually happened [Rom. 1:20].

   20. He deserves to be called a theologian, however, who comprehends the visible and manifest things of God seen through suffering and the cross.

   21. A theologian of glory calls evil good and good evil. A theologian of the cross calls the thing what it actually is.

   22. That wisdom which sees the invisible things of God in works as perceived by man is completely puffed up, blinded, and hardened.

   23. The law brings the wrath of God, kills, reviles, accuses, judges, and condemns everything that is not in Christ [Rom. 4:15].

   24. Yet that wisdom is not of itself evil, nor is the law to be evaded; but without the theology of the cross man misuses the best in the worst manner.

   *Luther's Works*, vol. 31, ed. Harold J. Grim (Philadelphia: Fortress Press 1957), 40–1.

   The editors are grateful for invaluable advice on the theology of the cross from Sheila Grant, Douglas Hall, and Harris Athanasiadis. See note 5 of the Introduction to Volume 1, p. xxxvi, for a list of their works on this subject.

3 Christian, ed., *George Grant: Selected Letters*, 121.

4 See 'Two Theological Languages' in *'Two Theological Languages' by George Grant and Other Essays in Honour of His Work*, ed. Wayne Whillier (Lewiston, NY: Edwin Mellen Press 1990), 14.

## Abstract

1 For a list of Oman's earlier theological writings (up to 1918) see Grant's bibliography on Oman (Appendix B, 394–5). For an account of Grant's own theology of the cross, see Sheila Grant, 'George Grant and the Theology of the Cross,' in *George Grant and the Subversion of Modernity: Art, Philosophy, Politics, Religion, and Education*, ed. Arthur Davis (Toronto: University of Toronto Press 1996), 243–62.

2 Rudolph Hermann Lotze (1817–1881), German philosopher, was a 'realist' in the sense that he believed there are real forms or structures of being that

are the path to God. They are not perceived by the senses, but rather are apprehended by estimating their value in a way that is beyond the scope of science. Lotze insisted that estimating value is not merely subjective but establishes *objective* value. He was the first thinker to use the language of values in the realm of religion. Grant refers, in the thesis, to 'axiological theists' (those who, like Lotze, find God through the study of values) and 'cosmological theists' (who find God through nature).

3  Friedrich Daniel Ernst Schleiermacher (1768–1834), German philosopher and leading Protestant theologian, argued that religion is the feeling of absolute dependence on the infinite. Oman translated and introduced an edition of his *On Religion: Speeches to Its Cultured Despisers* (1799); he approved of Schleiermacher's claim as a Romantic that we intuit the supernatural through feeling, considering it a healthy reaction against traditional natural theology, but he also felt that the tendency in Schleiermacher's thought towards cosmic pantheism was dangerous for a Christian theism of persons.

4  Albrecht Benjamin Ritschl (1822–1889), German Protestant theologian, argued that Christian faith is concerned with the maintenance of the worth of personal spirit against 'mere extension,' the objective conception of being favoured by modern philosophy and science. He defended personal spirit against conceptions of nature and human nature in Greek metaphysics, prompting Grant to defend Plato against 'his Christocentric scorn of metaphysics.' See footnote *, p. 200, where Grant chides the Platonist Oman for not admitting openly 'that his Ritschlian contempt for Greek metaphysics could no longer stand.' Ritschl also influenced Oman with his direct appeal back across the centuries to the experiences of Christians in the early Church. In chapter 1, p. 155, Grant discusses Oman's debt to Ritschl in *The Problem of Faith and Freedom in the Last Two Centuries*.

5  Herbert Henry Farmer (1892–1981), Presbyterian minister, educator, and theologian influenced by Schleiermacher and Ritschl. Grant is referring to the personalist account of nature in Farmer's *The World and God* (1935). See footnote †, p. 252, for a reference to that work. Farmer was a close friend of Oman's as well as being his student. Grant talked with him about Oman while working on the DPhil thesis. Farmer's writings also include *The Servant of the Word* (1930), and *God and Men* (1948).

6  The text has 'striving' lined out after the word 'without.'

7  John Laird (1887–1946), professor of philosophy at Aberdeen. See Grant's reference to the last chapter of Laird's *Mind and Deity* (1940) as the location of his argument about 'audit by reason alone' (footnote *, p. 354). According to Grant in his chapter 7, Laird proceeded to philosophical theology from 'natural evidence', while Oman denied the possibility of such 'objectivity.'

## Chapter 1

1  The lower case 'g' in the copy-text has been changed to the upper case to be consistent with Grant's usual practice in the thesis and elsewhere.

2  The Zeitgeist, or spirit of the age, obviously glorifies human achievement. Grant is here arguing that the Christian philosopher can communicate effectively to modern people without surrendering completely to that spirit. Oman and Grant believed that Pelagianism (like the modern spirit) weakens trust and patience and causes humans to seek security in their own achievements and emotions. Salvation is achieved by human will and effort as well as divine grace, according to its doctrine. The British monk Pelagius (c360–c420) argued that the doctrine of man's total depravity (original sin) had permitted an evasion of moral responsibility. St Augustine found his views heretical and had them condemned at the Councils of Carthage in 416 and 418.

3  John Richardson Illingworth (1848–1915), English clergyman and Hegelian philosopher. In *Personality, Human and Divine* (1894), for example, he claimed that the arguments for a personal God admit of continual adaptation to the ideas of each successive age (see note 1, page 218). See also 'The Incarnation in Relation to Development,' one of his two contributions to Bishop Charles Gore's *Lux Mundi* (1889).

4  Alfred North Whitehead (1861–1947), English mathematician and philosopher, was brought up in southern England (Kent) in a family concerned with education, religion, and local administration. His 'Autobiographical Notes' indicate that, though his father was an Anglican clergyman, faith did not play a major part in his early life or in his schooling at Sherborne and then Trinity College, Cambridge. See Paul Arthur Schilpp, ed., *The Philosophy of Alfred North Whitehead* (New York: Tudor 1941), 3–14. See also notes 19 and 20, below.

5  Andrew Seth Pringle-Pattison (1856–1931), Scottish Hegelian philosopher, wanted, as Grant says, to see that human individuality was not lost in the Absolute. See, for example, *Hegelianism and Personality* (1887). He also argued that intuitions of value, along with the principle of coherence, should be given a role in determining the nature of reality.

6  Samuel Wilberforce (1805–1873), conservative Bishop of Oxford, tried unsuccessfully to refute evolutionary theory with ridicule and mock politeness in a confrontation with T.H. Huxley (note 23) at the British Association for the Advancement of Science at Oxford in 1860.

7  William Robertson Smith (1846–1894), a Bible scholar and teacher in the Free Church of Scotland, was dismissed from his post because of the critical approach to Bible study he had learned while a student under Ritschl at

Göttingen. Smith argued that such study could be guided by faith, but critics in the Free Church maintained he was denying the divine authorship of the Bible. He was tried for heresy over his articles in journals and the *Encyclopaedia Britannica* and, though acquitted of heresy, was dismissed from his chair at the Free Church college at Aberdeen by the Assembly of the Church.

8  Francis Herbert Bradley (1846–1924) and Bernard Bosanquet (1848–1923), along with T.H. Green, belonged to a group of liberal Hegelians centred at Balliol College, Oxford, who tended in varying degrees towards a Burkean conservative politics (though both Green and Bosanquet were members of the Liberal party). Bradley taught philosophy and Bosanquet taught ancient history at Oxford.

9  Jansenism, named after the theologian Bishop Cornelius Jansen of Ypres (1585–1638), strongly emphasized the necessity of divine grace and predestination for salvation, in contrast to Pelagianism, which emphasized free will (see note 2). Jansenism spread over large parts of France, Belgium, Holland, Italy, and Germany in the seventeenth and eighteenth centuries but was condemned by Rome in 1641 and 1642. Grant, like Oman, was attracted to the most famous supporter of Jansenism, Blaise Pascal (see chap. 3, note 2), but he did not share Jansenism's moral austerity and aversion to philosophy.

10  Jacques-Bénigne Bossuet (1627–1704), priest and theologian who was counsellor to Louis XIV and tutor to Louis XV, argued for the supreme authority of the Church. This is the 'ecclesiasticism of Bossuet and the Jesuits' that Oman and Grant rejected. Bossuet also defended the divine right of monarchs and claimed that rebellion against legally constituted governments is criminal.

11  Joseph Butler (1692–1752), English moral philosopher and theologian, argued that conscience is a reflective and rational principle operating as one of many aspects of human nature. He defended the Christian position against Deism.

12  Bible scholars at the University of Tübingen such as Ferdinand Christian Baur (1792–1860) and David Friedrich Strauss (1808–74) applied Hegelian dialectical principles to the understanding of the historical origins of Christianity. Both Oman and Grant sided with Ritschlean personalism against the impersonalist critical-history approach.

13  John Henry, Cardinal Newman (1801–1890), in his *Apologia pro Vita Sua* (1864), exemplified, for Oman, a generation in reaction against the French Revolution who falsely lumped liberalism, rationalism, and revolution together, as the offspring of the Reformation. Newman's defence of the authority of the Roman Catholic Church, Oman thought, was a failure to assert the significance of the individual, with his responsibility, guilt, weak-

ness, and 'the need of victory.' It denied that human beings were worthy of what Oman, following Luther, called the 'glorious liberty of the children of God.'

14 The text contains the following sentence crossed out at this point: 'In his posthumous work *Honest Religion* he writes in an equally vague way about this subject.'

15 Tertullian, properly Quintus Septimius Florens Tertullianus (*c*.155–*c*.222), African church father, posed the famous rhetorical question 'What has Athens to do with Jerusalem?' in *De Praescriptione Haereticorum*, 7. His complete question was: 'What has Athens to do with Jerusalem, the Church with the Academy, the Christian with the heretic?' Tertullian meant that Christians do not need philosophy and should stand apart from the world and its ways of thinking. Grant argued that Christianity must communicate its case in philosophical language the world understands, although he sided with what he called Oman's 'quietist' resistance to participation in the state, rather than with his 'liberal' embrace of it. (The word 'quietism' as Grant used it does not mean a passive or apolitical withdrawal from the world, but rather a detachment from the purposes of the state when they conflict with Christian principles.)

16 Karl Barth (1886–1968), Swiss reformed theologian, along with some other members of his generation, revolted against the liberal theology of their teachers, which they felt could not respond adequately to the war. Barth argued, in works such as *Epistle to the Romans* (1919), that theology should be brought back to the revelation and word of God in opposition to the primacy given to human reason and culture in the modern world. See pp. 360–1 in chapter 7 for Grant's defence of the possibility of a philosophical theology (such as Oman's) against the critique of Barth. At the time he was writing the thesis, Grant apparently appreciated the early Barth's response to the war, but not his combative attack on philosophy.

17 Edward Morgan Forster (1879–1970), English novelist and critic, wrote a biography of G. Lowes Dickinson (1862–1932) entitled *Goldsworthy Lowes Dickinson* (1934), as Grant mentions. Forster was educated at Cambridge during the era of Dickinson, G.E. Moore, and G.M. Trevelyan. Dickinson lectured in political history at Cambridge from 1896 to 1920. He wrote *The Greek View of Life* in 1896.

18 Sir Joseph John Thomson (1856–1940), Cavendish professor of physics at Cambridge (1884–1919) and master of Trinity College (1918–40), discovered the electron in 1897 and received the Nobel Prize for Physics for his work on the conductivity of electricity through gases in 1906.
Ernest Rutherford (1871-1937), first Baron Rutherford, was Macdonald Professor at McGill University (1898–1907), professor of physics at Manchester

University (1907–19), and Cavendish Professor of physics at Cambridge after 1919.

Arthur Stanley Eddington (1882–1944), Professor of Astronomy at Cambridge (1913–44), contributed to the establishment of Einstein's theories in the scientific community.

19 Alfred North Whitehead (1861–1947) and Bertrand Russell (1872–1970) together published *Principia Mathematica* (3 vols., 1910–13). Whitehead taught at Cambridge (1902–10), then at the College of Science in South Kensington (1910–24), and Harvard (1924–47). Russell was at Trinity College, Cambridge, until 1916, when he was dismissed in connection with anti-war protests.

20 Grant praised Russell for filling his moral thought with the intensities of the modern world, even though he attacked Russell's view that philosophy cannot teach us how to live ('Pursuit of An Illusion: A Commentary on Bertrand Russell' [1952]. See volume 2 of the *Collected Works*); Whitehead's writings, on the other hand, he thought inadequately affirmed God 'as subsidiary to process' and tasted 'of secularized Anglicanism seeking a Harvard substitute for prayer' ('Justice and Technology' [1984, written 1975], reprinted in William Christian and Sheila Grant, eds. *The George Grant Reader* [Toronto: University of Toronto Press 1997], 441.)

George Edward Moore (1873–1958) was one of the principal forces in English moral philosophy at the turn of the century engaged in attacking idealism and naturalism while asking the question, in *Principia Ethica* (1902), 'What do we mean when we discuss "good"?' He taught at Cambridge (1898–1904; 1911–39) and edited the journal *Mind* (1921–47).

21 Charlie Dunbar Broad (1887–1971), professor of moral philosophy at Cambridge (1933–53), continued the ethical empiricist tradition of Russell and Moore. Grant hated the 'civilized' disdain for Christianity exemplified in this slight of those who 'hunger and thirst after righteousness' (See Mathew 5: 6).

22 Later in the thesis, Grant says of Professor Webb what he wishes to say about all of the six Christian Platonists who are grouped together here. They are Christians, but they tend to accept modern culture and thought rather than challenge and oppose it: 'Though there is ... similarity between Oman and Professor Webb's approach to Christian philosophy, the difference in their works is profound, because of their differing ethical tone. Oman has a much more vivid intuition of the gulf that lies between the demands of the Cross and the ethics of civilisation. Professor Webb is the gentle reconciler of Christianity with the best of the European tradition' (chap. 4, note *, p. 268).

Baron Friedrich von Hügel (1852–1909), Anglo-Austrian, Roman Catholic philosopher, later appreciated by Grant for his work on mysticism.

George Tyrrell (1861–1909), Roman Catholic modernist, excommunicated for criticizing Pius X's encyclical *Pascendi dominici gregis*.

John Cook Wilson (1849–1915), Wykeham Professor of Logic at Oxford, was concerned with what has affected the masses of mankind, meaning, for Grant, that philosophy has lost its power to challenge mass society.

Clement Charles Julian Webb (1865–1954), student of Cook Wilson's and later Oriel Professor of the Philosophy of the Christian Religion at Oxford.

William Temple (1881–1944), English theologian and Archbishop of Canterbury (1942–4) strongly influenced by neo-Hegelianism.

Edwyn Bevan (1870–1943), lecturer on Hellenistic history and literature at King's College, London.

23  Grant may have meant the resistance of conservative scientists such as Richard Owen (1804–1892), professor of comparative anatomy and superintendent at the British Museum, who was a bitter critic of evolutionary theory. Thomas Henry Huxley (1825–1895), zoologist, anatomist, and essayist, contributed to the elevation of the science of biology, and especially the Darwinian theory of evolution, to public prominence.

Herbert Spencer (1820–1903), social philosopher later called a 'social Darwinist,' attempted to apply the theory of evolution (interpreted as the survival of the fittest individuals) to all branches of knowledge.

24  Henri Bergson (1859–1941), French philosopher of evolution, taught at the Collège de France from 1901 to 1921. Grant is referring to *Time and Free Will: An Essay on the Immediate Data of Consciousness* (1899) and *Essay on the Immediate Given of Awareness* (1899).

25  Conwy Lloyd Morgan (1852–1936), English biologist and philosopher of evolution, taught in South Africa and then at Bristol. In *The Natural and the Supernatural*, Oman refers to Morgan as 'Spinoza turned biologist.' He thought Morgan made the mistake of submerging human striving in a biological version of Spinoza's 'intellectual love of God.'

26  The text has 'Celline' corrected to 'Céline,' but the Oxford carbon copy has not been corrected.

Louis-Ferdinand Céline (1894–1961) (Louis-Ferdinand Auguste Destouches). See note 30 in the 1942 Journal.

Possibly Alfred Rosenberg (1893–1946), the German ideologist of Nazism who was declared a war criminal at Nuremberg and hanged.

David Herbert Lawrence (1885–1930), English novelist. In later years Grant enjoyed and praised Lawrence, recommending his books to students; but he never found Lawrence's paganism compelling. It is worth noting that Lawrence, who had been raised with the Bible in a non-conformist household, published a short review of Oman's *The Book of Revelation* in the journal *The Adelphi* in April 1924 and later wrote his own work on the book of Revelation called *Apocalypse* in 1929.

27  Jacques Maritain (1882–1973), French neo-Thomist philosopher, studied under Bergson and then was converted to Catholicism in 1906. According to Sheila Grant, her husband considered Maritain's account of Luther in *Three Reformers* (1925) to be unfair, preferring the work of another neo-Thomist, Étienne Gilson.

28  James Henry Leuba (1868–1946), professor of psychology and pedagogy at Bryn Mawr College; according to Oman, he put forward a theory of religion as illusion of the Kantian type.

29  Sir James George Frazer (1854–1941), Scottish classicist and anthropologist, published *The Golden Bough* in 1911. As Oman saw it, Frazer discovered only part of the truth of early religion because he did not illuminate his data from the living religion of the present.

30  John Ellis McTaggart (1866–1925), British philosopher, taught at Cambridge (1897–1923). His Hegelian 'system of souls,' according to Oman, is only a rather poor substitute for Spinoza's 'one Substance,' failing to give freedom its due because it is thought to have too great a price in pain and evil.

31  Francis Crawford Burkitt (1864–1935) was Professor of Divinity at Cambridge during Oman's time there.

## Chapter 2

1  Frederick Robert Tennant (1866–1957), Cambridge theologian and philosopher of religion, in *Philosophical Theology* (1928) interpreted faith broadly as the volitional element in all knowledge, but argued it is insufficient by itself to give knowledge of reality.

2  Samuel Alexander (1859–1938), Manchester philosopher, claimed that time–space is the matrix of all reality. See *Space, Time, and Deity* (2 vols., 1920) as cited by Oman. Such a claim shows the influence of the 'Cartesian rationalist fallacy,' according to Oman. He argued that Cartesian rationalism is a method that excludes the supernatural (unlike the method employed by Whitehead).

3  Rudolph Otto (1869–1937), German philosopher and theologian, failed, according to Oman, to give an adequate account of the relation between moral holiness and religious awe in his *The Idea of the Holy* (1917). His account does not allow him to avoid a radical disjunction between rationality and irrationality in humans. See the discussion on pp. 210–12 below.

4  The copy-text has 'of' corrected to 'as,' but the Oxford carbon copy was not corrected.

5  St Bonaventure (Giovanni Fidanza) (1217–1274), Italian scholastic philosopher, was an Augustinian Platonist in orientation and was known as the

'seraphic doctor' because of his exemplary character. He was elected minister general of the Franciscan Order.

6  Wilhelm Windelband (1848–1915), German philosopher and historian of philosophy, was a disciple of Lotze and known for his attempt to extend the principles of Kantian criticism to the historical sciences. Oman reports that he was indebted more to Windelband's 'clear and calm exposition of "the holy" as the ground of moral ideals as well as of all religion, than to [Rudolph] Otto's fervour, "which often produces more heat than light".'

7  Ferdinand Kattenbusch (1851–1935), German philosopher, argued that moral holiness and awe were one, in both Judaism and Apostolic Christianity, and also that the weakness of Hegel-inspired theology lay in its submerging of the personality in infinite dependence.

8  John Baillie (1886–1960), Professor of Divinity at Edinburgh, refers on page 257 of *Our Knowledge of God* (1939) to 'Kant's later willingness, apparent in the *Opus Postumum*, to believe that in the challenge of the moral law God Himself is already present to us.' Sheila Grant notes that Grant found in the Baillie book the translation of the Luther's 21st Heidleberg Thesis that he frequently quoted. See Sheila Grant, 'George Grant and the Theology of the Cross,' in Arthur Davis, ed., *George Grant and the Subversion of Modernity* (Toronto: University of Toronto Press 1996), 243–62.

9  Max Scheler (1874–1928), German social philosopher. His criticism of Kant's ethics (and his criticism of Hartmann) is in *Formalism in Ethics and Non-Formal Ethics of Values* (1916), which is subtitled 'With Special Attention to Immanuel Kant's Ethics.' He argued that Kant's doctrine of formal ethics had to be refuted before an effective non-formal ethics could be articulated. Scheler sought to overcome the presumed relativism of values by arguing that they are non-temporal essences possessing objective validity. He also claimed that the concept of person (neither a natural being nor a spiritual entity) leads to the concept of God.
Nicolai Hartmann (1882–1950), German philosopher, published *The Structure of the Real World* (1940) in addition to *Ethics* (1932) (which is the work Grant cites for its realist criticism of Kant, similar to Oman's).

10  The copy-text has 'loose' corrected to 'lose,' but the Oxford carbon copy was not corrected.

11  Henri Bergson (1859–1941), French philosopher of evolution, taught at the Collège de France from 1901 to 1921. Bergson argued that God is the *Élan vital* which makes the process of evolution work and move towards an open future.Grant cites the 1945 French edition of *Two Sources of Morality and Religion* (1930).

12  As in note 10, the copy-text has 'loose' corrected to 'lose,' but the Oxford carbon copy was not corrected.

**Chapter 3**

1  William Ralph Inge (1860–1954), Dean of St Paul's Cathedral (1911–34), was a Christian Platonist who attacked the doctrine of progress while accepting the modern scientific account of the natural world. In this passage, Grant is contrasting Oman's insistence on a Christian account of nature with Inge's 'reconciliation' of Christianity with the scientific account of nature. Grant refers specifically to *God and the Astronomers* (1934), where Inge argues that the law of entropy points to a creation in time by some Power outside the degenerative process which science observes. (The second law of thermodynamics states that if no outside energy is applied to a system, its entropy – its state of disorder – will stay constant or increase, but never decrease.)

2  Blaise Pascal (1623–1662), French mathematician, philosopher, and theologian, was perhaps the most famous of the Jansenists (see note 9, chapter 1). Grant is concerned in this passage with Pascal's belief that true religion is beyond reason and even asserted in defiance of reason. Grant often read and was moved by Pascal, and later paid special attention to his account of the necessary and the Good. According to Sheila Grant, Grant was also moved by the novels of François Mauriac, whose position is said to be 'Jansenist.'

3  Martin Buber (1878–1965), Jewish existentialist philosopher and mystic, argued in *I and Thou* (1922) that there is a basic difference between relating to an object (I–It relation) and relating to a person (I–Thou relation). He believed the true relation to the living God is actualized when we address Him, not when we think about Him.

4  Matthew Arnold (1822–1888) wrote this famous phrase in 'Sonnet 2 – To a Friend.' Sophocles is the friend alleged to have seen life steadily and whole. Grant wrote many years later: 'We have been told that the saints in prayer can contemplate the whole steadily; it is reported that the philosophers can understand the meaning of the parts within the whole. But for the rest of us, seeing it steadily is not seeing it whole, and only a well-heeled bourgeois could have claimed that it was.' See George Grant, 'Céline's Trilogy,' in Arthur Davis, ed., *George Grant and the Subversion of Modernity: Art, Philosophy, Politics, Religion, and Education* (Toronto: University of Toronto Press 1996), 42.

5  The copy-text has this phrase from Matthew 7: 14 with 'strait' spelled 'straight.' Elsewhere in the text the phrase was corrected, but this instance had been overlooked.

6  The copy-text has 'loose' corrected to 'lose,' but the Oxford carbon copy was not corrected.

7  William James (1842–1910), American pragmatic philosopher and func-

tional psychologist, argued that objects are not duplicated in sense perception and that consciousness is not an entity but a function. James Ward (1843–1925), English philosopher and psychologist who taught at Cambridge during Oman's time there, argued that objects are generated in three phases in the mind from sense impression through percept to continuous image, and that we have only an inferred knowledge of ourselves.

## Chapter 4

1  The copy-text has 'all environment is related.' We changed the phrase to conform with 'those environments' in the next clause.
2  Charles Norris Cochrane (1889–1945), professor of Greek and Roman history in University College at the University of Toronto. Grant called Cochrane his teacher, meaning not that he had studied under him at Toronto, but that he had learned a great deal from his book *Christianity and Classical Culture* (1939). Grant refers to the last three chapters of Cochrane's book as the source of his criticism of Oman's account of Augustine (note †, pp. 324–5).
3  Samuel Johnson (1709–1784) defended common-sense realism about the existence of external objects on 6 August 1763, as recorded by Boswell: '... We stood talking for some time together of Bishop Berkeley's ingenious sophistry to prove the non-existence of matter, and that every thing in the universe is merely ideal. I observed, that though we are satisfied his doctrine is not true, it is impossible to refute it. I never shall forget the alacrity with which Johnson answered, striking his foot with mighty force against a large stone til he rebounded from it –"I refute it thus."' (New York: Everyman Edition, Knopf, 1992), 295–6.
4  John Bunyan (1628–1688), non-conformist English religious author and preacher, wrote *Grace Abounding to the Chief of Sinners* (1666) and *The Pilgrim's Progress* (1678), which, Grant felt, accurately portrayed the appalling difficulties free human beings experience seeking and meeting God, and then describing that experience, as Plato, Augustine, and Bonaventure also did.
5  The copy-text has 'In saying this.' We corrected the grammatical slip.
6  Norman Kemp Smith (1872–1958), professor of logic and metaphysics at Edinburgh. Grant is referring to Kemp Smith's *Is Divine Existence Credible?* (1931), Cook Wilson's paper 'Rational Grounds of Belief in God' (first drafted in 1897) in *Statement and Inference* (1926), vol. II, and Webb's *Divine Personality and Human Life* (1920). See note 22, chapter I, for Grant's critical remarks about Cook Wilson and C.C.J. Webb.
7  John Ruskin (1819–1900), English art critic and social thinker, argued in 'Of

The Pathetic Fallacy,' chapter 12 in *Modern Painters*, Vol III, that poets (and we ourselves) should be wary of endowing nature with human feelings when they (and we) ought better to receive nature as what it is. Oman may be referring to this argument.

8  Grant objected to Oman's oversimplified indentification of Kant with the human centred heresies, and Hegel with the overarching orthodoxies, because, for one thing, it tended to trivialize both Kant and Hegel along with Augustine and Calvin, and also to trivialize the human-centred 'modern heresies.' He deplored too easy refutations of Kant by believers when they underestimated the power of his argument. Arminianism is named after the Dutch theologian Jacobus Arminius (1560–1609), who opposed Calvin. He argued that human freedom still obtains in the state of grace, that the divine decree is contingent upon the individual's repentance or its absence, that believers may be certain of their salvation, and that the regenerate can live without sin. See note 2, chapter I, for 'pelagianism.'

9  Xenophanes (570–*c*.470 B.C.), Greek philosopher, argued that humans create the gods in their own image. If elephants had gods, they would be like elephants, if horses, like horses, and so on. He criticized Homer and Hesiod for attributing vice and crime to the gods and is considered a forerunner of Parmenides and the Eleatics since he argued that God (unlike the gods) is a changeless and unmoving unity, and that since God and nature are the same, change and movement are essentially illusory.

10  The editorial intervention is Grant's.

11  The copy-text has 'rights.' We have corrected this slip.

12  The copy-text has 'of' corrected to 'or,' but the Oxford carbon copy was not corrected.

13  The copy-text has 'difference' corrected to 'different,' but the Oxford carbon copy was not corrected.

14  Both copies have the words 'and freedom' struck through after the word 'universalism.'

15  Hastings Rashdall (1858–1924), theologian, philosopher, and historian, taught at Oxford, focusing primarily on the rational foundations of religion and ethics. He called his ethical position 'Ideal Utilitarianism' to distinguish it from Bentham's strict hedonism.

16  St Augustine's mother, Monica, was a fervent Christian who is recognized in Catholic tradition as a saint. In Book IX of the *Confessions*, Augustine gives a moving account of his mother's death in 387 and of her ability to forgive her husband's failings in a way that eventually drew the best from him. Grant may have been suggesting that Oman and Monica, because of their 'fine straight faith' and exemplary character, could not know the need to be forgiven as those of lesser faith know it.

**Chapter 5**

1 Adolph von Harnack (1851–1930), Lutheran church historian and theologian, is identified with the tradition of German liberal theology along with Ritschl (see Thesis Abstract, note 4).

2 In the copy-text 'others' has been corrected to 'other's.' We have corrected it to 'others'.

3 In the copy-text 'Knew' has been corrected to 'knew,' but the Oxford carbon copy was not corrected.

4 Charles Gore (1853–1932), Anglo-Catholic bishop and theologian, delivered the Bampton Lectures (1891) entitled *The Incarnation of the Son of God* in which he argued primarily for the divinity of Christ. He had earlier edited and published a controversial collection of essays called *Lux Mundi: a series of studies in the religion of the incarnation* (1889). J.R. Illingworth contributed (see chap. 1, note 3), and Gore argued that biblical inspiration had to be kept in context with the rest of the work of the Holy Spirit in the Church. Gore later was Bishop of Worcester (1901), Birmingham (1904), and Oxford (1911–19).

5 Albert Schweitzer (1875–1965), German medical missionary, musician, philosopher, and theologian, looked upon Jesus as a historical figure who believed the destruction of the world was imminent, and who must therefore introduce the Messianic age. Schweitzer's writings include *Paul and His Interpreters* (1912), *Christianity and the Religions of the World* (1923), and *The Quest for the Historical Jesus* (1926).

6 Rt Hon. Lord Eustace Sutherland Campbell Percy (1887–1958), Baron Percy of Newcastle, 1953, was in the British Diplomatic Service from 1909 to 1919, conservative MP for Hastings from 1921 to 1937, the parliamentary secretary to the Board of Health from 1923 to 1924, and president of the Board of Education from 1924 to 1929. In addition to *The Christian Congregation* (1945), cited in Grant's note, Lord Percy's works include *The Responsibilities of the League* (1920), *Education at the Crossroads* (1930), and *John Knox* (1937).

7 Arnold Joseph Toynbee (1889–1965), philosopher of history who taught at the London School of Economics. He states, for example, in 'My View of History,' that 'while civilizations rise and fall ... some purposeful enterprise, higher than theirs, may all the time be making headway, and, in a divine plan, the learning that comes through the suffering caused by the failures of civilizations may be the sovereign means of progress.' See *Civilization on Trial* (New York: Oxford University Press 1948), 15.

8 Thucydides (*c*.460–*c*.399 B.C.), Athenian historian, was a student of politics and a general commander of the Athenian forces in Thrace. His work *The*

*Peloponnesian War* projects the tragic inevitability of the destruction of the Greek city-states in that war.

Oswald Spengler (1880–1936), German author of *The Decline of the West* (1918). See note 4 in Grant's review of *The Machiavellians* by James Burnham.

9  William Manson (1882–1958) published *The Incarnate Glory, an Expository Study of the Gospel according to St John* (1923), *The Gospel of Luke* (1930), and *Jesus the Messiah, the Synoptic Tradition of the Revelation of God in Christ with special reference to Form-Criticism* (1943). For Professor Farmer, see note 5, Thesis Abstract.

10  J. Wilhelm Herrmann (1846–1922), German liberal Protestant theologian, emphasized that faith should be grounded in a direct experience of the reality of the life of Christ rather than in doctrine. He was a disciple of Ritschl and influenced Barth and Bultmann. For Ritschl see note 4, Thesis Abstract; for von Harnack see note 1.

Donald Macpherson Baillie (1887–1954), professor of Systematic Theology at St Andrews in Scotland. The full title of the book Grant is citing is *God Was in Christ: An Essay on Incarnation and Atonement* (1948).

11  Peter Taylor Forsyth (1848–1921), English Congregationalist minister and theologian, became principal of Hackney Theological College in 1901. He emphasized the place of grace in theology and stressed Christ's confession of God's holiness as the element in His experience that gives it atoning value. He was later thought to have anticipated Karl Barth's theology. Grant may be referring to Forsyth's *The Cruciality of the Cross* (London: Hodder and Stoughton 1909).

12  Athanasius (*c*.298–373), theologian, saint, Bishop of Alexandria (328), and one of the Doctors of the Church. His theology focused on the incarnation of God in Christ as the central principle of Christianity. In his dispute with the Arians, undertaken in defence of the doctrine of the trinity, he argued that the Father and the Son are of the same essence in contrast to the Arian view which subordinated the Son to the Father. The Council of Constantinople adjudicated the dispute in favour of Athanasius in 381.

13  The copy-text has the following sentence struck through after '... God's care for all men means': 'Oman would say that he at least cannot attempt to define why at that particular moment in history God revealed the true nature of His Mind.'

## Chapter 6

1  Richard Hooker (1553–1600), English theologian and political philosopher, drew upon various currents of medieval thought to explain the ecclesiastical and political institutions of Elizabethan England in his *Of the Laws of*

*Ecclesiastical Polity.* His purpose was to articulate a view of law supporting the relations of church and state as they had developed in the Church of England, while answering the objections of the Calvinists. Grant read Hooker later when he was more interested in the history of political philosophy, and expecially the influence of Calvinism in the genesis of twentieth century society. In *English-Speaking Justice* (1974) (p. 64) he quotes Hooker attacking Calvinist theological voluntarism in the name of the theologies of the Platonic world: 'They err who think that of the will of God to do this or that, there is no reason beside his will.'

2  Vladimir Sergeyevich Soloviev (1853–1900), Russian philosopher and mystic, attempted a synthesis of religious philosophy, science, and ethics in *The Crisis of Western Philosophy* (1874), *Lectures on Godmanhood* (1878), and *Foundations of Theoretical Philosophy* (1897 9).

3  Vatican Council I opened on 8 December 1869, and suspended sessions on 1 September 1870. On 18 July 1870 the council promulgated the constitution *Pastor aeternus,* which defined the jurisdictional primacy and infallibility of the Pope, shocking many liberal Christians at the time. The council strengthened the spiritual power of the papacy at a time when it was losing the temporal authority it had held for a millennium.

4  Alfred Firmin Loisy (1857–1940), French priest and biblical exegetist, best known for his modernist critiques of earlier scholars like Ernest Renan, for which he was eventually excommunicated. Oman cites from pages 122 and 150 of *The Gospel and the Church* (1902).

5  Karl Theodor Jaspers (1883–1973), German psychiatrist and philosopher, taught at Heidelberg (1921–37; 1945–7) and Basel (1948). Known as a philosopher of *Existenz,* he argued that human beings achieve *Existenz* when they become aware of themselves standing in their historical situation with an attitude of freedom and openness before what encompasses them, an attitude that transcends objective thought. Grant cites Jaspers's Geneva lecture entitled *Vom Europäischen Geist* (1946), translated and published by SCM as *The European Spirit* (1948).

6  See note 16, chapter 1.

7  The copy-text has the following sentence struck through at the end of this paragraph: 'Throughout history it has not been the "natural man" who has distrusted art and metaphysics.'

8  Rudolph Sohm (1841–1917), German canonist and church historian, concluded in *The Institutes of Roman Law* (1892) and *Outlines of Church History* (1895) that the development of ecclesiastical canon law had perverted the authentic Christian faith.

9  Gerard Manley Hopkins (1844–1889), English poet and churchman, always believed his poetic gifts should serve God and be subject to the discipline of

the church. He expressed this view in the poem that follows. Hopkins became a Catholic in 1866 and a Jesuit in 1868, ministered to various parish churches, and later taught Greek and Latin. His most famous poems include 'God's Grandeur,' 'The Windhover,' 'Carrion Comfort,' 'Pied Beauty,' and 'Hurrahing in Harvest.' Grant used Hopkins's poem 'That Nature Is a Heraclitean Fire and of the comfort of the Resurrection,' many years later in his classes on Christianity at McMaster University.

10 The lines are from 'To what serves Mortal Beauty?'

11 Leonard Hodgson (1889-1969), English theologian. On the subject of the Church, see also Hodgson's *Doctrine of the Church as held and taught in the Church of England* (1946). See Grant's footnote *, p. 298, chapter 5, where Grant praises Hodgson's argument for the relation of faith and philosophy.

12 John Morley (1838–1923), Gladstonian Liberal statesman, editor, and philosophical critic. Near the end of his career, as member of Asquith's cabinet in 1914, he opposed the decision to go to war with Germany. Morley had served as Chief Secretary for Ireland (1886 and 1892), and Secretary of State for India (1905), and written a life of Gladstone (1903). He was elevated to the peerage in 1908 as first Viscount Morley of Blackburn.

13 Rudyard Kipling (1865–1936), English poet, short-story writer, and novelist. 'McAndrew's Hymn' (1893) is a portrait of a ship's engineer that brings together toughness, Calvinist predestination, the love of hard work, and the love of steam technology.

14 William James (1842–1910), American psychologist and philosopher, discusses 'the contrast between the two ways of looking at life which are characteristic respectively of what we called the healthy-minded, who need to be born only once, and of the sick souls, who must be twice-born in order to be happy' (*The Varieties of Religious Experience* [1902; London: Longmans, Green, 1916], 166–7). James attributes this idea to Francis W. Newman, *The Soul: Its Sorrows and Aspirations*, 3d ed. [London, 1852], 89 and 91). See note 7, chapter 3.

15 The lines are from 'I wake and feel the fell of dark.'

## Chapter 7

1 John Maynard Keynes (1883–1946), English economist, in chapter 3 of *Tract on Monetary Reform* (1923) entitled 'Theory of Money and the Exchanges,' says the Quantity Theory is true 'in the long run,' and adds: 'But this *in the long run* is a misleading guide to current affairs. *In the long run* we are all dead. Economists set themselves too easy, too useless a task if in tempestuous seasons they can only tell us that when the storm is long past the ocean

is flat again.' See John Maynard Keynes, *Monetary Reform* (New York: Harcourt Brace 1924), 88.

2  Thomas Edward Lawrence (1888–1935), known as Lawrence of Arabia, discusses Christianity, Arab religion, and his own despair in chapters 3 and 63 of his most important work, *Seven Pillars of Wisdom* (privately published 1926, 1935). He contrasts the direct Arab experience of God with his own experience of a 'God [that] is so wistfully veiled from [him] by despair of [his] carnal unworthiness of Him and by the decorum of formal worship' (pp. 40–1). Grant may have been suggesting that Lawrence succumbed to despair because of a fear that joy was no longer possible for someone such as himself. We were unable to find any exact expression of fear that joy was an illusion.

3  See note 9, chapter 1.

4  The copy-text has 'proceeding' corrected to 'preceding,' but the Oxford carbon copy has not been corrected.

5  Emil Brunner (1899–1966), Swiss Protestant theologian, taught at Zurich. In contrast to Barth's crisis theology, he held that humans, though unable to provide their own salvation, were able to respond to God.

6  The copy-text has 'straight' corrected to 'strait,' but the Oxford carbon copy has not been corrected.

7  William McDougall (1871–1938), Anglo-American psychologist, taught at London, Oxford, Harvard, and Duke universities. For his account of 'feelings' and 'emotions' see chap. XII of his *Outlines of Psychology* (1923), titled 'The Derived Emotions,' 338–50. The 'derived emotions' include joy, sorrow, chagrin, disappointment, surprise, regret, remorse, confidence, hope, anxiety, despondency, and despair; they are distinguished by McDougall from 'primary' or 'blended' emotions.

8  Lady Julian or Juliana of Norwich (1342–1416), English mystic. This phrase is quoted from a passage which reads: 'Sin is behovely, but all shall be well, and all shall be well, and all manner of thing shall be well' (from chap. 27 of *Showings* or *Revelations of Divine Love*). Lady Julian received a series of visions on 8 May 1373. Her account of the visions, and of her meditations twenty years later, were published as the *Showings*. She was assured by her visions that everything is held in being by the love of God so that 'all will be well.'

## Appendix A

1  'Reiver' (or 'reaver') is a Scottish word for robber, plunderer, marauder, or raider.

2  Leopold von Ranke (1795–1886), German scientific historian, is best

known for his phrase 'wie es eigentlich gewesen ist' ('how it actually happened').

3  Auguste Comte (1789–1857), French philosopher and social theorist, usually regarded as the founding father of sociology. According to his positivist philosophy every science and every society must pass through theological and metaphysical stages on the way to the positive, scientific stage which is their proper goal.

4  Cornelis Petrus Tiele (1830–1902), Dutch historian of religion, made the distinction between religions of nature and ethical religions in order to show that the history of religion is the story of raising, for God, the ethical temple of universal humanity.
   Hermann Siebeck (1842–1920), German philosopher of religion who taught at Basel and Giessen. Oman appreciated Siebeck's work even though he disagreed with his way of classifying religions in terms of ethics.

5  The copy-text has 'others' corrected to 'other's'; we changed it to 'others'.

6  The copy-text has 'reflexion' corrected to 'awareness.'

7  Bernhard Ankermann (1859–1943), German historian of primitive religions, customs, and laws. Oman used his account of primitive religion (in *Lehrbuch der Religionsgeschichte*, Vol. I, ed. 4, editors A. Bertholet and E. Lehmann, pp. 131 ff.), as a starting point for his own account in *The Natural and the Supernatural*.

8  The copy-text has the word 'brilliantly' struck through before the word 'illuminates.'

9  Rabindranath Tagore (1861–1941), Indian poet, novelist, and philosopher, concentrated on central truths which mediate among all positions. According to Sheila Grant, her husband frequently used a prayer by Tagore when taking a service for students: 'Give me the supreme faith of love, this is my prayer; the faith of the life in death, of the victory in defeat, of the power hidden in the frailness of beauty, of the dignity of pain that accepts hurt but disdains to return it.' She and Grant both owned copies of a book of poems translated by Tagore into English prose entitled *Gitanjali* (1914). Grant's copy had originally been given to his mother by his father.
   Mahatma Gandhi (1869–1948), pacifist and leader of Indian independence, was assassinated in 1948. Grant, when he heard about the assassination, wrote in a letter that 'his being was of the quality that makes it possible for less clear lights like us to know where to go.' Grant never ceased in later years to admire Gandhi's exemplary wedding of pacifism with political action.

10  Grant here uses the word 'mysticism' in a broad sense when he includes Augustine and Gregory.
   Gregory I, the Great (*c*.540–604), Pope (590), saint, and father of the church,

was known as a great church administrator; as a reformer of the church, including its mass and liturgy; and for sending a religious mission to England.

Bernard of Clairvaux (1090–1153), French theologian, reformer, and saint (canonized in 1174), was Abbot of the Cistercian monastery of Clairvaux in Champagne. He was studious, ascetic, and eloquent, and his 'fervid piety' and living grasp of Christian doctrine contrasted with the scholasticism of the age. His fourth stage of love involves the annihilation of the self in a vision of God.

11 William James (1842–1910) (chap. 6, note 14) argued (in pragmatic terms) for the comforting truth of religious belief while criticizing its moral irresponsibility. Believers in the Absolute treat the temporal as if it were potentially the eternal and are able to drop the worry of our finite responsibility. 'In short, they mean that we have a right ever and anon to take a moral holiday, to let the world wag in its own way, feeling that its issues are in better hands than ours, and are none of our business.' (*Pragmatism* and *The Meaning of Truth* [Cambridge, Mass.: Harvard University Press 1975], 41 (further references to 'moral holiday': 43, 56, 171, and 289–90).

12 Grant thought Oman was wrong to argue that mysticism was antithetical to responsibility in the world. Grant cites examples of lives given to charity and contemplation that he thinks should obviously be considered 'responsible.'

St Catherine of Siena (Caterina Benincasa) (1347–1380), Italian mystic and saint (canonized 1461), became a Dominican at the age of sixteen, and is their patron saint.

St Teresa of Avila (1515–1582), Spanish mystic, was turned toward contemplation by conversion and entered a Carmelite convent at age forty.

St John of the Cross (1542–1592), Spanish mystic and poet in the Carmelite order, founded, with Teresa, a new branch of the order.

Jacob Boehme, or Jakob Böhme (1575–1624), German mystic and Lutheran religious philosopher, thought that God is the 'Ungrund,' the undifferentiated absolute. He had a profound effect on German romanticism, especially on F.W.J. Schelling.

13 Meister Eckhart (c.1260–1327/8), German mystic, and a Dominican who taught in Paris. The scintilla, or 'spark,' refers to the ground of the soul. Eckhart believed that through contemplation it is possible to attain to this uncreated and uncreatable ground.

# Appendix 1
# Upper Canada College, 1933–1936

A LAKE

A poem written at the age of fourteen. It appeared in 'In Between Times,'
Supplement to the *College Times*, edited by Giff Robertson, 1933.

It sparkles in the morning light,
It glimmers in the evening shade,
The greenish waters deep and clear,
Surrounded by the rocky shores,
On which pine, birch and poplar bright,
Grow, where in the spring the seed was laid,
At one end is a beavers weir,
O'er which the water gently pours.

1935
THE AMERICAN BREAKFAST TABLE

A short literary piece written at the age of sixteen. It appeared in 'In
Between Times,' Supplement to the *College Times*, 1935.

Mrs Dudley Copperplate was moved to the roots of her inmost soul.
Her husband had just announced that he had invested a large sum in a
motion picture company. The enormity of this offence seems obscure to
an ordinary stranger. But Mrs Copperplate was the President of the
'Legion of Decency' for Sackertown.

'We, the daughters of Liberty,' heaved Mrs Copperplate, 'are
attempting to lift the yoke of immorality from the shoulder of the

Youth of America while you invest your money in some lousy degrading Company which will pollute the minds of our children. You must get rid of those shares.' The shares were sold. From Texas to Maine, anxious husbands hurriedly sold their stock.

Herbert Lambon was beaming with joy. He was pointing at the morning paper in front of him with a finger which quivered with excitement. His wife came down-stairs and noticing his unusual good temper asked him what was the matter.

'I've won my bet; I've beaten Ed,' he cried, 'The President has fired the new Brain Trust. I bet Ed Bennett that they wouldn't last till the end of the month and they were kicked out before the fifteenth. The good old Democrats. I told you that they would save the country.'

'Can I go and see Bruno's jurors when they come to town?' pleaded the rash Jimmie Robinson to his mother.

'Of course not! Now why don't you want to see dear little Shirley Temple? Little sister and I went yesterday and thought that she was too cute.'

'Mum, why can't we see the Mae West picture instead of Shirley Temple's?'

'Don't be ridiculous. Why really! Imagine the child getting those terrible thoughts into his head at his age. What would happen next. Those Mae West pictures were alright for father and his friends but for the children!'


PICASSO

A poem written at the age of sixteen. It appeared in 'In Between Times,' Supplement to the *College Times*, edited by R.D. Hutchison, 1935.

On cubes and squares, Picasso
   The modern critic feeds.
'Oh isn't Pablo too sublime'
   'He soars, he builds, he leads.'

'To think that Spain produced this man!'
   With rapture they elate

Velasquez and El Greco are
  Completely out of date

'A one man revolution'
  'Our one and only light'
'My dear! of course! it is the vogue
  To be a Picassite.'


PEACE

This poem, handwritten and undated, seems to have been written while Grant was at Upper Canada College and possibly near the time he requested exemption from the cadet corps along with his friend and fellow pacifist, Michael Gelber.

Its echoing and far echoing sounds
Reach over earth to where on heaven's throne
Almighty God sits in his pomp alone
And when he sees he smiles
And when on his smile comes life
Which is our hope and our salvation.

# Appendix 2
## Excerpts from *Citizens' Forum* Program Study Bulletins, 1943–1944

Overall Title: 'Of Things to Come: A *Citizens' Forum* on Canada in the Post-war World'

Grant, at twenty-four, accepted a position as national secretary with the Canadian Association for Adult Education (CAAE). As part of his work, he collaborated with his colleague Jean Hunter Morrison writing study bulletins to accompany the weekly *Citizens' Forum* programs broadcast by the CBC. The bulletins were intended as guides for study and discussion in all the local Citizens' Forum chapters and were widely distributed across the country before each program.

The bulletins were found in the Archives of Ontario in the files relating to the CAAE for the *Citizens' Forum* period (CAAE papers F 1205, series B I and B II). Unfortunately, the CAAE papers do not help us with the question of Grant's and Morrison's respective contributions to the writing of the bulletins. It is possible that Grant did more of the writing on international questions, and Morrison more on domestic ones, since Grant's work at Queen's had focused on international relations, but we do not have any actual proof that this was the case. Nor do Morrison's other writings help us make a judgment, since they are not different enough in style from Grant's writings of the 1940s. A 'Report on the Citizens' Forum Programme – 1943–44' states that the bulletins 'were written after six months preliminary research on the part of the writers – George Grant (National Secretary of Citizens' Forum, former student at Queen's University and Rhodes Scholar studying law at Oxford) and Jean Hunter Morrison (Editor of *Food for Thought* and graduate of McGill with M.A., *magna cum laude*, in sociology). Each bulletin ... was checked as to accuracy by Dr John Robbins, Secretary of the Canadian Council on Education for Citizenship, and member of the staff of the Dominion Bureau of Statistics ... The average weekly distribution was 13,500 copies of each bulletin; 8,500 went to civilian groups, and 5,000 were purchased by the Canadian Legion Educational Services and used by listening groups in the Forces.'

Broadcasts featured three speakers, including such well-known Canadians as Charlotte Whitton, Paul Martin Sr, Frank Underhill, Frank Scott, Mrs Pierre Casgrain, Roland Michener, Reverend Endicott, Arthur Lower, Vernon Fowke, M.J. Coldwell, Bessie Touzel, and Grattan O'Leary. Grant was unhappy with the contribution of Morley Callaghan as moderator. In a letter to Corbett, dated 26 January 1944, he said: 'Listening to the broadcast last night, I had a feeling that Callaghan didn't know exactly what were the important points to be discussed in housing and therefore didn't get across a clear, interesting picture ... If this is to be an effective piece of education, I feel that somehow the CAAE must impress on Callaghan that it is not his woolly ideas that go over the air, but a well-planned and thought out script.'

The bulletins taken as a whole present a remarkable compendium of progressive Canadian thinking in the 1940s, dealing with unemployment, social security, health care, education, the constitution, agriculture, and external relations involving the United Nations, the Commonwealth, the Soviet Union, Asia, and the United States. Each was followed by sections of information and questions under the headings: MORE INFORMATION, FILMS, REPORT QUESTIONS, THINGS TO DO, AND QUESTIONS FOR FURTHER GROUP DISCUSSION. Each was dated to coincide with programs on consecutive Tuesdays from 7 December 1943 to 2 May 1944.

The editors have selected Bulletins No. 8 and 11, entitled 'One People – Two Cultures' and 'Canada in the Anglo-American World,' to be presented in their entirety, because of the importance of the French–English and Canada–United States themes for Canada, themes that are taken up by Grant twenty years later in *Lament for a Nation*. The remainder of the section includes excerpts from other bulletins to reflect the broad range of thought on domestic and foreign, economic and political matters that Grant and Morrison addressed, providing some evidence of Grant's 1943 positions on these matters for comparison with his later writings.

A list of the bulletin titles follows, including No. 6 and 14, which are missing from the collection in the archive:

Bulletin No. 1    The New Demand, The Right to Work
Bulletin No. 2    Public and Private Enterprise – A New Partnership?

Bulletin No. 3    Social Security
Bulletin No. 4    The Right to Be Healthy
Bulletin No. 5    The School Comes First
Bulletin No. 6    A Man's Own Castle [Missing]
Bulletin No. 7    The Constitutional Barrier
Bulletin No. 8    One People, Two Cultures
Bulletin No. 9    Canadians – World Citizens
Bulletin No. 10   Canada in the British Commonwealth
Bulletin No. 11   Canada in the Anglo-American World
Bulletin No. 12   The New Relationship with Soviet Russia
Bulletin No. 13   The Rise of Asia
Bulletin No. 14   Our Trade With the World [Missing]
Bulletin No. 15   The Fascist Nations in Defeat
Bulletin No. 16   The New World Order
Bulletin No. 17   The Soldier Comes Home
Bulletin No. 18   The People on the Land
Bulletin No. 19   Who Shapes the Future?
Bulletin No. 20   Action Now

**Excerpt from Bulletin No. 1**
**The New Demand, The Right to Work**
**Tuesday, 7 December**

All over the world a new demand has arisen: the right to work, usefully and creatively. One planning agency in the United States has put this as article I in A New Bill of Rights. Certainly it represents the most fundamental hope in the minds of ordinary people when they think of a better world after the war. For without jobs for all, the post-war period will hold nothing for them but despair.

Like other men of every nation, Canadians are worrying about what it will be like after the war. They are saying: if we can mobilize all our resources and manpower for a total war-effort, why can't we mobilize them for peace and plenty? Does it take a world war to find employment for all our young men? Workers in war-industry wonder where they will find a job when the war-orders cease; men in the forces – thousands and thousands of them – will be looking for work when demobilization day comes.

*The Hungry Thirties*

Probably the chief reason people are *demanding* that somehow the right to work must be *guaranteed* is because the dominant memory in everybody's experience is the joblessness of the 'thirties.

We might as well face the facts, right at the beginning, about this pre-war decade. Unless we realize the extent of our failure to provide full employment, we can't be realistic about the steps which need to be taken to ensure jobs for all after this war.

The depression hardly needs to be 'described.' It is etched on too many minds with the strong acid of suffering.

*Why the Depression?*

The results of the depression are certainly familiar to us all. But what causes depressions? How can they be prevented? What can we do to see that another one doesn't occur after this war?

There are many different theories about the cause. We won't attempt to review them here. There are, however, certain factors which obviously had a bearing on the last depression, whether or not they were the only causes.

*World Conditions:* The well-being of the whole Canadian economy depends on world markets where we can sell our surplus products. Before this war, Canada was the fifth largest exporting country in the world. A comparatively few products constitute the great bulk of exports: wheat and flour, pulp and paper, lumber, precious and base metals, fish. During the depression our total gross value of exports declined by 61.5% and our imports by 67.9%. In other words, we lost almost two-thirds of our foreign markets, because of the world's economic collapse. This naturally brought about a drastic shrinkage in our whole economy.

*Internal Factors:* Another factor in the depression was the monopolistic structure of our economy. As the Rowell-Sirois Report points out:[1]

Business organization has everywhere become increasingly monopolistic. In Canada, industry, commerce, and finance are highly centralized and in many branches a few enterprises dominate the field. Under such conditions the maintenance of prices is possible in the face of declining demands. The monopolistic producers may consider that they are better off by selling less at higher prices than by selling more at lower prices. Consequently, the burden tends to fall upon the workers who lose their jobs through the reduction in output and on the exporters whose costs are thus held rigid while their prices on world markets are sharply reduced.[2]

In other words, when world trade fell off sharply, monopolies tended to meet this contingency by retaining high prices and selling less. This produced several results. Employment dropped, and wages were lowered. With shrinking external markets and decreased purchasing power at home, profits were uncertain so business couldn't embark on a programme of expansion to reduce the unemployment.

Urban and industrial workers found their jobs disappearing or their wages dropping. The farmer kept on producing, but most of his machinery and supplies had to be bought from highly monopolistic concerns. He had to sell much of his produce either on the foreign market (as wheat) or to distributing companies (like packing plants, dairy concerns) where several enterprises dominate the entire field. Thousands of individual producers were dealing with a few large and powerful concerns. Hence, the farmers were faced with relatively fixed costs of equipment, and sharply lowered prices for their products.

So the farmer couldn't buy the goods manufactured by industrial workers, and city-workers couldn't afford enough food. In a similar deadlock in the United States, the government undertook to get things going again by increasing public purchasing power through government expenditures on public works. In Canada we did very little, and that only on an uncoordinated, spasmodic basis, to mitigate the effects of the depression by government investment. True, we could hardly expect to escape the effects of shrinking world trade – but we found no measures to break the vicious circle, or temper the severity of the suffering.

Previous to 1929, we had always discovered some great area of expansion which pulled us out of slumps – the wheatlands of the prairies, the mining frontiers in northern Quebec and Ontario, or the great pulpwood areas. In 1929 we hit bedrock. We could find no way of transforming a rapidly contracting economy into a once more expanding one. We could find no way – until the war came along.

...

**Excerpt from Bulletin No. 2**
**Public and Private Enterprise – A New Partnership**
**Tuesday, 14 December**

*After the War - What?*

Will government and business carry on this war-partnership into peace time, to achieve full employment?

There seems to be little expression of opinion in Canada now in favour of dropping the government's war-time controls immediately at the close of the war. Most business leaders are speaking in favour of a 'government–management offensive for full employment.'

*Government as Pinch-Hitter.* But what is to be the role of government in the new partnership that so many people are predicting? Is it to be merely a 'Pinch-hitter,' stepping in when a private enterprise economy gets into an emergency as one prominent spokesman for business suggests?

...

... varying points of view show clearly that this is a question which Canadians must weigh carefully, examining the arguments on both sides.

*Control – By Whom?*

Although, as we have seen, most sections of the Canadian population agree that at least some government intervention will have to continue after the war, there are differing views about in whose interest this control should and will be exercised. Will it be control by the people and for the people or control in the interests of some special group?

In a brief to the ... parliamentary committee, the Canadian Congress of Labour criticizes the dominance of big business in war-time controls. The issue, they claim, is not whether we shall have controls, but *who* will exercise the controls: representatives of big business alone, or representatives of organized labour, smaller business, farmers, and consumers as well.

...

The emphasis here is on *democratic* state control, with all sections of the population represented on both war-time and peace-time planning agencies.

...

**Excerpt from Bulletin No. 3**
**These Social Security Plans**
**Tuesday, 21 December**

Social security has become almost a catchword these days. There are many definite reasons why so many people are interested in social security at this time. They have known insecurity in the past, and they hope that somehow a better world after the war will do away with the worst depths of poverty. It actually means a guarantee on the part of the whole community that no one in the community will be allowed to fall below a certain standard of living. As a prominent United Nations leader has put it:

> The idea behind the social security system is that in so far as a person is unable to care for himself or herself then it is a collective responsibility to see that those things necessary for physical welfare and cultural life are made available to them.

First of all, social security planners assume that we shall somehow achieve relatively full employment, either by private enterprise, or private enterprise plus public works, paid for by the government. They recognize that without this, all plans for social security must fail. But they go on to claim that contingencies will be present, even if we have full employment, which must be met not by the individual but by the whole community. These plans are intended not to be a substitute for full employment, but supplementary to it. They fill the gaps employment does not touch.

Advocates of social security claim that in this day and age it is very largely outside the grasp of an individual by himself to achieve economic security. He has little control over wage levels. Sickness, sudden death, disability may strike him and cut off his earning power. He can do little either to prevent or meet these emergencies.

**Excerpt from Bulletin No. 5**
**The School Comes First**
**Tuesday, 18 January**

[Much of this fifth bulletin draws on the *Report of the Survey Committee of the Canada and Newfoundland Education Association*. There is unfortunately very little discussion of curriculum and specifically no mention of liberal education.]

The most telling characteristic of any society is *how it treats its children*. This reveals more about the nature of that society than any declarations or statistics. The standards actually achieved in nutrition, child protection, education, and so on, show very plainly what value a nation places on human life. Many recent books have portrayed the fascist ideal for children: submissive, fanatical soldiers in miniature. In the democratic countries a rising tide of concern about child welfare has been an earmark of the 20th century.

To-night we are going to discuss one aspect of child welfare: the educational system. Obviously, our schools are one of the great forces moulding each new generation of Canadians to a pattern which may be good or bad.

[The bulletin discusses inequality in the schools, particularly the disparity between rural and urban schools, and then takes up the question of discrimination.]

*Discrimination.* The third obstacle to equal opportunity suggested by the Survey Report is discrimination against children because of their racial or religious background. This is more difficult to pin down, in a concrete way, than our other problems. It is, however, equally important. It may exist in the attitudes of Anglo-Saxon children to the 'foreign' child. If a child starts life with his race or creed held against him, we clearly have no equality in our schools.

...

*Specialization.* One further point must be noted about our schools. We are barely beginning to adapt our education to the needs of the vocational life our children will lead. There are only a handful of technical schools in the cities. There are only a few schools offering courses adapted to the needs of boys and girls who will be living on the land. For the most part, our high schools give a course training people only for college entrance and for commercial life.

*Education and the War*

These lacks in our educational system have been emphasized by the war. We have been wasting manpower because we have not keyed our educational system to children's needs, because we have not provided equality of opportunity for all Canadian children. In wartime we have found ourselves tragically short of properly trained personnel – from doctors and dentists to draughtsmen. We have had to speed up our college courses, and set up special training on a temporary and sometimes haphazard basis. Many small schools in this country have not been able to open this year. They could find no teachers. The situation is so serious that teachers have been frozen in their profession.

...

**Bulletin No. 8**
**One People, Two Cultures**
**Tuesday, 8 February**

One big question-mark springs up in the minds of many English-Canadians when they think of the post-war period. Can we build a better world in cooperation with the French-Canadians? This is the subject we shall discuss tonight. It is a very touchy one. Feeling runs high among both French-Canadians and English-Canadians. There's hidden dynamite in this problem.

But the hidden fact of the matter is that whether we like it or not, we will have no security and no prosperity in Canada unless it is achieved for all Canadians, unless French- and English-Canadians build it together.

We shall perform a real service to our country if we are prepared to look quite frankly, and as objectively as possible, at some of the difficulties which beset French–English relationships at the present time. Only if we uncover the real difficulties can we attempt to deal with them. We must have good-will, of course, but it must be realistic rather than sentimental, or it will only be a further stumbling block.

It is plainly impossible in a few thousand words to do justice to our subject. We shall have to touch on only a few major points. Members of groups are urged to consult the books listed at the end. They represent many different points of view about French–English relations, and present the complete picture which we cannot even attempt to outline.

Since this study course is being used primarily by English-Canadians, we shall try to interpret some of the less obvious and more fundamental characteristics of French-Canadian life. To get to the real problems, we need to dig below the surface and see what social and historical developments underlie the misunderstandings we are all so concerned about.

*One-Third of the Nation*

One of our first tasks is to try to rid our minds of the conception of a 'typical' French-Canadian, which we probably all have. Most of us have rather limited contact, often second-hand at that, with these fellow citizens of ours, and we tend to draw vivid pictures of them, mainly as quaint and romantic 'habitants.'

A prominent American sociologist points out:

> ... the French-Canadians are a people. They number millions and are of many kinds: corporation lawyers, financiers, savants, sophisticates, artists, women of fashion, city slickers, criminals, as well as the rustic farmers of the Lower St Lawrence Valley, the woodsmen of the north, and the fishermen of the Gaspé Peninsula. In villages, towns, and cities are small merchants, artisans, and the honoured priests and professional men. (E.C.Hughes, *French Canada in Transition* [page 2])[3]

*The French-Canadian Culture.* Yet, with all this variety, there is an underlying 'pattern,' a culture which binds the diverse elements together, so that we can quite rightly speak of a French-Canadian society. It had its beginnings long before English-Canadians appeared on the scene at all. When New France was ceded to the British, they took over not merely a stretch of territory, but a national group with a language and culture of its own, settled in a certain clearly defined geographic area. The British were the 'new comers,' the 'invaders.' This struggling little colony was now under 'foreign' control; the gentlemen adventurers who had exploited the fur trade, the political functionaries, and the majority of the seigneurs returned to France, leaving only one major institution, the Roman Catholic Church, which became the centre of French Canadian community life.

When a French-Canadian looks back on his history, the dominant theme is a struggle to maintain national identity beginning at the time when the positions of power and authority passed into the hands of outsiders. All official ties with France were cut in 1759. (However, as Abbé Maheux points out,[4] already in 1759 there were thousands of French-Canadians whose families had been in the new land for 75 or 100 years, and who had lost touch entirely with France, regarding themselves simply as 'Canadiens'). French is his mother tongue; Quebec is his homeland.

It hardly needs to be pointed out that this is in extreme contrast to the background of English-speaking Canadians. We have come in streams from every corner of Europe, the British Isles, and the United States. Few families, even of Anglo-Saxon descent, have been here a hundred years, while Europeans have generally arrived within the last fifty years. With some justification, the French-Canadians think of themselves as the only group with a purely Canadian background. In fact, they call themselves *les Canadiens*, while Anglo-Saxons are to them *les Anglais*.

It is precisely this contrast which makes it seem so ridiculous to our French fellow-Canadians when we say: 'Why don't the French all speak English?' or 'Assimilation would settle everything.'

*Rural Background.* For the French-Canadian is part of a closely woven web of community life whose roots in this country go back beyond any of ours. He belongs to a people which has maintained its identity for generations under constant pressure from English and American cultural influences.

This French-Canadian society has had a rural base. But it has also had its town life and its townspeople; businessmen, artisans, professionals, and so forth. In 1941 only 471 out of every thousand persons employed in Quebec were engaged in agriculture, even though the spirit of French-Canada was predominantly rural.

Farm families sent most of their sons (except those who inherit the family farm, or who may be established on another farm nearby) into the professions and the towns. Family solidarity was maintained during the time the children remained under the family roof, working on the farm which would go intact to only one of the sons. Family connections, with all their extensive ramifications, gave the individual his standing in the community. Even though a man became a doctor or a priest, or kept a store, he still had roots in a particular rural family, with a farm still in family hands in some part of Quebec.

The goods and services which were dispensed by the townspeople were those which served a dominantly rural population. Even industry was closely linked with rural life; potasheries, tanneries, sawmills, carriage factories, carding mills, etc. These employed few workers and only small amounts of capital.

*Industry Comes to Quebec*

We can see that French-Canada over a period of many generations had developed a relatively stable world of its own based on a simple, self-sufficient economy with little contact outside its borders. Two things have more recently upset this balance.

*Natural Increase.* In French-Canada where the subdivision of farmlands of necessity ceased nearly a hundred years ago, only one son could inherit the family farm. By the 1870s most of the good farming land had been taken up in the province. Few families could afford professional training for more than one or two offspring, and yet all of them except the inheriting son had to find some means of livelihood elsewhere. This drove French-Canadians into the two main outlets which presented themselves, before the turn of the century: taking up land which the English with their smaller families were willing or forced to sell, and immigration to the United States textile towns, where there was an unlimited demand for cheap labour. To some extent, French-Canadians spread out also into other provinces, chiefly neighbouring Ontario and New Brunswick.

Incidentally, it could be noted here that the displacement of English population by French is more easily explained by this pressure of population on the land rather than by any plot on the part of all French-Canadians to drive out the English.

This high rate of natural increase had one outstanding result. In every generation a large number of young people had to find their livelihood outside the traditional French-Canadian system. Hence the clerical and lay leaders had to reach out towards these people in an attempt to keep them French-Canadian and Catholic in the midst of an alien government.

*Industrialization.* The other main factor disturbing the stability of French-Canada is the entrance of big industry into Quebec. In Canada, as in other parts of the world, the British served as the handmaidens of the industrial revolution. The mainstream of British immigration into Canada came well after the industrial revolution had given Britain a dominant place in world industry and trade. Before Canada could be settled on any extensive scale and her resources of wheat-land and timber and minerals could be exploited, communication and transportation had to be built. It was the English, rather than the French-Canadians who had the prerequisites for opening up and industrializing the country. They had family and political connections which gave them access to pools of capital in Britain and in the United States. In addition, accumulation of capital in Canada, based on the lumber and fur-trade carried on by the English, and on the retail trade developed by Yankee and British merchants who came to the new British colony in its early days, provided the money which was necessary for the development of industry, transportation, and mining.

On the other hand, French society, with its family goals, its non-acquisitive philosophy, its classical education, and its small enterprises closely tied to the rural economy, did not produce the capital, the connections, or the skills at industrial organization which would give French-Canadians a leading role in this new economic life.

By the turn of the century, when mass-production industry was well-established in the United States, when monopolies were growing apace in Great Britain, and when Canada had developed export trade and a far-flung national market for goods and services stretching to the Pacific Coast, Quebec offered a frontier for the expansion of industrialism.

For here were huge forest tracts, water powers, and a pool of surplus labour, unskilled in industry, but adaptable, and from industry's point of view, untainted with the evils of trade unionism and working-class struggles.

From 1900 on, big industries have broken into Quebec society. The out-standing ones are textiles, mining and metallurgy, and pulp and paper.

> Of course, there are even today many small industries, but they are overshadowed by these great new ones, which are financed by outside capital, run by imported managers and technicians, and whose products are sold in a national or even international market. (Hughes [page 25])

True, many of these industries are concentrated around Montreal. But a large number have been literally 'planted' in the middle of small French-Canadian towns, bringing in their own staff from managers down through foremen to an initial group of skilled workers, who are of course, all English-speaking. The French-Canadians have provided the 'hands.'

When industry, already organized, establishes either a major or a branch plant into the middle of a French-Canadian community, it draws into that community part of the pool of surplus labour which Quebec with its large families and its particular landholding system has been accumulating for years. The French-Canadians come in at the bottom of industry, with the top ranks all filled with people of an alien culture. There is no other way for the French-Canadians to come in, for there is no link between their small industrial enterprises typical of an earlier stage of capitalism, and these modern giants. Nor do professional skills and classical education prepare French-Canadians for taking many positions of authority in this new structure.

*Results of Industrialization.* The results of this new development in Quebec will only work themselves out in years. It will be apparent that this set of circumstances has had profound influence upon French-English relations.

First of all, large numbers of French-Canadians are being drawn into mass-production industry. This means they are being put in a situation where the traditional ambitions of the French-Canadian to own his own enterprise, farm or store, cannot be realized. It further exposes them to all the stresses and strains of mass-production economy, intensified by the fact that the rates of pay are smaller, hours longer, and working conditions poorer than in other parts of Canada. In other words a French-Canadian urban working class, with problems very similar to those of English-Canadian workers, has grown up. But the complicating factor is that the 'bosses' are English. That is, they speak another language, and come from the group which has been regarded as a traditional threat to French-Canadian continuity.

This new industrialization not only fails to contribute materially to the prosperity of the French-Canadian middle class; it actually noses them out of their former prestige and security, by introducing another social structure in which they have only minor places. By creating urban French 'masses,' with no property stake in the community, it threatens the values the middle class attach to individual proprietorship and family solidarity. It is not surprising then that from this middle class come many of the nationalist leaders, whose message is often a combination of exhortation to the working class to retain the traditional French piety and virtues, anti-trust sentiment and resentment of the English 'bosses,' and covert criticism of the French-Canadian educational system which does not prepare people to compete with the English in the higher positions of industry. The dominant theme is the age-old struggle to maintain national rights and customs, but the new threat is from industrialism under English control.

At the top of the social structure, however, one finds a handful of French-Canadians acting on boards of directors of large English concerns, with outlook and interest somewhat similar to those of their English colleagues. And at the bottom one finds an unprecedented growth since the beginning of the war of international trade unionism among the French-Canadian workers, which binds them directly with the English-Canadian working class.

## Possibilities of Unity

There is one major problem out of all this crisis through which French-

Canada is passing, as regards Canadian unity. Is real understanding and cooperation possible between French-Canadians and English?

Now there are many things which can be done to promote unity, many things which are suggested daily by people of genuine good-will: the English-Canadians should learn to speak French; there should be exchange scholarships, exchange of teachers, visits, conferences between the people of the two national groups. All of these suggestions are perfectly good ones. More contacts certainly would do something to break down the mutual suspicion and sheer lack of knowledge about each other. But such gestures of good-will by themselves will not solve the deep-lying resentments and fears on both side, which have been fostered, if not originated, by the particular circumstances under which the industrialization of Quebec has taken place.

The main question is whether English-Canadians and French-Canadians will discover that they both face the problems of achieving a society of peace and plenty in an industrial age which has bred widespread insecurity, wars, and depressions, as well as the most advanced civilization and the most abundant material goods which the world has ever known. If they find this is their common problem, then they may discover how to solve it in common. Or, it might be put the other way round: if they discover how to co-operate in wiping out inequality, ignorance, poverty, disease, and squalor, then they may find that the major causes of conflict can be solved.

The great task before us is to realize our potential greatness as a nation, the richness of cultural diversity which is ours. We shall accomplish this only if French- and English-Canadians work together to build a strong and united Canada.

**Excerpt from Bulletin No. 9**
**Canadians – World Citizens**
**Tuesday, 15 February**

*During the Depression.* A good example of how we depend on world markets is what happened to us in the depression. In the years after 1929 the insecurity, selfishness, and suspicion produced in great part by the last war, caught up with the world. Each nation tried to protect itself against others by cutting off its imports from other nations. The result was, of course, that between 1929 and 1931 the volume of world trade fell 40%. How did this affect us in Canada? We were particularly hard hit. Every Canadian who lived through the depression will remember what it meant. The price of wheat, our chief export commodity, fell from 1.08 to 35 cents a bushel. It doesn't take much figuring to see what that did to the western farmer. And the effect was of course not limited to one section of the country. The whole national income dropped lower and lower. Teachers and doctors, truck-drivers and ministers, farmers and shopkeepers earned less. The productive machinery of the country had been thrown completely out of gear by the loss of the world markets. This is not to argue that Canada could not have done much to make the effect of the depression less hard for its citizens – but it is a fact, to quote the Rowell-Sirois report once again, that 'it was the sharp fall in export prices which pushed Canada down the incline of the depression.' Events in the outside world did much to make deadly for Canadians those years after 1929.

...

... it seems that we are dependent on what happens in all continents. By now, most Canadians should agree that the refusal of England to surrender in June 1940 was in fact protecting us. The fight of the Russians at Stalingrad in 1942 was in truth a shield for us. In the economic sphere the tariffs put up by Americans and Europeans against our goods in the early 1930's affected the livelihood of thousands of Canadians. The other side of the picture is that what we do affects the rest of the world. The fact that there was a well-equipped Canadian division in England in 1940 was, as Winston Churchill said, a vital factor in the ability of the free world to survive. Our policy of tariff restriction carried out at Ottawa in 1932 affected many businesses in other lands. We have the choice then: we may co-operate in world arrangements or we may not. But we should recognize that whether we do or whether we do not, events in the rest of the world are still going to affect our lives at every turn. We are part of one world.

...

**Bulletin No. 11**
**Canada in the Anglo-American World**
**Tuesday, 29 February**

The other day a Canadian newspaper reported the tale that Canada makes its policy three days a week in Washington, three days a week in London, and once a week at home in Ottawa. This story puts in an exaggerated form something that is essentially true. In the past our most intimate relations to the rest of the world have been for the most part with the U.S.A. and Great Britain. Those two countries have in many ways dominated our lives. We have seen last week how Canada has developed in the British Commonwealth from a colony of Great Britain into an independent country in our own right. But this fact of being a free nation does not mean that we are free from the influence of the U.S.A. and Great Britain. As the Rowell-Sirois Report has said:

> Canada's position in both her trade and financial relations with the outside world is largely that of her position in relation to the U.S.A. and United Kingdom. This position is similar to that of a small man sitting in a big poker game. He must play for the full stakes, but with only a fraction of the capital resources of his two substantial opponents.[5]

What is the role of a small country in this interdependent world? Will we be merely dominated either by one or the other of the big powers? Or will we be able to support a policy of our own towards the world? This question faces all the smaller countries of the world. They are wondering if they are going to have much to say in what happens after the war or whether they are going to be swamped by the big powers who will lay down what is to be done.

Last week we have examined the relationship between Canada and Great Britain – as one of the two most important relationships between Canada and the outside world. Tonight we will examine the ways in which Canada is tied up with the U.S.A. and how that tie-up will affect Canada in the post-war world.

*Canada and the U.S.A.*

*North American Neighbours.* Canada and the U.S.A. cover between them most of North America. Through the centre of this continent stretches horizontally a border of 4000 miles. Across that border thousands of people flow each year. Probably more Canadians (both English- and French-speaking) have relatives in the U.S.A. than in Great Britain.

Motion pictures, magazines, radio programmes flood into Canada from across the line. Factors like these are hard to measure, but they make anything but close relations almost unthinkable. Going into many cities, on either side of the border, it is difficult to find much difference in ordinary everyday life.

*Trade.* The effects of our trade relations are easier to calculate. Before the war, over 40% of our exports went to United States and over 60% of our imports came from there. In per capita figures, our trade to the U.S.A. was worth between $30 and $40 a year to every Canadian.

The newsprint, lumber, and mining industries are particularly dependent on American markets. If they continue to grow in importance, as they have during the last few years, then our dependence on American markets will grow. The effect of this trade connection is clear. Many Canadians depend for their livelihood upon producing goods that are sold in the States. If the U.S. adopts a policy that prevents our goods being sold, then many of us would be thrown out of work.

*Investment.* A new country like Canada needed vast sums of capital to develop its resources. Before the last war most of that capital came from Great Britain. Since the last war, however, most of it has come from the U.S.A. Today there is more American capital in Canada than that of any other country – more than three billion dollars' worth. What that means to Canadian life is clear. Many of our productive resources are owned and controlled either directly or indirectly by Americans. This control gives them a large stake in the life of our country. Because of this capital investment, the owners of this wealth in the U.S.A. are vitally interested in what happens in Canada.

*Labour.* It is not only capital that has flowed across the border. Labour organizations are also established internationally. Both the A.F. of L. and the C.I.O., the two main parts of the American labour movement, have affiliated organizations in Canada.

*Defence.* In 1938, President Roosevelt said:

> The Dominion of Canada is part of the sisterhood of the British empire. I give you the assurance that the people of the United States will not stand

idly by if domination of Canadian soil is threatened by any other empire.[6]

This statement, made at a time when Hitler and the Japanese war lords were growing increasingly stronger, was clear evidence of the close interest of the two countries in common defence. As the common danger grew, the common agreement became stronger. In August 1940, Canada and the U.S.A. signed the Ogdensburg Agreement, by which a Permanent Joint Defence Board was created. Since then, the Canadian and American governments have the following Joint Committees – Material Co-ordination, Economic, War Production, Agriculture, and War Aid, while Canada is part of Combined Production and Resources Board and the combined Food Board along with the U.S.A. [and] Great Britain. Since the entrance of the U.S.A. into war after Pearl Harbor in December 1941, the war efforts of the two countries have been increasingly linked.

Part of the mutual defence programme has been the development on Canadian soil of vast projects by the American government. The most famous of these is the Alaskan Highway, which serves as a road to Tokyo. There are also the development of the large oil resources in the Canadian North West and many other smaller projects. These will all serve to bring American influence deeper into Canadian life. The story is told that when one telephones the American army in Edmonton, the answer sometimes is 'American army of occupation.'

*After the War*

In December 1942, the two countries exchanged views on post-war planning, in which they stressed the benefit that had come to both countries from the co-operation during the war and their decision to continue that into the years of peace. 'Our governments,' it was stated, 'have in large measure similar interests in post-war international economic policy ... They will seek to furnish to the world concrete evidence of the ways in which two neighbouring countries that have a long experience of friendly relations, may promote by agreed action their mutual interests to the benefit of themselves and other countries.'

This is an affirmation that after the war the Canadian and American governments will work closely together.

What are the future prospects of Canadian–American relations?

*Co-operation.* The first point is that we must co-operate with the U.S.A. On the most practical basis, twelve million people living on the same continent with a hundred and thirty million have little choice except co-operation. For one thing, our economies are so linked that for Canada to pursue policies not friendly to the U.S.A. would be extremely difficult. Of course our connection is also rooted in friendship as well.

We are, as we have said, an American nation. We cannot forget this. One practical means of co-operating as an American nation is as a member of the Pan-American Union. Where most of the other American republics have co-operated to insure hemisphere solidarity, Canada has up to now never been a member of this organization. Today we find that many Canadians feel we should join this union, not only to help our co-operation with the U.S.A., but to bring us closer to the Latin American republics. In a recent session of Parliament, members of all parties came out in favour of this step. There are some, however, who feel that we should not concentrate too closely on this hemisphere at the expense of our relations with the other parts of the world.

*Not Domination.* Will our relations be on the basis of co-operation and friendship, or domination? For instance, it seemed to many Canadians that the recent proposals of President Roosevelt on civil aviation did not take into consideration Canadian interests.[7] Canada, a small nation, was to be a landing field used for the greater convenience of the large powers that surround her. The same thing might be true in many spheres. For instance, in the midst of the depression, the U.S.A. put through the Smoot–Hawley tariff that cut off American markets to Canadian goods. The result of this action was that thousands of Canadians were thrown out of work, and Canadian agriculture lost an important market. How can we ensure that, in the future, relations with our southern neighbour do not result in Canada getting the raw end of the deal because she is not powerful enough to support her case. In the last ten years, the policies of Good Neighbours pursued by the Roosevelt regime in Washington have done much to quiet the fears of Canadians and Latin American countries that the U.S.A. will try to dominate this continent.

*Co-operation with the Rest of the World.* Can we be sure that co-operation with the U.S.A. is part of a fuller co-operation with the rest of the world? Canada is not only a North American nation, it is part of what Wendell Wilkie has called our 'One World.'[8] Canada is a member of certain international organizations – the British Commonwealth and the United Nations. We have seen how we are developing a new relationship with the U.S.S.R. across the Pole and with the Orient across the Pacific. How are we then going to see that our co-operation with the U.S.A. is related to a policy of co-operation with the rest of the world?

*End of isolation.* A recent Gallup poll showed that over 70% of American opinion was in favour of some kind of international organization. If this opinion remains stable, it will bring to an end the policy of isolation that kept the U.S.A. out of world affairs for so long. President Roosevelt has affirmed this as the policy of the American government when he said:

> When we have helped to end the curse of Hitlerism we shall help to establish a new peace, which will give to decent people everywhere a better chance to live and prosper in security and in freedom and in faith.[9]

## The Anglo-American World

Though there are growing signs that a majority of the American people have in the last years given up their traditional isolationism, there have been some who are afraid that they will substitute for this an attempt to dominate the world. In the early days of the war, some leading U.S. newspapers and magazines talked about the coming 'American century,' when the world would be run from Washington, with Great Britain as a junior partner. A leading member of the American Cabinet, Secretary to the Navy Knox, said, in February 1941: 'To put it bluntly, we must join our force and power to that of Great Britain, another peace-loving nation, to stop aggression which might lead to a world-wide disturbance at its beginnings. We must for an interregnum of "one hundred years instruct the world in the fundamentals of international law".'[10] There was much talk of how the U.S.A. and Great Britain must have sufficient power to dominate both Europe and Asia, and be able to do what they liked in these continents. Some experts even recommended that the

U.S.A. should prevent China from getting too powerful after the war, by backing Japan against her. In Europe, we should support anything that would stop the growing power of Russia.

A prominent American summed this attitude up when he said:

> Whatever the outcome of the war, America has embarked upon a career of imperialism, both in world affairs, and in every other aspect of her life. Even though, by our aid, England should emerge from this struggle without defeat, she will be so impoverished economically and so crippled in prestige that it is improbable she will be able to maintain the dominant position in world affairs which she has occupied so long. At best, England will become a junior partner in a new Anglo-Saxon imperialism, in which economic resources and the military and naval strength of the United States will be the centre of gravity. (Virgil Jordan)[11]

As late as 1942, Mrs Luce, the wife of a prominent American journalist, and member of the U.S. Congress, talked about international goodwill as 'Globalony' and said the only thing for the U.S.A. was to concentrate on its own interests throughout the world.[12]

Recently, however, this kind of attitude to the future of the world has given way before a concept of international co-operation. President Roosevelt affirmed that the world of the future was a world free from want and fear, dominated by no single group of nations, but the whole world working together. Anthony Eden, the British Foreign Secretary, backed this statement up.[13] Henry Wallace, the Vice-President of the U.S.A., attacked the idea of mastery of the world by a single power when he said:

> Those who write the peace must think of the whole world. There can be no privileged peoples. We ourselves in the United States are no more a master race than the Nazis.[14]

The signing of the Declaration of the United Nations in January 1942, by all the free nations of the world, large and small, was evidence to the world that a policy of attempted domination was at an end.

*Teheran, Cairo, and Moscow.* This policy of co-operation with the rest of the world rather than domination was carried into practical effect, in the autumn of 1943, when the leaders of Great Britain and the U.S.A. met with Chiang-Kaishek at Cairo and later with Stalin at Teheran. Earlier these four powers of the United Nations had issued a joint declaration at Moscow that they would work together in the war and in the building of a just peace all over the world. The unanimity of these conferences may not have been complete, but the fact that the American government put its name to their joint declaration is a vast step towards real international organization. Few Canadians would doubt the willingness of any country to co-operate internationally that would sign declarations such as these.

Canada is part of the Anglo-American world. We have seen that. She is part of the British Commonwealth. She is a North American neighbour to the U.S.A. She has in the past done much to bring the U.S.A. and Great Britain together. Now as the future is being made by the co-operation of the Anglo-American powers with China and the U.S.S.R., we must see how Canada fits into this widening picture of the United Nations. Next week we will discuss 'The New Relationship with Soviet Russia' and how we are to build up new friendship with the great republics across the Pole. The week after we will discuss 'The Rise of Asia' and how Canada with its borders on the Pacific faces the awakening power of the Orient.

[Editor's Note: Each bulletin included a bibliography and discussion questions. The following was printed with Bulletin No. 11.]

*More Information*

*Canada an American Nation*: J.W. Dafoe, New York, 1935. An analysis of Canada's position and destiny by the late journalist.

*U.S. Foreign Policy: Shield of the Republic*, Walter Lippman. Pocket book edition, 39¢. A famous American columnist writes of the need for American intervention in world affairs – a conservative view.

*Make This the Last War*: Michael Straight, New York, 1943. A plea for a United Nations policy to save the world from war – a progressive view.

*The Unguarded Frontier*: Edgar McInnis, 1942. A scholarly history of Canadian-American relations.

*Canada–United States Cooperation*: available free of charge from the War-time Information Board, Ottawa. A factual description of our co-operation with the U.S.A.

*Anglo-American Economic Policy*: Behind the Headlines Series. Available from the Canadian Association for Adult Education, 198 College Street, Toronto, for 10¢. A description of Anglo-American economic co-operation and the implications for Canada.

*The Inter-American System: a Canadian view.* J.P. Humphrey, Macmillan, 1942.

*Canada and the Pan-American Union*: a plea for Canada to co-operate with the rest of the hemisphere.

*Films*

*Road to Tokyo.* Building of the Alaska Highway. (Running time - 18 minutes)

*Smoke and Steel.* A complete story of the new industries which have been developed in Canada during the war. (Running time – 20 minutes)

*Report Questions*

1. What factors have in the past tied us closely to the U.S.A.? Which of these factors will continue to influence us in the future?
2. Should Canada be a member of the Pan-American Union?
3. What should be the future of projects launched during the war in Canada by American government capital? (e.g., the Alaska Highway, the Canol oil project, etc.)

*Further Questions*

1. Would you be in favour of the War Boards that have jointly planned war production for the U.S. and Canada being continued into the post-war period for the planning of peace-time production?
2. Why do you think labour has found it necessary to organize internationally across the boundary of the United States and Canada?

3. What rights should Canada guard as to her future place in international civil aviation?
4. Certain American thinkers have described the post-war period as the American century. What do you think is meant by such statements? What effect do such ideas have on the peace of the world and the future of Canada?

*Next Week: The New Relationship With Soviet Russia*

**Excerpt from Bulletin No. 15**
**The Fascist Nations in Defeat**
**Tuesday, 28 March**

Our future relationships with the enemy countries must be thought out carefully. It is easy to find solutions that will please our passions; but they must be *reasonable* solutions if they are to lay the basis for world security. After the last war we failed to turn our victory into a lasting and just peace. This time we cannot risk another failure. As Dorothy Thompson has written, 'The eternal dilemma of war and peace is that the mentality engendered by war is rarely if ever the mentality capable of constructing a lasting peace.'[15] Let us be careful that this time our feelings of the moment do not jeopardize our chance of obtaining a peaceful world.

...

The important question regarding the future of the fascist nations is just this: can the Allied Nations achieve unity in their policy toward them? As we have already pointed out, the U.S.S.R. sponsors a Free German Committee that is committed to build a democratic Germany. Great Britain and the U.S.A. have never officially given support to a movement of that kind. If in the case of Germany the U.S.S.R. entered from the east with one policy and the Anglo-American armies entered from the west, what would happen? Obviously this would threaten the kind of conflict that might spoil all our plans for a peaceful world ...

**Excerpt from Bulletin No. 16**
**The New World Order**
**Tuesday, 4 April**

*Power Block Politics*

The stage is set then for the emergence of a new world order. We can achieve what we all want. That is not to say, however, that we will achieve it. In the past a world order has too often been placed secondary to the attempt of one block to achieve advantage over another. Nations competed against each other in terms of power. National economies competed against each other, hoping to get privilege and prosperity for themselves at the expense of others. These power blocks were sometimes known more pleasantly as 'the balance of power' in the world. There are signs in some quarters that that kind of thinking still exists, and that some still want to create a world where one group of nations will be in competition against another group. In the past this has been the road to depression and finally to war. The competing blocks of power driving against each other, eventually met in armed conflict. There seems little doubt that if we think and act in the same terms, we will reach the same place as we did in the past. Only if we realize that we live in one world and that we can all gain from each other's gain will we achieve a stable society. This is not idealism, it is plain common sense. We are living in one world. If we decide to split it up into conflicting and competing camps, we need have little hope of achieving unity, prosperity, and peace in that world. Only if we recognize it as one world, will we achieve the new world order we want.

...

*In Our Own Interest*

Finally it must be repeated that the new world order is not other people's business. It is ours. It is fine to talk of the place of Great Britain or the U.S.S.R. in a new world order, but what is more important is to see what Canada can do and then to see that we do it. 'The fireproof house' we were told about between the wars has proved inflammable. Today we are up to our necks in war. And if we let there be a next time,

Canada will be even more deeply involved. We are at the air routes centre of the world. We are situated between two of the great powers, the U.S.S.R. and the U.S.A. We are closely linked with another, Great Britain. If we cannot build the new world order, the next war may not be in far away Poland or remote Manchuria, it may be here in our own backyard. The new world order is not something we are building out of the kindness of our hearts to help the Chinese or the Europeans, it is something which is in the interest of every Canadian. Let us see what we as members of our democracy can do to promote that interest.

**Excerpt from Bulletin No. 17**
**The Soldier Comes Home**
**Tuesday, 11 April**

In this war Canadian civilians have time and time again expressed a keen consciousness of the debt we owe to the fighting men who are defending Canada in the waters of the Atlantic, the mountains of Italy, and skies over Germany. This gratitude is displayed in the widespread determination that after this war veterans will not tramp the streets in a vain search for work, nor be forced to sell knick-knacks from door to door.

*Social Readjustment*

While all these measures we have been discussing are of first importance in preparing for demobilization day, there is a further and perhaps more delicate problem – the social readjustment of returned men. Hundreds of thousands of Canadian citizens have been plucked out of the family and community setting in which they grew up.

For instance, one of the dominant characteristics of this old life was the premium placed on competition. It was every man for himself, except where such associations as cooperatives or trade unions demanded group loyalty.

But in the services, particularly in actual combat, it must be 'each for all and all for each.' Cooperation and discipline rather than competition are the virtues on which successful action and life itself depend. Squadron-Leader Vlastos has put this point very well:

Over and over again I have heard men who were in the last war say that never since have they known anything like the comradeship of the trenches. They would see it in this war at almost any operational squadron. It is not the effect of talking about comradeship. Even the most inspired talk about comradeship cannot produce it – only living together, working for the same purpose. They are well acquainted with that. Cooperation is an absolute demand of their daily existence. And it is not distorted by arbitrary economic and social divisions. Whether a man's father is a wealthy business man or was on the relief rolls is a secondary matter. Men meet as persons and not as symbols of social power. And they are judged by what they have in them to contribute to the common task.

That is why there is no racial or ethnic problem among the men who are doing the actual fighting. There are plenty of such tensions elsewhere. But they do not exist where men work together, as say, in a bomber crew. Frictions between RAF and RCAF, between French and English Canadians, Jews, and Gentiles, etc., are smoothed out under the iron pressure of cooperation, and differences are more apt to enrich comradeship than destroy it.[16]

Now in Canada during the war, some of the conflicts which divided us have been smoothed out under the over-riding objective of defeat-·ing the Fascist nations. Not all of them by any means – for we in Canada have been far away from the firing line. But we have found a new degree of national unity built around war-objectives.

When the soldier comes home will he find in Canada a new sense of comradeship, a new determination to preserve unity and work together for a better world? If he doesn't, great will be the disillusionment, and great the difficulty of fitting into 'normal' life. It is in precisely such circumstances that veterans turn back to their ties with fellow-soldiers, and band together against the society which fails to satisfy their needs or to give them a place. It is no accident that Hitler's earliest followers were the hungry, bitter veterans of defeated Germany.

...

We have discussed the relation of men in the services to labour, in some detail, not because it is the only problem to be faced in the social readjustments which must follow the war – but because it is one of the most perilous. This is the sphere where pro-fascist elements can most easily stir up conflict and threaten national unity. Racial prejudice is another such breeding ground for strife. Only with the utmost degree of national unity can we build a secure peace. Civilians and service men alike must see that nothing shatters this unity.

...

## Excerpt from Bulletin No. 19
## Who Shapes the Future?
## Tuesday, 25 April

As the post-war period comes ever more swiftly towards us, Canadians are reaching a greater measure of agreement about post-war objectives than ever before. Farmers, labour, professional and business organizations have expressed themselves in favour of social security plans, re-housing schemes, planning for full employment, and so on. There is little disagreement now among the Canadian people about the nature of our post-war objectives.

There is, however, some uncertainty about how we shall achieve these ends. Almost everyone assumes that there will have to be extensive government planning and control for at least the period of transition from war to peace. Most of our schemes for improvement, health insurance, better educational facilities, and so forth, simply can't be carried out unless there is over-all planning and co-ordination. In many cases the money will have to be collected by the government either at the national or provincial level.

...

Many people have fears [that] arise out of a sense of frustration, of powerlessness to have any effect over the social forces which mould our lives. Their reaction is that of the little man tossed around by currents which he doesn't understand. Rightly or wrongly many people feel that governments push the individual around – that the nation's affairs are run from Ottawa, and the ordinary man doesn't have much to say in what goes on. Full employment, monetary stabilization, the balance of trade – matters like this seem so complicated that the average man doesn't know what to think about them.

*New Times, New Ways*

This is a common reaction to the increasing complexity and interdependence of life in the 20th century. Modern scientific developments in transportation, communication, and methods of producing goods have created a world in which events in far-off lands have devastating and mysterious effects on our own daily lives. We no longer spend our days within the bounds of a narrow community. In our sprawling cities and large towns we hardly know our neighbours personally, let alone the people who represent us in Parliament. Our security is smashed overnight by a depression or a war. Governments take action on problems which seem remote from what we know about in our own experience. Innumerable boards and agencies are set up in Ottawa, and their long arm reaches right into our household life.

This gulf which seems to have arisen between the people and their government is one of the greatest perils which we face.

...

History has proved that unless everyone plays his part in a democracy, it will wither and die. The Fascists have been jeering at us for years, saying that we aren't really democracies at all, that we're run by the wealthy and the Jews. They say that the idea of everyone taking part in the running of society is absurd and impossible. They say we need a Leader. And their propaganda sometimes falls on receptive ears.

For a great many people the central question on the agenda of the future is not: *should there be planning?* but rather: *in whose interest, and by whom, will the planning be done* – by a minority group or by the people as a whole? Will the Canadian people achieve mastery over their own destiny, and shape the future in a pattern which will contribute to the well-being of all?

## Participation in Government

The first fact to be recognized is that unless we understand a thing, we can't control it. A man has to know how the gears work before he can drive a car. He has to know what will happen when he presses his foot on the accelerator, or he will find himself against a telegraph pole.

In public affairs many of us didn't understand how things worked. For example, we didn't foresee that shutting foreign goods out of our markets would mean that other countries couldn't find money to buy the things we were making, and our own factories would eventually have to close down. There are certain elementary facts about the way our economic system works which we must grasp, or we won't be able to make it go in the direction we want it to.

Many of the social and economic problems we shall have to tackle are not really as complicated as they appear to be. Experts may use a difficult vocabulary when they talk about full employment. Actually, this problem is simply the question of how our manpower can be fully harnessed to use our resources to meet our needs.

...

**Excerpt from Bulletin No. 20**
**Action Now**
**Tuesday, 2 May**

*Action in the Community*

Post-war planning doesn't stop at the national or even the provincial level. Dozens of cities and towns in Canada have their own post-war planning committees. Here, in the community, all of us can participate in shaping the world that is to be. In fact, if democracy is to work at all, it must be effective on the community level.

International, national, and provincial government planning is of course important, but the welfare of our own community depends ultimately on us. Large scale plans become real to us when we see how they affect our own localities. They will be effective only if the needs and responsibilities of people in all communities are recognized.

Take housing, for instance. The government at Ottawa intends to initiate a housing programme and all the political parties are in favour of new and better housing for Canada. But if we are really to get good homes and decent neighbourhoods for ourselves, then it is up to the citizens of a community to see that local plans meet local needs. This means action.

Good blueprints are still not enough. Only the citizens of a community can see that plans are put into effect. This also means actions.

Citizens' Forums have recognized this. Reports from all over the country indicate that many are undertaking action projects that they feel are necessary in their community. Some are doing it as a group; others are accomplishing it within the organizations they belong to – through their trade unions, home and school clubs, their business associations, their local YMCAs or YWs, and in many other ways. They are finding out that their discussion together has made them more effective citizens.

Citizens' Forum groups have discovered that to carry out plans, they must unite with other groups and organizations. This unity often takes the form of community councils, with representatives from all parts of a locality. Men from service clubs and professional associations, members of trade unions, librarians, recreation leaders, and many others are banding together to see how they can meet their common problems. They know that if democracy is to be fully achieved, it must work right here in their own backyard. To this end there must be action now!

## Notes for Appendix 2

1 *The Rowell–Sirois Report* (3 vols) contained the conclusions of the Royal Commission on Dominion–Provincial Relations in 1940. The commission was established unilaterally by the federal government to re-examine 'the economic and financial basis of Confederation and the distribution of legislative powers in the light of the economic and social developments of the last 70 years.' The report recommended the transfer of taxation power to the federal government, which was to assume responsibility for unemployment insurance and contributory pensions and for provincial debts incurred in the Depression.

2 See Donald V. Smiley, ed., *The Rowell–Sirois Report: An Abridgement of Book I of the Royal Commission Report on Dominion-Provincial Relations* (Toronto: McClelland and Stewart 1963), ch. VI.

3 Everett Cherrington Hughes (1897–1983), educator and author as well as sociologist, taught at McGill (1927–38), Chicago (1938–60), Brandeis (1961–8), and Boston College (1968–76). He published *French Canada in Transition* with the University of Chicago Press and Toronto's W.J. Gage Press in 1943 (reprinted 1963), and also *Where People Meet: Racial and Ethnic Frontiers* (1952), and *Men and Their Work* (1958).

4 Abbé Arthur Maheux, O.B.E. (1884–1967), Canadian history professor at Laval, published *French Canada and Britain: A New Interpretation* (1942), *Canadian Unity: What Keeps Us Apart?* (1944), containing 'radio addresses given to English-speaking Canadians,' as well as *Problems of Canadian Unity* (1944), the book to which Grant refers (pp. 41-2).

5  Smiley, ed., *The Rowell–Sirois Report*, 161.
6  This passage is quoted from an address delivered at Queen's University on 18 August 1938. See Samuel Rosenman, ed., *The Public Papers and Addresses of Franklin D. Roosevelt*, vol. 7 (London: Macmillan 1941), 493.
7  The position of Canada can be found in Hansard 1943, 1798: 'The Canadian Government strongly favours a policy ... best calculated to serve not only the immediate national interests of Canada ['Trans-Canada Air Lines is the sole agency which may operate international air services'] but also our over-riding interest in the establishment of an international order [International Air Transport Authority under the United Nations proposed in April 1944] which will prevent the outbreak of an international world war.' The *Montreal Gazette*, 11 July, reported as follows: 'Early in July [1944] the US Civil Aeronautics Board announced 20 air routes which it "tentatively con cluded" would be desireable [*sic*] for post-war operation by United States air carriers. There are powerful interests [principally 16 American airlines who have secured the support of their government] who do not wish any international control of aviation restricting their "freedom of the air".' See S.G. Cameron, 'International Air Transport,' *Canadian Forum* 24 (Oct. 1944): 155–9. See also 'What Roosevelt Meant: Air Showdown Drawing Close,' *Canadian Aviation* 16 (Nov. 1943): 56; and 'The Coming Struggle for Air Control,' *Canadian Forum* 24 (Apr. 1944): 8–9.
8  Wendell Wilkie (1892–1944), Democratic businessman who opposed Roosevelt's New Deal, ran unsuccessfully for president as a Republican in 1940.
9  This passage is quoted from the Navy Day Address on World Affairs delivered in Washington, D.C., on 27 October 1941. See B.D. Zevin, ed., *Nothing to Fear: The Selected Addresses of Franklin Delano Roosevelt, 1932–1945*, (Freeport, NY: Books for Libraries Press Reprint 1970), 298.
10  William Franklin Knox (1874–1944), journalist and politician, became editor and publisher of the *Chicago Daily News* in 1931. He ran as Republican vice-presidential candidate with Landon against Roosevelt and was made secretary of the navy by President Roosevelt in 1940. He was responsible for the inquiry into naval disaster at Pearl Harbor.
11  Virgil Jordan (1892–1965), economist, author, and publicist, was president (1932–48) and chancellor (1949–63) of the National Industrial Conference Board. He wrote *The World Crisis and American Business Management* (1940) and *America in 1992* (1942).
12  Clare Boothe Luce (1903–1987), American socialite and wit, was associate editor of *Vogue* magazine and American ambassador to Italy. In 1935, she married millionaire publisher and editor Henry Robinson Luce (1898–1967), who founded *Time* magazine (1923), *Fortune* magazine (1930), and *Life* magazine (1936).

13  Sir Robert Anthony Eden (1897–1977), first Earl of Avon, 1961, Foreign
    Secretary 1900–45, led the British delegation to the San Francisco Confer-
    ence in 1945 and was deputy leader of the opposition from 1945 to 1951,
    returning to the foreign office under Churchill in 1951. He succeeded
    Churchill as prime minister in 1955 and incurred the wrath of the United
    Nations and the United States when he ordered troops to occupy the Suez
    Canal Zone in 1956.

14  Henry Agard Wallace (1888–1965), American agriculturist and statesman,
    was nominated in 1940 as vice-president with Roosevelt, whose New Deal
    policy he supported. He was chairman of the Board of Economic Warfare
    (1941–5) when he made the statement Grant quotes. Wallace makes the
    same point in 'Practical Religion in the World of Tomorrow' in *Christian
    Bases of World Order* (Freeport: Books for Librairies Press 1943), 9–20.

15  Dorothy Thompson (1893–1961), American newspaper columnist, lecturer,
    and radio commentator. Grant's probable source was one of her columns at
    the *New York Herald Tribune*, called 'On the Record,' which appeared three
    days weekly and was syndicated with 151 papers. She was also editorial
    writer at the *Ladies' Home Journal* and her second husband (1928–41) was
    Sinclair Lewis.

16  Gregory Vlastos (1907–1991), Christian socialist and classics and philoso-
    phy professor, taught at Queen's University (1931–48), Cornell (1948–55),
    and Berkeley (1976–82). During the war he was a Squadron Leader in the
    Canadian Air Force, working at the Wartime Information Board editing
    *Canadian Affairs,* a fortnightly magazine prepared by that board for distri-
    bution among the services and civilians. His publications during the war
    include *A Christian New Order* (1944).

# Appendix 3
# Radio and Television Broadcasts
# by George Grant
# Canadian Broadcasting Corporation

The list was compiled from CBC records and from Dr Grant's letters. It is as complete as available records allow.

49/11/01  'On Human Happiness': A talk on the radio series *Points of View*.

52/12/16  'On *Waiting on God*': A review on radio of Simone Weil's book *Waiting on God*.

52/[full date unavailable] An appearance on the radio program series *Critically Speaking*.

54/06/02  A first appearance on the television quiz program *Fighting Words*, with Moderator Nathan Cohen, in which participants must identify the authors of, and discuss, controversial quotations. During most of the period from 1952 to 1962 the television programs were repeated on radio station CBL two days after the televised version.

54/10/26  'Charles Cochrane': A thirty-minute talk on the radio series *Anthology*.

55/08/19  'The Atomic Age and the Mind of Men': A talk given at the Couchiching Conference and later broadcast on CBC radio.

55/11/09  'Jean Paul Sartre': A talk given on the radio series *CBC Wednesday Night*, later published in *Architects of Modern Thought*.

56/08/27    Another appearance on the television series *Fighting Words*, with the radio version two days later.

58/01/06    'Philosophy in the Mass Age': A talk on the radio series *University of the Air*, the first of nine talks later revised and published as *Philosophy in the Mass Age*.

58/01/13    'The Ancient and the Modern World': A talk on the radio series *University of the Air*, the second of nine talks.

58/01/20    'Natural Law': A talk on the radio series *University of the Air*, the third of nine talks.

58/01/27    'The Rebellion of Enlightenment': A talk on the radio series *University of the Air*, the fourth of nine talks.

58/02/03    'The Ethics of Marxism': A talk on the radio series *University of the Air*, the fifth of nine talks.

58/02/17    'A Criticism of the Progressive Spirit: Middle-Class Morality': A talk on the radio series *University of the Air*, the sixth of nine talks.

58/02/24    'The American Pragmatic Spirit': A talk on the radio series *University of the Air*, the seventh of nine talks.

58/03/03    ''The Limits of Freedom': A talk on the radio series *University of the Air*, the eighth of nine talks.

58/03/10    George Grant answers questions from listeners: A talk on the radio series *University of the Air*, the last of nine talks in the 'Philosophy in the Mass Age' programs.

58/11/05    'Dostoevski': A talk given on the radio series *CBC Wednesday Night*, later published in *Architects of Modern Thought*. The series was introduced by John A. Irving.

59/01/11    An appearance on *Fighting Words,* with the radio version two days later on 59/01/13.

59/02/08    An appearance on *Fighting Words,* with the radio version two days later on 59/02/10.

59/03/05    'Belief': A sixty-minute program prepared from interviews by George Grant of Miss Bessie Touzel, Dr Keith MacDonald, Dr Victorin Voyer, Dr Wilder Penfield, Mr W.J.Bennett, Robertson Davies, Mrs Viola Halpenny, and Mr Archie Bennett on the television series *Explorations.*

59/10/18    An appearance on *Fighting Words.*

59/12/27    'Christ what a Planet!': A ten-minute talk on the radio series *Our Special Speaker,* reviewing the year 1959.

60/01/10    An appearance on *Fighting Words.*

60/05/22    An appearance on *Fighting Words.*

61/01/10    An appearance on *Fighting Words.*

61/07/12    'Four Philosophers, Part 1: Plato – 'Belief and What it is'': A thirty-minute television drama with commentary by George Grant on the series *Explorations.*

61/07/19    'Four Philosophers, Part 2: St Augustine – Belief and what it is': A thirty-minute television drama with commentary by George Grant on the series *Explorations.*

61/07/26    'Four Philosophers, Part 3: Hume': A thirty-minute drama with commentary by George Grant on the series *Explorations.*

61/08/02    'Four Philosophers, Part 4: Kant': A thirty-minute drama with commentary by George Grant on the series *Explorations.*

61/11/06    'What is History? – No.2': A talk on the radio series *University of the Air*.

61/11/21    'Carl Gustav Jung': A thirty-minute talk on the radio series *CBC Wednesday Night*, later published in *Architects of Modern Thought*.

61/12/18    'What Is History?': A thirty-minute talk on the radio series *University of the Air*, in which George Grant is one of three professors discussing E.H. Carr.

62/09/?     'On Peter Fechter': A short talk on radio about a man who had been shot while trying to cross the Berlin Wall.

63/01/08    'The Best of All Possible Beasts': A panel discussion on the human brain and the computer in the field of memory was held, with George Grant, two physiologists, a neurosurgeon, and Dr Keith MacDonald, a physicist, on the television series *Science Review*.

63/10/07    'Crime and Corruption': A talk on the radio series *Preview Commentary*, later published in *Christian Outlook*.

65/06/27    'The Future of Canadian Nationhood': A defence by George Grant of the thesis of *Lament for a Nation* on the television series *Venture*.

65/10/10    'Revolution and Response': A speech delivered to the U of T International Teach-in on the radio series *CBC Sunday Night*.

65/10/21    'Talking with Diefenbaker': A television broadcast with George Grant talking with John Diefenbaker on the series *Political Telecasts*.

65/11/21    'Power and Society': A program with George Grant as host and Professor John Porter as guest on the series *Extension – Educational Television*.

65/11/28   'Power in Practice': A program with George Grant as host
and Professor John Porter as guest on the series *Extension –
Educational Television*.

65/12/05   'Leadership and Power': A program with George Grant as
host and Professor J.H. Aitchison as guest on the series
*Extension – Educational Television*.

65/12/12   'The MP and Parliament': A program with George Grant as
host and Pauline Jewett and Gordon Fairweather as guests
on the series *Extension – Educational Television*.

65/12/19   'Politics and the Professor': A program with George Grant
as host and Pauline Jewett as guest on the series *Extension –
Educational Television*.

65/12/26   'Politics in Society': A program with George Grant as host
and Professor John Meisel as guest on the series *Extension –
Educational Television*.

66/01/02   'Parties in Canada': A program with George Grant as host
and Professor Gad Horowitz as guest on the series *Extension – Educational Television*.(On 9, 16, 23, and 30 Jan., the
series continued with Gad Horowitz as host and Ramsay
Cook, Charles Taylor, and Brough MacPherson as guests.)

66/01/07   George Grant talking to graduate students about *Lament for
a Nation* and Canada on the radio series *1967 And All That*.

66/02/07   'Political Action in Canada': A program with Gad Horowitz as host and George Grant as guest (co-host) on the
series *Extension – Educational Television*.

66/02/14   'A Canadian Identity': A program with Gad Horowitz as
host and George Grant as guest on the series *Extension –
Educational Television*.

66/02/20   Segment (g) about the Edmonton Teach-in on Canadian
Identity with George Grant among the speakers on the television series *This Hour Has Seven Days* (Program no. 42).

66/06/02   George Grant is interviewed by Adrienne Clarkson about
the effects of modern technology on man's ideas, on the
television series *First Person*.

66/07/30   The radio broadcast of the Couchiching Conference, 'Great
Societies and Quiet Revolutions,' includes George Grant.

66/07/31   The radio broadcast of the Couchiching Conference, 'Great
Societies and Quiet Revolutions,' includes George Grant.

66/08/07   'Comments on the Great Society': Excerpts from a speech
by George Grant delivered at the 35th annual Couchiching
Conference, 'Great Societies and Quiet Revolutions'. The
speech was later published in *Great Societies and Quiet Revolutions*, edited by John Irwin (Toronto: Canadian Broadcasting Corporation 1967), pp. 71–6.

66/08/14   'The British Fact': George Grant is among those interviewed by Larry Zolf in a thirty-minute program on the
series *Compass*.

67/01/01   George Grant talks about Canada, *Lament for a Nation*, and
Diefenbaker, on the television series *Sunday*.

67/03/09   A program which includes extracts from an address by
George Grant on nationalism in the modern world on the
radio series *Second Century Week*.

67/08/13   George Grant talks about Duff Roblin and Dalton Camp on
the television series *The Other Eye*.

69/11/12   'Massey Lectures': A thirty-minute talk on the radio series
*Ideas*, the first of five, later published by the CBC as *Time as
History*.

69/11/19     'Massey Lectures': A thirty-minute talk on the radio series *Ideas*, the second of five, entitled 'Time as History.'

69/11/26     'Massey Lectures': A thirty-minute talk on the radio series *Ideas*, the third of five, entitled 'Time as History.'

69/12/03     'Massey Lectures': A thirty-minute talk on the radio series *Ideas*, the fourth of five, entitled 'Time as History.'

69/12/10     'Massey Lectures': A thirty-minute talk on the radio series *Ideas*, the fifth of five, entitled 'Time as History.'

69/12/17     'A dialogue in which Dr.Grant's theme and the suggestion that God is dead are discussed and challenged by theologian, Dr Charles Malik ... a Lebanese diplomat ...,' on the radio series *Ideas* as a sequel to the 'Time as History' programs. This dialogue was not included in the book *Time as History*, but it is included in the set of long-playing records issued by the CBC for their International Transcription Service.

71/12/07     'To Be a Tory': George Grant is among those interviewed by Larry Zolf in this one-hour documentary on the Tories on the television series *Tuesday Night*.

73/01/28     'Lessons of Vietnam War': A phone-in discussion of the lessons Canadians have learned from the war, on the radio series *Cross-Country Check-Up*, includes comments by George Grant.

73/08/05     Ramsay Cook interviews George Grant on the Second World War, French-Canadian nationalism, and the problem of feeling at home in a homogeneous technological world on the television series *Impressions*.

73/10/10     A program includes George Grant discussing *Lament for a Nation*, Canada, Lester Pearson, and 'mental health state' on the radio series *This Country in the Morning*.

74/03/05    A program on the need for changing attitudes: George
Grant on the Gross National Product in the light of re-
evaluated goals, the James Bay Project, and Quebec, on the
television series *Canada Tomorrow.*

75/03/27    'The Technological Imperative': The fourth of five lectures
in the 'Beyond Industrial Growth' series on the radio series
*Ideas.* The lecture was originally delivered at the University
of Toronto on 31 Jan.1975, and later published under the
title 'The computer does not impose on us the ways it
should be used,' in *Beyond Industrial Growth*, edited by
Abraham Rotstein (Toronto: University of Toronto Press
1976), pp. 117–31. A revised version of this same essay
appeared as 'Thinking about Technology' in *Technology and
Justice* (Toronto: Anansi 1986), pp. 11–34.

77/10/20    Segment (e) of a ninety-minute program. Peter Gzowski
interviews Peter Newman, Dalton Camp, and George
Grant discussing Diefenbaker's memoirs on the television
series *90 Minutes Live.*

80/02/13    'The Owl and the Dynamo': A one-hour profile of George
Grant produced by Vincent Tovell and narrated by William
Whitehead on the television series *Spectrum.*

87/05/31    'George Grant Profile': Linden MacIntyre reports from
Halifax on the television series *Sunday Morning.* Clips of
George Grant on Canada, Diefenbaker, Vietnam, Abortion,
Mozart, Technology, Conversion, walking in the park, and
[the fact that he is a] believer not [a] pessimist.

88/02/13    'On the Morgenthaler decision': A five-minute talk on the
radio series *Commentary.* Sheila Grant says letters request-
ing copies of the script came in from all over Canada.

88/09/28    'Tribute to George Grant,' by David Cayley, during hour
three of the radio series *Morningside.*

88/10/02    'Reflections': Tributes to George Grant and bp Nichol, with clips from the 87/05/31 program, on the television series *Sunday Morning*.

89/08/24    'Tribute to George Grant,' by David Cayley (repeat of 28 Sept. 1988) on hour three of the radio series *Morningside*.

# Appendix 4
# Editorial and Textual Principles and Methods Applied in Volume 1

The purpose of the edition is to provide readers with a complete collection of reliable reading texts. Editorial interventions identify the sources of the writings; explain Grant's allusions to persons, places, and events; and describe any changes made to the writings during the preparation of the volume. They consist of headnotes, annotations, and a chronology of Grant's life. A general index of names and topics is included in each of the first six volumes of the edition.

## Copy-text

The material included in this volume did not pose difficult questions regarding the versions that ought to be chosen as copy-text, that is, the closest to the author's intentions and preferences. No second versions of these particular writings have survived, as far as we know. Hence the copy-texts consist of published works, with two exceptions: the handwritten journal, which has not been printed (in its entirety) before now; and the doctoral (DPhil) thesis, which was originally typewritten with one carbon copy.

## Accuracy of the text

We have corrected the human and mechanical errors that occurred in the process of scanning the documents into computer files. In addition, we have checked the original sources of Grant's quotations for accuracy.

## Headnotes

We have provided short headnotes for each piece of writing to identify its source and date. For the special case of the DPhil thesis, we decided to provide a substantial introduction to help readers to see the work in the context of Grant's thought as a whole. We have also written a longer headnote for the appendix containing the *Citizens' Forum* bulletins, and one sectional headnote has been included for the writings of the Canadian Association for Adult Education period. All headnotes are in sans serif type to distinguish them from Grant's writings.

## Annotations

Annotations are intended to supplement and clarify Grant's references in as unobtrusive a way as possible. The notes have been kept concise. They identify persons, events, or places that might puzzle or confuse some readers. Again we ask for patience from those readers who find that some of the notes give information that seems obvious to them.

In the DPhil thesis, where many annotations appear along with Grant's original notes, we have reproduced Grant's as footnotes and ours as notes at the end of the thesis. There was no need (in this volume) for textual notes that explain revision and emendation of texts. Minor textual notes are included in the annotations.

## Appendices

There are four appendices in this volume. They include the Upper Canada College writings, set apart because they are the work of youth; the Bulletins, set apart because they are collaborative works; the list of CBC broadcasts, which extends in time beyond the period covered by this volume; and this explanation of textual matters.

## Correction, Regularization, Standardization, and House Style

When we judged that absolutely no question of meaning was at stake, we silently corrected minor typographical and punctuation errors in Grant's texts. Whenever we judged that a correction might affect the meaning of the text, the error has simply been flagged with [*sic*]. We have corrected mistakes that obviously occurred because of an oversight by either Grant or the typists who worked on the original works. For example, Grant regularly used the expression 'that is' without a following comma. We have added commas in such cases. Grant's frequent substitution of 'loose' for 'lose' has been corrected. His own corrections of the copy-text have been noted when they were not also made to the carbon copy at Oxford, or when we judged they were significant. We have restored the full title of books where Grant referred to them with abbreviated titles as in '*The N and S*' for '*The Natural and the Supernatural.*' All foreign words have been italicized.

In the case of the journal and the DPhil thesis, however, we have retained Grant's spelling and punctuation because we judged they were essential parts of his voice in the time and place he was writing. We have kept his spelling of words with -ise endings that now tend to be -ize endings and his use of 'reflexion,' for example. To conform with Grant's preferred usage in the thesis, 'analyse' is spelt with an 's' not a 'z', and all instances of 'judgement' have been changed to 'judgment.' Grant's use of 'Humian' for what is now usually 'Humean' and of 'Tolstoi' rather than 'Tolstoy' have not been changed. His quotations from Oman have been checked for accuracy and amended to conform with the original.

In the few cases where he departed from his usual practice, we have regularized Grant's usage of capitals in his own writing and in his quotations of Oman. Capitalization was important for Grant, though he was not always consistent. He states in a note that he himself is retaining Oman's different use of the upper case when he quotes him. Oman capitalizes 'Natural' and 'Supernatural,' for example, where Grant does not (except in the Oman quotations). Grant reserves capitals in this context for God and His attributes.

Apart from the exceptions mentioned, texts adhere to the University of Toronto Press house style. We have used the inverted style for dates, except in the case of the Journal, where we retained Grant's style. Single quotation marks are used; quotation marks are removed from displayed quotations; punctuation is placed inside closing quotation marks in accordance with the prevailing modern practice; dashes are removed when put beside a comma; periods have been removed from abbreviations such as 'Dr' and 'St'; hyphens are added or removed in accordance with current practice; and, finally, the serial comma is used. Such regularization, standardization, and house-style emendations have been done silently, without annotation.

We left Grant's bibliographic references as they were, except for making slight changes to clarify references a modern reader might not otherwise understand. In the bibliography of the DPhil thesis, we made minor structural changes in the interest of readability, putting the titles of essays and articles by Oman at the head of their entries and simplifying the format of the book-review section.

## Selection of unpublished work

This volume presented no difficult decisions concerning the choice of unpublished works. Since no notebooks or lectures from the first two years at Dalhousie have survived as far as we know, and since no drafts of the other works were found in Grant's papers, the journal of 1942 and the DPhil thesis of 1950 are the only works in question from this period.

## Transcription of written material

The only handwritten manuscript prepared for this volume is the 1942 journal. We worked with the photocopy that William Christian made from the original in the Grant–Parkin papers. The transcription was prepared by four editors. We have tried to keep the unfinished quality of the original by retaining the informal punctuation and avoiding grammatical corrections. We have checked the finished text against the original by having one person read the original while another corrected the computerized version.

# Index